AMERICAN CONSTITUTIONAL HISTORY

AMERICAN CONSTITUTIONAL HISTORY

With an Introduction by Leonard W. Levy

Selections from the
Encyclopedia of the American Constitution
Edited by
Leonard W. Levy, Kenneth L. Karst, and
Dennis J. Mahoney

MACMILLAN PUBLISHING COMPANY

NEW YORK

Collier Macmillan Publishers

LONDON

Macmillan Publishing Company
866 Third Avenue, New York, NY 10022

Collier Macmillan Canada, Inc.

Library of Congress Catalog Card Number: 89-7949

Printed in the United States of America

printing number

1 2 3 4 5 6 7 8 9 10

Library of Congress Cataloging-in-Publication Data

Encyclopedia of the American Constitution. Selections.
    American constitutional history : selections from the Encyclopedia
of the American Constitutions / Leonard W. Levy, Kenneth L. Karst,
and Dennis J. Mahoney, editors ; with an introduction by Leonard W.
Levy.
      p.   cm.
   Bibliography: p.
   ISBN 0-02-897231-7
   1. United States—Constitutional history. I. Levy, Leonard
Williams, 1923- .   II. Karst, Kenneth L.   III. Mahoney, Dennis J.
IV. Title.
KF4541.A2E53   1989
342.73'02303—dc20
[347.3022303]   89-7949
                                          CIP

CONTENTS

INTRODUCTION

Professor Felix Frankfurter once remarked that "the Supreme Court is the Constitution." Justice Felix Frankfurter, as if in disagreement, declared that the "ultimate touchstone of constitutionality is the Constitution itself, not what we have said about it."[1] The ultimate, however, is far off. What counts is what the Supreme Court has said about the Constitution—in nearly 500 volumes thus far.

The Constitution itself plays a mere secondary role in American constitutional law. When, for example, the Court had to construe the First Amendment's injunction against establishments of religion, Justice Robert H. Jackson candidly observed that it was "idle to pretend that this task is one for which we can find in the Constitution one word to help us as judges to decide where the secular ends and the sectarian begins in education."[2] Justices who look to the Constitution for more than a puzzling, if majestic, phrase might just as well turn to the comic strips for all the guidance they will find on how to decide most of the great cases that involve national public policy, whether the question relates to legislature veto, sodomy, school prayers, abortion, legislative apportionment, environmental protection, racial segregation, the exclusionary rule, the regulation of utility rates, affirmative action, subversive activities, commercial speech, the curtailment of crop production, Medicaid, the seizure of steel mills, stock frauds, or sex discrimination. There is not a word in the Constitution about these or most of the subjects of great import with which the Court must deal. That fact, paradoxically, is a great strength of the Constitution, accounting in part for its longevity and vitality.

The Framers of the Constitution also had a genius for studied imprecision and calculated ambiguity. Their Constitution, expressed in very generalized terms, resembled Martin Chuzzlewit's grandnephew, who had no more than "the first idea and sketchy notion of a face." It thereby permitted, even encouraged, nay, necessitated, continuous reinterpretation and adaptation. Men trained in the common law would habitually avoid minute specifications that became obsolete with a change in the particular circumstances for which they were adopted; such men would tend rather to formulate principles that are expansive and comprehensive in nature. The principles themselves, not their framers' understanding and application of them, were meant to endure.

In determining "whether a provision of the Constitution applies to a new subject matter," declared Justice Harlan Fiske Stone,

it is of little significance that it is one with which the framers were not familiar. For in setting up an enduring framework of government they undertook to carry out for the indefinite future, and in all the vicissitudes of the changing affairs of men, those fundamental principles which the instrument itself discloses. Hence we read its words, not as we read legislative codes which are subject to continuous revision with the changing course of events, but as the revelation of the great purposes which were intended to be achieved by the Constitution as a continuing instrument of government.[3]

Thus the commerce clause applies to satellite communication, racial discrimination in motels, stolen cars, stock exchange transactions, and the wages of window washers. The Constitution, designed for an eighteenth-century rural society, serves as well today as ever, perhaps better than ever, because an antiquarian historicism that would freeze its original meanings, even if discernible, has not guided its interpretation and was not intended to. As Justice Oliver Wendell Holmes once said, "The present has a right to govern itself, so far as it can. . . . Historical continuity with the past is not a duty, only a necessity."[4]

The document itself, with all amendments, clearly delineates the structure of American national government but only roughly maps the contours of power. We know unmistakably that there is to be a President whose term of office is four years; but what is "the executive power" with which the President is vested? Chief Justice John Marshall happily noted that the Constitution has none of the "prolixity of a legal code"; it has, rather, the virtue of muddy brevity, a mere 7,000 words, including amendments. Scarcely 2 percent of the verbiage possesses any significance in constitutional law. Almost without exception, these are the purposefully ambiguous or vague words, like general welfare, due process of law, probable cause, unreasonable search, commerce among the states, speedy trial, liberty, equal protection, impartial jury, obligation of contracts, privileges and immunities, establishment of religion, necessary and proper, cruel and unusual punishment, and direct taxes. Other words of crucial importance in constitutional law are not even in the Constitution, including use immunity, clear and present danger, self-incrimination, fair trial, war power, executive agreement, public purpose, exigent circumstances, separate but equal, liberty of contract, reasonable doubt, separation of church and state, double jeopardy, interstate commerce, right to privacy, strict scrutiny, fair return, and police power. They are judicial glosses. In large measure we have an unwritten constitution whose history is the history of judicial review. James Beck made the point by comparing the work of the Supreme Court to that of a "continuous constitutional convention" that adapts the original charter by reinterpretation, making its duties "political in the highest sense of the word, as well as judicial."[5]

The Constitution's power of survival derives also from the fact that it incorporates and symbolizes the political values of a free people. It creates a representative, responsible government empowered to serve the general welfare at the same time that it keeps the government bitted and bridled. "In framing a government which is to be administered by men over men," noted Madison in *The Federalist* #51, "the great difficulty lies in this; you must first enable the government to control the governed; and in the next place oblige it to control itself." The Constitution deals with great powers, many of them undefined, but they are separated and distributed, checked and balanced, limited and prohibited. At the same time, most notably through the Bill of Rights and the great Reconstruction amendments, the Constitution requires that the game shall be played freely and fairly, with the judiciary as the umpire. "The great ideals of liberty and equality," wrote Justice Benjamin Cardozo, "are preserved against the assaults of opportunism, the expediency of the passing hour, the erosion of small encroachments, the scorn and derision of those who have no patience with general principles, by enshrining them in constitutions, and consecrating to the task of their protection a body of defenders."[6] Charles Evans Hughes's much quoted remark, that "the Constitution is what the judges say it is," expressed only half his thought; he added, much like Cardozo, "and the judiciary is the safeguard of our liberty and of our property under the Constitution."[7]

Constitutional law is the product of the entire federal judiciary, not just of the Supreme Court. Indeed, the history of constitutional law would be as illuminating as the dark side of the moon without also considering the participation of the nonjudicial branches of the government. The President makes constitutional history when, by simple executive order, he authorizes the internment of 70,000 American citizens of Japanese descent; or sends troops to Little Rock or Oxford, Mississippi; or ends racial discrimination in the armed forces, or in private employment under government contract, or in federally assisted housing projects; or establishes a loyalty-security program among government employees. The Congress makes constitutional history more obviously and with far greater frequency via the legislative process. Nevertheless, constitutional law is peculiarly the product of the Supreme Court. The President, Congress, and administrative agencies help make constitutional history; they even help make constitutional law, but only in the first instance. The sovereign people may even amend the Constitution itself, but unless they abolish judicial review, the Supreme Court still has the last word, for it construes not only the validity of the exercise of power by the other branches of government; it construes also the meaning of the Constitution. The point is implicit in Justice Holmes's quotation from the exaggerated remark by Bishop Hoadly to the effect that the final authority to interpret the law, rather than its maker, is the real sovereign.[8]

As de Tocqueville observed long ago, almost every public issue in the United States sooner or later becomes a subject for judicial resolution.[9] Frankfurter, echoing the thought a century later, declared that most of the problems of modern society, "whether of industry, agriculture, of finance, or racial interactions or the eternal conflict between liberty and authority, become in the United States sooner or later legal problems for ultimate solution by the Supreme Court."[10] Thus trivial disputes between private litigants may be argued in terms of fundamental principles of government by judges and lawyers, and matters of the highest policy go to the courts for judgment, though the case itself may be insignificant in terms of the interest of the immediate parties. For example, on the outcome of the claim of a Mr. Norman for $15.60 against the Baltimore and Ohio Railroad depended the financial policy of the United States, involving some one hundred billion dollars and a possible 60 percent increase in the national debt in the midst of a depression.[11] The role of the government in the economy, the relation of the individual to the state and of the states to the nation, the system of justice, and the legal standards of equality are among the subjects of our constitutional law. Its study is ennobled by an alliance with history, with statecraft, with the evolution of popular institutions of government, and with human rights.

Nearly every significant decision of the Supreme Court deals with rights or with power, whether government power or private power. Constitutional government is, by definition, limited government, a system of regularized restraints upon power; there is therefore an inevitable and enduring tension between the exercise of powers allegedly vested and limitations allegedly breached. In some periods in the history of constitutional law the Supreme Court tends to emphasize the affirmative aspects of power, in other periods its limitations. In each of the periods of the Court's history, certain characteristic doctrines and precedents prevail, only to be abandoned or distinguished in a later period; as some wag once said, a distinguished case is one that is no longer distinguished. The Court also seems always to have special interests to protect. In one period it might be the Union or the state police power; in another, corporations or organized labor; in still another, radicals, black Americans, or the criminally accused.

The first or formative period is identifed with the chief-justiceship of John Marshall. When John Jay, one of his predecessors who had resigned from the Court to run for state office, declined reappointment as chief justice, he said that the Court was fatally lacking in power. Marshall took the job and no one thereafter could make the same complaint. During Marshall's long tenure of office, the Court asserted the power of judicial review, precariously over Congress and firmly over the states, establishing the supremacy of the Constitution and federal law. A partisan organ of the national government, the Court's nationalistic opinions conjured up the image of screaming eagles and Old Glory on the rise. Marshall also made the Court, in Max Lerner's phrase, "the strategic link between capitalism and constitutionalism."[12] His nationalism, which was both real and enduringly constructive in *McCulloch v. Maryland* and *Gibbons v. Ogden,* was more frequently a guise for the invalidation of state statutes that trenched on private property. Doctrines of vested rights, derived from extraconstitutional sources, found lodgment mainly in the contract clause.

Under Roger B. Taney's chief-justiceship, which was marred by the aberrational *Dred Scott* decision, the Court deviated only slightly from the course set by Marshall. Its vigorous exercise of judicial review and extension of its jurisdiction into unprecedented fields fortified the national judicial power. Less inclined to see state legislation as an assault upon the supremacy of the union, the Taney Court refused to let unused national powers serve as a rationale for the invalidation of state acts not in operative conflict with national acts. It behaved more like an impartial arbitrator between states and nation than like a strident champion of the latter. Despite some rhetoric about community rights and public welfare, property rights vested by contract were usually treated as if sacred, and corporate business was encouraged and protected. The trend, if not the tone, of decision was rather conservative.

In the third period of the Court's history, from the close of the Civil War to the 1890s, the state police power enjoyed its greatest triumphs, despite threatening judicial language that laid the groundwork for new doctrines of constitutional limitations. The contract clause, although revealed to have weaknesses, still served as the principal justification for the invalidation of much regulatory legislation. During this time the Court struck down or eviscerated most of a comprehensive congressional program for the protection of civil rights, making corporations rather than black Americans the chief beneficiary of the Fourteenth Amendment. Judicial interpretation eroded away the historic meanings of due process of law as a protection of the rights of the criminally accused, and engrafted a new economic substance to due process, making it a device for keeping man's relation to his Gold as private as possible.

From 1895 to 1936, the period of relative "judicial supremacy," the Court acted as if it were a superlegislature or third chamber, and the due process clause became the most formidable weapon in the armory of judicial review. Brooks Adams tartly observed that the historic purpose of the federal judiciary seemed to be to "dislocate any comprehensive body of legislation, whose effect would be to change the social status." This same patrician, with his contempt for the profit-hungry captains of industry, remarked: "The capitalist, as I infer, regards the constitutional form of government which exists in the United States, as a convenient method of obtaining his own way against a majority."[13] The Supreme Court arrogantly, artlessly, and inconsistently manipulated doctrines of constitutional law against an array of statutory reforms that sought to protect consumers, trade unions, farmers, unorganized workers, women, and children from the exploitation and abuses of economic enterprise. The high point of the Court's attempt to control public policy was reached during seventeen months of 1935–1936 in a massive and unprecedented judicial assault against a single administration. No less than twelve acts of Congress, parts of a systematic program to combat economic and social disaster, were held unconstitutional. Public opinion, though opposed to packing the Court, was outraged. The Court-packing plan failed largely because the Court, in the spring of 1937, made a timely, strategic retreat, validating the observation that it could read election returns, even if belatedly. During this long era from 1895 to 1936, critics of the Court, liberals and democrats of both parties, lambasted it for its activism and propounded arguments that the reactionary Court was oligarchic; they contended that it should devote itself to self-restraint, so that popular government might have its way.

President Franklin D. Roosevelt reconstructed the Court by placing it in the control of its critics, including Hugo L. Black, Felix Frankfurter, Robert H. Jackson, and William O. Douglas, who remade constitutional law out of the dissenting opinions of Oliver Wendell Holmes, Louis D. Brandeis, and Harlan F. Stone. The great issues of the 1930s were quickly settled. Outworn and reprehensible precedents fell like cold clinkers through an open grate. The new Court also junked economic due process and doctrines constricting government powers. At the same time that the Court emancipated both federal and state governmental powers, it vitalized the constitutional law of human rights. Cases involving free speech, the claims of the criminally accused, equality, racial justice, and expansion of the political process dominated, then overwhelmed, the Court's docket. The supreme tribunal at last caught up with folklore: it became the protector of civil rights and civil liberties, sometimes anticipating rather than following the election returns. Liberal intellectuals and scholars, as well as spokesmen for racial, religious, and ethnic minorities and women, warmed themselves in the glowing approval that the Court's opinions provided to them. People who had once castigated the Court for its undemocratic propensities discovered that it stood, in many respects, in the vanguard of social revolution. The political branches, by default as in the cases involving the rights of the criminally accused, reapportionment, and racial discrimination, took their leads from the Court. Once conservative activist, it had become liberal activist. Judicial review possessed new attractions.[14]

While liberals welcomed the new trend of decision, conservatives found it repugnant, leveling charges that the Court had coddled communists and criminals, outlawed God from the public schools, legislated morality and sociology in its desegregation decisions, and intruded into the "political thicket" of legislative apportionment. Liberals rushed to the Court's protection, defending it against such charges as irresponsible, misleading, and misunderstanding. By no coincidence the argument harmonizing judicial review and democracy seems to have originated during the McCarthy period, when majoritarian excesses invited thoughtful but overwrought liberals to reconsider the benefits of judicial intervention. Then *Brown v. Board of Education* (1954) became the watershed case in modern history, and modern constitutional law developed feverishly under the aegis of the Warren Court.

The Burger Court deeply disappointed ultraconservatives.[15] It sniped at the Warren Court but carried on in much the same way. It did not overturn *Miranda v. Arizona*[16] or the exclusionary rule.[17] It extended the principle of one person, one vote, even when racial criteria served as the basis for reapportionment.[18] It backed enforced school busing to achieve integration in the public schools.[19] It advanced the cause of sexual equality by invalidating a variety of sexual classifications.[20] It rejected the principle of racial color blindness and supported racial quotas as well as affirmative action.[21] It did little to permit the censorship of blatant, commercialized pornography.[22] It disallowed publicly financed field trips, instructional aids, and specialized auxiliary services for parochial school children.[23] It denied the constitutionality of a state act requiring the posting in every public school room of an enlargement of the Ten Commandments.[24] It disapproved of inherent executive power to eavesdrop electronically on domestic "subversives."[25] It sharply restricted the use of capital punishment and reversed the death sentences of hundreds of convicted murderers by finding that the death penalty, though not unconstitutional per se, was inflicted arbitrarily and capriciously when the juries received inadequate judicial guidance.[26] Even worse than its softness on the death penalty, according to ultraconservatives, the Burger Court made a most heinous and wholly unforgivable decision in *Roe v. Wade* (1973), one doubtlessly saturated with judicial activism: the Court sustained the right of a woman to an abortion in the early stages of pregnancy.[27]

The Court is most likely, nowadays, to be sensitive to the scholarly commentators and the law reviews. Chief Justice Hughes called the journals the "fourth estate of the law."[28] Responsible, informed critics have often led the way during this period of modern constitutional law. The Justices are also far more conscious of constitutional history and the mistakes of their predecessors. They rarely decide a case without first canvassing the journals to determine whether the issue has been discussed by some extramural authority from whom some wisdom may be gleaned. Students of constitutional law, no less than the Justices themselves, must know constitutional history. Although the Court will no longer hold unconstitutional a statute fixing maximum hours for labor or prohibiting racial discrimination in public facilities, the early cases are indispensable to any understanding of current constitutional law. Modern judicial tolerance is an outgrowth of yesterday's judicial intolerance; judicial humility is the child of judicial arrogance.

LEONARD W. LEVY

NOTES

1. *Graves v. New York*, 306 U.S. 466, 491 (1939).

2. *McCollum v. Board of Education*, 334 U.S. 203, 237–238 (1948).

3. *United States v. Classic*, 313 U.S. 299, 315–316 (1941).

4. Oliver Wendell Holmes, *Collected Legal Papers* (New York, 1920), p. 139.

5. James M. Beck, *The Constitution of the United States* (New York, 1922), p. 221. The phrase "continuous constitutional convention" has been used independently by other writers, e.g., Henry S. Commager, "Constitutional History and the Higher Law," in Conyers Read, ed., *The Constitution Reconsidered* (New York, 1938), p. 231; and Robert H. Jackson, *The Struggle for Judicial Supremacy* (New York, 1941), pp. x–xi. Members of the Supreme Court, including Louis D. Brandeis, Hugo Black, Byron R. White, and Warren Burger, have also used the term.

6. Benjamin N. Cardozo, *The Nature of the Judicial Process* (New Haven, 1921), pp. 92–93.

7. Charles Evans Hughes, *Addresses and Papers* (New York, 1908), pp. 139–140.

8. Hoadly said, "Whatever hath an absolute authority to interpret any written or spoken laws, it is he who is truly the lawgiver, to all intents and purposes, and not the person who first wrote or spoke them." Quoted in James B. Thayer, "The Origin and Scope of the American Doctrine of Constitutional Law," *Harvard Law Review* 7 (1893): 152.

9. Alexis de Tocqueville, *Democracy in America*, Henry S. Commager, ed., trans. Henry Reeve (New York, 1947), p. 177.

10. Felix Frankfurter, "The Supreme Court," in Sydney D. Bailey, ed., *Aspects of American Government* (London, 1950), p. 35.

11. *Perry v. United States*, 294 U.S. 330 (1935). See the discussion in Jackson, *Struggle for Judicial Supremacy*, pp. 96–103.

12. Lerner, "John Marshall and the Campaign of History," *Columbia Law Review* 39 (1939): 403. The essay is reprinted in Leonard W. Levy ed., *American Constitutional Law: Historical Essays* (New York, 1969).

13. Brooks Adams, *The Theory of Social Revolutions* (New York: Macmillan, 1914), pp. 214, 218.

14. Compare Henry Steele Commager's *Majority Rule and Minority Rights* (1943) with his lectures seventeen years later on "Democracy and Judicial Review," in his *Freedom and Order* (New York, 1966), pp. 3–51, which conclude, like Rostow, "It is as an educational institution that the Court may have its greatest contribution to make to the understanding and preservation of liberty."

15. Vincent Blasi, ed., *The Burger Court: The Counter-Revolution That Wasn't* (New Haven, 1983), is a good account by various constitutional scholars. For ultraconservative accounts, see Christopher Wolfe, *The Rise of Modern Judicial Review: From Constitutional Interpretation to Judge-made Law* (New York, 1968), pp. 258–322, and Lino A. Graglia, "Constitutional Theory: The Attempted Justification for the Supreme Court's Liberal Political Program," *Texas Law Review 65* (1987):789–798.

16. Miranda v. Arizona, 384 U.S. 436 (1966).

17. Harris v. New York, 401 U.S. 222 (1971); United States v. Calandra, 414 U.S. 338 (1974); United States v. Leon, 468 U.S. 897 (1984).

18. United Jewish Organizations v. Carey, 430 U.S. 144 (1977).

19. Columbus Board of Education v. Penick, 443 U.S. 449 (1979); Dayton Board of Education v. Brinkman, 443 U.S. 526 (1979).

20. Califano v. Goldfarb, 430 U.S. 199 (1977), and Califano v. Westcott, 433 U.S. 76 (1979).

21. United Steelworkers Union v. Weber, 443 U.S. 193 (1979), and Fullilove v. Klutznick, 448 U.S. 448 (1980).

22. Miller v. California, 413 U.S. 15 (1973), and Young v. American Mini Theatres, 427 U.S. 50 (1976).

23. Meek v. Pittenger, 421 U.S. 349 (1975); Wolman v. Walter, 433 U.S. 229 (1977).

24. Stone v. Graham, 449 U.S. 39 (1980).

25. United States v. United States District Court, 407 U.S. 297 (1972).

26. Furman v. Georgia, 408 U.S. 238 (1972).

27. Roe v. Wade, 410 U.S. 113 (1973).

28. Quoted by Chester A. Newland, "Legal Periodicals and the United States Supreme Court," *Midwest Journal of Political Science* (February 1959): 59.

PUBLISHER'S NOTE

The essays in this volume form an overview of American constitutional history, from colonial times up to and including the Burger Court. They are chosen from the four-volume set of the *Encyclopedia of the American Constitution,* which Macmillan published in 1986.

In these articles the reader will find certain words, names, and court cases set in small capital letters. This cross-referencing system was used in the *Encyclopedia* to refer to separate entries on those subjects. Readers of this volume who want to find out more about these topics will want to consult the *Encyclopedia of the American Constitution* for further information. In addition, each essay has a bibliography that will aid the reader in pursuing his or her own study of the subject.

This volume is the first of a planned series on topics of constitutional interest. We are publishing the series to make the contents of the *Encyclopedia of the American Constitution* more readily accessible to students. Future volumes will treat the subjects of civil rights, criminal justice, and the Bill of Rights, among others.

ABOUT THE EDITOR

Leonard W. Levy was formerly Earl Warren Professor of American Constitutional History at Brandeis University. Since 1970, he has been at Claremont Graduate School where he is Andrew W. Mellon All-Claremont Professor of Humanities and Chairman of the Graduate Faculty of History. In 1969 he won the Pulitzer Prize for *Origins of the Fifth Amendment* (reissued by Macmillan in 1986). Mr. Levy is Editor-in-Chief of the *Encyclopedia of the American Constitution* (Macmillan, 1986). He has written and edited more than a score of books on the Constitution, among them *The Establishment Clause: Religion and the First Amendment* (Macmillan, 1986) and *Original Intent and the Framers' Constitution* (Macmillan, 1988).

CONSTITUTIONAL HISTORY BEFORE 1776

Edmund S. Morgan

The opening words of the United States Constitution, "We the People," startled some of the old revolutionaries of 1776. PATRICK HENRY, after expressing the highest veneration for the men who wrote the words, demanded "What right had they to say, *We the People.* . . . Who authorized them to speak the language of *We, the People,* instead of *We, the States?* " It was a good question and, as Henry knew, not really answerable. No one had authorized the members of the CONSTITUTIONAL CONVENTION to speak for the people of the United States. They had been chosen by the legislatures of thirteen sovereign states and were authorized only to act for the governments of those states in redefining the relationships among them. Instead, they had dared not only to act for "the people of the United States" but also to proclaim what they did as "the supreme law of the land," supreme apparently over the actions of the existing state governments and supreme also over the government that the Constitution itself would create for the United States. Because those governments similarly professed to speak and act for the people, how could the Constitution claim supremacy over them and claim it successfully from that day to this, however contested in politics, litigation, and civil war? The answer lies less in logic than in the centuries of political experience before 1787 in which Englishmen and Americans worked out a political faith that gave to "the people" a presumptive capacity to constitute governments.

The idea that government originates in a donation by the people is at least as old as classical Greece. Government requires some sort of justification, and a donation of power by the governed or by those about to be governed was an obvious way of providing it. But such a donation has seldom if ever been recorded as historical fact, because it is virtually impossible for any substantial collection of people to act as a body, either in conveying powers of government or in prescribing the mode of their exercise. The donation has to be assumed, presumed, supposed, imagined—and yet be plausible enough to be acceptable to the supposed donors.

In the Anglo-American world two institutions have lent credibility to the presumption. The first to emerge was the presence in government of representatives chosen by a substantial portion of the people. With the powers of government thus shared, it became plausible to think of the representatives and the government as acting for the people and deriving powers from them. But as these popular representatives assumed a dominant position in the government, it was all too easy for them to escape from the control of those who chose them and to claim unlimited power in the name of the almighty people. A second device was necessary to differentiate the inherent sovereign powers of the people from the limited powers assigned to their deputed agents or representatives. The device was found in written CONSTITUTIONS embodying the people's supposed donation of power in specific provisions to limit and define the government.

Such written constitutions were a comparatively late development; the United States Constitution was one of the first. They came into existence not simply out of the need to specify the terms of the putative donation of power by the people but also out of earlier attempts by representatives or spokesmen of the people to set limits to governments claiming almighty authority from a different source. Although the idea of a popular donation was an ancient way of justifying government, it was not the only way. Indeed, since the fall of Rome God had been the favored source of authority: earthly rulers, whether in church or state, claimed His commission, though the act in which He granted it remained as shadowy as any donation by the people. Up to the seventeenth century, the persons who spoke for the people spoke as subjects, but they spoke as subjects of God as well as of God's lieutenants. While showing a proper reverence for divinely ordained authority, they expected those commissioned by God to rule in a godlike manner, that is, to abide by the natural laws (discernible in God's government of the world) that were supposed to guide human conduct and give force to the specific "positive" laws of nations derived from them. Even without claiming powers of government, those who spoke for the people might thus set limits to the powers of government through "fundamental" laws that were thought to express the will of God more reliably than rulers who claimed His commission. The link is obvious between such FUNDAMENTAL LAWS and written constitutions that expressed the people's will more reliably than their elected representatives could. The one grew out of the other.

Written constitutions were a deliberate invention, designed to overcome the deficiencies of representative government, but representative government itself was the unintended outcome of efforts by kings to secure and extend their own power. The story begins with the creation of the English House of Commons in the thirteenth century, when the English government centered in a hereditary king who claimed God-given authority but had slender means for asserting it. The king, always in need of funds, summoned two representatives from each county and from selected boroughs (incorporated towns) to come to his court for the purpose of consenting to taxes. He required the counties and boroughs in choosing representatives, by some unspecified electoral process, to give them full powers of attorney, so that no one could later object to what they agreed to. Although only a small part of the adult population shared in the choice of representatives, the House of Commons came to be regarded as having power of attorney for the whole body of the king's subjects; every man, woman, and child in the country was held to be legally present within its walls.

The assembly of representatives, thus created and identified with the whole people, gradually acquired an institutional existence, along with the House of Lords, as one branch of the king's Parliament. As representatives, the members remained subjects of the king, empowered by other subjects to act for them. But from the beginning they were somewhat more than subjects: in addition to granting the property of other subjects in taxes, they could petition the king for laws that would direct the actions of government. From petitioning for laws they moved to making them: by the sixteenth century English laws were enacted "by authority" of Parliament. Theoretically that authority still came from God through the king, and Parliament continued to be an instrument by which English monarchs consolidated and extended their government, never more so than in the sixteenth century. But in sharing their authority with Parliament the kings shared it, by implication, with the people. By the time the first American colonies were founded in the early seventeenth century, the king's instrument had become a potential rival to his authority, and the people had become a potential alternative to God as the immediate source of authority.

The potential became actual in the 1640s when Parliament, discontented with Charles I's ecclesiastical, military, and fiscal policies, made war on the king and itself assumed all powers of government. The Parliamentarians justified their actions as agents of the people; and at this point the presumption of a popular origin of government made its appearance in England in full force. The idea, which had been overshadowed for so long by royal claims to a divine commission, had been growing for a century. The Protestant Reformation had produced a contest between Roman Catholics and Protestants for control of the various national governments of Europe. In that contest each side had placed on the people of a country the responsibility for its government's compliance with the will of God. The people, it was now asserted, were entrusted by God with creating proper governments and with setting limits on them to insure protection of true religion. When the limits were breached, the people must revoke the powers of rulers who had betrayed their trust. For Roman Catholics, Protestant rulers fitted the definition, and vice versa.

When Englishmen, mostly Protestant, challenged their king, who leaned toward Catholicism, these ideas were ready at hand for their justification, and the House of Commons had long been recognized as the representative of the people. The House, the members now claimed, to all intents and purposes *was* the people, and the powers of the people were supreme. Both the king and the House of Lords, lacking these powers, were superfluous. In 1649 the Commons killed the king, abolished the House of Lords, and made England a republic.

By assuming such sweeping powers the members of the House of Commons invited anyone who felt aggrieved by their conduct of government not only to question their claim to represent the people but also to draw a distinction between the powers of the people themselves and of the persons they might choose, by whatever means, to represent them.

The first critics of the Commons to draw such a distinction were, not surprisingly, the adherents of the king, who challenged the Commons in the public press as well as on the field of battle. The House of Commons, the royalists pointed out, had been elected by only a small fraction of the people, and even that fraction had empowered it only to consent to positive laws and taxes, not to alter the government. Parliament, the royalists insisted, must not be confused with the people themselves. Even if it were granted that the people might create a government and set limits on it in fundamental laws, the House of Commons was only one part of the government thus created and could not itself change the government by eliminating the king or the Lords.

More radical critics, especially the misnamed Levellers, called not only for a reform of Parliament to make it more truly representative but also for a written "Agreement of the People" in which the people, acting apart from Parliament, would reorganize the government, reserving certain powers to themselves and setting limits to Parliament just as Parliament had formerly set limits to the king. Although the Levellers were unsuccessful, other political leaders also recognized the need to elevate supposed acts of the people, in creating a government and establishing its fundamental laws, above acts of the government itself. They also recognized that even a government derived from popular choice needed a SEPARATION OF POWERS among legislative, executive, and judicial branches, not merely for convenience of administration but in order to prevent government from escaping popular control.

Although the English in these years generated the ideas that have guided modern republican government, they were unable to bring their own government into full conformity with those ideas. By the 1650s they found that they had replaced a monarch, whose powers were limited, first with a House of Commons that claimed unlimited powers and refused to hold new elections, and then with a protector, Oliver Cromwell, whose powers knew only the limits of his ability to command a conquering army. In 1660 most Englishmen were happy to see the old balance restored with the return of a hereditary king and an old-style but potent Parliament to keep him in line. In 1688 that Parliament again removed a king who seemed to be getting out of control. This time, instead of trying to eliminate monarchy, they replaced one king with another who promised to be more tractable than his predecessor. William III at the outset of his reign accepted a parliamentary declaration of rights, spelling out the fundamental laws that limited his authority.

JOHN LOCKE, in the classic defense of this "Glorious Revolution," refined the distinction made earlier by the Levellers between the people and their representatives. Locke posited a SOCIAL COMPACT in which a collection of hitherto unconnected individuals in a "state of nature" came together to form a society. Only after doing so did they enter into a second compact in which they created a government and submitted to it. This second compact or constitution could be broken—the government could be altered or replaced—without destroying the first compact and throwing the people back into a state of nature. Society, in other words, came before government; and the people, once bound into a society by a social compact, could act without government and apart from government in order to constitute or change a government.

Locke could point to no historical occurrence that quite fitted his pattern. Even the Glorious Revolution was not, strictly speaking, an example of popular constituent action; rather, one branch of an existing government had replaced another branch. And the Declaration of Rights, although binding on the king, was no more than an act of Parliament that another Parliament might repeal. Moreover, the authority of the king remained substantial, and he was capable of extending his influence over Parliament by appointing members to lucrative government offices.

Locke's description of the origin of government nevertheless furnished a theoretical basis for viewing the entire British government as the creation of the people it governed. That view was expressed most vociferously in the eighteenth century by the so-called commonwealthmen, who repeated the call for reforms to make Parliament more representative of the whole people and to reduce the king's influence on its members. But it was not only commonwealthmen who accepted Locke's formulation. By the middle of the eighteenth century the doctrine of the divine right of kings was virtually dead in England, replaced by the sovereignty of the people, who were now accepted as the immediate source of all authority whether in king, lords, or commons.

In England's American colonies the idea that government originates in the people had been familiar from the outset, nourished not only by developments in England but also by the special conditions inherent in colonization. Those conditions were politically and constitutionally complex. The colonies were founded by private individuals or corporations under charters granted by the king, in which Parliament had no part. In the typical colony the king initially conveyed powers of government to the founders, who generally remained in England and directed the enterprise through agents. As time went on, the king took the powers of government in most colonies to himself, acting through appointed governors. But whether the immediate source of governmental authority in a colony rested in the king or in royally authorized corporations or individual proprietors, it proved impossible to govern colonists at 3,000 miles' distance without current information about changing local conditions. That kind of information could best be obtained through a representative assembly of the settlers, empowered to levy taxes and make laws. As a result, in each of England's colonies, within a short time of the founding, the actual settlers gained a share in the choice of their governors comparable to that which Englishmen at home enjoyed through their Parliament.

England's first permanent colony in America, Virginia, was the first to exhibit the phenomenon. The Virginia Company of London, which founded the colony in 1607 and was authorized to govern it in 1609, did so for ten years without participation of the actual settlers. The results were disastrous, and in 1618 the company instructed its agents to call a representative assembly. The assembly met in 1619, the first in the present area of the United States. When the king dissolved the Virginia Company and resumed governmental authority over the colony in 1624, he declined to continue the assembly, but the governors he appointed found it necessary to do so on their own initiative until 1639, when the king recognized the need and made the Virginia House of Burgesses an official part of the government.

In most other colonies representatives were authorized from the beginning or came into existence spontaneously when colonists found themselves beyond the reach of existing governments. The Pilgrims who landed at Plymouth in 1620 provided for their own government by the MAYFLOWER COMPACT, with a representative assembly at its center. The initial governments of Rhode Island and Connecticut began in much the same way. In these Puritan colonies religious principle worked together with pragmatic necessity to emphasize the popular basis of government. Puritans believed that government, though ordained by God, must originate in a compact (or covenant) between rulers and people, in which rulers promised to abide by and enforce God's laws, while the people in return promised obedience. Even in Massachusetts, where from the beginning the government rested officially on a charter from the king, Governor John Winthrop took pains to explain that he regarded emigration to Massachusetts as a tacit consent to such a covenant on the part of everyone who came. The emigrants themselves seem to have agreed; and because the king's charter did not spell out the laws of God that must limit a proper government, the representative assembly of the colony in 1641 adopted the MASSACHUSETTS BODY OF LIBERTIES, which did so.

The model for the colonial representative assemblies was the House of Commons of England; but from the beginning the colonial assemblies were more representative than the House of Commons, in that a much larger proportion of the people shared in choosing them. In England REPRESENTATION was apportioned in a bizarre fashion among the towns and boroughs, with nearly empty villages sending members while many populous towns sent none. In the colonies, although the extension of representation did not everywhere keep up with the spread of population westward, the imbalance never approached that in England, where virtually no adjustments to shifts of population were made after the sixteenth century and none at all between 1675 and the nineteenth century. And while in England a variety of property qualifications and local regulations excluded the great majority of adult males from voting, in the colonies, because of the abundance of land and its widespread ownership, similar restrictions excluded only a minority of adult males.

In addition to its broader popular base, representation in the colonies retained more of its original popular function than did the English counterpart. Representatives in both England and the colonies were initially identified more with a particular group of subjects than with their rulers. As representatives assumed a larger and larger role in government, they necessarily came to consider themselves as acting more in an authoritative capacity over the whole people and less as the designated defenders of their immediate constituents. This conception grew more rapidly in England, as the power of the king declined and that of Parliament increased, than it did in the colonies, where representatives continued to champion the interests of their constituents against unpopular directives from England. The divergence in the American conception of representation was to play a key role both in the colonies' quarrel with England and in the problems faced by the independent Americans in creating their own governments.

By 1763, when France surrendered its North American possessions, Great Britain stood at the head of the world's greatest empire. But the place of the American colonists in that empire remained constitutionally uncertain. Officially their governments still derived authority not from popular donation but directly or indirectly from the king. In two colonies, Rhode Island and Connecticut, the king had conveyed power to the free male inhabitants to choose their own governor, governor's council, and legislative assembly. In two more the king had conveyed governmental power to a single family, the Penns in Pennsylvania and the Calverts in Maryland, who exercised their authority by appointing the governor and his council. In the rest of the colonies the king appointed the governor and (except in Massachusetts) his council, which in all colonies except Pennsylvania doubled as the upper house of the legislature. Thus in every colony except Rhode Island, Connecticut, and Massachusetts, a representative assembly made laws and levied taxes, but neither the governor nor the members of the upper house of the legislature owed their positions even indirectly to popular choice.

It might have been argued that the king himself owed his authority to some sort of popular consent, however tacitly expressed, but it would have been hard to say whether the people who gave that consent included those living in the colonies. It would have been harder still to say what relationship the colonists had to the king's Parliament. In England the king's subordination to Parliament had become increasingly clear. It was Parliament that recognized the restoration of Charles II in 1660; it was Parliament that, in effect, deposed James II in 1688; it was Parliament that placed George I on the throne in 1714 and established the succession of the House of Hanover. Insofar as England's kings ruled Great Britain after 1714 they ruled through Parliament. But they continued to rule the colonies through royal governors and councils, and Parliament still had no hand officially in the choice of royal governors and councils or in the formulation of instructions to them.

Because each colony had its own little parliament, its representative assembly, the people of each colony could have considered themselves as a separate kingdom and a separate people, separate not only from the people who chose the representative assemblies of the other colonies but separate also from the people of Great Britain who chose the British Parliament. If any colonist thought that way—and probably few did before the 1760s or 1770s—he would have had to consider a complicating fact: the British Parliament did on occasion legislate for the colonies and the colonies submitted to that legislation, most notably to the Navigation Acts of 1660 and 1663, which limited the trade of the colonies for the benefit of English merchants. Did this submission mean that the people of the colonies, who elected no representatives to Parliament, were subordinate to, as well as separate from, the people of Great Britain?

In one sense the answer had to be yes: if the king was subordinate to Parliament and the colonists were subordinate to the king, that would seem to make the colonists subordinate to Parliament and thus to the people who elected Parliament. But since Parliament had so seldom legislated for the colonies, it could be argued that the colonists' subordination to it was restricted to those areas where it had in fact legislated for them, that is, in matters that concerned their trade. In other areas, they would be subordinate to Parliament only through the king, and the subordination of the colonial representative assemblies to the king was by no means unlimited. Through the taxing power the colonial assemblies had achieved, over the years, a leverage in the operation of their respective governments comparable to that which had raised Parliament above the king in Great Britain. To be sure, they had not arrived at so clear a position of superiority over their royal governors as Parliament enjoyed over the king. For example, while Queen Anne was the last monarch to veto an act of Parliament, royal governors regularly vetoed acts of colonial assemblies; and even an act accepted by the king's governor could still be vetoed by the king himself. The assemblies nevertheless enjoyed considerable power; by refusing to authorize taxation or to appropriate funds, they could thwart royal directives that they considered injurious to the interests or rights of their constituents. And in some ways they enjoyed a greater independence of royal influence than did Parliament. Because there were few sinecures or places of profit in colonial governments within the appointment of the king or his governors, it was difficult for a governor to build a following in an assembly through patronage.

Despite its constitutional and political ambiguities the British imperial system worked. It continued to work until the power of Parliament collided with the power of the colonial assemblies, thus requiring a resolution of the uncertainties in their relationship. The collision occurred when Parliament, facing a doubled national debt after the Seven Years War, passed the Revenue Act of 1764 (usually called the Sugar Act), levying duties on colonial imports, and the Stamp Act of 1765, levying direct taxes on legal documents and other items used in the colonies. In these acts, probably without intending to, Parliament threatened to destroy the bargaining power through which the colonial assemblies had balanced the authority of the king and his governors. If Parliament could tax the colonists directly, it might free the king's governors from dependence on the assemblies for funds and ultimately render the assemblies powerless.

In pamphlets and newspaper articles the colonists denounced the new measures. The assemblies, both separately and in a STAMP ACT CONGRESS, to which nine colonies sent delegates, spelled out in resolutions and petitions what they considered to be fundamental constitutional rights that Parliament had violated. In doing so the assemblies were obliged to define their constitutional relationship to Parliament with a precision never before required.

Parliament, it must be remembered, had been regarded for centuries as the bulwark of English liberties. It was the representative body of the English people, and through it the English had tamed their king as no other Europeans had. To question its supremacy might well seem to be a reactionary retreat toward absolute monarchy by divine right. The colonists were therefore hesitant to deny all subordination to Parliament. Yet, if they were to enjoy the same rights that other British subjects enjoyed in Great Britain, they must reserve to their own assemblies at the very least the power to tax. They acknowledged, therefore, the authority of Parliament to legislate for the whole empire as it had hitherto done in regulating colonial trade, but they drew a distinction between the power to legislate and the power to tax.

The colonists associated legislation with the sovereign power of a state, and they wanted to consider themselves as remaining in some still undefined way under the sovereign power of the British government. But taxation had from the time of England's first Parliaments been a function of representatives, authorized by those who sent them to give a part of their property to the king in taxes. Taxation, the colonial assemblies affirmed, was not a part of the governing or legislative power, but an action taken in behalf of the king's subjects. This distinction could be seen, they pointed out, in the form given to Parliamentary acts of taxation: such acts originated in the House of Commons and were phrased as the gift of the commons to the king.

Now the difference between American and British conceptions of representation began to appear. The colonists did not think of the English House of Commons as representing them, for no county or town or borough in the colonies sent members. The British government had never suggested that they might, and the colonists themselves rejected the possibility as impracticable. Given their conception of the representative's subservient relation to his constituents, it would have been impossible, they felt, to maintain adequate control over representatives at 3,000 miles' distance. Thus the colonists had not authorized and could not authorize any representative in Parliament to give their property in taxes. When Parliament taxed them, therefore, it deprived them of a fundamental right of Englishmen, sacred since before the colonies were founded. For a Parliament in which the colonists were not represented to tax them was equivalent to the king's taxing Englishmen in England without the consent of the House of Commons. The colonists called in vain on English courts to nullify this violation of fundamental law.

In answering the colonial objections, British spokesmen did not claim that the colonists could be taxed without the consent of their representatives. Thomas Whately, speaking for the ministry that sponsored the taxes, went even further than the colonists by denying that any legislation affecting British subjects anywhere could be passed without consent of their representatives. But he went on to affirm what to the colonists was an absurdity, that the colonists were represented in the House of Commons. Although they did not choose members, they were *virtually* represented by every member chosen in Britain, each of whom was entrusted with the interests not merely of the few persons who chose him but of all British subjects. The colonists were represented in the same way as Englishmen in towns that sent no members, in the same way also as English women and children.

However plausible this reasoning may have been to Englishmen, to the colonists it was sheer sophistry. They made plain in resolutions of their assemblies, as for example in Pennsylvania, "That the only legal Representatives of the Inhabitants of this Province are the Persons they annually elect to serve as Members of Assembly." Pamphlets and newspapers were even more scathing in rejecting the pretensions of Parliament to represent Americans. In Massachusetts JAMES OTIS asked, "Will any man's calling himself my agent, representative, or trustee make him so in fact?" On that basis the House of Commons could equally pretend "that they were the true and proper representatives of all the common people upon the globe." (See TAXATION WITHOUT REPRESENTATION.)

In reaction to the objections of the colonists and of the English merchants who traded with them, Parliament in 1766 repealed the Stamp Act and revised the Sugar Act. But at the same time it passed a Declaratory Act, affirming its right to legislate for the colonies "in all cases whatsoever." The framers of the act deliberately omitted specific mention of the power to tax, but in the following year Parliament again exercised that presumed power in the TOWNSHEND ACTS, levying more customs duties on colonial imports. The colonists again mounted protests, but they were still reluctant to deny all Parliamentary authority over them and clung to their distinction between legislation and taxation, which the great William Pitt himself had supported (unsuccessfully) in Parliamentary debate. Parliament, they said, could regulate their trade, even by imposing customs duties, but must not use the pretext of trade regulation for the purpose of raising revenue.

Once again the colonial protests, backed by boycotts, secured repeal of most of the offending taxes, but once again Parliament reaffirmed the principle of its unlimited power, not in a declaration, but by retaining a token tax on tea. The colonists, relieved of any serious burden, were left to ponder the implications of their position. In one sense Parliament was treating them as part of a single people, over all of whom, whether in England or elsewhere, Parliament reigned supreme. In rejecting the notion that they were, or even could be, represented in Parliament, the colonists implied that they were a separate people or peoples.

A reluctance to face this implication had prompted their continued recognition of some sort of authority in Parliament. If Parliament in the past had secured the rights of Englishmen, was it not dangerous (as Whately had indeed said it was) to rely instead on the powers of their own little assemblies? If they were a separate people, or peoples, not subject to Parliament, would they not be foregoing the rights of

Englishmen, the very rights they were so vigorously claiming? Could they expect their own assemblies to be as effective defenders of those rights as the mighty British Parliament?

As the quarrel over taxation progressed, with the Boston Tea Party of 1773 and Parliament's punitive Coercive Act of 1774 against Massachusetts, more and more Americans overcame the doubts raised by such questions. The Coercive Acts regulated trade with a vengeance by interdicting Boston's trade, and the acts also altered the government of Massachusetts as defined by its royal charter (ending the provincial election of the governor's council), thereby showing once and for all that guarantees given by the king could not stand before the supremacy claimed by Parliament. In the treatment of Massachusetts the other colonies read what was in store for them, and the various colonial assemblies sent delegates to the FIRST CONTINENTAL CONGRESS in 1774 in order to concert their response.

As in the earlier Stamp Act Congress, the delegates had to determine what they considered to be the limits of Parliament's authority. This time, abandoning their distinction between legislation and taxation (which Parliament had never recognized), they denied that Parliament had or had ever had constitutional authority over them. As a last conciliatory gesture, they expressed a willingness voluntarily to submit to bona fide regulations of trade, but made clear that Parliament had no constitutional right to make such regulations. Following the lead given in tracts by JOHN ADAMS, JAMES WILSON, and THOMAS JEFFERSON, they elevated their separate representative assemblies to a constitutional position within their respective jurisdictions equal to that of Parliament in Great Britain. The only remaining link connecting them with the mother country was their allegiance to the same king, who must be seen as the king of Virginia, Massachusetts, and so on, as well as of England, Scotland, Wales, and Ireland. (Ireland, it was noted, also had its separate Parliament.) Over his peoples beyond the seas the king exercised his powers through separate but equal governments, each with its own governor, council, and representative assembly.

The king did not, of course, rule by divine right. In the colonies as in England he derived his authority from the people themselves, that is, from the separate consent or constituent act of each of the peoples of his empire. John Adams of Massachusetts, perceiving the need to identify such an act, pointed to the Glorious Revolution of 1688 as an event in which each of the king's peoples participated separately. "It ought to be remembered," he said, "that there was a revolution here, as well as in England, and that we as well as the people of England, made an original, express contract with King William." That contract, as Adams and other colonists now saw it, limited royal power in the same way it was limited in England and guaranteed in each colony the exclusive legislative and taxing authority of the representative assembly.

Although the First Continental Congress gave a terminal clarity to the colonists' views of their constitutional position in the empire, it looked forward uncertainly toward a new relationship among the colonies themselves. The membership of the Congress reflected the uncertainty. Some of the members had been chosen by regularly constituted assemblies; others had been sent by extralegal conventions or committees; and a few were self-appointed. What authority, if any, the members had was not clear. Given the view of representation that had guided colonial reaction to Parliamentary taxation, no one was ready to claim for Congress the powers denied to Parliament. Though delegates from every colony except Georgia were present, they had not been chosen by direct popular elections and therefore were not, by their own definition, representatives. At best, as one of them put it, they were "representatives of representatives."

Yet they had not come together simply for discussion. Boston was under military occupation and Massachusetts was under military government. Regular royal government throughout the colonies was fast approaching dissolution. It was time for action, and the Congress took action. Without pausing to determine by what authority, it adopted an ASSOCIATION forbidding not only exports to and imports from Great Britain but also the consumption of British goods. And it called for the creation of committees in every county, city, and town to enforce these restrictions.

In the misnamed Association (membership in which was scarcely voluntary) the Congress took the first steps toward creating a national government separate from that of the (not yet independent) states. If the members believed, as presumably they did, that the authority of government derives from the people, they implied, perhaps without quite realizing what they were doing, that there existed a single American people, distinct not only from the people of Great Britain but also from the peoples of the several colonies and capable of conveying a political authority distinct from that either of Great Britain or of the several colonies.

The implication would not become explicit until the Constitution of 1787, but the Second Continental Congress, which assembled in May 1775, looked even more like the government of a single people than had the First. Fighting had already broken out in April between British troops and Massachusetts militiamen, and Congress at once took charge of the war and began the enlistment of a Continental Army. It sent envoys to France to seek foreign assistance. It opened American commerce to foreign nations. It advised the peoples of the several colonies to suppress all royal authority within their borders. And finally, after more than a year of warfare, it declared the independence of the United States.

Despite the boldness of these actions, the DECLARATION OF INDEPENDENCE itself betrayed the ambiguities that Americans felt about their own identity. It unequivocally put an end to royal authority (parliamentary authority had already been rejected) and consequently to all remaining connection with the people of Great Britain. But it was not quite clear whether the independence thus affirmed was of one people, or of several, or of both one and several. While the preamble spoke of "one people" separating from another, the final affirmation was in the plural, declaring that "these United Colonies are, and of Right ought to be Free and Independent States." Yet in stating what constituted free and independent statehood, the Declaration specified only "power to levy war, conclude peace, contract alliances, establish commerce." These were all things, with the possible exception of the last, that had been done or would be done by the Congress.

But if the Congress sometimes acted like the government of a single free and independent state, the members still did not recognize the implication that they represented a single free and independent people. They did not consider their Declaration of Independence complete until it had been ratified by each of the separate states whose freedom and independence it declared. And when they tried to define their own authority, they found it difficult to reach agreement. ARTICLES OF CONFEDERATION, first drafted in 1776, were not ratified by the several states until 1781. The Articles entrusted Congress with the powers it was already exercising but declined to derive those powers from a single American people. The old local committees of the Association of 1774, tied directly to Congress, were now a thing of the past, and the enactments of Congress became mere recommendations, to be carried out by the various states as they saw fit.

Even before the Declaration of Independence, in response to the recommendation of the Congress, the states had begun to create governments resting solely on the purported will of the people within their existing borders. In every state a provisional government appeared, usually in the form of a provincial congress resembling the old colonial representative assembly. In most of the states, beginning with Virginia in June 1776, these provincial congresses drew up and adopted, without further reference to the people, constitutions defining the structure of their governments and stating limitations on governmental powers in bills of rights. In every case the constitution was thought or proclaimed to be in some way an act of the people who were to be governed under it, and therefore different from and superior to acts of representatives in a legislative assembly. But often the provincial congress that drafted a state constitution continued to act as the legislative body provided in it. Although a constitution might affirm its own superiority to ordinary legislation, the fact that it was created by legislative act rendered doubtful its immunity to alteration by the body that created it.

A similar doubt surrounded the principle, also enunciated in most of the constitutions, that (as in Virginia) "The legislative, executive, and judiciary departments shall be separate and distinct, so that neither exercise the powers properly belonging to the other." The several provincial congresses that drafted the constitutions inherited the aggressiveness of the colonial assemblies against executive and, to a lesser degree, judicial powers, which had hitherto rested in an overseas authority beyond their reach. In spite of the assertion of the separation of powers, and in spite of the fact that executives and judges would now derive authority solely from the people they governed, the state constitutions generally gave the lion's share of power in government to the representative assemblies.

The result was to bring out the shortcomings of the view of representation that had directed the colonists in their resistance to British taxation. For a decade the colonists had insisted that a representative must act only for the particular group of persons who chose him. They occasionally recognized but minimized his responsibility, as part of the governing body, to act for the whole people who were to be governed by the laws he helped to pass. Now the representative assemblies were suddenly presented with virtually the entire powers of government, which they shared only with a weak executive and judiciary and with a Continental Congress whose powers remained uncertain, despite Articles of Confederation that gave it large responsibilities without the means to perform them. Undeterred by any larger view of their functions, too many of the state assemblymen made a virtue of partiality to their particular constituents and ignored the long-range needs not only of their own state but of the United States.

The solution lay ahead in 1787. By 1776 the inherited ingredients of the settlement then adopted were in place. A rudimentary distinction between the constituent actions of a putative people and the actions of their government had been recognized, though not effectively implemented, in the state governments. All government officers were now selected directly or indirectly by popular choice, with their powers limited, at least nominally, by a reservation to the people of powers not specifically conveyed. And a national center of authority, not quite a government but nevertheless acting like a government, was in operation in the Continental Congress.

What was needed—and with every passing year after 1776 the need became more apparent—was a way to relieve popular government from the grip of short-sighted representative assemblies. Two political inventions filled the need. The first was the constitutional convention, an assembly without legislative powers, entrusted solely with the drafting of a constitution for submission to popular ratification, a constitution that could plausibly be seen as the embodiment of the popular will superior to the ordinary acts of representative assemblies. Massachusetts provided this invention in 1779, in the convention that drafted the state's first constitution. (See MASSACHUSETTS CONSTITUTION.)

The first invention made way for the second, which was supplied by JAMES MADISON and his colleagues at Philadelphia in 1787. They invented the American people. It was, to be sure, an invention waiting to be made. It had been prefigured in the assumptions behind the Continental Association and the Declaration of Independence. But it reached fulfillment only in the making of the Constitution. By means of a national constitutional convention the men at Philadelphia built a national government that presumed and thus helped to create an American people, distinct from and superior to the peoples of the states.

The idea of popular SOVEREIGNTY was, as we have seen, an old one, but only occasionally had it dictated the formation of popular governments, governments in which all the officers owed their positions directly or indirectly to popular election. Though the idea surfaced powerfully in the England of the 1640s and 1650s, it eventuated there in a restored monarchy, and it won only partial recognition in England's Revolution of 1688. In the American Revolution it had seemingly found full expression in thirteen separate state governments, but by 1787 the actions of those governments threatened once again to discredit the whole idea. The signal achievement of the constitutional convention was expressed in the opening words of the document it produced: "We the People of the United States." The United States Constitution rescued popular sovereignty by extending it. It inaugurated both a new government and a new people.

Bibliography

ADAMS, WILLI PAUL   1980   *The First American Constitutions.* Chapel Hill: University of North Carolina Press.

BAILYN, BERNARD   1967   *The Ideological Origins of the American Revolution.* Cambridge, Mass.: Harvard University Press.

———   1968   *The Origins of American Politics.* New York: Knopf.

FIGGIS, JOHN NEVILLE   1914   *The Divine Right of Kings.* Cambridge: At the University Press.

GREENE, JACK P.   1963   *The Quest for Power.* Chapel Hill: University of North Carolina Press.

KANTOROWICZ, ERNST H.   1957   *The King's Two Bodies.* Princeton: N.J.: Princeton University Press.

LABAREE, LEONARD W.   1930   *Royal Government in America.* New Haven, Conn.: Yale University Press.

McIlwain, Charles H.   1923   *The American Revolution.* New York: Macmillan.

Morgan, Edmund S. and Morgan, Helen M.   1953   *The Stamp Act Crisis.* Chapel Hill: University of North Carolina Press.

Pocock, John G. A.   1957   *The Ancient Constitution and the Feudal Law.* Cambridge: At the University Press.

Russell, Conrad   1979   *Parliaments and English Politics 1621–1629.* Oxford: Clarendon Press.

Schuyler, Robert L.   1929   *Parliament and the British Empire.* New York: Columbia University Press.

Skinner, Quentin   1978   *The Foundations of Modern Political Thought.* Cambridge: At the University Press.

Tucker, Robert W. and Hendrickson, David C.   1982   *The Fall of the First British Empire.* Baltimore: Johns Hopkins University Press.

CONSTITUTIONAL HISTORY, 1776–1789

Leonard W. Levy

On July 4, 1776, King George III wrote in his diary, "Nothing of importance this day." When the news of the DECLARATION OF INDEPENDENCE reached him, he still could not know how wrong he had been. The political philosophy of SOCIAL COMPACT, NATURAL RIGHTS, and LIMITED GOVERNMENT that generated the Declaration of Independence also spurred the most important, creative, and dynamic constitutional achievements in history; the Declaration itself was merely the beginning. Within a mere thirteen years Americans invented or first institutionalized a bill of rights against all branches of government, the written CONSTITUTION, the CONSTITUTIONAL CONVENTION, FEDERALISM, JUDICIAL REVIEW, and a solution to the colonial problem (admitting TERRITORIES to the Union as states fully equal to the original thirteen). RELIGIOUS LIBERTY, the SEPARATION OF CHURCH AND STATE, political parties, SEPARATION OF POWERS, an acceptance of the principle of equality, and the conscious creation of a new nation were also among American institutional "firsts," although not all these initially appeared between 1776 and 1789. In that brief span of time, Americans created what are today the oldest major republic, political democracy, state constitution, and national constitution. These unparalleled American achievements derived not from originality in speculative theory but from the constructive application of old ideas, which Americans took so seriously that they constitutionally based their institutions of government on them.

From thirteen separate colonies the Second Continental Congress "brought forth a new nation," as ABRAHAM LINCOLN said. In May 1776, Congress urged all the colonies to suppress royal authority and adopt permanent governments. On that advice and in the midst of a war the colonies began to frame the world's first written constitutions. When Congress triggered the drafting of those constitutions, Virginia instructed its delegates to Congress to propose that Congress should declare "the United Colonies free and independent states." Neither Virginia nor Congress advocated state sovereignty. Congress's advice implied the erection of state governments with sovereign powers over domestic matters or "internal police."

On June 7, 1776, Congressman RICHARD HENRY LEE of Virginia

introduced the resolution as instructed, and Congress appointed two committees, one to frame the document that became the Declaration of Independence and the other to frame a plan of confederation—a constitution for a continental government. When Lincoln declared, "The Union is older than the States, and in fact created them as States," he meant that the Union (Congress) antedated the states. The Declaration of Independence, which stated that the colonies had become states, asserted the authority of the "United States of America, in General Congress, Assembled."

The "spirit of '76" tended to be strongly nationalistic. The members of Congress represented the states, of course, and acted on their instructions, but they acted for the new nation, and the form of government they thought proper in 1776 was a centralized one. As a matter of fact BENJAMIN FRANKLIN had proposed such a government on July 21, 1775, when he presented to Congress "ARTICLES OF CONFEDERATION and perpetual Union." Franklin urged a congressional government with an executive committee that would manage "general continental Business and Interests," conduct diplomacy, and administer finances. His plan empowered Congress to determine war and peace, exchange ambassadors, make foreign alliances, settle all disputes between the colonies, plant new colonies, and, in a sweeping omnibus clause, make laws for "the General Welfare" concerning matters on which individual colonies "cannot be competent," such as "our general Commerce," "general Currency," the establishment of a post office, and governance of "our Common Forces." Costs were to be paid from a common treasury supplied by each colony in proportion to its male inhabitants, but each colony would raise its share by taxing its inhabitants. Franklin provided for an easy amendment process: Congress recommended amendments that would become part of the Articles when approved by a majority of colonial assemblies. Franklin's plan of union seemed much too radical in July 1775, when independence was a year away and reconciliation with Britain on American terms was the object of the war. Congress simply tabled the Franklin plan.

As the war continued into 1776, nationalist sentiment strengthened. THOMAS PAINE's *Common Sense* called for American independence and "a Continental form of Government." Nationalism and centralism were twin causes. JOHN LANGDON of New Hampshire favored independence and "an American Constitution" that provided for appeals from every colony to a national congress "in everything of moment relative to governmental matters." Proposals for a centralized union became common by the spring of 1776, and these proposals, as the following representative samples suggest, tended to show democratic impulses. Nationalism and mitigated democracy, not nationalism and conservatism, were related. A New York newspaper urged the popular election of a national congress with a "superintending power" over the individual colonies as to "all commercial and Continental affairs," leaving to each colony control over its "internal policy." A populistic plan in a Connecticut newspaper recommended that the congress be empowered to govern "all matters of general concernment" and "every other thing proper and necessary" for the benefit of the whole, allowing the individual colonies only that which fell "within the territorial jurisdiction of a particular assembly." The "Spartacus" essays, which newspapers in New York, Philadelphia, and Portsmouth printed, left the state "cantons" their own legislatures but united all in a national congress with powers similar to those enumerated by Franklin, including a paramount power to "interfere" with a colony's "provincial affairs" whenever required by "the good of the continent." "Essex" reminded his readers that "the strength and happiness of America must be Continental, not Provincial, and that whatever appears to be for the good of the whole, must be submitted to by every Part." He advocated dividing the colonies into many smaller equal parts that would have equal representation in a powerful national congress chosen directly by the people, including taxpaying widows. Carter Braxton, a conservative Virginian, favored aristocratic controls over a congress that could not "interfere with the internal police or domestic concerns of any Colony . . . ."

Given the prevalence of such views in the first half of 1776, a representative committee of the Continental Congress probably mirrored public opinion when it framed a nationalist plan for confederation. On July 12, one month after the appointment of a thirteen-member committee (one from each state) to write a draft, JOHN DICKINSON of Pennsylvania, the committee chairman, presented to Congress a plan that borrowed heavily from Franklin's. The Committee of the Whole of Congress debated the Dickinson draft and adopted it on August 20 with few changes. Only one was significant. Dickinson had proposed that Congress be empowered to fix the western boundaries of states claiming territory to the Pacific coast and to form new states in the west. The Committee of the Whole, bending to the wishes of eight states with extensive western claims, omitted that provision from its revision of the Dickinson draft. That omission became a stumbling block.

On August 20 the Committee of the Whole reported the revised plan of union to Congress. The plan was similar to Franklin's, except that Congress had no power over "general commerce." But Congress, acting for the United States, was clearly paramount to the individual states. They were not even referred to as "states." Collectively they were "the United States of America"; otherwise they were styled "colonies" or "colony," terms not compatible with sovereignty, to which no reference was made. Indeed, the draft merely reserved to each colony "sole and exclusive Regulation and Government of its internal police, in all matters that shall not interfere with the Articles of this Confederation." That crucial provision, Article III, making even "internal police" subordinate to congressional powers, highlighted the nationalist character of the proposed confederation.

The array of congressional powers included exclusive authority over war and peace, land and naval forces, treaties and alliances, prize cases, crimes on the high seas and navigable rivers, all disputes between states, coining money, borrowing on national credit, Indian affairs, post offices, weights and measures, and "the Defence and Welfare" of the United States. Congress also had power to appoint a Council of State and civil officers "necessary for managing the general Affairs of the United States." The Council of State, consisting of one member from each of the thirteen, was empowered to administer the United States government and execute its measures. Notwithstanding this embryonic executive branch, the government of the United States was congressional in character, consisting of a single house whose members were to be elected annually by the legislatures of the colonies. Each colony cast one vote, making each politically equal in Congress. On all important matters, the approval of nine colonies was required to pass legislation. Amendments to the Articles needed the unanimous approval of the legislatures of the various colonies, a provision that later proved to be crippling.

The Articles reported by the Committee of the Whole provoked dissension. States without western land claims opposed the omission of the provision in the Dickinson draft that gave Congress control over western lands. Large states opposed the principle of one vote for each state, preferring instead proportionate representation with each delegate voting. Sharp differences also emerged concerning the rule by which each state was to pay its quota to defray common expenses. Finally some congressmen feared the centralizing nature of the new government. Edward Rutledge of South Carolina did not like "the Idea of destroying all Provincial Distinctions and making every thing of the most minute kind bend to what they call the good of the whole. . . ." Rutledge resolved "to vest the Congress with no more Power than what is absolutely necessary." JAMES WILSON of Pennsylvania could declare that Congress represented "all the individuals of the states" rather than the states, but ROGER SHERMAN of Connecticut answered, "We are representatives of states, not individuals." That attitude would undo the nationalist "spirit of '76."

Because of disagreements and the urgency of prosecuting the war, Congress was unable to settle on a plan of union in 1776. By the spring of 1777 the nationalist momentum was spent. By then most of the states had adopted constitutions and had legitimate governments. Previously, provisional governments of local "congresses," "conventions," and committees had controlled the states and looked to the Continental Congress for leadership and approval. But the creation of legitimate state governments reinvigorated old provincial loyalties. Local politicians, whose careers were provincially oriented, feared a strong central government as a rival institution. Loyalists no longer participated in politics, local or national, depleting support for central control. By late April of 1777, when state sovereignty triumphed, only seventeen of the forty-eight congressmen who had been members of the Committee of the Whole that adopted the Dickinson draft remained in Congress. Most of the new congressmen opposed centralized government.

James Wilson, who was a congressman in 1776 and 1777, recalled what happened when he addressed the Constitutional Convention on June 8, 1787:

Among the first sentiments expressed in the first Congs. one was that Virga. is no more. That Massts. is no more, that Pa. is no more &c. We are now one nation of brethren. We must bury all local interests and distinctions. This language continued for some time. The tables at length began to turn. No sooner were the State Govts. formed than their jealousy & ambition began to display themselves. Each endeavored to cut a slice from the common loaf, to add to its own morsel, till at length the confederation became frittered down to the impotent condition in which it now stands. Review the progress of the articles of Confederation thro' Congress & compare the first and last draught of it [Farrand, ed., Records, I, 166–67].

The turning point occurred in late April 1777 when Thomas Burke of North Carolina turned his formidable localist opinions against the report of the Committee of the Whole. Its Article III, in his words, "expressed only a reservation [to the states] of the power of regulating the internal police, and consequently resigned every other power [to Congress]." Congress, he declared, sought even to interfere with the states' internal police and make its own powers "unlimited." Burke accordingly moved the following substitute for Article III, which became Article II of the Articles as finally adopted: "Each State retains its sovereignty, freedom and independence, and every power, jurisdiction and right, which is not by this confederation expressly delegated to the United States in Congress assembled." Burke's motion carried by the votes of eleven states, vitiating the powers of the national government recommended by the Committee of the Whole.

In the autumn of 1777 a Congress dominated by state-sovereignty advocates completed the plan of confederation. Those who favored proportionate representation in Congress with every member entitled to vote lost badly to those who favored voting by states with each state having one vote. Thereafter the populous wealthy states had no stake in supporting a strong national government that could be controlled by the votes of lesser states. The power of Congress to negotiate commercial treaties effectively died when Congress agreed that under the Articles no treaty should violate the power of the states to impose tariff duties or prohibit imports and exports. The power of Congress to settle all disputes between states became merely a power to make recommendations. The permanent executive branch became a temporary committee with no powers except as delegated by the votes of nine states, the number required to adopt any major measure. Congress also agreed that it should not have power to fix the western boundaries of states claiming lands to the Pacific.

After the nationalist spurt of 1776 proved insufficient to produce the Articles, the states made the Confederation feckless. Even as colonies the states had been particularistic, jealous, and uncooperative. Centrifugal forces originating in diversity—of economics, geography, religion, class structure, and race—produced sectional, provincial, and local loyalties that could not be overcome during a war against the centralized powers claimed by Parliament. The controversy with Britain had produced passions and principles that made the Franklin and Dickinson drafts unviable. Not even these nationalist drafts empowered Congress to tax, although the principle of no TAXATION WITHOUT REPRESENTATION had become irrelevant as to Congress. Similarly, Congress as late as 1774 had "cheerfully" acknowledged Parliament's legitimate "regulation of our external commerce," but in 1776 Congress denied that Parliament had any authority over America, and by 1777 Americans were unwilling to grant their own central legislature powers they preferred their provincial assemblies to wield. Above all, most states refused to repose their trust in any central authority that a few large states might dominate, absent a constitutionally based principle of state equality.

Unanimous consent for amendments to the Articles proved to be too high a price to pay for acknowledging the "sovereignty" of each state, although that acknowledgment made Maryland capable of winning for the United States the creation of a national domain held in common for the benefit of all. Maryland also won the promise that new states would be admitted to the union on a principle of state equality. That prevented the development of a colonial problem from Atlantic to Pacific, and the NORTHWEST ORDINANCE OF 1787 was the Confederation's finest and most enduring achievement.

The Constitution of 1787 was unthinkable in 1776, impossible in 1781 or at any time before it was framed. The Articles were an indispensable transitional stage in the development of the Constitution. Not even the Constitution would have been ratified if its Framers had submitted it for approval to the state legislatures that kept Congress paralyzed in the 1780s. Congress, representing the United States, authorized the creation of the states and ended up, as it had begun, as their creature. It possessed expressly delegated powers with no means of enforcing them. That Congress lacked commerce and tax powers was a serious deficiency, but not nearly so crippling as its lack of sanctions and the failure of the states to abide by the Articles. Congress simply could not make anyone, except soldiers, do anything. It acted on the states, not on people. Only a national government that could execute its laws independently of the states could have survived.

The states flouted their constitutional obligations. The Articles obliged the states to "abide by the determinations of the United States, in Congress assembled," but there was no way to force the states to comply. The states were not sovereign, except as to their internal police and tax powers; rather, they behaved unconstitutionally. No foreign nation recognized the states as sovereign, because Congress possessed the external attributes of sovereignty especially as to FOREIGN AFFAIRS and WAR POWERS.

One of the extraordinary achievements of the Articles was the creation of a rudimentary federal system. It failed because its central government did not operate directly on individuals within its sphere of authority. The Confederation had no independent executive and judicial branches, because the need for them scarcely existed when Congress addressed its acts mainly to the states. The framers of the Articles distributed the powers of government with remarkable acumen, committing to Congress about all that belonged to a central government except, of course, taxation and commercial regulation, the two powers that Americans of the Revolutionary War believed to be part of state sovereignty. Even ALEXANDER HAMILTON, who in 1780 advocated that Congress should have "complete sovereignty," excepted "raising money by internal taxes."

Congress could requisition money from the states, but they did not pay their quotas. In 1781 Congress requisitioned $8,000,000 for the next year, but the states paid less than half a million. While the Articles lasted, the cumulative amount paid by all the states hardly exceeded what was required to pay the interest on the public debt for just one year.

Nationalists vainly sought to make the Articles more effective by both interpretation and amendment. Madison devised a theory of IMPLIED POWERS by which he squeezed out of the Articles congressional authority to use force if necessary against states that failed to fulfill their obligations. Congress refused to attempt coercion just as it refused to recommend an amendment authorizing its use. Congress did, however, charter a bank to control currency, but the opposition to the exercise of a power not expressly delegated remained so intense that the bank had to be rechartered by a state. Congress vainly sought unanimous state consent for various amendments that would empower it to raise money from customs duties and to regulate commerce, foreign and domestic. In 1781 every state but Rhode Island approved an amendment empowering Congress to impose a five percent duty on all foreign imports; never again did an amendment to the Articles come so close to adoption.

Only four states ratified an amendment authorizing a congressional embargo against the vessels of any nation with whom the United States had no treaty of commerce. Congress simply had no power to negotiate commercial treaties with nations such as Britain that discriminated against American shipping. Nor had Congress the power to prevent states from violating treaties with foreign nations. In 1786 JOHN JAY, Congress's secretary of foreign affairs, declared that not a day had passed since ratification of the 1783 treaty of peace without its violation by at least one state. Some states also discriminated against the trade of others. Madison likened New Jersey, caught between the ports of Philadelphia and New York, "to a cask tapped at both ends." More important, Congress failed even to recommend needed amendments. As early as 1784 Congress was so divided it defeated an amendment that would enable it to regulate commerce, foreign and domestic, and to levy duties on imports and exports. Often Congress could not function for lack of a quorum. The requisite number of states was present for only three days between October 1785 and April 1786. In 1786 Congress was unable to agree on any amendments for submission to the states.

The political condition of the United States during the 1780s stagnated partly because of the constitutional impotence of Congress and the unconstitutional conduct of the states. The controversy with Britain had taught that liberty and localism were congruent. The 1780s taught that excessive localism was incompatible with nationhood. The Confederation was a necessary point of midpassage. It bequeathed to the United States the fundamentals of a federal system, a national domain, and a solution to the colonial problem. Moreover the Articles contained several provisions that were antecedents of their counterparts in the Constitution of 1787: a free speech clause for congressmen and LEGISLATIVE IMMUNITY, a PRIVILEGES AND IMMUNITIES clause, a clause on the extradition of FUGITIVES FROM JUSTICE, a FULL FAITH AND CREDIT clause, and a clause validating United States debts. The Confederation also started an effective government bureaucracy when the Congress in 1781 created secretaries for foreign affairs, war, marine, and finance—precursors of an executive branch. When the new departments of that branch began to function in 1789, a corps of experienced administrators, trained under the Articles, staffed them. The courts established by Congress to decide prize and admiralty cases as well as boundary disputes foreshadowed a national judiciary. Except for enactment of the great Northwest Ordinance, however, the Congress of the Confederation was moribund by 1787. It had successfully prosecuted the war, made foreign alliances, established the national credit, framed the first constitution of the United States, negotiated a favorable treaty of peace, and created a national domain. Congress's accomplishments were monumental, especially during wartime, yet in the end it failed.

By contrast, state government flourished. Excepting Rhode Island and Connecticut, all the states adopted written constitutions during the war, eight in 1776. Madison exultantly wrote, "Nothing has excited more admiration in the world than the manner in which free governments have been established in America, for it was the first instance, from the creation of the world that free inhabitants have been seen deliberating on a form of government, and selection of such of their citizens as possessed their confidence to determine upon and give effect to it."

The VIRGINIA CONSTITUTION OF 1776, the first permanent state constitution, began with a Declaration of Rights adopted three weeks before the Declaration of Independence. No previous bill of rights had restrained all branches of government. Virginia's reflected the widespread belief that Americans had been thrown back into a state of nature from which they emerged by framing a social compact for their governance, reserving to themselves certain inherent or natural rights, including life, liberty, the enjoyment of property, and the pursuit of happiness. Virginia's declaration explicitly declared that as all power derived from the people, for whose benefit government existed, the people could reform or abolish government when it failed them. On the basis of this philosophy Virginia framed a constitution providing for a bicameral legislature, a governor, and a judicial system. The legislature elected a governor, who held office for one year, had no veto power, and was encumbered by an executive council. The legislature chose many important officials, including judges.

Some states followed the more democratic model of the PENNSYLVANIA CONSTITUTION OF 1776, others the ultraconservative one of Maryland, but all state constitutions prior to the MASSACHUSETTS CONSTITUTION OF 1780 were framed by legislatures, which in some states called themselves "conventions" or assemblies. Massachusetts deserves credit for having originated a new institution of government, a specially elected constitutional convention whose sole function was to frame the constitution and submit it for popular ratification. That procedure became the standard. Massachusetts's constitution, which is still operative, became the model American state constitution. The democratic procedure for making it fit the emerging theory that the sovereign people should be the source of the constitution and authorize its framing by a constitutional convention, rather than the legislature to which the constitution is paramount. Massachusetts was also the first state to give more than lip service to the principle of separation of powers. Everywhere else, excepting perhaps New York, unbalanced government and legislative supremacy prevailed. Massachusetts established the precedent for a strong, popularly elected executive with a veto power; elsewhere the governor tended to be a ceremonial head who depended for his existence on the legislature.

The first state constitutions and related legislation introduced significant reforms. Most states expanded VOTING RIGHTS by reducing property qualifications, and a few, including Vermont (an independent state from 1777 to 1791), experimented with universal manhood suffrage. Many state constitutions provided for fairer apportionment of REPRESENTATION in the legislature. Every southern state either abolished its ESTABLISHMENT OF RELIGION or took major steps to achieve separation of church and state. Northern states either abolished SLAVERY or provided for its gradual ending. Criminal codes were made more humane. The confiscation of Loyalist estates and of crown lands, and the opening of a national domain westward to the Mississippi, led to a democratization of landholding, as did the abolition of feudal relics such as the law of primogeniture and entail. The pace of democratic change varied from state to state, and in some states it was nearly imperceptible, but the Revolution without doubt occasioned constitutional and political developments that had long been dammed up under the colonial system.

The theory that a constitution is supreme law encouraged the development of judicial review. Written constitutions with bills of rights and the emerging principle of separation of powers contributed to the same end. Before the Revolution appellate judges tended to be dependents of the executive branch; the Revolution promoted judicial independence. Most state constitutions provided for judicial tenure during good behavior rather than for a fixed term or the pleasure of the appointing power. Inevitably when Americans believed that a legislature had exceeded its authority they argued that it had acted unconstitutionally, and they turned to courts to enforce the supreme law as law. The dominant view, however, was that a court holding a statute unconstitutional insulted the sovereignty of the legislature, as the reactions to HOLMES V. WALTON (1780) and TREVETT V. WEEDEN (1786) showed. COMMONWEALTH V. CATON (1782) was probably the first case in which a state judge declared that a court had power to hold a statute unconstitutional, though the court in that case sustained the act before it. In RUTGERS V. WADDINGTON (1784) Alexander Hamilton as counsel argued that a state act violating a treaty was unconstitutional, but the court declared that the judicial power advocated by counsel was "subversive of all government." Counsel in *Trevett* also contended that the court should void a state act. Arguments of counsel do not create precedents but can reveal the emergence of a new idea. Any American would have agreed that an act against a constitution was void; although few would have agreed that courts have the final power to decide matters of constitutionality, that idea was spreading. The TEN POUND ACT CASES (1786) were the first in which an American court held a state enactment void, and that New Hampshire precedent was succeeded by a similar decision in the North Carolina case of BAYARD V. SINGLETON (1787). The principle of MARBURY V. MADISON (1803) thus originated at a state level before the framing of the federal Constitution.

The Constitution originated in the drive for a strong national government that preceded the framing of the Articles of Confederation. The "critical period" of 1781–1787 intensified that drive, but it began well before the defects of the Articles expanded the ranks of the nationalists. The weaknesses of the United States in international affairs, its inability to enforce the peace treaty, its financial crisis, its helplessness during SHAYS' REBELLION, and its general incapacity to govern resulted in many proposals—in Congress, in the press, and even in some states—for national powers to negotiate commercial treaties, regulate the nation's commerce, and check state policies that adversely affected creditor interests and impeded economic growth. Five states met at the Annapolis Convention in 1786, ostensibly to discuss a "uniform system" of regulating commerce, but those who masterminded the meeting had a much larger agenda in mind—as Madison put it, a "plenipotentiary Convention for amending the Confederation."

Hamilton had called for a "convention of all the states" as early as 1780, before the Articles were ratified, to form a government worthy of the nation. Even men who defended state sovereignty conceded the necessity of a convention by 1787. William Grayson admitted that "the present Confederation is utterly inefficient and that if it remains much longer in its present State of imbecility we shall be one of the most contemptible Nations on the face of the earth. . . ." LUTHER MARTIN admitted that Congress was "weak, contemptibly weak," and Richard Henry Lee believed that no government "short of force, will answer." "Do you not think," he asked GEORGE MASON, "that it ought to be declared . . . that any State act of legislation that shall contravene, or oppose, the authorized acts of Congress, or interfere with the expressed rights of that body, shall be *ipso facto* void, and of no force whatsoever?" Many leaders, like THOMAS JEFFERSON, advocated executive and judicial branches for the national government with "an appeal from state judicatures to a federal court in all cases where the act of Confederation controlled the question. . . ." RUFUS KING, who also promoted a "vigorous Executive," thought that the needed power of Congress to regulate all commerce "can never be well exercised without a Federal Judicial." A consensus was developing.

The Annapolis Convention exploited and nurtured that consensus when it recommended to all the states and to Congress that a constitutional convention to "meet at Philadelphia on the second Monday in May next (1787), to take into consideration the situation of the United States, to devise such further provisions as shall appear to them necessary to render the constitution of the federal government adequate to the exigencies of the Union. . . ." Several states, including powerful Virginia and Pennsylvania, chose delegates for the Philadelphia convention, forcing Congress to save face on February 21, 1787, by adopting a motion in accord with the Annapolis recommendation, although Congress declared that the "sole and express purpose" of the convention was "revising the articles of confederation."

The CONSTITUTIONAL CONVENTION OF 1787, which formally organized itself on May 25, lasted almost four months, yet reached its most crucial decision almost at the outset. The first order of business was the nationalistic VIRGINIA PLAN (May 29), and the first vote of the Convention, acting as a Committee of the Whole, was the adoption of a resolution "that a *national* Government ought to be established consisting of a *supreme* legislative, Executive and Judiciary" (May 30). Thus the Convention immediately agreed on abandoning, rather than amending, the Articles; on writing a new Constitution; on creating a national government that would be supreme; and on having it consist of three branches.

The radical character of this early decision may be best understood by comparing it with the Articles. The Articles failed mainly because there was no way to force the states to fulfill their obligations or to obey the exercise of such powers as Congress did possess. "The great and radical vice in the construction of the existing Confederation," said Alexander Hamilton, "is the principle of legislation for states or governments, in their corporate capacities, and as contradistinguished from the individuals of which they consist." The Convention remedied that vital defect in the Articles, as George Mason pointed out (May 30), by agreeing on a government that "could directly operate on individuals." Thus the framers solved the critical problem of sanctions by establishing a national government that was independent of the states.

On the next day, May 31, the Committee of the Whole made other crucial decisions with little or no debate. One, reflecting the nationalist bias of the Convention, was the decision to establish a bicameral system whose larger house was to be elected directly by the people rather than by the state legislatures. Mason, no less, explained, "Under the existing confederacy, Congress represent the States not the people of the States; their acts operate on the States, not on the individuals. The case will be changed in the new plan of Government. The people will be represented; they ought therefore to choose the Representatives." Another decision of May 31 was to vest in the Congress the sweeping and undefined power, recommended by the Virginia Plan, "to legislate in all cases to which the separate States are incompetent; or in which the harmony of the U.S. may be interrupted by the exercise of individual [state] legislation; to negative all laws passed by the several States contravening in the opinion of the National Legislature the articles of Union, or any treaties subsisting under the authority of the Union." Not a state voted "nay" to this exceptionally nationalistic proposition. Nor did any state oppose the decision of the next day to create a national executive with similarly broad, undefined powers.

After deliberating for two weeks, the Committee of the Whole presented the Convention with its recommendations, essentially the adoption of the Virginia Plan. Not surprisingly, several of the delegates had second thoughts about the hasty decisions that had been made. ELBRIDGE GERRY reiterated "that it was necessary to consider what the people would approve." Scrapping the Articles contrary to instructions and failing to provide for state equality in the system of representation provoked a reconsideration along lines described by WILLIAM PATERSON of New Jersey as "federal" in contradistinction to "national." Yet injured state pride was a greater cause of dissension than were the powers proposed for the national government. Some delegates were alarmed, not because of an excessive centralization of powers in the national government but because of the excessive advantages given to the largest states at the expense of the others. Three states—Virginia, Massachusetts, and Pennsylvania—had forty-five percent of the white population in the country. Under the proposed scheme of proportionate representation, the small states feared that the large ones would dominate the others by controlling the national government.

On June 15, therefore, Paterson submitted for the Convention's consideration a substitute plan. It was a small states plan rather than a STATES' RIGHTS one, for it too had a strong nationalist orientation. Contemplating a revision, rather than a scrapping, of the Articles, it retained the unicameral Congress with its equality of state representation, thus appeasing the small states. But the plan vested in Congress one of the two critical powers previously lacking: "to pass Acts for the regulation of trade and commerce," foreign and interstate. The other, the power of taxation, appeared only in a stunted form; Congress was to be authorized to levy duties on imports and to pass stamp tax acts. Except for its failure to grant full tax powers, the PATERSON PLAN proposed the same powers for the national legislature as the finished Constitution. The Plan also contained the germ of the national SUPREMACY CLAUSE of the Constitution, Article Six, by providing that acts of Congress and United States treaties "shall be the supreme law of the respective States . . . and that the Judiciary of the several States shall be bound thereby in their decisions, any thing in the respective laws of the Individual States to the contrary notwithstanding." The clause also provided for a federal judiciary with extensive jurisdiction and for an executive who could muster the military of the states to compel state obedience to the supreme law. Compulsion of states was unrealistic and unnecessary. Paterson himself declared that the creation of a distinct executive and judiciary meant that the government of the Union could "be exerted on individuals."

Despite its nationalist features, the Paterson Plan retained a unicameral legislature, in which the states remained equal, and the requisition system of rising a revenue, which had failed. "You see the consequence of pushing things too far," said John Dickinson of Delaware to Madison. "Some of the members from the small States wish for two branches in the General Legislature and are friends to a good National Government; but we would sooner submit to a foreign power than submit to be deprived of an equality of suffrage in both branches of the Legislature, and thereby be thrown under the domination of the large states." Only a very few dissidents were irreconcilably opposed to "a good National Government." Most of the dissidents were men like Dickinson and Paterson, "friends to a good National Government" if it preserved a wider scope for small state authority and influence.

When Paterson submitted his plan on June 15, the Convention agreed that to give it "a fair deliberation" it should be referred to the Committee of the Whole and that "in order to place the two plans in due comparison, the other should be recommitted." After debating the two plans, the Committee of the Whole voted in favor of reaffirming the original recommendations based on the Virginia Plan "as preferable to those of Mr. Paterson." Only three weeks after their deliberations, had begun the Framers decisively agreed, for the second time, on a strong, independent national government that would operate directly on individuals without the involvement of states.

But the objections of the small states had not yet been satisfied. On the next day, Connecticut, which had voted against the Paterson Plan, proposed the famous GREAT COMPROMISE: proportionate representation in one house, "provided each State had an equal voice in the other." On that latter point the Convention nearly broke up, so intense was the conflict and deep the division. The irreconcilables in this instance were the leaders of the large-state nationalist faction, otherwise the most constructive and influential members of the Convention: Madison and James Wilson. After several weeks of debate and deadlock, the Convention on July 16 narrowly voted for the compromise. With ten states present, five supported the compromise, four opposed (including Virginia and Pennsylvania), and Massachusetts was divided. The compromise saved small-state prestige and saved the Convention from failure.

Thereafter consensus on fundamentals was restored, with Connecticut, New Jersey, and Delaware becoming fervent supporters of Madison and Wilson. A week later, for example, there was a motion that each state should be represented by two senators who would "vote per capita," that is, as individuals. Luther Martin of Maryland protested that per capita voting conflicted with the very idea of "the States being represented," yet the motion carried, with no further debate, 9–1.

On many matters of structure, mechanics, and detail there were angry disagreements, but agreement prevailed on the essentials. The office of the presidency is a good illustration. That there should be a powerful chief executive provoked no great debate, but the Convention almost broke up, for the second time, on the method of electing him. Some matters of detail occasioned practically no disagreement and revealed the nationalist consensus. Mason, of all people, made the motion that one qualification of congressmen should be "citizenship of the United States," and no one disagreed. Under the Articles of Confederation, there was only state citizenship; that there should be a concept of national citizenship seemed natural to men framing a constitution for a nation. Even more a revelation of the nationalist consensus was the fact that three of the most crucial provisions of the Constitution—the taxing power, the NECESSARY AND PROPER CLAUSE, and the supremacy clause—were casually and unanimously accepted without debate.

Until midway during its sessions, the Convention did not take the trouble to define with care the distribution of power between the national government and the states, although the very nature of the "federal" system depended on that distribution. Consensus on fundamentals once again provides the explanation. There would be no difficulty in making that distribution; and, the framers had taken out insurance, because at the very outset, they had endorsed the provision of the Virginia Plan vesting broad, undefined powers in a national legislature that would act on individuals. Some byplay of July 17 is illuminating. ROGER SHERMAN of Connecticut thought that the line drawn between the powers of Congress and those left to the states was so vague that national legislation might "interfere . . . in any matters of internal police which respect the Government of such States only, and wherein the general welfare of the United States is not concerned." His motion to protect the "internal police" of the states brought no debaters to his side and was summarily defeated; only Maryland supported Connecticut. Immediately after, another small-state delegate, GUNNING BEDFORD of Delaware, shocked even EDMUND RANDOLPH of Virginia, who had presented the Virginia Plan, by a motion to extend the powers of Congress by vesting authority "to legislate in all cases for the general interest of the Union." Randolph observed, "This is a formidable idea indeed. It involves the power of violating all the laws and constitution of the States, of intermeddling with their police." Yet the motion passed.

On July 26 the Convention adjourned until August 6 to allow a Committee on Detail to frame a "constitution conformable to the Resolutions passed by the Convention." Generously construing its charge, the committee acted as a miniature convention and introduced a number of significant changes. One was the explicit enumeration of the powers of Congress to replace the vague, omnibus provisions adopted previously by the Convention. Although enumerated, these powers were liberally expressed and formidable in their array. The committee made specific the spirit and intent of the Convention. Significantly the first enumerated power was that of taxation and the second that of regulating commerce among the states and with foreign nations: the two principal powers that had been withheld from Congress by the Articles. When the Convention voted on the provision that Congress "shall have the power to lay and collect taxes, duties, imposts and excises," the states were unanimous and only one delegate, Elbridge Gerry, was opposed. When the Convention next turned to the commerce power, there was no discussion and even Gerry voted affirmatively.

Notwithstanding its enumeration of the legislative powers, all of which the Convention accepted, the Committee on Detail added an omnibus clause that has served as an ever expanding source of national authority: "And to make all laws that shall be necessary and proper for carrying into execution the foregoing powers." The Convention agreed to that clause without a single dissenting vote by any state or delegate. The history of the great supremacy clause, Article Six, shows a similar consensus. Without debate the Convention adopted the supremacy clause, and not a single state or delegate voted nay. Finally, Article One, Section 10, imposing restrictions on the economic powers of the states with respect to paper money, ex post facto laws, bills of credit, and contracts also reflected a consensus in the Convention. In sum, consensus, rather than compromise, was the most significant feature of the Convention, outweighing in importance the various compromises that occupied most of the time of the delegates.

But why was there such a consensus? The obvious answer (apart from the fact that opponents either stayed away or walked out) is the best: experience had proved that the nationalist constitutional position was right. If the United States was to survive and flourish, a strong national government had to be established. The Framers of the Constitution were accountable to public opinion; the Convention was a representative body. That its members were prosperous, well-educated political leaders made them no less representative than Congress. The state legislatures, which elected the members of the Convention, were the most unlikely instruments for thwarting the popular will. The Framers, far from being able to do as they pleased, were not free to promulgate the Constitution. Although they adroitly arranged for its ratification by nine state ratifying conventions rather than by all state legislatures, they could not present a plan that the people of the states would not tolerate. They could not control the membership of those state ratifying conventions. They could not even be sure that the existing Congress would submit the Constitution to the states for ratification, let alone for ratification by state conventions that had to be specially elected. If the Framers got too far astray from public opinion, their work would have been wasted. The consensus in the Convention coincided with an emerging consensus in the country that recaptured the nationalist spirit of '76. That the Union had to be strengthened was an almost universal American belief.

For its time the Constitution was a remarkably democratic document framed by democratic methods. Some historians have contended that the Convention's scrapping of the Articles and the ratification process were revolutionary acts which if performed by a Napoleon would be pronounced a coup d'état. But the procedure of the Articles for constitutional amendment was not democratic, because it allowed Rhode Island, with one-sixtieth of the nation's population, to exercise a veto power. The Convention sent its Constitution to the lawfully existing government, the Congress of the Confederation, for submission to the states, and Congress, which could have censured the Convention for exceeding its authority, freely complied—and thereby exceeded its own authority under the Articles! A coup d'état ordinarily lacks the deliberation and consent that marked the making of the Constitution and is characterized by a military element that was wholly lacking in 1787. A Convention elected by the state legislatures and consisting of many of the foremost leaders of their time deliberated for almost four months. Its members included many opponents of the finished scheme. The nation knew the Convention was considering changes in the government. The proposed Constitution was made public, and voters in every state were asked to choose delegates to vote for or against it after open debate. The use of state ratifying conventions fit the theory that a new fundamental law was being adopted and, therefore, conventions were proper for the task.

The Constitution guaranteed to each state a republican or representative form of government and fixed no property or religious qualifications on the right to vote or hold office, at a time when such qualifications were common in the states. By leaving voting qualifications to the states the Constitution implicitly accepted such qualifications but imposed none. The Convention, like the Albany Congress of 1754, the Stamp Act Congress, the Continental Congresses, and the Congresses of the Confederation, had been chosen by state (or colonial) legislatures, but the Constitution created a Congress whose lower house was popularly elected. When only three states directly elected their chief executive officer, the Constitution provided for the indirect election of the President by an ELECTORAL COLLEGE that originated in the people and is still operative. The Constitution's system of separation of powers and elaborate CHECKS AND BALANCES was not intended to refine out popular influence on government but to protect liberty; the Framers divided, distributed, and limited powers to prevent one branch, faction, interest, or section from becoming too powerful. Checks and balances were not undemocratic, and the Federalists were hard pressed not to apologize for checks and balances but to convince the Anti-Federalists, who wanted far more checks and balances,

that the Constitution had enough. Although the Framers were not democrats in a modern sense, their opponents were even less democratic.
Those opponents sought to capitalize on the lack of a BILL OF RIGHTS,
and RATIFICATION OF THE CONSTITUTION became possible only because
leading Federalists committed themselves to amendments as soon as
the new government went into operation. At that time, however, Anti-
Federalists opposed a Bill of Rights because it would allay popular fears
of the new government, ending the chance for state sovereignty amendments.

Although the Framers self-consciously refrained from referring to
slavery in the Constitution, it recognized slavery, the most undemocratic
of all institutions. That recognition was a grudging but necessary price
of Union. The THREE-FIFTHS CLAUSE of Article I provided for counting
three-fifths of the total number of slaves as part of the population of a
state in the apportionment of REPRESENTATION and DIRECT TAXATION.
Article IV, section 2, provided for rendition of fugitive slaves to the
slaveholder upon his claim. On the other hand, Article I, section 9,
permitted Congress to abolish the slave trade in twenty years. Most
delegates, including many from slaveholding states, would have preferred
a Constitution untainted by slavery; but Southern votes for ratification
required recognition of slavery. By choosing a Union with slavery, the
Convention deferred the day of reckoning.

The Constitution is basically a political document. Modern scholar-
ship has completely discredited the once popular view, associated with
CHARLES BEARD, that the Constitution was undemocratically made to
advance the economic interests of personalty groups, chiefly creditors.
The largest public creditor at the Convention was Elbridge Gerry, who
refused to sign the Constitution and opposed its ratification, and the
largest private creditor was George Mason who did likewise. Indeed,
seven men who either quit the Convention in disgust or refused to
sign the Constitution held public securities that were worth over twice
the holdings of the thirty-nine men who signed the Constitution. The
most influential Framers, among them Madison, Wilson, Paterson,
Dickinson, and Gouverneur Morris, owned no securities. Others, like
Washington, who acted out of patriotism, not profit, held trifling amounts.
Eighteen members of the Convention were either debtors or held property that depreciated after the new government became operative. On
crucial issues at the Convention, as in the state ratifying conventions,
the dividing line between groups for and against the Constitution was
not economic, not between realty and personalty, or debtors and creditors, or town and frontier. The restrictions of Article I, section 10, on
the economic powers of the states were calculated to protect creditor
interests and promote business stability, but those restrictions were not
undemocratic; if impairing the obligations of contracts or emitting bills

of credit and paper money were democratic hallmarks, the Constitution left Congress free to be democratic. The interest groups for and against the Constitution were substantially similar. Economic interests did influence the voting on ratification, but no simple explanation that ignores differences between states and even within states will suffice, and many noneconomic influences were also at work. In the end the Constitution was framed and ratified because most voters came to share the vision held by Franklin in 1775 and Dickinson in 1776; those two, although antagonists in Pennsylvania politics, understood for quite different reasons that a strong central government was indispensable for nationhood.

Bibliography

ADAMS, WILLI PAUL   1980   *The First American Constitutions.* Chapel Hill: University of North Carolina Press.

BEARD, CHARLES   1935   *An Economic Interpretation of the Constitution of the United States.* New York: Macmillan.

BROWN, ROBERT E.   1956   *Charles Beard and the Constitution: A Critical Analysis of "An Economic Interpretation of the Constitution."* Princeton, N.J.: Princeton University Press.

BURNETT, EDMUND C.   1941   *The Continental Congress.* New York: Macmillan.

CROSSKEY, WILLIAM W. and JEFFREY, WILLIAM, JR. 1980   *Politics and the Constitution in the History of the United States.* Volume III: "The Political Background of the Federal Convention." Chicago: University of Chicago Press.

FARRAND, MAX, ed.   1937(1966)   *The Records of the Federal Convention of 1787.* New Haven, Conn.: Yale University Press.

JENSEN, MERRILL   1940   *The Articles of Confederation.* Madison: University of Wisconsin Press.

KENYON, CECILIA, ed.   1966   *The Antifederalists.* Indianapolis: Bobbs-Merrill.

McDONALD, FORREST   1958   *We the People: The Economic Origins of the Constitution.* Chicago: University of Chicago Press.

McLAUGHLIN, ANDREW C.   1905   *The Confederation and the Constitution, 1783–1789.* New York: Harper & Brothers.

MURPHY, WILLIAM P.   1967   *The Triumph of Nationalism: State Sovereignty, the Founding Fathers, and the Triumph of the Constitution.* Chicago: Quadrangle Books.

RACOVE, JACK N.   1979   *The Beginnings of National Politics: An Interpretation of the Continental Congress.* New York: Knopf.

WARREN, CHARLES   1928   *The Making of the Constitution.* Boston: Little, Brown.

CONSTITUTIONAL HISTORY, 1789–1801

Merrill D. Peterson

GEORGE WASHINGTON was inaugurated the first President of the United States on April 30, 1789, in New York City. The First Congress, having been elected in February, was already at work. Most of the members were supporters of the Constitution. Fifty-four of them had sat either in the CONSTITUTIONAL CONVENTION or in one of the state ratifying conventions; only seven were Anti-Federalists. A new government had been established. But in 1789 it was only a blueprint. The first business of the President and Congress was to breathe life into the Constitution. For a document of some 5,000 words, the Constitution was remarkably explicit and complete. Yet it left a great deal to the discretion and decision of the men entrusted with its care. They, too, were "founding fathers," for they transformed words engrossed on parchment into living institutions and defined the terms of debate on the Constitution.

JAMES MADISON was the Federalist leader in the House of Representatives, where most of the formative legislation of the new government originated. Among the first statutes were those establishing the three executive departments: state, treasury, and war. Madison wrote into his bill for the department of state a provision authorizing the President to remove the department head, thereby precipitating the first congressional debate over interpretation of the Constitution. The document was clear on the President's power to appoint, with the advice and consent of the Senate, but silent on his power to remove executive officers. Removal being the reverse of appointment, some congressmen argued that it should follow the same course. But Madison contended, successfully, that the President's responsibility to see that the laws were faithfully executed necessarily included the removal power. The action of the House set an enduring precedent. Thus it was that in the first year of the new government an UNWRITTEN CONSTITUTION, unknown to the Framers, grew up alongside the written constitution. (See APPOINTING AND REMOVAL POWER.)

Article II, it was sometimes said, had been framed with General Washington in mind; and so great was the confidence in him that Congress showed little jealousy of the chief executive. The act creating the treasury department, however, made its head responsible to Congress as well as to the President. This was recognition that "the power of the purse" was fundamentally a legislative power, and therefore the secretary of the treasury must answer to Congress in financial matters.

The JUDICIARY ACT OF 1789, which gave life to Article III, originated in the Senate. The act provided for an elaborate system of federal courts, created the office of ATTORNEY GENERAL, and in Section 25 authorized the Supreme Court to review on APPEAL decisions of state courts concerning questions of federal law involving the United States Constitution and the laws and treaties made under it. None of this had been settled in the Constitution itself, though Federalists said that Article III together with the SUPREMACY CLAUSE of Article VI implicitly sanctioned Section 25.

The Federalists, with Madison in the lead, kept the promise made during the ratification campaign to add a BILL OF RIGHTS to the Constitution. Even before North Carolina and Rhode Island entered the new union, Congress approved twelve amendments and sent them to the states. Ten were ratified and on December 15, 1791, became part of the Constitution. In the founding of the nation the Bill of Rights was important less because it secured fundamental rights and liberties against the national government, which was without DELEGATED POWER in this sphere, than because it strengthened public confidence in the government without impairing its powers as many Anti-Federalists had wished.

The principal executive offices were filled by THOMAS JEFFERSON at state, ALEXANDER HAMILTON in the treasury, Henry Knox in the war department, and EDMUND RANDOLPH as the part-time attorney general. The unity of the executive was one of the claims made for it in THE FEDERALIST. Washington worked closely with his subordinates, and depended on them for initiative and advice, but there was never any doubt that the executive power belonged exclusively to him. The Constitution made no provision for a "cabinet," nor was one contemplated at first. The President seemed to think, on the basis of the ADVICE AND CONSENT clause, that the Senate was meant to function as an advisory council. In August he appeared personally in the Senate to ask its advice on a proposed treaty with an Indian tribe. But the process proved awkward and cumbersome. It was not repeated. The President, instead, conducted his business with the Senate in writing, and met his need for collective consultation and advice, particularly in FOREIGN AFFAIRS, through the development of the cabinet. By 1793 it was an established institution. There were suggestions in the First Congress of a movement toward a generalized ministerial responsibility on the model of the treasury act; but this did not materialize. On the whole, the first presidency decisively enforced the theory of SEPARATION OF POWERS, associated with congressional government, rather than the ministerial responsibility characteristic of parliamentary government. In 1791 the President exercised the

VETO POWER for the first time. The veto was potentially a means for controlling legislation, but Washington did not use it in that fashion (he vetoed only one other measure in eight years), and in the first forty years of the government Presidents used the veto sparingly.

The most important political and constitutional issues of Washington's first administration arose out of Hamilton's financial program. Exploiting his special relationship with Congress—conceiving of himself, indeed, as a kind of prime minister—Hamilton submitted a series of reports to Congress recommending measures to put the country's fiscal house in order, strengthen the government by appealing to the cupidity of the moneyed class, and stimulate the commercial and manufacturing sectors of the economy. His plan to fund the national debt at face value raised questions of equity between debtor and creditor interests but did not present a constitutional issue. The expectation of funding on the part of creditor groups had, of course, been a vital source of Federalist support for the Constitution. But Hamilton's plan also called for the assumption of the state debts. This proposal surprised many and aroused intense opposition in Congress, especially among Southerners sensitive to Anti-Federalist fears of undue concentration of power in the national government. Madison opposed Hamilton's plan, though on other grounds, and in doing so disclosed a division in the Federalist ranks on the direction of the new government. He was joined by his Virginia friend, Jefferson, who had just taken up his duties as secretary of state in the spring of 1790. Both were disposed to be conciliatory on this issue, however, and entered into a sectional bargain with Hamilton that would fix the permanent seat of government on the Potomac in exchange for the necessary southern votes to secure passage of the assumption bill. Still, the compromise failed to quiet Anti-Federalist fears. In December the Virginia legislature adopted a series of resolutions condemning the assumption of state debts as inimical to federal and republican institutions and pointedly questioning the constitutionality of the measure. Hamilton responded angrily. "This," he said, "is the first symptom of a spirit which must either be killed, or will kill the Constitution."

The constitutional question was brought to the fore a few months later on the bill to charter the BANK OF THE UNITED STATES. A national bank, as conceived and proposed by Hamilton, would function as the financial arm of the government and multiply the active capital of the country by mounting a large paper circulation. Because three-fourths of the initial bank capital would come in the form of public securities— securities issued to fund the debt—the institution was obviously an integral part of the funding system and would directly benefit the same creditor class. Madison vigorously opposed the bill in the House, less on grounds of policy than on grounds of unconstitutionality. The power to incorporate a bank was not among the powers delegated to Congress, nor could it be considered NECESSARY AND PROPER to execute those powers. But Congress adopted the bill and sent it to the President. Uncertain whether to sign or return it, Washington first sought the attorney general's opinion, which was adverse, and then requested Jefferson's. The secretary of state agreed with Madison and offered an even more emphatically STRICT CONSTRUCTION of the Constitution. The government was one of strictly delegated powers, as declared in the TENTH AMENDMENT still in the course of ratification. "To take a single step beyond the boundaries thus specifically drawn around the powers of Congress," Jefferson warned, "is to take possession of a boundless field of power, no longer susceptible to definition." To these objections Hamilton replied in a powerful opinion founded on the doctrine of IMPLIED POWERS. "Every power vested in a government is in its nature *sovereign,* and included, by *force* of the *term,* a right to employ all *means* requisite and fairly applicable to the attainment of the *ends* of such power, and which are not precluded by restrictions and exceptions specified in the Constitution . . ." (italics in original). The utility of a national bank in the execution of powers to tax, borrow money, and regulate commerce could not be denied. It was decisive in Hamilton's judgment. Washington concurred, and signed the Bank Bill into law.

In his Report on Manufactures, presented to the Second Congress, Hamilton extended his nationalist program by way of the GENERAL WELFARE CLAUSE. Believing that extensive domestic manufactures were necessary to the wealth and welfare of the nation, Hamilton proposed a comprehensive system of aid and encouragement—tariffs, bounties, inspections, export controls, drawbacks—which he justified under the power to provide for the general welfare. No legislation resulted from the report, but it produced consternation in opposition ranks. "If not only the *means,* but the *objects* [of the government] are unlimited," Madison wrote, "The parchment had better be thrown into the fire at once" (italics in original). Virginia's two senators introduced constitutional amendments to limit the application of the clause to the ENUMERATED POWERS and deny the power of Congress to charter corporations.

Although the widening debate took its shape from the constitutional question, it involved much more. It involved the conflict of economic interests: debtors and creditors, landed property and fluid capital, the mass of people engaged in agriculture, and the enterprising class of merchants, bankers, and manufacturers. The fact that the former tended to be concentrated in the South, the latter in the Northeast, particularly in the coastal cities, gave the conflict a sectional character as well. The debate also involved competing strategies of economic development in the new nation, as well as contrasting ideas of the nature of freedom, the Union, and republican government. To an extent, certainly, the conflict was epitomized in the clash between the leading cabinet secretar-

ies, Jefferson and Hamilton, who increasingly appeared as t
nists of opposing doctrines and parties in the public eye. On
the other idolized governance. One located the strength of th
in the diffuse energies of a free society, the other in the con
of the government's power. One believed that private interest corrupted
public good, the other conscripted private interest for public benefit.
One viewed the Constitution as a superintending rule of political action,
the other, as a point of departure for heroic statesmanship. In the balance
between authority and liberty, Hamilton was an apologist for the former,
Jefferson for the latter. Hamilton feared most of the ignorance and
turbulence of the people, while Jefferson preached "trust the people"
and feared rulers independent of them.

The division on foreign policy deepened the division on domestic
policy. Jefferson, Madison, and those who began to call themselves Republicans opposed British power and influence and openly championed
the French Revolution. Hamilton and the Federalists, on the other hand,
relied upon British trade, credit, and power to nurture American development; they feared the contagion of French ideas. The controversy over
foreign policy assumed a constitutional dimension after Britain and
France went to war in 1793. President Washington issued a proclamation
pledging "a conduct friendly and impartial" toward the belligerents and
warning citizens against hostile acts. Jefferson opposed this PROCLAMA-
TION OF NEUTRALITY, as it came to be known, principally because it
tended to defeat his foreign policy objectives to oppose Britain and
support France. As an ally, France had a right to expect friendship
from the United States; Britain, on the other hand, might have been
made to pay a price for American neutrality, as in recognition of "free
ships make free goods" and related guarantees of neutral rights. Viewing
a declaration of neutrality as the negative side of a DECLARATION OF
WAR, Jefferson also held that the proclamation invaded the authority
of Congress. The popular reception of the new French minister to the
United States, Edmond Genet, fueled criticism of the proclamation.
Genet himself took advantage of this sentiment by arming privateers in
American ports and issuing military commissions to American citizens.
Hamilton, under the pseudonym "Pacificus," wrote a series of newspaper
articles in defense of the presidential proclamation. Broadly construing
Article II, Hamilton maintained that all executive power is vested in
the President unless specifically qualified or withheld. The power to
declare war belonged to Congress, of course, but did not preclude unilateral actions by the President bearing on the exercise of that power. To
Republicans such a power looked suspiciously like the British royal prerogative in foreign affairs. Taking up his pen in reply, Madison, as
"Helvidius," argued that all matters touching on the WAR POWER are
necessarily legislative; the executive, therefore, cannot initiate a course

of action that, in effect, confronts Congress with a *fait accompli*. Whatever the abstract merits of Madison's argument, it gave too little weight to realities in the conduct of foreign affairs, which inevitably favored the executive.

In the absence of statute, executive officers decided difficult questions of neutrality as they arose. Thus it was that the cabinet became a permanent institution. Jefferson and Hamilton were usually at odds, causing many split decisions. On July 18, 1793, the officers submitted to the Supreme Court a list of twenty-nine questions about international law. The Justices declined to rule, however, thereby setting a precedent against ADVISORY OPINIONS. The cabinet hammered out its own ADMINISTRATIVE LAW of neutrality, which prevailed until Congress convened and enacted the Neutrality Act of 1794.

Long before that the firebrand French minister had been recalled and Jefferson had retired from the government, ensuring Hamilton the same ascendancy in foreign affairs he had earlier enjoyed in domestic affairs. The upshot was JAY'S TREATY, negotiated in London in November 1794 and ratified by the Senate six months later. The treaty preserved peace with Britain but, in Republican opinion, at the cost of submission to British maritime power and risk of war with France. Like every great issue of Washington's presidency, the treaty caused significant constitutional debate. Because some provisions required appropriations to carry them into effect, the treaty came under the scrutiny of the House of Representatives. In this connection a Republican majority demanded that the President lay before the House a copy of the instructions given to JOHN JAY and other pertinent documents. The President emphatically rejected the call, holding that the House had no constitutional power with respect to treaties. The House, after reiterating its position and carefully differentiating the appropriation power from the TREATY POWER, which it disclaimed, proceeded to vote the money requested by the President.

The protracted battle over Jay's Treaty set the stage for the presidential election of 1796. Washington's decision to retire after two terms lifted the last restraint on partisanship, and two infant POLITICAL PARTIES, each with its own standard bearer, JOHN ADAMS for the Federalists, Jefferson for the Republicans, contested the election. The Constitution had been intended to work without parties. Parties, the Framers reasoned, fed the natural turbulence of the populace and served the ambitions of demagogues; they caused implacable rivalries in legislative councils, usurping the place of reason and moderation; they introduced whole networks of partisan allegiance at cross-purposes with the national welfare. Washington had attempted to govern independently of parties, but in an increasingly polarized political environment even he became a partisan. When the Republicans sought to channel popular enthusiasm for the French cause into "democratic societies," Washington publicly condemned the societies as illicit political engines, thereby betraying intolerance of political opposition from outside the constitutional channels of authority. WASHINGTON'S FAREWELL ADDRESS pointedly warned the people against the "baneful" effects of parties. The Republicans, however, were rapidly discovering in party organization outside the government the appropriate means for wresting power from the Federalists who, in their eyes, were the real bane of the country.

Adams was elected President by a slender ELECTORAL COLLEGE majority. Crisis with France, mounting since the British treaty, set the course of the administration. Angrily denouncing French decrees against American commerce, Adams sent a special commission to negotiate in Paris under threat of war. Intriguing agents of the French foreign ministry demanded money as the price of negotiations. The Americans indignantly refused. This affair—the XYZ Affair—then exploded in the United States, and the Federalists converted foreign crisis into domestic crisis. Under cover of whipped-up war hysteria, they assailed the patriotism of the Republicans, portraying them as Jacobin disorganizers in the country's bowels whose ultimate treachery only awaited the signal of an invading French army. Although the President refrained from asking for a declaration of war, he inflamed the war spirit. Congress abrogated the French treaties, expanded the army, established the Navy Department, and authorized an undeclared naval war against France. The Republicans fought this policy to no avail. Two years later the Supreme Court, in a prize case, *Bas v. Tingey* (1800), upheld the power of the government to make war without declaring it.

The war hysteria found domestic expression in the ALIEN AND SEDITION ACTS. The Republicans attacked the laws restrictive of ALIENS on grounds of policy and the Alien Act, in particular, for violating the Constitution by authorizing the President summarily to deport aliens deemed dangerous to the nation. The Sedition Act, the Republicans argued, was without congressional authority and directly violated the FIRST AMENDMENT. Despite the smokescreen of war, TREASON, and subversion, Republicans believed that the law aimed at suppressing their presses and crippling their party. Political freedom, as well as FREEDOM OF SPEECH and FREEDOM OF THE PRESS, was at stake. When the federal courts, manned by partisan Federalist judges, cooperated in enforcing the Sedition Act, closing off the judicial channel of redress, Jefferson and Madison turned to two Republican state legislatures to arouse opposition. The VIRGINIA AND KENTUCKY RESOLUTIONS interposed the authority of these states to declare the Alien and Sedition Acts unconstitutional and urged other states to join in forcing their repeal. The resolutions were especially significant as landmark statements of the THEORY OF THE UNION as a compact of sovereign states and of the right of a state, whether by

INTERPOSITION or NULLIFICATION, to judge the constitutionality of acts of Congress. Northern state legislatures, in response, rejected the theory together with the appeal. Although the resolutions contributed to rising popular opposition against the administration, they did not force repeal of the hated laws. Whatever their later significance for the issue of STATES' RIGHTS and Union—the constitutional issue over which the Civil War would be fought—the resolutions originated in a struggle for political survival and addressed the fundamental issue of freedom and self-government descending from the American Revolution.

The foreign crisis passed in 1800. Adams seized the olive branch extended by France, broke with the Hamiltonian faction in his administration, and dispatched another commission to negotiate peace. The result was the Convention of 1800, which restored normal relations and formally terminated the Franco-American alliance of 1778. From the standpoint of the "war system," Adams's decision to make peace drove a sword into the Federalist party. In the ensuing presidential election, Hamilton and his friends conspired to defeat Adams.

The election of 1800 was bitterly contested by two organized political parties. The Republicans achieved unprecedented unity behind their ticket of Jefferson and AARON BURR. By party organization and electioneering tactics they turned the election of the President into a test of public opinion. This, of course, made a mockery of the Constitution, under which a body of electors separated from the people was to choose the President and vice-president. Electoral tickets became party tickets, and every presidential elector became an agent of the popular majority that elected him.

Jefferson won a decisive victory over Adams. Although the Federalists swept New England, took two of the small middle states (New Jersey and Delaware), and picked up scattered votes in three others, the Republicans won everything else, south, west, and north. The electoral vote, 73–65, failed to reflect the wide Republican margin at the polls. But the victory was jeopardized by political developments that played havoc with the electoral system. Under the Constitution each elector cast two votes for different candidates; the one with the most votes became President, while the runner-up became vice-president. The rise of political parties made the system an anachronism, for electors chosen on a party ticket would cast both votes for the party candidates, thereby producing a tie between them. So it happened in 1800: Jefferson and Burr received an equal number of electoral votes. The choice was thus thrown into the House of Representatives. There the lame-duck Federalist majority plotted to annul the popular verdict either by creating an interregnum or by dealing Burr into the presidency. Finally, on the thirty-sixth ballot, the stalemate was broken and Jefferson was elected.

The new Republican majority moved rapidly to amend the Constitution to prevent a similar occurrence in the future. The TWELFTH AMEND-MENT (1804) provided for separate ballots for President and vice-president. The elaborate machinery devised by the Framers for the election of the President was thus radically revised in response to changing political realities. Not only was this an effective use of the AMENDING PROCESS, but it seemed to suggest frequent change by amendment in the future. However, the next amendment of the Constitution came only after the passage of sixty-one years and the convulsions of civil war.

Bibliography

BUEL, RICHARD, JR.   1972   *Securing the Revolution: Ideology and American Politics, 1789–1815*. Ithaca, N.Y.: Cornell University Press.
MALONE, DUMAS   1962   *Jefferson and the Ordeal of Liberty*. Boston: Little, Brown.
MILLER, JOHN C.   1960   *The Federalist Era: 1789–1801*. New York: Harper & Row.
STOURZH, GERALD   1970   *Alexander Hamilton and the Idea of Republican Government*. Stanford, Calif.: Stanford University Press.
WHITE, LEONARD D.   1948   *The Federalist: A Study in Administrative History, 1789–1801*. New York: Free Press.

SUPREME COURT, 1789–1801

Leonard W. Levy

On January 8, 1801, twelve days before President JOHN ADAMS appointed JOHN MARSHALL as Chief Justice, a Jeffersonian newspaper reported: "JOHN JAY, after having thru' decay of age become incompetent to discharge the duties of Governor, has been appointed to the sinecure of Chief Justice of the United States. That the Chief Justiceship is a sinecure needs no other evidence than that in one case the duties were discharged by one person who resided at the same time in England, and by another during a year's residence in France." The one in France was OLIVER ELLSWORTH, sent there by President Adams as a special ambassador to negotiate peace. Ellsworth had recently resigned, and Jay, whose appointment as Ellsworth's successor had been confirmed by the Senate, had himself been the first Chief Justice, whom President GEORGE WASHINGTON had sent to England to negotiate a treaty that bore Jay's name. The chief justiceship was no sinecure: although the Supreme Court then met for only two short terms a year, the Justices also served as circuit court judges, and riding circuit was extremely arduous. When Jay was offered the position again, he declined it because of the circuit responsibilities and because the Court had neither "the energy, weight and dignity" necessary for it to support the national government nor "the public confidence and respect."

Jay's judgment was harsh although the Court did have problems, some of its own making. All the Justices were Federalists; their decisions EN BANC or on circuit seemed partisan—pro-Administration, pro-English, or procreditor—and they presided at trials under the infamous Sedition Act, whose constitutionality they affirmed. But the Court was not responsible for most of its difficulties. It had no official reporter (ALEXANDER J. DALLAS's unofficial reports first appeared in 1798) and the press publicized only a few of the Court's decisions. The public knew little about the Court, and even members of its own bar were unfamiliar with its decisions. Nothing better symbolizes the nation's neglect of the Court than the fact that when the United States government moved to Washington, D.C., in late 1800, the Court had been forgotten. Not only did it lack a building; it had no courtroom. Congress hastily provided a small committee room in the basement of the Senate wing of the Capitol for the Court to meet.

The Court's beginnings were hardly more auspicious, however distinguished its membership. At its first term in February 1790 it had nothing to do except admit attorneys to its bar, and it shortly adjourned. It began as a court without a reporter, litigants, a docket, appeals, or decisions to make. It was chiefly an appellate court whose APPELLATE JURISDICTION scarcely matched the breadth of the JUDICIAL POWER OF THE UNITED STATES stated in Article III. Congress in the JUDICIARY ACT OF 1789 had authorized the Court to review state court decisions that denied claims based on federal law, including the Constitution. Review was not authorized when the state court upheld a claim of federal right. The system of appellate jurisdiction thus permitted the Supreme Court to maintain federal law's supremacy but not its uniform interpretation. The Court's review of civil decisions of the lower federal courts was limited to cases involving more than $2,000 in controversy, and it could not review criminal cases from those courts. Congress had stingily authorized the Court to hear cases in its appellate capacity in order to keep it weak, to prevent centralization of judicial powers, to preserve the relative importance of state courts, and to insulate the Court from many matters that concerned ordinary citizens. For its first two years it heard no cases, and it made no substantive decisions until 1793. Its docket never got crowded. Dallas reported less than seventy cases for the pre-Marshall Court, and fewer than ten percent of them involved constitutional law. The Court was then first a COMMON LAW court, second a court of ADMIRALTY AND MARITIME JURISDICTION.

Although its members were able, the pre-Marshall Court had difficulty attracting and keeping them. When Marshall became Chief Justice, only WILLIAM CUSHING of the original six Justices appointed by Washington remained. Robert H. Harrison, one of the original six, was confirmed but declined appointment, preferring instead the chancellorship of Maryland. JAMES IREDELL accepted Harrison's place, so that the first Court consisted of Chief Justice Jay and Justices Cushing, JOHN BLAIR, JOHN RUTLEDGE, JAMES WILSON, and Iredell. Rutledge performed his circuit duties but had never attended a session of the Court when he resigned after two years to become chief justice of South Carolina. CHARLES C. PINCKNEY and Edward Rutledge declined appointment to John Rutledge's seat, preferring to serve in their state legislature. THOMAS JOHNSON accepted that seat but resigned it in less than two years because circuit riding was too strenuous. WILLIAM PATERSON succeeded him. The February 1794 term was Jay's last. That he reentered New York politics after negotiating JAY'S TREATY says something about the Court's prestige at the time. So too does the fact that ALEXANDER HAMILTON preferred private practice to the chief justiceship. At that point, John Rutledge, who had quit the Court, applied for the post vacated by Jay. Washington appointed Rutledge, who attended the August 1795 term of the Court when it decided only two cases. The Senate, having reconvened, rejected him because of his opposition to Jay's Treaty. Washington offered the chief justiceship to PATRICK HENRY who declined it. The President then named Justice Cushing, whom the Senate confirmed; but he too declined, preferring to remain Associate Justice. In 1796, Oliver Ellsworth became Chief Justice but quit after four years. John Blair retired early in 1796 and Washington again had to fill a vacancy on the Court. After EDMUND RANDOLPH refused the position, SAMUEL CHASE accepted. In 1798, Wilson became the first Justice to die in office. RICHARD PETERS refused to be considered for the position, and John Marshall also declined. Adams then appointed BUSHROD WASHINGTON, and after Iredell died in 1798, he appointed ALFRED MOORE, who resigned within five years. When Ellsworth resigned and Jay declined reappointment, even though the Senate confirmed him, Adams turned to Marshall. The rapid turnover in personnel during the Court's first decade did not ease its work or enhance its reputation.

Jeffersonians grumbled about the Court's Federalist constitutional theories, but Jay kept his Court out of politics and established its independence from the other branches of the government. That achievement and the Court's identification of its task as safeguarding the supreme law of the land kept the Court a viable institution, despite its many problems during the first decade, and laid the groundwork for the achievements of the MARSHALL COURT.

Late in 1790, Virginia's legislature denounced as unconstitutional the bill for national assumption of state debts. Washington allowed Hamilton to send a copy of the Virginia resolves to Jay and to inquire whether the various branches of the government should employ their "collective weight . . . in exploding [Virginia's STRICT CONSTRUCTION] principles." Hamilton warned that Virginia had shown "the first symptom of a spirit which must either be killed or it will kill the Constitution of the United States." However, Jay, who privately advised Washington and drafted his PROCLAMATION OF NEUTRALITY, recognized the difference between a judicial pronouncement and an extrajudicial one. The Court, strongly believing in the principle of SEPARATION OF POWERS, would not express ex officio opinions except in judicial cases before it. Jay calmly declined the executive's invitation.

Similar principles motivated the Justices when confronted by Congress's Invalid Pensioners' Act of 1792 which required the circuit courts to pass on the pension applications of disabled veterans, subject to review by the secretary of war and Congress. Justices Wilson and Blair together with Judge Peters on circuit in the district of Pennsylvania, having refused to pass on an application from one Hayburn, explained their conduct in a letter to the President. They could not proceed because first, the business directed by the statute was not judicial in nature, there being no constitutional authority for it, and second, because the possible revision of the Court's judgment by the other branches of government would be "radically inconsistent with the independence" of the judiciary. In their circuits, Jay, Cushing, and Iredell similarly explained that a judicial decision must be a final decision. HAYBURN'S CASE (1792), which was not really a "case" and in which nothing was judicially decided, was important because the Court, in Wilson's words, affirmed "a principle important to freedom," that the judicial branch must be independent of the other branches.

Similarly, Jay established another principle vital to the Court's independent, judicial, and nonpolitical character when he declined Washington's request for an ADVISORY OPINION. That request arose out of apparent conflicts between American treaty obligations to France and the Proclamation of Neutrality. The French commissioned privateers in American ports and established prize courts to condemn vessels captured by those privateers. Washington sought the Court's opinion on twenty-nine questions involving international law and treaty interpretation, in connection with the French practices. Jay, relying again on the principle of separation of powers, observed that the Court should not "extra-judicially" decide questions that might come before it in litigation. Thus, by preserving its purely judicial character, the Court was free to decide some of those questions when real cases posed them. From the beginning, the Court staked its power and prestige on its special relationship to the supreme law of the land, which it safeguarded, expounded, and symbolized.

The pre-Marshall Court also exercised the power of JUDICIAL REVIEW. The Justices on circuit quickly held state acts unconstitutional for violating the supreme law of the land. Jay and Cushing on circuit in the district of Connecticut held that that state, by adversely affecting debts owed to British creditors, had violated the treaty of peace with Britain; Iredell in Georgia and Paterson in South Carolina made similar decisions. The Justices held that United States treaties were superior to state laws. The Supreme Court confronted the issue in WARE v. HYLTON (1796). With Iredell alone dissenting, the Court rejected the arguments of John Marshall, making his only appearance before the Justices, as counsel for the debtor interests of Virginia. He opposed "those who wish to impair the sovereignty of Virginia" and contended first that the Constitution had not authorized the Court to question the validity of state statutes and, second, that a treaty could not annul them. SERIATIM opinions by Chase, Paterson, Wilson, and Cushing held otherwise.

In *Clarke* v. *Harwood* (1797) the Court ruled that *Ware* "settled" the question before it. *Clarke* was the Court's first decision against the validity of a state act in a case arising on a WRIT OF ERROR to a state court under section 25 of the Judiciary Act of 1789. Section 25 authorized the Court to reverse or affirm state decisions that denied rights claimed under United States treaties. Maryland's high court, relying on a state statute sequestering debts owed to British creditors, had barred a claim based on the treaty of peace with Britain. By reversing the Maryland court, the Supreme Court in effect voided the state act. However, the Court rarely heard cases on a writ of error to a state court. Indeed, it had not decided its first such case until shortly before *Clarke*. In *Olney v. Arnold* (1796) the Court had reversed a Rhode Island decision that misconstrued a revenue act of Congress. The Court's power of reviewing state decisions under Section 25 did not become controversial until 1814. (See MARTIN v. HUNTER'S LESSEE, 1816.) During the Court's first decade, judicial review of state legislation was uncontested, and it was exercised.

On circuit the Justices also struck down state acts as violating the CONTRACT CLAUSE of the Constitution. The first such decision occurred in 1792 in CHAMPION AND DICKASON v. CASEY, which voided a Rhode Island state law. Given the hullaballoo in that state when its own judiciary was suspected of having voided a state act in TREVETT v. WEEDEN (1787), the meek acceptance of the 1792 decision showed the legitimacy of judicial review over the states.

In HYLTON v. UNITED STATES (1796) the Court for the first time determined the constitutionality of an act of Congress, ruling that an EXCISE on carriages, not being a DIRECT TAX, was valid even if not apportioned among the states. Those hoping for the Court to hold the federal excise unconstitutional were Jeffersonians; they did not then or at any time during the Court's first decade challenge the legitimacy of the Court's power to refuse to enforce an unconstitutional statute. Until the debate on the repeal of the JUDICIARY ACT OF 1801 (see JUDICIARY ACTS OF 1802), scarcely anyone opposed judicial review, whether over state or over congressional legislation. *Hayburn's Case* in 1792 was misunderstood throughout the nation. Not only did Attorney General Randolph believe that the Court had annulled an act of Congress; so did Congress. The House established an investigating committee, "this being the first instance in which a Court of Justice had declared a law of Congress unconstitutional." Jeffersonians gleefully praised the Justices and hoped the Court would extend the precedent by holding unconstitutional other congressional legislation that promoted Hamilton's economic programs. Later, Jeffersonians in Sedition Act trials sought to persuade the Justices on circuit that they should declare the statute void. Repeatedly during the first decade, bills arose in Congress that provoked members in both houses to state that the Court should and would hold them unconstitutional. The way to the doctrine of judicial review announced in MARBURY v. MADISON (1803) was well paved, and the opposition to the Court's opinion did not derive from its assumption of a power to void an act of Congress.

Another major theme in the work of the Court during its first decade was nationalism. Once again, the Marshall Court built on what the Jay and Ellsworth Courts had first shaped. The early Courts helped vindicate the national character of the United States government, maintain the supremacy of the nation over the states, and keep the states from undermining the new constitutional system. On circuit duty the Justices frequently lectured federal GRAND JURIES, inculcating doctrines from THE FEDERALIST, and these grand jury charges were well publicized in the newspapers. In one of his charges, Jay, in 1790, having declared, "We had become a Nation," explained why national tribunals became necessary for the interpretation and execution of national law, especially in a nation accustomed only to state courts and state policies. Circuit court opinions striking down state laws in violation of the contract clause or federal treaties preached nationalism and national supremacy. Many of the criminal prosecutions before the federal circuit courts during the first decade were connected with national suppression of the WHISKEY REBELLION and the FRIES REBELLION. Similarly, prosecutions under the Sedition Act were intended to vindicate the reputations of Congress and the President.

The development of a FEDERAL COMMON LAW OF CRIMES, expanding the jurisdiction of the national courts, fit the nationalist pattern. Whether the courts could try nonstatutory offenses was a question that first arose in Henfield's case (1793). Wilson maintained that an American citizen serving on a French privateer commissioned in an American port and attacking ships of England, with whom the United States was at peace, had committed an indictable offense under the Proclamation of Neutrality, the law of nations, and the treaty with England, even though Congress had not made his act a crime.

The same nationalist pattern unified several of the Court's opinions in cases dealing with various issues. In CHISHOLM v. GEORGIA (1793) the Court's holding, that its jurisdiction extended to suits against a state by citizens of another state, was founded on nationalist principles as well as on the text of Article III. Wilson, for example, began with the principles that the people of the United States form a nation, making ridiculous the "haughty notions of state independence, state SOVEREIGNTY, and state supremacy." "As to the purposes of the Union," he said, "therefore, Georgia is not a sovereign state." Jay's opinion also stressed "the national character" of the United States and the "inexpediency" of allowing state courts to decide questions that involved the performance of national treaties. The denunciation of the Court for its "consolidation of the Union" and its "annihilation of the sovereignty of the States" led to the ELEVENTH AMENDMENT, which was intended to nullify *Chisholm*.

In *Glass v. Sloop Betsy* (1794) the Court supported the government's neutrality policy by ruling that France, after capturing a neutral ship, could not hold or award her as a prize in an American port. Only the

United States courts could determine the lawfulness of prizes brought into its ports, and no foreign nation controlled its admiralty law or could subvert American rights under international law. In *Penhallow v. Doane* (1795) the Court resolved an old dispute over the ownership of a prize. One party's claims relied on decisions of a New Hampshire court, the other's on a decision of a prize court established by the old Congress of the Confederation. Paterson, in the Supreme Court's principal opinion, upheld the lower federal courts, which had decided against the state court and claimed jurisdiction. No nation, he said, had recognized the states as sovereign for the purpose of awarding prizes. The old Congress had been the supreme council of the nation and center of the Union, he claimed, whose sovereignty was approved by the people of America and recognized by foreign nations. The federal courts succeeded to that sovereignty in prize matters. New Hampshire angrily remonstrated against the "destruction" of its sovereignty but the Court's ruling prevailed.

Its decision in *Hylton v. United States* gave life to the government's revenue powers. When the Court upheld federal treaties as paramount to state laws, in *Ware v. Hylton* (1796), Chase, in the principal opinion for the Court, indulged in fanciful nationalism when declaring, "There can be no limitation on the power of the people of the United States. By their authority the State Constitutions were made."

Other notable cases of the first decade were VAN HORNE'S LESSEE v. DORRANCE (1794) and CALDER v. BULL (1798), in which the Court laid the foundation for the judicial doctrine of VESTED RIGHTS, which it developed further in contract clause and HIGHER LAW decisions during Marshall's chief justiceship. Although the Court was left out of the planning for the new national capital, it had been enunciating doctrines— of judicial review, national supremacy, and vested rights—that helped shape the United States and would in time make the judicial branch of government impossible to ignore.

Bibliography

CURRIE, DAVID P.   1981   The Constitution in the Supreme Court: 1789–1801. *University of Chicago Law Review* 48:819–885.

GOEBEL, JULIUS   1971   *Antecedents and Beginnings.* Vol. I of the *Oliver Wendell Holmes Devise History of the Supreme Court,* ed. Paul Freund. New York: Macmillan.

HAINES, CHARLES GROVE   1944   *The Role of the Supreme Court in American Government and Politics, 1789–1835.* Berkeley: University of California Press.

HENDERSON, DWIGHT F.   1971   *Courts for a New Nation.* Washington, D.C.: Public Affairs Press.

WARREN, CHARLES   1923   *The Supreme Court in United States History.* Vol. I. Boston: Little, Brown.

CONSTITUTIONAL HISTORY, 1801–1829

Merrill D. Peterson

THOMAS JEFFERSON entered the presidency in 1801 with a rhetoric of return to constitutional first principles. Inaugurated in the new permanent capital on the Potomac, he offered a brilliant summation of these principles together with a lofty appeal for restoration of harmony and affection. "We are all republicans: we are all federalists," he declared. He hoped to achieve "a perfect consolidation" of political sentiments by emphasizing principles that ran deeper than party names or doctrines. He spoke of preserving "the whole constitutional vigor" of the general government yet called for "a wise and frugal government, which shall restrain men from injuring one another, which shall leave them otherwise free to regulate their own pursuits of industry and improvement, and shall not take from the mouth of labor the bread it has earned." Jefferson never doubted that "constitutional vigor" and individual liberty were perfectly compatible, indeed that the strength of republican government rested upon the freedom of the society. He named "absolute acquiescence in the decisions of the majority the vital principle of republics, from which there is no appeal but to force." This principle demanded freedom of opinion and debate, including the right of a minority to turn itself into a new majority, as the Republican party had done. "If there be any among us," Jefferson said, alluding to the delusions of 1798, "who would wish to dissolve this Union or to change its republican form, let them stand undisturbed as monuments of the safety with which error may be tolerated where reason is left free to combat it." He thus announced a commitment to ongoing change through the democratic process. Because of that commitment the Constitution became an instrument of democracy, change became possible without violence or destruction, and government went forward on the continuing consent of the governed.

The "revolution of 1800," as Jefferson later called it, introduced no fundamental changes in the structure or machinery of the general government but made that government a more effective instrument of popular leadership. Jefferson himself possessed great popular authority. Combining this with the constitutional authority of the office, he overcame Whiggish monarchical fears and gave the presidency a secure place in the republican system. Jefferson dominated his administration more surely and completely than even GEORGE WASHINGTON had done. The cabinet, which was composed of moderate Republicans, enjoyed unprecedented harmony, stability, and unity. It was the main agency of policy and decision making.

Jefferson also dominated Congress. For the first time, in 1801, the Republicans controlled both houses of Congress. The Federalists were a shrinking minority, though by no means powerless. In republican theory Congress should control the executive. Jefferson honored the theory in official discourse. Thus he declined to appear before Congress in person and sent his annual "State of the Union" message to be read by a clerk, setting a precedent that remained unbroken for 112 years. Practically, however, Jefferson recognized that the government demanded executive leadership if any majority, Federalist or Republican, was to carry out its program. How could he overcome the constraints of republican theory and the constitutional SEPARATION OF POWERS? The solution was found partly through the personal influence Jefferson commanded and partly through a network of party leadership outside constitutional channels. As the unchallenged head of the Republican party, Jefferson acted with an authority he did not possess, indeed utterly disclaimed, in his official capacity. Leaders of both houses of Congress were the President's political lieutenants. Despite the weak structural organization of the Republican party in Congress—the only formal machinery was the presidential nominating caucus which came into being every four years—the party was a pervasive functional reality. The President was chief legislator as well as chief magistrate. Nearly all the congressional legislation during eight years originated with the President and his cabinet. Lacking staff support, Congress depended on executive initiatives and usually followed them. Federalists complained of the "backstairs" influence of the President; eventually some Republicans, led by JOHN RANDOLPH, rebelled. But the system of presidential leadership worked with unerring precision during Jefferson's first term. It faltered during his second term when the Republicans, with virtually no opposition to contend with, began to quarrel among themselves; and it would not work at all under Jefferson's successor, JAMES MADISON, who lacked Jefferson's popular prestige and personal magnetism.

In matters of public policy, the Jefferson administration sought reform within the limits of moderation and conciliation. More doctrinaire Republicans, still infected with Anti-Federalism, were not satisfied with a mere change of leadership and demanded restrictive constitutional amendments to place the true principles of government beyond reversal or contradiction. While rejecting this course, Jefferson was never entirely happy with the consequences of his temporizing policies. Republican reform was bottomed on fiscal policy. The Hamiltonian system of public debt, internal taxes, and a national bank was considered an evil of the first magnitude. Secretary of the Treasury ALBERT GALLATIN developed a plan to extinguish the debt, which had increased under the Federalists, by large annual appropriations, yet, amazingly, reduce taxes at the same time. All internal taxes would be repealed and government would depend solely on revenue from the customs houses. The plan required deep retrenchment, especially in the army and navy departments. Of course, it was premised on peace. Congress embarked on it; and although the debt was dramatically reduced during the next seven years, the plan was initially upset by the exigencies of the Tripolitan War, then derailed by the Anglo-American crisis that led to the War of 1812. Jefferson agonized over ALEXANDER HAMILTON's fiscal system. "When the government was first established," he wrote in 1802, "it was possible to have kept it going on true principles, but the contracted, English, half-lettered ideas of Hamilton destroyed that hope in a bud. We can pay off his debt in 15 years, but we can never get rid of his financial system. It mortifies me to be strengthening principles which I deem radically vicious, but the vice is entailed on us by the first error. . . . What is practicable must often control pure theory." A case in point was the Bank of the United States. Jefferson thought it an institution of "the most deadly hostility" to the Constitution and republican government. Yet he tolerated the Bank, in part because its charter ran to 1811 (when Republicans would refuse to renew it) and also because Gallatin found the bank highly useful to the government's operations.

Jefferson's "war on the judiciary" featured three main battles and several skirmishes, ending in no very clear outcome. The first battle was fought over the JUDICIARY ACT OF 1801. Republicans were enraged by this blatantly partisan measure passed in the waning hours of JOHN ADAMS's administration. It created a new tier of courts and judgeships, extended the power of the federal judiciary at the expense of state courts, and reduced the number of Supreme Court Justices beginning with the next vacancy, thereby denying the Republicans an early opportunity to reshape the Court. Jefferson promptly targeted the act for repeal. The Federalists had retreated to the judiciary as a stronghold, he said, from which "all the works of Republicanism are to be beaten down and erased." The Sedition Act had demonstrated the prostration of the judiciary to partisan purposes. After taking office Jefferson acted to pardon victims of the act, which he considered null and void, and to drop pending prosecutions. He often spoke of making judges more responsible to the people, perhaps by periodic review of their tenure; and although he recognized the power of JUDICIAL REVIEW, he did not think it binding on the executive or the legislature. According to his theory of "tripartite balance" each of the coordinate branches of government is supreme in its sphere and may decide questions of constitutionality for itself. The same theory was advanced by Republicans in Congress, as against the Federalist claim of exclusive power of the Supreme Court to declare legislation unconstitutional. Congress did not settle this issue; but after heated debate it repealed the offensive act and, with minor exceptions, returned the judiciary to its previous footing.

The second battle involved the case of MARBURY v. MADISON (1803). Although the Supreme Court's decision would later be seen as the cornerstone of judicial review, the case was understood at the time primarily as a political duel between the President and the Court, one in which Chief Justice JOHN MARSHALL took a gratuitous stab at the executive but then deliberately backed away from a confrontation he knew the Court could not win.

The third battle featured the IMPEACHMENT of federal judges. In 1803 Congress impeached, tried, and convicted Judge JOHN PICKERING of the district court in New Hampshire. The case was a hard one because Pickering's bizarre conduct on the bench stemmed from intoxication and possible insanity; but in the absence of any constitutional authorization for the removal of an incompetent judge, the Republicans took the course of impeachment and convicted him of "high crimes and misdemeanors." The subsequent impeachment of Supreme Court Justice SAMUEL J. CHASE was clearly a political act. A high-toned Federalist, Chase had earned Republican enmity as the convicting judge in several SEDITION trials and by harangues to grand juries assailing democracy and all its works. Nevertheless, his trial in the Senate ended in a verdict of acquittal in 1805. Jefferson and the Republican leaders turned away from impeachment in disgust. Although it may have produced salutary restraint in the federal judiciary, and enhanced the President's role as a popular leader, neither impeachment nor any other Jeffersonian action disturbed the foundations of judicial power.

During his second term, Jefferson used the TREASON trial of AARON BURR to renew the attack on the judiciary but without success. The former vice-president was charged with treason for leading a military expedition to separate the western states from the Union. Determined to convict him, Jefferson again faced an old enemy, John Marshall, who presided in the trial at Richmond. At Burr's request, Marshall subpoenaed Jefferson to appear in court with papers bearing on the case. Jefferson refused, citing his responsibility as chief executive. "The Constitution enjoins his constant agency in the concerns of six millions of people. Is the law paramount to this, which calls on him on behalf of a single one?" he asked. The court backed off. Nothing required Jefferson's presence. He offered to testify by deposition, but this was not requested. When the trial ended in Burr's acquittal, Jefferson denounced its whole conduct as political. He laid the proceedings before Congress and urged that body to furnish some remedy for judicial arrogance and error. Several Republican state legislatures instructed their delegations to seek amendment making judges removable on the address of both houses of Congress. Both President and Congress were preoccupied with FOREIGN AFFAIRS in the fall of 1807, however, and nothing came of this effort.

The first foreign crisis of the Jefferson administration culminated in the LOUISIANA PURCHASE. It was an ironic triumph for a President, an administration, and a party that made a boast of constitutional purity. For the Constitution made no provision either to acquire foreign territory or, as the purchase treaty mandated, to incorporate that territory and its inhabitants into the Union. Jefferson, therefore, proposed to sanction the acquisition retroactively by amendment of the Constitution. Actually, such an authorization was the lesser part of the amendment he drafted; the larger part undertook to control the future of the Trans-Mississippi West by prohibiting settlement above the thirty-third parallel. But neither part interested congressional Republicans, and Jefferson, though he said failure of the amendment made the Constitution "a blank paper by construction," acquiesced. A revolution in the Union perforce became a revolution in the Constitution as well. The expansion of the treaty-making power was only the beginning of the revolution. A series of acts for the government of the new territory vested extraordinary power in the President; and the President proposed, with the sanction of a constitutional amendment, a national system of INTERNAL IMPROVEMENTS to unite this far-flung "empire of liberty."

The foreign crisis of Jefferson's second administration continued under Madison and finally terminated in the War of 1812. With the formation of the Third Coalition against Napoleonic France in 1805, all Europe was engulfed in war. The United States became the last neutral nation of consequence—to the profit of its carrying trade. Unfortunately, each side, the British and the French, demanded the trade on its own terms, and submission to one side's demands entailed conflict with the other. Britain, the dominant sea power, was the greater problem. British ships attacked American carriers under interpretations of rules of blockade, contraband, and neutral commerce that were rejected by the United States. Britain claimed the right of impressment of seamen aboard American ships on the ground that they were actually British subjects who had deserted from His Majesty's Navy and shipped aboard American vessels with government connivance. There was some truth in this claim, but thousands of American citizens were, in fact, impressed by Britain. And every seizure was a stinging reminder of past colonial servitude. Diplomatic efforts to settle these issues proved abortive. Relations rapidly deteriorated after the *Chesapeake-Leopard* Affair in June 1807. The attack of HMS *Leopard* on an American naval vessel after its captain refused to permit boarding and search for deserters inflamed the entire country against Britain. Jefferson might have taken the country to war. Instead, in December, he proposed, and Congress swiftly passed, the EMBARGO ACT. Essentially a self-blockade of American commerce, the act was in some part a preparation for war and in some part an experiment to test the theory of "peaceable coercion." The idea that the United States might enforce reason and justice on European belligerents by withholding its commerce was a first principle of Jeffersonian statecraft. Under the trial now begun, that idea failed. While the policy had comparatively little effect abroad, it produced serious economic, political, and perhaps even constitutional damage at home.

The embargo raised a host of constitutional issues, all hotly debated by Federalists and Republicans, though the parties seemed to have changed places. First, and broadest, was the issue of the commerce power. Republicans said the power to regulate commerce included the power to prohibit it. Federalists, who were closely allied with eastern merchants and shipmasters, limited regulation to encouragement and protection. Yet it was a Federalist, John Davis, the United States District Judge for Massachusetts, who upheld the constitutionality of the embargo on a broad view of the commerce power backed up by the "inherent SOVEREIGNTY" of the United States. Second, wholesale violation of the embargo in the Lake Champlain region led the President to proclaim an insurrection and authorize military force to suppress it under the same law George Washington had earlier used to put down the WHISKEY REBELLION over Republican opposition. Third, enforcement of the embargo required ever tighter measures of control. The fourth in the series of five embargo acts empowered customs collectors to search without a SEARCH WARRANT and to detain vessels merely on suspicion of intent to violate the law. The FOURTH AMENDMENT, a part of the Bill of Rights, was thus jeopardized. Fourth, before Congress adjourned in April 1808 it authorized the President to suspend the embargo against either or both belligerents—an unprecedented DELEGATION OF POWER. Federalists, of course, denounced the embargo in terms that recalled the VIRGINIA AND KENTUCKY RESOLUTIONS.

A storm of protest in New England led Congress, at the end of Jefferson's presidency, to repeal the embargo. The Non-Intercourse Act, which replaced it, reopened trade with all the world except Britain and France. That course, too, failed; and for the next three years under the new president, Madison, the country drifted toward war. In the end, war was declared because both diplomacy and "peaceable coercion" had failed to resolve the conflict over neutral rights. But that conflict was a symbol of much more: the honor and independence of the nation, the freedom of its commerce, the integrity of American nationality, the survival of republican government. The war was thus morally justified as the second war for American independence. The nation was ill-prepared for war, however, and its conduct produced one disaster after another. One section of the Union, New England, vigorously opposed the war from the start.

This opposition gave rise to the principal constitutional controversy of the time. The governors of the New England states challenged congressional power to provide for organizing and calling forth the militia. The chief justice of Massachusetts's highest court advised the governor that the right to decide when the militia should be called belonged to him, not to Congress or the President; and later, in 1814, when the militia was activated it was in the state rather than the national service. Years later, in *Luther v. Mott* (1827), the Supreme Court fully sustained national authority over the militia. Interference with the prosecution of the war was accompanied by a steady stream of denunciation. Madison called this a "seditious opposition," but unlike his Federalist predecessors he made no move to restrain or suppress it. Ultra-Federalists had been hinting at disunion since the Louisiana Purchase threatened New England's power in the Union; some of them had plotted to establish a Northern Confederacy in 1804. Now, a decade later, Federalist delegates from all the New England states met secretly in the HARTFORD CONVENTION, not to plot disunion, for moderate forces were in control, but to organize resistance against "Mr. Madison's War." Resolutions adopted by the convention recommended a series of constitutional admendments, including elimination of the THREE-FIFTHS CLAUSE for the apportionment of representation and direct taxes, limitation of presidential tenure to one term, a two-thirds vote in Congress to admit new states and to declare war, and the disqualification of naturalized citizens from federal office.

The commissioners of the Hartford Convention arrived in Washington with their resolutions in the midst of jubilation over the Battle of New Orleans. They were ridiculed, of course; and from this nadir the Federalist party never recovered. News of the Peace of Ghent quickly followed. While it resolved none of the issues over which the war had begun, the treaty placed American independence on impregnable foundations and confirmed the strength of republican government. The American people erased the shame from a war so meager in victories, so marked by defeat, division, and disgrace, and put upon it the face of glory. In December 1815 Madison laid before Congress a nationalistic program that featured measures, such as a national bank, formerly associated with the defeated party. Yet the program was not a case of "out-Federalizing Federalism." The Republican nationalism that matured with the Peace of Ghent had nothing to do with Federalist nationalism, with its vitiating Anglophobia, its narrow class and sectional views, and its distrust of popular government. The American political experiment had vindicated itself, exorcising earlier fears for its survival and making possible the incorporation of principles of national improvement and consolidation into the Republican party.

A new era dawned in American politics in 1815. For a quarter-century the nation had directed its industry and commerce toward a Europe ravaged by war and revolution; now that era had ended, and with it the opportunity of rearing American prosperity on the misfortunes of the Old World. For almost as long, government had been carried on by party spirit; now one of the two parties, the Federalist, around which the rivalry of men, issues, and principles had turned, ceased to be a factor in national affairs, and it was by no means clear what political force would replace the force of party. A country that had hugged the Atlantic seaboard and sought its prosperity in foreign trade was about to explode in the Trans-Appalachian West. During the next six years five new western states would enter the Union. A wider Union and the rise of the West as a self-conscious section raised difficult problems of economic development, constitutional principle, and political power. Since its Revolutionary birth the nation had enjoyed astonishing continuity of leadership. Thomas Jefferson, author of the Declaration of Independence, was a gray eminence at Monticello; James Madison, Father of the Constitution, was the President who had finally, irrevocably, secured that independence in a second war against Great Britain. But a new generation of political leaders had burst on the scene during the war, and the fate of the nation now lay in their hands.

Nearly all Republicans united on the program of national improvement and consolidation that Madison laid before the Fourteenth Congress in December. This "Madisonian Platform" proceeded from an enlarged view of the general government's responsibility for the nation's welfare. A national bank had previously been recommended to Congress as an agency for financing the war. Now, facing the chaos of runaway state banking, Madison recommended it as a permanent institution to secure the constitutional object of a stable and uniform national currency. Madison, of course, had opposed the original Bank of the United States as unconstitutional, and Republicans in Congress had defeated its recharter in 1811. But conditions and needs had changed, and Madison, with most of these same Republicans, considered that experience had settled the question of constitutionality in favor of a national bank. The Madisonian platform called for continuing in peacetime high tariff duties on imports in order to protect the infant industries that had grown up behind the sheltering wall of war and embargo. The President called for a comprehensive system of internal improvements—roads and canals to bind the nation together, secure its defenses, and facilitate internal commerce. Any deficiency of constitutional power should be overcome by amendment. In a final appeal to the liberality of American patriotism, Madison proposed the establishment of a national university, in Washington, which would be "a central resort of youth and genius from every part of their country, diffusing on their return examples of those national feelings, those liberal sentiments, and those congenial manners which contribute cement to our union and strength to [its] great political fabric."

Congress responded with legislation to charter a national bank, establish a system of tariff protection, and create a permanent fund for financing a vast network of roads, canals, and other improvements. The last measure, dubbed the Bonus Bill because the fund was founded on the bonus to be paid for the bank charter, was vetoed by Madison on constitutional grounds in the last act of his presidency. In this surprising retreat to the doctrine of strict construction, Madison delivered the first shock to the postwar nationalism he had himself championed. His successor, JAMES MONROE, took the same position on internal improvements, holding that a constitutional amendment was necessary to authorize them. Republican leaders in Congress disagreed. They found sufficient constitutional warrant to build as well as to fund internal improvements in the commerce, post road, and general welfare clauses, and they declined to seek an amendment lest by the failure to obtain it the Constitution be weakened. In the end, however, Monroe conceded the unlimited power of Congress to appropriate money for internal improvements, while continuing to deny the power to construct and operate them. This concession provided a constitutional justification for the General Survey Act of 1824. Although the same argument supported important projects in the ensuing administration, no national system of internal improvements was ever realized. In the absence of constructive national action, the several states embarked upon ambitious projects of their own (New York's Erie Canal, for instance, begun in 1817); and soon the government even relinquished its one great enterprise, the National Road, to the states.

The period of Monroe's presidency was signalized as "The Era of Good Feelings." This reflected the dissolution of old party ties and feelings. The Republican party had become the grand party of the nation. In 1820 Monroe ran unopposed for reelection and only one erratic electoral vote was cast against him. But his success had little to do with party or popularity, nor did it translate into effective power and leadership. Power and leadership had shifted to Congress, particularly to the House of Representatives where HENRY CLAY had converted the office of speaker from that of an impartial moderator to one of policymaking leadership. To an extent, certainly, executive power receded because foreign affairs had taken a distant second place to domestic affairs on the nation's agenda. Interestingly, Monroe is best remembered not for any initiative or achievement in domestic affairs but for a masterly stroke of foreign policy, the Monroe Doctrine. But Clay even challenged the President in foreign policy; and congressional ascendancy owed much to the boldness and address of young leaders like Clay who sought to command the popular feeling and power of the country. Partly for this reason the postwar Republicans consensus was soon shattered and "good feelings" vanished on the winds of change. Great issues, such as the Missouri Compromise, split the nationalizing Republican party along its sectional seams. The Panic of 1819, which led to the first major depression in the country's history, released powerful currents that shriveled the bright hopes of 1815.

Although the Panic of 1819 broke banks, bankrupted merchants, idled workers, and emptied factories everywhere, it was centered in American agriculture, especially in the freshly burgeoning lands of the South and West. Many purchasers of these lands had availed themselves of the credit allowed by the Harrison Land Act of 1800. Also important to frontier farmers and planters, of course, was bank credit. State banks had generally met this need, but now they were aided and abetted by the new Bank of the United States, which established most of its branches in the South and West. Agricultural prices collapsed worldwide in 1818. A severe contraction of bank credit followed. The Bank of the United States barely survived, and did so only at the expense of bankrupting many thousands of farmers, merchants, and local bankers. Several western states enacted legislation in the interest of debtors. The controversy over the constitutionality of debtor relief laws rocked Kentucky for a decade. All along the frontier, in wheat lands and in cotton lands, people tended to blame their troubles on the Bank. There were calls for repeal of its charter, and state legislatures acted to restrain "The Monster." Ohio levied a prohibitive tax on resident branches; when it was not paid the state auditor seized $100,000 of the Bank's funds, thereby giving birth to the case of OSBORN v. THE BANK OF THE UNITED STATES (1824). Wherever the depression caused hostility to the Bank, it weakened the spring of support for economic nationalism generally. To nationalist leaders, on the other hand, the depression offered further confirmation of the colonial character of the American economy and pointed up the imperative need for higher protective tariffs and other government assistance to bring about a flourishing "home market" for the products of American industry. This AMERICAN SYSTEM, as Clay named it, had its fulfillment in the Tariff of 1824.

While the Panic was at its height, in March 1819, the Supreme Court handed down its unanimous decision in McCULLOCH v. MARYLAND, upholding the constitutionality of the Bank and its freedom to operate without state interference. Chief Justice John Marshall drew upon the Hamiltonian doctrine of IMPLIED POWERS not only for the congressional authority to charter a bank but also for a sweeping vindication of national supremacy. In the same momentous term, which established the high-water mark of judicial nationalism, the court invoked the CONTRACT

CLAUSE to strike down laws of two states. In DARTMOUTH COLLEGE v. WOODWARD it extended the protection of that clause to corporate charters; and in STURGES v. CROWNINSHIELD it struck down a New York law for the relief of debtors whose contracts antedated the law. Quite aside from their implications for national versus state authority, all these decisions placed the court unreservedly on the side of propertied interests against popular majorities in state legislatures.

The Bank case, in particular, provoked attack on the Supreme Court and more broadly on the growth of national power. In Virginia opposition to the Supreme Court, which Jefferson called a "subtle corps of sappers and miners constantly working under ground to undermine the foundations of our confederated fabric," sparked revival of the STATES' RIGHTS doctrines of the Virginia and Kentucky Resolutions and offered powerful reinforcement of the state's challenge to the court's appellate jurisdiction. The challenge had ridden on an old case involving the confiscation of Loyalist lands during the American Revolution. Taking the case on appeal from the Virginia Court of Appeals, the Supreme Court had overturned the state's confiscation law and found for the right of the English heir. To this Judge SPENCER ROANE, head of the Virginia court, responded by denying the Supreme Court's appellate jurisdiction, declaring section 25 of the Judiciary Act of 1789 unconstitutional, and refusing to execute the Supreme Court's decree. The court again took up the case, MARTIN v. HUNTER'S LESSEE (1816), and through Justice JOSEPH STORY reasserted the constitutionality of the appellate jurisdiction over state courts together with the judicial supremacy that went with it. But for the Bank case the controversy would have been quickly forgotten. As Marshall observed, however, that case "roused the Sleeping Giant of Virginia." Under the pseudonym "Hampden," in the columns of the Richmond *Enquirer,* Roane advanced a DUAL FEDERALISM philosophy of the Constitution. Under it there could be no ultimate appeal from the state courts to the Supreme Court. Marshall replied at length as "Friend of the Constitution" in the Alexandria *Gazette.* The veteran Old Republican JOHN TAYLOR of Caroline expounded the Virginia doctrines *ad nauseum* in *Construction Construed and Constitutions Vindicated* (1820). The doctrines still had a long course to run, but the controversy over appellate jurisdiction drew to a close in COHENS v. VIRGINIA (1821). In this arranged case Virginia became the defendant when the Cohens appealed their conviction in state court to the Supreme Court under Section 25. The Virginia assembly adopted resolutions backing the state cause. Surprisingly, perhaps because the case resulted in a nominal victory for the state, Marshall's broad assertion of national judicial supremacy provoked no official reaction in Virginia, and opposition collapsed in 1822.

The Missouri Compromise was enacted in the midst of these events and communicated its own passions to them. The proposal to restrict slavery in Missouri as a condition of statehood raised difficult questions about the constitutional authority of Congress, the nature of the Union, the future of the West, the morality of slavery, and the sectional balance of power. Congress had previously restricted SLAVERY IN THE TERRITORIES. That power was not seriously in dispute. But the Missouri constitution would provide for slavery, and it was by no means clear that Congress could overrule it, especially as slavery had always been considered an institution under local jurisdiction. The compromise resolved the issue by allowing Missouri to enter the Union as a slave state. A new problem arose, however, when the proffered Missouri constitution contained a provision for excluding "free negroes and mulattoes" from the state. Opponents of the compromise charged that this violated the PRIVILEGES AND IMMUNITIES clause of the United States Constitution, because Negroes who were citizens of northern states would be denied citizenship in Missouri. Laboriously, a new compromise had to be constructed to save the original one. Under it Missouri would be admitted to the Union only after the legislature agreed, despite the constitutional provision, never to pass a law that might abridge the privileges and immunities of citizens. Missouri acquiesced and gained admission to the Union in August 1821. Not for many years would the harmony of the Union again be disturbed by slavery. The Missouri Compromise, therefore, contributed mightily to peace and union. Yet to Thomas Jefferson, contemplating the exclusion of slavery above the 36' 30" parallel, the compromise was "like a fire-ball in the night," sounding "the knell of the Union." "It is hushed, indeed, for the moment. But this is a reprieve only, not the final sentence. A geographical line, once conceived and held up to the angry passions of men, will never be obliterated; and every new irritation will mark it deeper and deeper."

The Republican consensus vanished during Monroe's second term. The Missouri question had raised fears of sectional parties and politics that were not dispelled by the compromise. The growth of the West, with a maturing sectional consciousness of its own, and the scramble of economic interests for the bounty and favor of the general government put the National Republican system under heavy strain. While nationalists continued to believe that the Union would survive and prosper only through measures of consolidation, growing numbers of Republicans, inspired by the Virginia "Old Republicans," believed consolidation must tear the Union apart. They called for return to Jeffersonian austerity and states' rights.

In this unstable political environment, the contest for the presidential succession was especially disturbing. Monroe's chief cabinet officers, JOHN QUINCY ADAMS, William H. Crawford, and JOHN C. CALHOUN, were in the race from the start, and they were soon joined by Henry Clay and ANDREW JACKSON. In the absence of a single dominant leader or a clear line of succession, such as the Virginia dynasty had afforded, the Republican party split into personal followings and factions. The congressional caucus of the party, which had been the mechanism for nominating candidates for President and vice-president, could no longer be relied upon. The caucus itself had become an issue. In an increasingly democratic electorate it was assailed as a closed, elitist institution. Politicians grew wary of the caucus but saw no obvious substitute for it. "We are putting to the proof the most delicate part of our system, the election of the Executive," DANIEL WEBSTER remarked. What was most distressing about the present contest, among men nourished on traditional Whig fears of executive power, was that it made the presidency the center of gravity in the government. Great issues of public policy were submitted to the artifice and caprice of presidential politics; and senators and representatives, if elected on the basis of presidential preferences, must necessarily compromise their independence. This threatened subordination of the legislative to the executive power was an inversion of the proper constitutional order.

Given the multiplicity of candidates, each with his own following, and none able to command a majority of votes, the election of the President inevitably wound up in the House of Representatives. There Clay, the speaker, having been eliminated, threw his support to Adams, who was chosen over Jackson, the popular vote leader. Adams's subsequent appointment of Clay as secretary of state, the cabinet post which had furnished the President for the third successive time, brought cries of "corrupt bargain" from the Jacksonians, and from this canard the Adams administration never recovered. Boldly, in his first message to Congress, Adams proposed to rally the country behind a great program of national improvement, one which took conventional internal improvements—rivers and harbors, roads and canals—only as a starting point. "Liberty is power," Adams declared. A nation of liberty should be a nation of power, provided, of course, power is used beneficently. The Constitution presents no obstacle. Indeed, to refrain from exercising legitimate powers for good ends would be treachery to the people. "While foreign nations less blessed with that freedom which is power . . . are advancing with gigantic strides in the career of public improvement," Adams said, "were we to slumber in indolence or to fold up our arms and proclaim to the world that we are palsied by the will of our constituents, would it not be to cast away the bounties of Providence and doom ourselves to perpetual inferiority?"

In response to the message, all the old artillery of states' rights and STRICT CONSTRUCTION was hauled out and turned on the administration. Liberty is power? What dangerous nonsense. Liberty is the jealous restraint of power. Individuals, not governments, are the best judges of their own interests; and the national interest consists only in the aggregate of individual interests. These ideas had been employed in the attack on the American System. Now they entered deeply into the ideology of the emerging Jacksonian coalition. A new recruit to the coalition was Vice-President Calhoun, who began to shed the liberality and nationalism that had characterized his political career. In part, certainly, he was influenced by the rising states' rights frenzy in South Carolina. This movement was orchestrated by Calhoun's enemies in the Crawford faction. In 1825 they drove through the legislature resolutions declaring the protective tariff and federal internal improvements unconstitutional. This "Revolution of 1825," as it came to be known, showed how far out of step Calhoun was with the opinion of his state, and he hurried to catch up.

In Congress the anticonsolidation movement provided most of the rhetoric and some of the substance of opposition on every issue with the administration but was especially evident in debates on the judiciary and the tariff. Report of a bill in the House to reorganize the federal judiciary, mainly by the addition of three circuits—and three new judges—in the West, furnished a forum for advocates of reforming the judiciary. There was still no consensus on the role and authority of the Supreme Court. The Court had been a powerful ally of consolidation. Between 1816 and 1825 it had ruled in favor of national power seventeen times and of states' rights only six times, when they were at issue; and by 1825 it had invalidated in whole or in part the statutes of ten states. Various measures, most of them involving constitutional amendment, had been offered to curb judicial power: the withdrawal of opinions, or removal of Justices, on the address of both houses of Congress; the requirement of seriatim opinions; the use of the Senate as a tribunal of last resort on federal questions; and the repeal of section 25 of the Judiciary Act. All were aired in the 1826 debate. Nothing of substance emerged; the reorganization bill itself, after passing the House, failed in the Senate. Yet the debate, which was the "last hurrah" of reform, may have contributed to the increasing moderation of the Marshall Court after 1825.

The tariff had been a constitutional issue since the great debate on the American System in 1824. The power to tax, Virginia congressman PHILIP P. BARBOUR had then argued, was not a power to promote one industry over another, nor did any such power exist in the Constitution. Controversy was reignited three years later by demands for additional protection, particularly on behalf of the rising wool and woolens industry of the Northeast. Jacksonian politicians, who came into control of the new Congress, could not ignore the demand. Under the leadership of MARTIN VAN BUREN of New York they framed a tariff bill that was a political stratagem rather than a serious piece of economic legislation. Moreover, they persuaded their southern friends to go along with the bill on the spurious plea that it would finally fail because of provisions designed to trigger overwhelming New England opposition, thereby enabling the Jacksonians to claim credit in the North for protectionist efforts without inflicting further injury on the South. But in the Senate, where it was named the Tariff of Abominations, the bill was amended to become less objectionable to New England, and its great spokesman, Webster, heretofore a free-trader, dramatically declared his support. The TARIFF ACT OF 1828 became law. The South felt betrayed. In South Carolina, which had grasped the flagging torch of states' rights from Virginia, there were demands to "calculate the value of the Union." The legislature, in December, enacted a series of resolutions declaring the tariff oppressive and unconstitutional. It also published the South Carolina Exposition and Protest, which Calhoun had authored secretly at the invitation of a legislative committee. The Exposition repeated, with some elaboration, the litany of antitariff arguments South Carolina radicals had been urging for several years and it offered the first authoritative statement of "the Carolina doctrine" of nullification.

A motley coalition—western agrarians, southern planters, northern democrats—swept Andrew Jackson into the presidency in 1828. His inaugural address gave no clear sign of the direction his administration would take; but the dominant pressure of the men, ideas, and interests gathered around the President was toward dissolution of the National Republican platform and toward the rebirth of party government on specious Jeffersonian principles.

Bibliography

ADAMS, HENRY   1891–1893   *History of the United States during the Administrations of Jefferson and Madison.* 9 Vols. New York: Scribner's.

BEVERIDGE, ALBERT J.   1919   *The Life of John Marshall,* vol. IV. Boston: Houghton Mifflin.

CUNNINGHAM, NOBLE E., JR.   1978   *The Process of Government under Jefferson.* Princeton, N.J.: Princeton University Press.

DANGERFIELD, GEORGE   1952   *The Era of Good Feeling.* New York: Harcourt, Brace.

GOODRICH, CARTER, ED.   1967   *The Government and the Economy: 1783–1861.* Indianapolis: Bobbs-Merrill.

JOHNSTONE, ROBERT M., JR.   1978   *Jefferson and the Presidency: Leadership in the Young Republic.* Ithaca, N.Y.: Cornell University Press.

KETCHAM, RALPH   1984   *Presidents above Party: The First American Presidency, 1789–1829.* Chapel Hill: University of North Carolina Press.

SOFAER, ABRAHAM D.   1976   *War, Foreign Affairs and Constitutional Power: The Origins.* Cambridge, Mass.: Ballinger.

TURNER, FREDERICK JACKSON   1906   *Rise of the New West, 1819–1829.* New York: Macmillan.

WHITE, LEONARD D.   1951   *The Jeffersonians: A Study in Administrative History, 1801–1829.* New York: Macmillan.

MARSHALL COURT

(1801–1835)

Leonard W. Levy

In 1801 the Supreme Court existed on the fringe of American awareness. Its prestige was slight, and it was more ignored than respected. On January 20, 1801, the day President JOHN ADAMS nominated JOHN MARSHALL for the chief justiceship, the commissioners of the DISTRICT OF COLUMBIA informed Congress that the Court had no place to hold its February term. The Senate consented to the use of one of its committee rooms, and Marshall took his seat on February 4 in a small basement chamber. At the close of 1809, Benjamin Latrobe, the architect, reported that the basement had been redesigned to enlarge the courtroom and provide an office for the clerk and a library room for the Justices. In 1811, however, Latrobe reported that the Court "had been obliged to hold their sittings in a tavern," because Congress had appropriated no money for "fitting up and furnishing the Court-room. . . ." After the British burned the Capitol in 1814 Congress again neglected to provide for the Court. It held its 1815 term in a private home, and for several years after met in temporary Capitol quarters that were "little better than a dungeon." The Court moved into permanent quarters in 1819. In 1824 a New York correspondent described the Court's Capitol chamber: "In the first place, it is like going down cellar to reach it. The room is on the basement story in an obscure part of the north wing. . . . A stranger might traverse the dark avenues of the Capitol for a week, without finding the remote corner in which Justice is administered to the American Republic." He added that the courtroom was hardly large enough for a police court.

The Supreme Court, however, no longer lacked dignity or respect. It had become a force that commanded recognition. In 1819 a widely read weekly described it as so awesome that some regarded it with reverence. That year THOMAS JEFFERSON complained that the Court had made the Constitution a "thing of wax," which it shaped as it pleased, and in 1824 he declared that the danger he most feared was the Court's "consolidation of our government." Throughout the 1820s Congress debated bills to curb the Court, which, said a senator, the people blindly adored— a "self-destroying idolatry." ALEXIS DE TOCQUEVILLE, writing in 1831, said: "The peace, the prosperity, and the very existence of the Union are vested in the hands of the seven Federal judges. Without them, the Constitution would be a dead letter. . . ." Hardly a political question arose, he wrote, that did not become a judicial question.

Chief Justice Marshall was not solely responsible for the radical change in the Court's status and influence, but he made the difference. He bequeathed to the people of the United States what it was not in the political power of the Framers of the Constitution to give. Had the Framers been free agents, they would have proposed a national government that was unquestionably dominant over the states and possessed a formidable array of powers breathtaking in flexibility and scope. Marshall in more than a figurative sense was the supreme Framer, emancipated from a local constituency, boldly using his judicial position as an exalted platform from which to educate the nation to the true meaning, his meaning, of the Constitution. He wrote as if words of grandeur and power and union could make dreams come true. By the force of his convictions he tried to will a nation into being.

He reshaped the still malleable Constitution, giving clarification to its ambiguities and content to its omissions that would allow it to endure for "ages to come" and would make the government of the Union supreme in the federal system. Marshall is the only judge in our history whose distinction as a great nationalist statesman derives wholly from his judicial career. Justice OLIVER WENDELL HOLMES once remarked, "If American law were to be represented by a single figure, sceptic and worshipper alike would agree without dispute that the figure could be one alone, and that one, John Marshall." That the Court had remained so weak after a decade of men of such high caliber as JOHN JAY, OLIVER ELLSWORTH, JAMES WILSON, JAMES IREDELL, WILLIAM PATERSON, and SAMUEL CHASE demonstrates not their weakness but Marshall's achievement in making the Court an equal branch of the national government.

Until 1807 he cast but one of six votes, and after 1807, when Congress added another Justice, but one of seven. One Justice, one vote has always been the rule of the Court, and the powers of anyone who is Chief Justice depend more on the person than the office. From 1812, BUSHROD WASHINGTON and Marshall were the only surviving Federalists, surrounded by five Justices appointed by Presidents Thomas Jefferson and JAMES MADISON; yet Marshall dominated the Court in a way that no one has ever since. During Marshall's thirty-five-year tenure, the Court delivered 1,106 opinions in all fields of law, and he wrote 519; he dissented only eight times. He wrote forty of the Court's sixty-four opinions in the field of constitutional law, dissenting only once in a constitutional case. Of the twenty-four constitutional opinions for the Court that he did not write, only two were important: MARTIN v. HUNTER'S LESSEE (1816), a case in which he did not sit, and OGDEN v. SAUNDERS (1827), the case in which he dissented. He virtually monopolized the constitutional cases for himself and won the support of his associates, even though they were members of the opposing political party.

Marshall's long tenure coincided with the formative period of our constitutional law. He was in the right place at the right time, filling, as Holmes said, "a strategic place in the campaign of history." But it took the right man to make the most of the opportunity. Marshall had the character, intellect, and passion for his job that his predecessors lacked. He had a profound sense of mission comparable to a religious "calling." Convinced that he knew what the Constitution should mean and what it was meant to achieve, he determined to give its purposes enduring expression and make them prevail. The Court was, for him, a judicial pulpit and political platform from which to address the nation, to compete, if possible, with the executive and legislative in shaping public opinion.

Marshall met few of the abstract criteria for a "great" judge. A great judge should possess intellectual rectitude and brilliance. Marshall was a fierce and crafty partisan who manipulated facts and law. A great judge should have a self-conscious awareness of his biases and a determination to be as detached as human fallibility will allow. In Marshall the judicial temperament flickered weakly; unable to muzzle his deepest convictions, he sought to impose them on the nation, sure that he was right. He intoxicated himself with the belief that truth, history, and the Constitution dictated his opinions, which merely declared the law rather than made the law. A great judge should have confidence in majority rule, tempered by his commitment to personal freedom and fairness. Marshall did not think men capable of self-government and inclined to favor financial and industrial capitalism over most other interests. A great judge should have a superior technical proficiency, modified by a sense of justice and ethical behavior beyond suspicion. Marshall's judicial ethics were not unquestionable. He should have disqualified himself in MARBURY v. MADISON (1803) because of his negligent complicity. He overlooked colossal corruption in FLETCHER v. PECK (1810) to decide a land title case by a doctrine that promoted his personal interests. He wrote the opinion in McCULLOCH v. MARYLAND (1819) before hearing the case. Marshall's "juridical learning," as Justice JOSEPH STORY, his reverent admirer and closest colleague, conceded, "was not equal to that of the great masters in the profession. . . ." He was, said Story, first, last, and always, "a Federalist of the good old school," and in the maintenance of its principles "he was ready at all times to stand forth a determined advocate and supporter." He was, in short, a Federalist activist who used the Constitution to legitimate predetermined results. A great judge should have a vision of national and moral greatness, combined with respect for the federal system. Marshall had that—and an instinct for statecraft and superb literary skills. These qualities, as well as his activism, his partisanship, and his sense of mission, contributed to his inordinate influence.

So too did his qualities of leadership and his personal traits. He was generous, gentle, warm, charming, considerate, congenial, and open. At a time when members of the Court lived together in a common boarding house during their short terms in Washington, his charismatic personality enabled him to preside over a judicial family, inspire loyalty, and convert his brethren to his views. He had a cast-iron will, an astounding capacity for hard work (witness the number of opinions he wrote for the Court), and formidable powers of persuasion. He thought audaciously in terms of broad and basic principles that he expressed axiomatically as absolutes. His arguments were masterful intellectual performances, assuming that his premises were valid. Inexorably and with developing momentum he moved from an unquestioned premise to a foregone conclusion. Jefferson once said that he never admitted anything when conversing with Marshall. "So sure as you admit any position to be good, no matter how remote from the conclusion he seeks to establish, you are gone." Marshall's sophistry, according to Jefferson, was so great, "you must never give him an affirmative answer or you will be forced to grant his conclusion. Why, if he were to ask me if it were daylight or not, I'd reply, 'Sir, I don't know. I can't tell.' " Marshall could also be imperious. He sometimes gave as the OPINION OF THE COURT a position that had not mustered a majority. According to one anecdote, Marshall is supposed to have said to Story, the greatest legal scholar in our history, "That, Story, is the law. You find the precedents."

The lengthy tenure of the members of the Marshall Court also accounts for its achievements. On the pre-Marshall Court, the Justices served briefly; five quit in a decade. The Marshall Court lasted—BROCKHOLST LIVINGSTON seventeen years, THOMAS TODD nineteen, GABRIEL DUVALL twenty-four, WILLIAM JOHNSON thirty, Bushrod Washington thirty-one, and Marshall outlasted them all. Story served twenty-four years with Marshall and ten more after his death; SMITH THOMPSON served fifteen years with Marshall and eight years after. This continuity in personnel contributed to a consistent point of view in constitutional doctrine—a view that was, substantially, Marshall's. From 1812, when the average age of the Court's members was only forty-three, through 1823—twelve successive terms—the Court had the same membership, the longest period in its history without a change, and during that period the Marshall Court decided its most important cases except for *Marbury*.

Marshall also sought to strengthen the Court by inaugurating the practice of one Justice's giving the opinion of the Court. Previously the Justices had delivered their opinions SERIATIM, each writing an opinion in each case in the style of the English courts. That practice forced each Justice to take the trouble of understanding each case, of forming his opinion on it, and showing publicly the reasons that led to his judgment. Such were Jefferson's arguments for seriatim opinions; and Marshall understood that one official opinion augmented the Court's strength by giving the appearance of unity and harmony. Marshall realized that even if each Justice reached similar conclusions, the lines of argument and explanation of doctrine might vary with style and thought of every individual, creating uncertainty and impairing confidence in the Court as an institution. He doubtless also understood that by massing his Court behind one authoritative opinion and by assigning so many opinions to himself, his own influence as well as the Court's would be enhanced. Jefferson's first appointee, Justice Johnson, sought to buck the practice for a while. He had been surprised, he later informed Jefferson, to discover the Chief Justice "delivering all the opinions in cases in which he sat, even in some instances when contrary to his own judgment and vote." When Johnson remonstrated in vain, Marshall lectured him on the "indecency" of judges' "cutting at each other," and Johnson soon learned to acquiesce "or become such a cypher in our consultations as to effect no good at all." Story, too, learned to swallow his convictions to enhance the "authority of the Court." His "usual practice," said Story, was "to submit in silence" to opinions with which he disagreed. Even Marshall himself observed in an 1827 case, by which time he was losing control of his Court, that his usual policy when differing from majority was "to acquiesce silently in its opinion."

Like other trailblazing activist judges, Marshall squeezed a case for all it was worth, intensifying its influence. For Marshall a constitutional case was a medium for explaining his philosophy of the supreme and FUNDAMENTAL LAW, an occasion for sharing his vision of national greatness, a link between capitalism and CONSTITUTIONALISM, and an opportunity for a basic treatise. Justice Johnson protested in 1818, "We are constituted to decide causes, and not to discuss themes, or digest systems." He preferred, he said, to decide no more in any case "than what the case itself necessarily requires." Ordinary Justices decide only the immediate question on narrow grounds; but Marshall, confronted by some trivial question—whether a justice of the peace had a right to his commission or whether peddlers of lottery tickets could be fined—would knife to the roots of the controversy, discover that it involved some great constitutional principle, and explain it in the broadest possible way, making the case seem as if the life of the Union or the supremacy of the Constitution were at stake. His audacity in generalizing was impressive; his strategy was to take the highest ground and make unnerving use of OBITER DICTA; and then, as a matter of tactics, almost unnoticeably decide on narrow grounds. *Marbury* is remembered for Marshall's exposition of JUDICIAL REVIEW, not for his judicial humility in declining JURISDICTION and refusing to issue the WRIT OF MANDAMUS. COHENS V. VIRGINIA

(1821) is remembered for Marshall's soaring explication of the supremacy of the JUDICIAL POWER OF THE UNITED STATES, not for the decision in favor of Virginia's power to fine unlicensed lottery ticket peddlers. GIBBONS v. OGDEN (1824) is remembered for its sweeping discourse on the COMMERCE CLAUSE of the Constitution, not for the decision that the state act conflicted with an obscure act of Congress.

Marshall's first major opinion, in *Marbury*, displayed his political cunning, suppleness in interpretation, doctrinal boldness, instinct for judicial survival, and ability to maneuver a case beyond the questions on its face. Having issued the show cause order to Madison, the Court seemingly was in an impossible position once Jefferson's supporters called that order a judicial interference with the executive branch. To decide for Marbury would provoke a crisis that the Court could not survive: Madison would ignore the Court, which had no way to enforce its decision, and the Court's enemies would have a pretext for IMPEACHMENT. To decide against Marbury would appear to endorse the illegal acts of the executive branch and concede that the Court was helpless. Either course of action promised judicial humiliation and loss of independence. Marshall therefore found a way to make a tactical retreat while winning a great strategic victory for judicial power. After upbraiding the executive branch for violating Marbury's rights, Marshall concluded that the Court had no JURISDICTION in the case, because a provision of an act of Congress conflicted with Article III. He held that provision unconstitutional by, first, giving it a sweeping construction its text did not bear and, second, by comparing it to his very narrow construction of Article III. Thus he reached and decided the great question, not argued by counsel, whether the Court had the power to declare unconstitutional an act of Congress. By so doing he answered from the bench his critics in Congress who, now that they were in power, had renounced judicial review during the debate on the repeal of the JUDICIARY ACT OF 1801. Characteristically Marshall relied on no precedents, not even on the authority of THE FEDERALIST #78. Significantly, he chose a safe act of Congress to void— section 13 of the JUDICIARY ACT OF 1789, which concerned not the province of the Congress or the President but of the Supreme Court, its authority to issue writs of mandamus in cases of ORIGINAL JURISDICTION. But Marshall's exposition of judicial review was, characteristically, broader than the holding on section 13. Jefferson, having been given no stick with which to beat Marshall, privately fumed: "Nothing in the Constitution has given them a right to decide for the Executive, more than to the Executive to decide for them," he wrote in a letter. "The opinion which gives to the judges the right to decide what laws are constitutional, and what not, not only for themselves in their own sphere of action, but also for the Legislature and Executive also, in their spheres, would make the judiciary a despotic branch."

The Court did not dare to declare unconstitutional any other act of Congress which remained hostile to it throughout Marshall's tenure. STUART V. LAIRD (1803), decided shortly after *Marbury,* upheld the repeal of the Judiciary Act of 1801. (See JUDICIARY ACTS OF 1802.) A contrary decision would have been institutionally suicidal for the Court. Marshall's opinion in *Marbury* was daring enough; in effect he courageously announced the Court's independence of the other branches of the government. But he was risking retaliation. Shortly before the arguments in *Marbury,* Jefferson instructed his political allies in the House to start IMPEACHMENT proceedings against JOHN PICKERING, a federal district judge; the exquisite timing was a warning to the Supreme Court. Even earlier, Jeffersonian leaders in both houses of Congress openly spoke of impeaching the Justices. The threats were not idle. Two months after *Marbury* was decided, Justice Chase on circuit attacked the administration in a charge to a GRAND JURY, and the House prepared to impeach him. Senator WILLIAM GILES of Virginia, the majority leader, told Senator JOHN QUINCY ADAMS that not only Chase "but all the other Judges of the Supreme Court," except William Johnson, "must be impeached and removed." Giles thought that holding an act of Congress unconstitutional was ground for impeachment. "Impeachment was not a criminal prosecution," according to Giles, who was Jefferson's spokesman in the Senate. "And a removal by impeachment was nothing more than a declaration by Congress to this effect: you hold dangerous opinions, and if you are suffered to carry them into effect, you will work the destruction of the Union. We want your offices for the purposes of giving them to men who will fill them better."

Intimidated by Chase's impending impeachment, Marshall, believing himself to be next in line, wrote to Chase that "impeachment should yield to an APPELLATE JURISDICTION in the legislature. A reversal of those legal opinions deemed unsound by the legislature would certainly better comport with the mildness of our character than a removal of the Judge who has rendered them unknowing of his fault." Less than a year after his *Marbury* opinion the fear of impeachment led an anguished Marshall to repudiate his reasoning and favor Congress as the final interpreter of the Constitution. Fortunately the greatest crisis in the Court's history eased when the Senate on March 1, 1805, failed to convict Chase on any of the eight articles of impeachment. Marshall and his Court were safe from an effort, never again repeated, to politicize the Court by making it subservient to Congress through impeachment.

The Court demonstrated its independence even when impeachment hung over it. In *Little v. Barreme* (1804) Marshall for the Court held that President Adams had not been authorized by Congress to order an American naval commander to seize a ship sailing from a French port. Justice Johnson on circuit vividly showed his independence of the President who had appointed him. To enforce the EMBARGO ACTS, Jefferson had authorized port officers to refuse clearance of ships with "suspicious" cargoes. In 1808 Johnson, on circuit in Charleston, ordered the clearance of a ship and denounced the President for having exceeded the power delegated by the Embargo Acts. Jefferson could not dismiss as partisan politics Johnson's rebuke that he had acted as if he were above the law. Justice Brockholst Livingston, another Jefferson appointee, also had occasion in 1808 to show his independence of the President. Jefferson supported a federal prosecution for TREASON against individuals who had opposed the embargo with violence. Livingston, who presided at the trial, expressed "astonishment" that the government would resort to a theory of "constructive treason" in place of the Constitution's definition of treason as levying war against the United States and he warned against a "precedent so dangerous." The jury speedily acquitted. After the tongue-lashing from his own appointees, Jefferson won an unexpected victory in the federal courts in the case of the brig *William* (1808). Federal district judge John Davis in Massachusetts sustained the constitutionality of the Embargo Acts on commerce clause grounds. Davis, a lifelong Federalist, showed how simplistic was Jefferson's raving about judicial politics.

The evidence for the Court's nonpartisanship seems plentiful. For example, Justice Story, Madison's appointee, spoke for an independent Court in *Gelston v. Hoyt* (1818), a suit for damages against government officials whose defense was that they had acted under President Madison's orders. Story, finding no congressional authority for these orders, "refused an extension of prerogative" power and added, "It is certainly against the general theory of our institutions to create discretionary powers by implication. . . ."

On the other hand, the Court supported the theory of IMPLIED POWERS in *McCulloch v. Maryland* (1819), which was the occasion of Marshall's most eloquent nationalist opinion. *McCulloch* had its antecedent in *United States v. Fisher* (1804), when the Court initially used BROAD CONSTRUCTION to sustain an act of Congress that gave to the government first claim against certain insolvent debtors. Enunciating the DOCTRINE of implied powers drawn from the NECESSARY AND PROPER CLAUSE, Marshall declared that Congress could employ any useful means to carry out its ENUMERATED POWER to pay national debts. That the prior claim of the government interfered with state claims was an inevitable result, Marshall observed, of the supremacy of national laws. Although a precursor of *McCulloch, Fisher* attracted no opposition because it did not thwart any major state interests.

When the Court did confront such interests for the first time, in UNITED STATES v. JUDGE PETERS (1809), Marshall's stirring nationalist passage, aimed at states that annulled judgments of the federal courts,

triggered Pennsylvania's glorification of state sovereignty and denunciation of the "unconstitutional exercise of powers in the United States
Courts." The state called out its militia to prevent execution of federal
judgments and recommended a constitutional amendment to establish
an "impartial tribunal" to resolve conflicts between "the general and
state governments." State resistance collapsed only after President Madison backed the Supreme Court. Significantly, eleven state legislatures,
including Virginia's, censured Pennsylvania's doctrines and endorsed
the Supreme Court as the constitutionally established tribunal to decide
state disputes with the federal courts.

The *Judge Peters* episode revealed that without executive support
the Court could not enforce its mandate against a hostile state, which
would deny that the Court was the final arbiter under the Constitution
if the state's interests were thwarted. The episode also revealed that if
other states had no immediate stake in the outcome of a case, they
would neither advance doctrines of state sovereignty nor repudiate the
Court's supreme appellate powers. When Virginia's high court ruled
that the appellate jurisdiction of the Supreme Court did not extend to
court judgments and that section 25 of the Judiciary Act of 1789 was
unconstitutional, the Marshall Court, dominated by Republicans, countered by sustaining the crucial statute in *Martin v. Hunter's Lessee* (1816).
Pennsylvania and other states did not unite behind Virginia when it
proposed the constitutional amendment initiated earlier by Pennsylvania,
because *Martin* involved land titles of no interest to other states. The
fact that the states were not consistently doctrinaire and became aggressive only when Court decisions adversely affected them enabled the
Court to prevail in the long run. A state with a grievance typically stood
alone. But for the incapacity or unwillingess of the Court's state enemies
to act together in their proposals to cripple it, the great nationalist decisions of the Marshall Court would have been as impotent as the one
in *Worcester v. Georgia* (1832). *Worcester* majestically upheld the supreme
law against the state's despoliation of the Cherokees, but President AN-
DREW JACKSON supported Georgia, which flouted the Court. Even Georgia, however, condemned the SOUTH CAROLINA ORDINANCE OF NULLIFICA-
TION, and several state legislatures resolved that the Supreme Court
was the constitutional tribunal to settle controversies between the United
States and the states.

The Court made many unpopular decisions that held state acts
unconstitutional. *Fletcher v. Peck,* which involved the infamous Yazoo
land frauds, was the first case in which the Justices voided a state act
for conflict with the Constitution itself. *Martin v. Hunter's Lessee,* which
involved the title to the choice Fairfax estates in Virginia, was only the
first of a line of decisions that unloosed shrill attacks on the Court's
jurisdiction to decide cases on a WRIT OF ERROR to state courts. In *McCulloch*

the Court supported the "monster monopoly," the Bank of the United States chartered by Congress, and held unconstitutional a state tax on its Baltimore branch. In *Cohens* the Court again championed its supreme appellate powers under section 25 of the Judiciary Act of 1789 and circumvented the ELEVENTH AMENDMENT. In STURGES V. CROWNINSHIELD (1819) the Court nullified a state bankruptcy statute that aided victims of an economic panic. In GREEN V. BIDDLE (1821) the Court used the CONTRACT CLAUSE when voiding Kentucky acts that supported valuable land claims. In OSBORN V. BANK OF THE UNITED STATES (1824) it voided an Ohio act that defied *McCulloch* and raised the question whether the Constitution had provided for a tribunal capable of protecting those who executed the laws of the Union from hostile state action.

When national supremacy had not yet been established and claims of state sovereignty bottomed state statutes and state judicial decisions that the Court overthrew, state assaults on the Court were inevitable, imperiling it and the Union it defended. Virginia, the most prestigious state, led the assault which Jefferson encouraged and SPENCER ROANE directed. Kentucky's legislature at one point considered military force to prevent execution of the *Green* decision. State attacks were vitriolic and intense, but they were also sporadic and not united. Ten state legislatures adopted resolutions against the Marshall Court, seven of them denouncing section 25 of the 1789 Act, which was the jurisdictional foundation for the Court's power of judicial review over the states. In 1821, 1822, 1824, and 1831 bills were introduced in Congress to repeal section 25. The assault on the Court was sharpest in the Senate, whose members were chosen by the state legislatures. Some bills to curb the Court proposed a constitutional amendment to limit the tenure of the Justices. One bill would have required seriatim opinions. Others proposed that no case involving a state or a constitutional question could be decided except unanimously; others accepted a 5–2 vote. One bill proposed that the Senate should have appellate powers over the Court's decisions.

Throughout the 1820s the attempts to curb the Court created a continuing constitutional crisis that climaxed in 1831, when Marshall despondently predicted the repeal of section 25 and the dissolution of the Union. In 1831, however, the House, after a great debate, defeated a repeal bill by a vote of 138–51; Southerners cast forty-five of the votes against the Court. What saved the Court was the inability of its opponents to mass behind a single course of action; many who opposed section 25 favored a less drastic measure. The Court had stalwart defenders, of course, including Senators DANIEL WEBSTER and JAMES BUCHANAN. Most important, it had won popular approbation. Although the Court had enemies in local centers of power, Americans thrilled to Marshall's paeans to the Constitution and the Union and he taught them to identify the Court with the Constitution and the Union.

A perceptible shift in the decisions toward greater tolerance for state action also helped dampen the fires under the Court in Marshall's later years. The coalition that Marshall had forged began to dissolve with the appointments of Justices Smith Thompson, JOHN MCLEAN, and HENRY BALDWIN. BROWN V. MARYLAND (1827), MARTIN V. MOTT (1827), AMERICAN INSURANCE COMPANY V. CANTER (1828), WESTON V. CHARLESTON (1829), CRAIG V. MISSOURI (1830), and the CHEROKEE INDIAN CASES (1832) continued the lines of doctrine laid down by the earlier Marshall Court. But the impact of new appointments was felt in the decisions of *Ogden v. Saunders* (1827), WILLSON V. BLACKBIRD CREEK MARSH COMPANY (1829) and PROVIDENCE BANK V. BILLINGS (1830). In Marshall's last decade on the Court, six decisions supported nationalist claims against seventeen for state claims. During the same decade there were ten decisions against claims based on VESTED RIGHTS and only one sustaining such a claim. The shift in constitutional direction may also be inferred from the inability of the Marshall Court, because of dissension and illness, to resolve CHARLES RIVER BRIDGE V. WARREN BRIDGE, MAYOR OF NEW YORK V. MILN, and BRISCOE V. BANK OF KENTUCKY, all finally decided in 1837 under Marshall's successor against the late Chief Justice's wishes. Before his last decade the only important influence on the Court resulting from the fact that Republicans had a voting majority was the repudiation of a FEDERAL COMMON LAW OF CRIMES.

What was the legacy of the Marshall Court? It established the Court as a strong institution, an equal and coordinate branch of the national government, independent of the political branches. It established itself as the authoritative interpreter of the supreme law of the land. It declared its rightful authority to hold even acts of Congress and the President unconstitutional. It maintained continuing judicial review over the states to support the supremacy of national law. In so doing, the Court sustained the constitutionality of the act of Congress chartering the Bank of the United States, laying down the definitive exposition of the doctrine of implied powers. The Court also expounded the commerce clause in *Gibbons v. Ogden* (1824), with a breadth and vigor that provided the basis for national regulation of the economy generations later. Finally, the Court made the contract clause of the Constitution into a bulwark protecting both vested rights and risk capital. *Fletcher* supported the sanctity of public land grants to private parties, encouraging capital investment and speculation in land values. NEW JERSEY V. WILSON (1812) laid down the doctrine that a state grant of tax immunity constituted a contract within the protection of the Constitution, preventing subsequent state taxation for the life of the grant. DARTMOUTH COLLEGE V. WOODWARD (1819) protected private colleges and spurred the development of state universities; it also provided the constitutional props for the expansion of the private corporation by holding that a charter of incorporation is entitled to protection of the contract clause. The Marshall Court often relied on nationalist doctrines to prevent state measures that sought to regulate or thwart corporate development. Just as national supremacy, judicial review, and the Court's appellate jurisdiction were often interlocked, so too the interests of capitalism, nationalism, and judicial review were allied. Time has hardly withered the influence and achievements of the Marshall Court.

Bibliography

BAKER, LEONARD   1974   *John Marshall.* New York: Macmillan.

BEVERIDGE, ALBERT J.   1919   *The Life of John Marshall.* Vols. 3 and 4. Boston: Houghton Mifflin.

CORWIN, EDWARD S.   1919   *John Marshall and the Constitution: A Chronicle of the Supreme Court.* New Haven: Yale University Press.

HAINES, CHARLES G.   1944   *The Role of the Supreme Court in American Government and Politics, 1789–1835.* Berkeley: University of California Press.

HASKINS, GEORGE LEE and JOHNSON, HERBERT Q.   1981   *Foundations of Power: John Marshall, 1801–1815.* Volume 2 of the *Oliver Wendell Holmes Devise History of the Supreme Court of the United States.* New York: Macmillan.

KONEFSKY, SAMUEL J.   1964   *John Marshall and Alexander Hamilton.* New York: Macmillan.

MORGAN, DONALD G.   1954   *Justice William Johnson: The First Great Dissenter.* Columbia: University of South Carolina Press.

WARREN, CHARLES   1923   *The Supreme Court in United States History,* 3 vols. Boston: Little, Brown.

CONSTITUTIONAL HISTORY, 1829–1848

William M. Wiecek

Constitutional change in the Jacksonian era began with the Virginia CONSTITUTIONAL CONVENTION of 1829–1830, and climaxed in the election controversies of 1848. Between these dates, the American people tried to renovate their constitutional order, especially with respect to the great issues of FEDERALISM, democratization, and slavery.

Virginia's venerable Constitution of 1776, like other early constitutions, had come to enshrine the related evils of malapportionment and disfranchisement. THOMAS JEFFERSON denounced these and other defects in the document from the founding of the commonwealth to his death. His criticism produced the convention of 1829, where the badly underrepresented Western delegates demanded reform, including white manhood suffrage and a REAPPORTIONMENT that would fairly represent the growing population of their region. The convention was a showcase of Virginia's political leadership, including as delegates JAMES MADISON (who had also been a delegate at the 1776 convention), JOHN MARSHALL, JAMES MONROE, JOHN RANDOLPH, as well as emergent conservative leaders like JOHN TYLER, Benjamin Watkins Leigh, and Abel Parker Upshur. The conservatives from the tidewater region, representing the interests of slaveholders, held the reformers at bay, conceding only a limited modification of the old freehold suffrage to include householders and leaseholders, far less than the taxpayer-militia qualification representing a compromise conceded by the western delegates. Reapportionment similarly fell short of western demands, as the convention adopted a complex system of regional representation. The conservative triumph on these two issues was assured partly because many delegates heeded Leigh's warning that reform would produce "the annihilation of all state rights." Implicit in this response were fears for the security of slavery. Those fears were bloodily confirmed by Nat Turner's 1831 slave insurrection in Southampton County, and reawakened the next year as the Virginia General Assembly debated and ultimately voted down a proposal for the gradual abolition of slavery.

Slavery, only hinted at in the 1828 Virginia debates, soon surfaced as a constitutional topic throughout the South. In *State v. Mann* (1829) Chief Judge Thomas Ruffin of the North Carolina Supreme Court held that the absolute subjection characteristic of slavery was "essential to the value of slaves as property, to the security of the master, and [to] the public tranquility." The South Carolina Court of Appeals later held that "a slave can invoke neither MAGNA CHARTA nor COMMON LAW. . . . In the very nature of things, he is subject to despotism." The political counterpart of this new proslavery jurisprudence was the "positive good" thesis, first advanced by South Carolina Governor George McDuffie in 1835 and amplified thereafter by JOHN C. CALHOUN in the United States Senate.

Southern judicial and political leaders found themselves compelled to erect defenses for the internal security of slavery after 1830 in part because a new cadre of abolitionists appeared in the northern states, led at first by William Lloyd Garrison. Repudiating both gradualism and projects for the colonization of free blacks in Liberia, this new generation of antislavery workers demanded the immediate and uncompensated abolition of slavery. They tried their hand at constitutional challenges to slavery. Although they conceded that the federal government had no power to interfere with slavery in the states, they found many areas for legitimate federal action, such as exclusion of slavery from the territories, abolition of slavery in the DISTRICT OF COLUMBIA, abolition of the interstate slave trade, and refusal to admit new slave states. At the state level, they sought, unsuccessfully, to have slavery declared unconstitutional in New Jersey, persuaded the Massachusetts and New York legislatures to enact PERSONAL LIBERTY LAWS, and provided invaluable support for fugitive slave rescues. In 1832, when they got their first taste of constitutional litigation in the Connecticut prosecution of Prudence Crandall, they attempted to define and secure the rights of free blacks under the PRIVILEGES AND IMMUNITIES CLAUSE of Article IV, section 2, of the Constitution.

By 1830 it was obvious that the South Carolinians were counting the costs of the Union, and weighing their alternatives. The fundamental concepts of state SOVEREIGNTY and the right of SECESSION were commonplace at the time. Thus in the Webster-Hayne debates of 1830, South Carolina Senator Robert Y. Hayne was closer to orthodoxy than DANIEL WEBSTER when he supported a cluster of theories derived or extrapolated from the VIRGINIA AND KENTUCKY RESOLUTIONS of 1798–1799: he condemned the consolidationist tendencies of the federal government, asserted state sovereignty, insisted on a STRICT CONSTRUCTION of the Constitution, reiterated the compact theory of the Union (by which the Constitution and the national Union were the creation of a compact of sovereign states), and defended the legitimacy of INTERPOSITION and NULLIFICATION. Webster's famous rhetorical reply is better known but less analytical than other rebuttals by EDWARD LIVINGSTON, JOHN QUINCY ADAMS, and JOSEPH STORY between 1830 and 1833. These maintained that sovereignty had effectively been transferred to the national government by the Constitution, that the Union created thereby was perpetual, and that secession was extralegal. In his *Commentaries on the Constitution* (1833), Story flatly denied that the Constitution was a compact among sovereign states. James Madison joined his venerable voice to theirs, condemning all theories of nullification as perversions of the doctrines he and Thomas Jefferson had propounded in 1798 and 1799. All maintained that because the Union was perpetual, it was therefore indissoluble. But John Quincy Adams had the ominous last word when he wrote in 1831 that "it is the odious nature of [this] question that it can be settled only at the cannon's mouth." South Carolina's attempted nullification of the TARIFF ACT of 1828 and its 1832 revision forced a resolution of these conflicts that came close to the mode Adams had predicted.

Though ostensibly aimed at the tariff, and the larger but more nebulous problem of the "consolidation" of the federal government's powers, the nullification controversy at its heart concerned the security and perpetuity of slavery. The tariff controversy nonetheless provided a convenient vehicle for the Carolinians to reconfirm their traditional THEORIES OF THE UNION and state sovereignty. In November 1832 a specially elected convention adopted the SOUTH CAROLINA ORDINANCE OF NULLIFICATION, which prohibited collection of the tariff and appeals to the United States Supreme Court. President ANDREW JACKSON responded with his "Proclamation to the People of South Carolina," drafted by Secretary of State Livingston, which refuted nullification theories, asserted federal supremacy, insisted on obedience to federal laws, warned that "Disunion by armed force is treason," and, surprisingly in view of his Bank Veto Message five months earlier, maintained that the Supreme Court was the proper and final arbiter of disputes under the United States Constitution and laws. The FORCE ACT of 1833 gave teeth to the proclamation, while a compromise tariff assuaged Carolina's nominal grievance. The Carolinians suspended, then rescinded the ordinance of nullification, which had been universally condemned by other states. But the state convention consoled itself with the empty gesture of a second ordinance nullifying the Force Act. On this equivocal note, the nullification crisis dissolved. Both sides in reality suffered a long-term defeat. Nationalists led by Jackson had failed to quash ideas of state sovereignty and secession; Calhoun and the nullifiers had failed to forge a united front of slave states and had promoted the federal "consolidation" they feared and condemned.

The second party system, emergent at the time of the nullification crisis, produced its own constitutional controversies. HENRY CLAY had announced the basis of what he called the AMERICAN SYSTEM in 1824: a protective tariff, federal aid to INTERNAL IMPROVEMENTS, and support for the second Bank of the United States. In a decade this became the program of the Whig Party. Jacksonian Democrats denounced all three elements as being of dubious constitutionality. In 1830 President Andrew Jackson vetoed the MAYSVILLE ROAD BILL partly because he doubted that federal aid for internal improvements, at least those lying wholly within a state, was constitutional. Two years later, in his veto of the recharter bill for the second Bank of the United States, he similarly expressed reservations about the constitutional power of Congress to charter a bank. He brushed aside the binding force of Chief Justice John Marshall's decision on the subject in McCULLOCH v. MARYLAND (1819) by asserting that "the authority of the Supreme Court must not, therefore, be permitted to control the Congress or the Executive when acting in their legislative capacities. . . ." In 1833 Jackson ordered his subordinates to remove all federal deposits from the bank, and to redistribute them in selected state-chartered banks.

The democratization of American politics was advanced by the Whigs' development of mass electioneering techniques in the 1840 presidential campaign. Whig success was short-lived, however, because of President William Henry Harrison's death in 1841. JOHN TYLER, a conservative Virginia Democrat, succeeded to the office, and in doing so established the important precedent that he was not merely the "acting President" but President in fact. One of the few positive accomplishments of the Whigs' brief accession to power was the enactment of the nation's second Bankruptcy Act in 1841. Its repeal in 1843 returned the matter of insolvency legislation to the states, where it was to remain until 1898. Direction of the nation's economy was to remain chiefly the responsibility of the states until the Civil War. (See BANKRUPTCY POWER.)

In the 1830s the states encouraged and subsidized economic development in numerous ways. Their role was almost entirely promotional; during the Jacksonian era, they essayed only the most diffident beginnings of ECONOMIC REGULATION. The state legislatures granted charters and franchises for banking, insurance, railroad, and manufacturing CORPORATIONS. Encouraged by the remarkable but unduplicated success of New York's Erie Canal in the 1820s, other states provided direct financial support for construction of turnpikes, canals, and railroads.

State jurists likewise supported economic development, sometimes by creating whole new domains of law (torts, nonmarine insurance), and sometimes by reworking traditional legal doctrines to provide instrumentalist approaches supportive of entrepreneurs. In 1831 Chancellor Reuben Walworth of New York upheld the power of the legislature to grant EMINENT DOMAIN powers to railroads, and Chief Justice LEMUEL SHAW of the Massachusetts Supreme Judicial Court afterward approved the extension of that power to manufacturing corporations as well. Chief Judge JOHN BANNISTER GIBSON of the Pennsylvania Supreme Court helped refashion the law of contracts in favor of the doctrine of *caveat emptor,* an impersonal and seller-oriented approach presumably suited to a national market. The new orientation of the law of contracts and sales emphasized the autonomy of the individual and private will, dismissing earlier insistence on equitable dealing and community standards of fairness.

But the public law of the states in the 1830s was not exclusively concerned with succoring nascent industrial capitalism. In fact, the common law itself, as well as its judicial exemplars, came under reformist attack. In the Jacksonian period, the movement toward an elective judiciary decisively gained ground, as Mississippi led the way in 1832 by making its entire bench elective. Other states followed suit, so that by the twentieth century only the federal judiciary remained wholly appointive and life-tenured. An even stronger assault on judge-made law emerged from the movement to codify all laws. Even legal conservatives like Joseph Story conceded that some restatement of law in certain areas (EVIDENCE, criminal law, and commercial law) might be both feasible and useful. More thoroughgoing codifiers, such as Edward Livingston and Robert Rantoul, condemned the common law as antidemocratic, mysterious, and prolix.

Meanwhile, the controversy over slavery intensified. From 1835 to 1840, mobs in all sections of the country harassed abolitionists and free blacks. The beleaguered abolitionists, for their part, mounted a propaganda campaign against slaveholding by weekly mailings of abolitionist literature throughout the South. Democrats and southern political leaders reacted violently, with Postmaster General Amos Kendall condoning destruction of mail in Charleston. President Jackson recommended congressional prohibition of abolitionist mailing in the southern states, but Senator John C. Calhoun objected, partly because such federal legislation would invade rights reserved to the states. The controversy dissipated when abolitionists redirected their energies to a petition campaign, garnering signatures throughout the north on petitions to Congress demanding various antislavery measures, such as abolition in the District of Columbia, interdiction of the interstate slave trade, and refusal to annex the slaveholding republic of Texas or to admit new slave states.

Abolitionists were active in legal-constitutional efforts against slavery at the state level, too. In Massachusetts, they scored a striking victory against the ingress of sojourners' slaves in COMMONWEALTH V. AVES (1836), when Chief Justice Shaw expounded an American version of the doctrine of SOMERSET'S CASE (King's Bench, 1772). Shaw held that a sojourning slave could not be held in slavery against her will in Massachusetts because no state law supported slavery and because the "all men are free and equal" provision of the 1780 Massachusetts Declaration of Rights was "precisely adapted to the abolition of negro slavery." Abolitionists enjoyed less success the next year in Ohio and Pennsylvania, however. Chief Judge Gibson held in 1837 that, under the Pennsylvania constitution, blacks were not "freemen" and hence could not vote. A state constitutional convention meeting that year took no action to reverse this holding. In Ohio, the abolitionist lawyers SALMON P. CHASE and JAMES G. BIRNEY developed an impressive range of legal and constitutional arguments in *Matilda's Case* (1837) to demonstrate that the 1793 federal Fugitive Slave Act was unconstitutional under the FOURTH AMENDMENT, the Fifth Amendment's DUE PROCESS clause, and the NORTHWEST ORDINANCE's guarantees of TRIAL BY JURY and HABEAS CORPUS. These arguments failed then, but they furnished an impressive stock of ideas to expanding ABOLITIONIST CONSTITUTIONAL THEORY.

At the national level, defenders of slavery launched a counterattack against this assault. The United States House of Representatives in 1836 adopted the first of the congressional "gag resolutions," declaring that all petitions coming into the House as a result of the antislavery petition campaign would be automatically tabled, without being referred or read. In subsequent years, the Senate adopted a similar rule, and the House made it a standing rule. But the gags proved insufficient bars to the determined evasions of a handful of antislavery congressmen, led by John Quincy Adams, who repeatedly introduced antislavery petitions. (See CIVIL LIBERTIES AND THE SLAVERY CONTROVERSY.)

Observing such assaults on slavery with alarm, Calhoun introduced into the Senate in 1837 a series of resolutions that in effect restated the nature of the Union and slavery's relation to it. These resolutions condemned antislavery agitation as "subversive"; declared that the federal government was the "common agent" of the states, bound to protect all their institutions, including slavery; that slavery was an "essential element" in the organization of the Union; that any congressional interference with slavery in the District of Columbia or the territories would be an "attack on the institutions" of the slave states; and that Congress could not discriminate against the interests of the slave states in the territories. Congress declined to adopt the last two, but its endorsement of the others threatened to give the slave states a constitutional predominance in the Union.

Abolitionists responded with innovative constitutional thinking of their own. In 1839 the hitherto unified movement began to split apart. The antislavery mainstream became involved in political action, forming the Liberty Party. They conceded exclusive state power over slavery in the states where it existed, but called for congressional action elsewhere, as, for example, by refusing to admit new slave states and by repealing the Fugitive Slave Act. Two splinter groups of the movement challenged this moderate position. Followers of William Lloyd Garrison, embracing the theological doctrine of perfectionism, by 1842 came to denounce the Constitution as a proslavery compact, and called for disunion. Radical abolitionists, led by the New York lawyer Alvan Stewart, discarded previous assumptions about slavery's legitimacy and contended that slavery was everywhere unconstitutional as a violation of various constitutional provisions, including the Fifth Amendment's due process clause (considered both in procedural and substantive senses), Article IV's guarantee of a REPUBLICAN FORM OF GOVERNMENT, and the same article's privileges and immunities clause.

Abolitionists harked back to the DECLARATION OF INDEPENDENCE and to the tenets of republican ideology of the Revolutionary era. So did contemporary suffrage reformers in Rhode Island, who faced the same problems of malapportionment and disenfranchisement as had Virginia two decades earlier. After concluding that the existing conservative regime would never concede reform, they called an extralegal constitutional convention to modernize the state's constitution, which until then had been the 1662 Charter. This "People's Constitution" was ratified by universal male suffrage. Its supporters then elected a new government for the state, with Thomas W. Dorr as governor. The existing regime refused to cede power, so for several months in 1842, Rhode Island had two governments, each claiming a different source of constitutional legitimacy: the Dorrites, a do-it-yourself, implicitly revolutionary popular sovereignty; and the extant regime, legality backed by force. With behind-the-scenes support of President Tyler, the regular government suppressed its opponents, then inaugurated the substance of what the reformers had demanded. The failure of the Dorr Rebellion demonstrated that the guarantees of self- government and equality in the Declaration of Independence would not be taken literally or programmatically in the Jacksonian era.

Constitutional change came to other states less turbulently in the 1840s. In neighboring Massachusetts, Chief Justice Shaw placed the Supreme Judicial Court in the forefront of legal and constitutional innovation in a series of decisions from 1842 to 1850 that created new doctrines and revolutionized old ones. In COMMONWEALTH V. HUNT (1842) Shaw legitimated labor union organization in the United States. The Philadelphia and New York *Cordwainers Cases* (1806, 1810), reaffirmed by New York decisions in the mid-1830s, had held labor organization and strikes to be CRIMINAL CONSPIRACIES at common law and illegal under state statutes prohibiting injury to commerce. But in *Hunt,* Shaw held that neither the objectives of the workers nor their means—unions and strikes—were inherently unlawful. Because it removed the taint of per se illegality from unions, the *Hunt* decision has been extravagantly called the "Magna Carta of organized labor."

Another Shaw decision of the same year, *Farwell v. Boston and Worcester Railroad,* proved as damaging to the cause of industrial workers as *Hunt* had been beneficial. In exempting an employer from liability for the injury to one of its employees caused by the negligence of another employee, Shaw enunciated the fellow-servant rule that stood as a bar to recovery in such situations.

Because Massachusetts was in the vanguard of industrialization, Shaw had an opportunity to influence the law of railroads and common carriers more than any other contemporary jurist, leading one scholar to conclude that he "practically established the railroad law for the country." In cases involving eminent domain and taxation, Shaw held railroads to be "a public work, established by public authority" whose property is held "in trust for the public." Shaw thereby hoped to secure legislative benefits granted railroads, while at the same time leaving open the possibility of some degree of public control through legislation. Yet he was solicitous to exempt railroads from forms of liability that would have drained investment capital.

The temperance movement proved to be as prolific a source of judicial lawmaking as innovations in transportation technology. Throughout the antebellum period, state appellate courts had kept alive the HIGHER LAW tradition enunciated by Justice SAMUEL CHASE in his opinion in CALDER V. BULL (1798). State judges, especially those of Federalist and Whig antecedents, readily struck down various state laws for the inconsistency with "the great principles of eternal justice" or "the character and genius of our government." In his *Commentaries on the Constitution* (3rd ed., 1858), Joseph Story summed up "the strong current of judicial opinion" that "the fundamental maxims of a free government seem to require, that the rights of personal liberty and private property should be held sacred." The Delaware Supreme Court used such nebulous concepts derived from the nature of republican government to void a local-option PROHIBITION statute in 1847. Higher law constitutional doctrine became all the more important after the United States Supreme Court's 5–4 decision in the LICENSE CASES (1847), upholding Massachusetts, Rhode Island, and New Hampshire statutes taxing and regulating liquor imported from outside the state. This trend culminated in the celebrated case of WYNEHAMER V. PEOPLE (1856), where the New York Court of Appeals struck down a state prohibition statute under the state constitution's LAW OF THE LAND and due process clauses.

Chief Justice Shaw was the author of a doctrine that provided a powerful offset to such higher law tendencies: the POLICE POWER. In COMMONWEALTH V. ALGER (1951) he stated that all property is held "under the implied liability that . . . use of it may be so regulated, that it shall not be injurious . . . to the rights of the community." He accorded the legislature sweeping power to subject property to "reasonable limitations." After the Civil War, the police power doctrine constituted the basis for an alternative to the dogmas of SUBSTANTIVE DUE PROCESS and FREEDOM OF CONTRACT.

Courts were by no means the sole font of constitutional innovation in the 1840s. State legislatures and constitutional conventions also modified the constitutional order. Reflecting the movement of the age from status to contract, as noted by Sir Henry Maine, the state legislatures in the 1840s extended some measure of control to married women over their own property through the married women's property acts. State courts sometimes reacted with hostility to these measures, seeing them either as a deprivation of the husband's property rights protected by higher law or as deranging gender and marital relationships.

Four New England states experimented with embryonic railroad regulatory commissions (Rhode Island, 1839; New Hampshire, 1844; Connecticut, 1850; Massachusetts, various ad hoc special commissions), but none of these proved successful or permanent. New York in the 1840s had to confront the legal consequences of the emergent nativist controversy. Roman Catholics sought public funding for parochial schools and objected to use of the King James Bible for devotional sessions in public schools. Nativists, for their part, demanded that the predominantly Catholic immigrants of the period be disfranchised.

The most significant state constitutional event of the decade was the drafting and ratification of the New York Constitution of 1846. This document was a compendium of constitutional trends of the era and profoundly influenced subsequent constitutions, especially those of Michigan and Wisconsin. It capped the decade's long movement toward general incorporation acts by restricting the granting of special corporate charters, and, for good measure, made all legislation respecting corporations, both general and special, subject to repeal or amendment at any time. It put to rest the controversies of the rent wars of the previous decade by abolishing all feudal real property tenures and perpetual leases, converting all long-term leaseholds into freeholds. It made the entire New York bench elective, and required appointment of a three-member commission to draw up a reformed procedural code.

Despite the sweep of innovation in the 1846 New York Constitution and its daughters in the west, the needs of certain groups in American society remained unmet. Chief among these were women. Feminists convened in Seneca Falls, New York, in 1848 and issued a manifesto on women's rights modeled on the Declaration of Independence, demanding VOTING RIGHTS, the recognition by law of full legal capacity, revision of male-biased divorce laws, access to the professions and to educational opportunity, and abolition of all discriminatory legislation.

Blacks in the northern states were no better off. After 1842, their situation, especially in areas near the slave states, became more precarious because of Justice Story's opinion in PRIGG v. PENNSYLVANIA (1842), upholding the constitutionality of the Fugitive Slave Act of 1793 and striking down inconsistent state legislation. After *Prigg,* most state personal liberty laws, such as those assuring jury trial to alleged fugitives or extending the writ of habeas corpus to them, were suspect. Abolitionists seized on a Story dictum in *Prigg,* stating that the states did not have to assist in fugitive recaptures under the federal act. They induced several state legislatures to enact statutes prohibiting state facilities from being used for temporary detention of alleged fugitives.

The slavery question briefly returned to Congress in 1842, in the form of the "*Creole* Resolutions" offered by Representative Joshua Giddings (Whig, Ohio). Slaves aboard the *Creole,* an American-flag vessel, mutinied on the high seas and made their way to the Bahamas, where most of them were freed by British authorities. Secretary of State Daniel Webster protested and demanded compensation for the liberated slaves. Giddings, despite the gag rule, introduced resolutions setting forth the *Somerset* -based position that the slaves had merely resumed their natural status, freedom, and could not be reenslaved. The federal government lacked authority to protect or reimpose their slave status, which was derived solely from Virginia law and hence confined to this JURISDICTION. The House defeated the resolutions and censured Giddings. But he was reelected by a landslide, in effect forcing and winning a REFERENDUM on his antislavery positions. This, together with the earlier and ignominious failure of an effort to censure Representative John Quincy Adams for flouting the gag, led to the demise of the gag rules in both houses in 1844.

Such inconclusive sparring between slavery and abolition might have gone on indefinitely had it not been for the Mexican War. But proslavery ambitions to expand into the southwestern empire fundamentally altered the character of the American Union, destabilizing extant constitutional settlements and requiring new constitutional arrangements to replace the now obsolete MISSOURI COMPROMISE.

ANNEXATION OF TEXAS had been controversial ever since Texan independence in 1836. When the issue reestablished itself on the national agenda in 1844, opponents of annexation, including Daniel Webster, Joseph Story, and John Quincy Adams, argued that annexation was not constitutionally permissible under the territories clause of Article IV, section 3, because previous annexations had been of dependent territories of sovereign nations, whereas Texas was itself an independent nation. Proponents dismissed this as an insignificant technicality, under the broad reading of the FOREIGN AFFAIRS power by Chief Justice Marshall in AMERICAN INSURANCE CO. V. CANTER (1828). Political opposition blocked ratification of an annexation treaty until President Tyler hit on the expedient of annexation by JOINT RESOLUTION of both houses, which required only a majority vote in each, rather than the two-thirds required for treaties in the Senate. Texas was thereby annexed in 1845.

Annexation hastened the deterioration of relations with Mexico, but Tyler was cautious and circumspect in his deployment of American forces in the areas disputed between Mexico and the United States. But the new President, JAMES K. POLK, ordered American ground forces into the area. After Mexican forces captured American soldiers, and the United States declared war, the question of the extent of the President's power to order American troops into combat areas reappeared regularly in congressional debates over military appropriations. In 1847, Whig Representative ABRAHAM LINCOLN offered the SPOT RESOLUTIONS, demanding to know the spot on American soil where, according to Polk, Mexican troops had attacked Americans. This led to House passage of a resolution early in 1848 declaring that the Mexican War had been "unconstitutionally begun by the President." Military victories and the TREATY OF GUADALUPE HIDALGO (1848) obviated this partisan measure, without providing any resolution to the question originally debated by James Madison and ALEXANDER HAMILTON in the Helvidius-Pacificus exchange of 1793 over whether there is an inherent executive prerogative that would embrace the power to commit troops to belligerent situations without explicit authorization by Congress. (See WAR, FOREIGN AFFAIRS, AND THE CONSTITUTION.)

In 1846, northern public opinion coalesced with remarkable unity behind the WILMOT PROVISO, which would have prohibited the extension of slavery into any territories to be acquired as a result of the Mexican War. Alarmed by the extent and fervor of grassroots support for such exclusion in the free states, administration Democrats and southern political leaders offered three alternatives to it, plus an expedient designed to depoliticize the whole question. The earliest proposal was to extend the old Missouri Compromise line of 36° 30′ all the way to the Pacific coast with slavery excluded north of the line and permitted south of it. After a short-lived flurry of interest in 1847, this suggestion withered. The northern Democratic alternative to the Wilmot Proviso was widely known as POPULAR SOVEREIGNTY or, pejoratively, "squatter sovereignty." First proposed by Vice-President George M. Dallas and then associated with Michigan Senator Lewis Cass, popular sovereignty called on Congress to refrain from taking any action concerning SLAVERY IN THE TERRITORIES, leaving it to the settlers of the territories to determine the future of slavery there. The idea's principal appeal derived from its superficial and simplistic democratic appearance. But its vitality was due to an ambiguity that could not be indefinitely postponed, namely, *when* were the settlers to make that determination? By the southern interpretation, that decision could not be made until the eve of statehood, by which time, presumably, slaveholders could avail themselves of the opportunity of settling there with their slaves and thus give the territory a proslavery impetus it would never lose. (All prior American territorial settlements had either guaranteed property rights in extant slaves, such as the LOUISIANA PURCHASE TREATY, or, like the Northwest Ordinance, had left existing pockets of slavery undisturbed as a practical matter despite their theoretical prohibition of slavery.) The northern assumption concerning popular sovereignty was that the territorial settlers could make their choice concerning slavery at any time in the territorial period, a position unacceptable to the South, which correctly believed that such an interpretation would exclude slavery.

The third alternative was embodied in resolutions offered by Calhoun in 1847. He proposed that the territories were the common property of all the states, and that Congress therefore could not prohibit citizens of any state from taking their property (including slaves) with them when they migrated into a territory. He also asserted that Congress could not refuse to admit a new state because it permitted slavery. After Calhoun's death in 1850, others advocated that Congress would have to protect the rights of slaveholders in all territories.

This selection of alternatives naturally influenced the presidential election of 1848. Democrats nominated Cass, thus providing some oblique endorsement of popular sovereignty, with its yet unresolved ambiguity. Whigs nominated the apolitical General ZACHARY TAYLOR and refused to endorse any party position at all on the various alternatives. Disgruntled elements of both parties in the northern states joined hands with the moderate, political-action abolitionists of the Liberty party to form the Free Soil party, which adopted the Wilmot Proviso as its basic plank, supplemented by the old Liberty party program of "divorce" of the federal government from support of slavery. Free Soil was an implicitly racist program, calling for the exclusion of all blacks from the territories to keep them open to white settlement, but that made it no less abominable to southern political leaders. The Whig victory in 1848 on its nonplatform merely postponed the resolution of what was rapidly becoming an urgent constitutional confrontation.

The American Union was in a far different condition in 1848 from what it had been at the onset of the Jacksonian era. The nation had increased in geographical extent by half. Such an immense increase necessitated a new or wholly revised constitutional order that could accommodate, if possible, the conflicting sectional expectations for the future of the western empire. All major constitutional events that had occurred at the national level since 1831 had made John Quincy Adams's prediction of that year all the more pertinent: the questions came ever closer to being settled at the cannon's mouth.

Bibliography

BLOOMFIELD, MAXWELL   1976   *American Lawyers in a Changing Society, 1776–1876*. Cambridge, Mass.: Harvard University Press.

DUMOND, DWIGHT L.   1961   *Antislavery: The Crusade for Freedom in America*. Ann Arbor: University of Michigan Press.

FRIEDMAN, LAWRENCE M.   1973   *A History of American Law*. New York: Simon & Schuster.

HAAR, CHARLES M., ED.   1965   *The Golden Age of American Law*. New York: Braziller.

HORWITZ, MORTON J.   1977   *The Transformation of American Law, 1780–1860*. Cambridge, Mass.: Harvard University Press.

HURST, JAMES WILLARD   1956   *Law and the Conditions of Freedom in the Nineteenth-Century United States*. Madison: University of Wisconsin Press.

HYMAN, HAROLD M. and WIECEK, WILLIAM M.   1982   *Equal Justice under Law: Constitutional Development, 1835–1875*. New York: Harper & Row.

LEVY, LEONARD W.   1957   *The Law of the Commonwealth and Chief Justice Shaw: The Evolution of American Law, 1830–1860*. Cambridge, Mass.: Harvard University Press.

WIECEK, WILLIAM M.   1977   *The Sources of Antislavery Constitutionalism in America, 1760–1848*. Ithaca, N.Y.: Cornell University Press.

ZAINALDIN, JAMIL   1983   *Law in Antebellum Society: Legal Change and Economic Expansion*. New York: Knopf.

CONSTITUTIONAL HISTORY, 1848–1861

Don E. Fehrenbacher

In American constitutional history, the years 1848 to 1861 ordinarily appear as a prelude to revolution, a time of intense controversy without significant change. Yet in at least two respects this impression is mistaken. First, constitutional change, though minimal in the national government, was widespread and vigorous among the states during the antebellum period. Second, if the structure of party politics is included (as it should be) in one's purview of the American constitutional system, then the 1850s, like the 1860s, were a decade of revolution.

Powerful social forces exerted pressure upon the constitutional order at mid-century. Mass immigration reached its first crest, with more than two million persons arriving in the years 1849–1854. This great influx caused much concern about the effects of ethnic diversity upon the quality of national life and upon the American experiment in self-government. At the same time, the progress of industrialization and business enterprise was rapidly changing the economic face of the agricultural nation for which the Constitution had been written. The railroads alone, as they tripled their mileage in the 1850s and thus accelerated their transformation of domestic commerce, confronted government with a host of new issues and problems, ranging from the regulation of capital formation to the determination of corporate liability in tort law. Still another major force at work was the continuing westward expansion of American SOVEREIGNTY and American people. The United States in 1848 was a transcontinental nation that had acquired forty percent of all its territory in the preceding three years. Occupation and assimilation of this new Western empire, extending from the mouth of the Rio Grande to the waters of Puget Sound, would absorb much national energy throughout the rest of the century. The process in itself placed no heavy strains upon the constitutional system. For the most part, it required only the further use of already tested forms and practices, such as territorial organization. But in the antebellum period, westward expansion became irredeemably entangled with still another formidable social force—the increasingly ominous sectional conflict over slavery.

The federal government, while extending its rule to the Pacific Ocean in the antebellum period, underwent little structural change.

The Constitution had not been amended since 1803. Far fewer amendments than usual were proposed from 1848 to 1860, and none of them passed either house of Congress. (Prominent among those introduced were proposals for the popular election of senators and postmasters.) During the secession winter of 1860–1861, however, Congress received nearly two hundred proposed amendments. Most of them were aimed at dampening the crisis by offering concessions or guarantees to the South on such subjects as SLAVERY IN THE TERRITORIES and the DISTRICT OF COLUMBIA, the domestic slave trade, FUGITIVE SLAVES, and the right to travel with slaves in free states. Only one of these efforts proved successful to the point of passing both houses, but RATIFICATION in the states had scarcely begun before it was interrupted and canceled by the outbreak of hostilities. This abortive "Thirteenth Amendment" would have forbidden any amendment authorizing Congress to interfere with slavery as it existed in the states, thereby presumably fixing a double lock on the constitutional security of the institution. (See CORWIN AMENDMENT.)

Besides formal amendment, constitutional change may be produced by other means, such as legislative enactment and judicial decision. Congress altered the structure of the executive branch in 1849, for instance, by establishing a Department of the Interior. To it were transferred a number of agencies previously housed in other departments, notably those administering PATENTS, public lands, military pensions, and Indian affairs. Congress in 1849 also created the new office of "assistant secretary" for the Treasury Department, adding a similar position to the Department of State four years later. The federal bureaucracy as a whole grew appreciably in the antebellum period, but largely because of the necessary expansion of the postal system. Of the 26,000 civilian employees in 1851 and 37,000 in 1861, eighty percent were in the postal service. Only six percent performed their duties in the capital. On the eve of the Civil War, the whole Washington bureaucracy numbered about 2,200. The Department of State got along throughout the 1850s with a staff of thirty persons or fewer. The presidency remained a very simple affair with practically no official staff. Not until 1857 did Congress provide funds even for a private secretary and a messenger.

The federal government accepted few new responsibilities during the antebellum period. Enlargement of its role was inhibited by the economic principle of laissez-faire, by the constitutional principles of STRICT CONSTRUCTION and FEDERALISM, and by the inertial influence of custom. Most of the governmental activity affecting the lives of ordinary citizens was carried on by the states and their subdivisions. Any effort to extend national authority usually met resistance from Southerners worried about the danger of outside interference with slavery. Congressional reluctance to expand federal power is well illustrated in the history of the first successful telegraph line, run between Washington and Baltimore in the mid-1840s. Built with federal money and put in commercial operation as a branch of the postal system, it was very soon turned over to private ownership. When Congress did occasionally become venturesome, presidential disapproval might intervene. JAMES K. POLK and Franklin Pierce, citing constitutional reasons, vetoed several INTERNAL IMPROVEMENTS bills. JAMES BUCHANAN expressed similar scruples in vetoing homestead legislation and land grants for the support of colleges. Sometimes a new social problem or need did evoke federal intervention, such as laws providing for safety inspection of steamboats and for minimum health standards on ocean-going passenger ships. Perhaps most significant was the expanded use of federal subsidies, in the form of land grants or mail contracts, to support railroad construction, steamship lines, and overland stagecoach service to the Pacific.

Although the three branches of the federal government remained fairly stable in their relationships to one another during the antebellum period, there was some shift of power from the presidency to Congress. The change is commonly viewed as a decline in presidential leadership, but it must be attributed to other factors as well, including the intensity of the sectional conflict. Congress could quarrel violently over slavery, then arrange some kind of truce, and thus perform admirably its function as a deliberative assembly. The President, on the other hand, could take no vigorous action, make no substantial proposal in respect of slavery without infuriating one side or the other.

For various reasons, none of the Presidents between ANDREW JACKSON and ABRAHAM LINCOLN served more than a single term, and only one, MARTIN VAN BUREN, was even renominated. Polk's energetic foreign policy and successful prosecution of the war with Mexico strengthened the presidency for a time, but by 1848 sectional strains and party dissension had put his administration in disarray. Zachary Taylor and Millard Fillmore were committed as Whigs to the principle of limited executive power. They did not exercise the VETO POWER, for instance, and were the last Presidents in history to refrain from doing so. Taylor, to be sure, proved unexpectedly stubborn on the slavery issue and seemed headed for a collision with Congress until his sudden death in the summer of 1850 cleared the way for compromise. During the great sectional crisis of 1846–1850, the Senate reached its peak of oratorical splendor and national influence. JOHN C. CALHOUN, HENRY CLAY, and DANIEL WEBSTER were the most famous men in America, and the outstanding political figure of the decade that followed was not a President but a senator—STEPHEN A. DOUGLAS. Most of the leading cabinet members of the 1840s and 1850s (Webster, Calhoun, Buchanan, Robert J. Walker, John M. Clayton, JEFFERSON DAVIS, Lewis Cass) were recruited directly from the Senate. Lincoln, after his election in 1860, filled the three top cabinet positions with Republican senators. The appearance of presidential weakness in the 1850s was therefore partly a reflection of senatorial prestige.

If Pierce and Buchanan were among the most ineffectual of American Presidents, as they are commonly portrayed, it was not for lack of trying to be otherwise. Both men regarded themselves as Jacksonian executives. Together they exercised the veto as often as Jackson in his two terms (though Pierce's negatives were usually overridden). Both took stern attitudes toward groups whom they labeled rebellious— namely, the free-state forces in Kansas and the Mormons in Utah. Both conducted a vigorously expansionist foreign policy, having in mind especially the acquisition of Cuba. Both made energetic use of patronage to coerce votes from Congress on critical measures—the KANSAS-NE-BRASKA ACT in 1854 and the admission of Kansas with a proslavery constitution in 1858. (See LECOMPTON CONSTITUTION.) Their fatal mistake was in misjudging the moral and political strength of the antislavery crusade. Seeking to discredit and dissipate the movement rather than accommodate it, they pursued policies that disastrously aggravated the sectional conflict and thereby brought the Presidency into disrepute. Then, in the final crisis of 1860–1861, Buchanan's constitutional scruples and his reluctance to use presidential power without specific congressional authorization lent substance to the *fainéant* image that history has fixed upon him. Again, as in 1850, the fate of the country seemed to rest primarily with the Senate, and when compromise failed in that body, little hope remained for peaceable preservation of the Union.

Meanwhile, the Supreme Court had tried its hand at resolving the slavery question and in the process had reasserted its power to review congressional legislation. The famous decision in DRED SCOTT V. SAND-FORD (1857) invalidated a law that had been repealed three years earlier— the 36°30' restriction of the MISSOURI COMPROMISE. Consequently, it did not put the Court into confrontation with Congress. Like the policies of Pierce and Buchanan, however, the decision outraged antislavery opinion and aggravated the sectional conflict. Thus the Court, like the presidency, entered the Civil War with lowered prestige.

At the level of state rather than national government, antebellum Americans acted very much in accord with the Jeffersonian credo that every generation should write its own fundamental law. The period 1830 to 1860 has been called "the high water mark for the making of constitutions among the states." During those three decades, ten new states framed their first constitutions, and eighteen of the other twenty-four revised their constitutions by means of conventions. In addition, many states added amendments from time to time through legislative action. The voters of Massachusetts, for instance, rejected a new constitution drafted by a convention in 1853, but they approved of six amendments in 1855, three in 1857, one in 1859, and two in 1860.

State constitutions became longer in the antebellum period, not only describing in greater detail the structure and functions of government but also incorporating many specific instructions and prohibitions intended to set public policy and control the substance of governmental action. The machinery for constitutional change remained heterogeneous, generally cumbersome, and, in some states, poorly defined. There was a clear trend, however, toward popular participation at every stage. Typically, voters decided whether a convention should be called, elected its members, and passed judgment on its handiwork. Legislative amendment, which bypassed the convention process and often had to be approved by two successive legislatures, was always submitted to the voters for ratification.

Democratization of the state constitutional systems, begun earlier in the century, proceeded unremittingly during the antebellum period. Two major categories of change were further extension of the franchise and further lengthening of the list of elective offices. With but a few exceptions, the old religious and property-holding qualifications for suffrage disappeared, although some states continued to require that voters be taxpayers. Under nativist influence, Connecticut in 1855 and Massachusetts in 1857 sought to curtail immigrant participation in politics by installing an English literacy test. But a stronger contrary tendency, exemplified in the constitutions of Wisconsin (1848), Michigan (1850), Indiana (1851), and Kansas (1859), was to expand the immigrant vote by enfranchising foreigners as soon as they had declared their intention to become citizens. Women were everywhere excluded from the polls, except in a few local elections, and blacks could vote only in a half-dozen northeastern states, but white male suffrage had become almost universal. The shift from appointive to elective offices was most dramatic in the case of the judiciary. Until 1846, only a few states had elective judgeships of any kind, and only in Mississippi were all judges elected. In that year both New York and Iowa followed the Mississippi example, and then the rush began. By 1861, twenty-four of the thirty-four states had written the election of judges into their constitutions, though in five of them the change did not extend to their supreme courts.

The antebellum state constitutions, like those written earlier, were primarily constructive. They established or redesigned systems of government and endowed them with appropriate powers. But in many there was also a conspicuous strain of negativism, reflecting disillusionment with state government and a determination to curb extravagance, corruption, and favoritism. Notably, the framers often placed new restrictions on legislative authority, particularly with reference to public finance, banks, and corporations. These subjects were political issues, of course, but then every CONSTITUTIONAL CONVENTION became to some extent a party battle. As a rule, Democrats were more hostile than their opponents to corporate enterprise and government promotion of it. Attitudes varied according to local circumstances, however, and much depended upon which party in the state had the upper hand at the time. The states of the Old Northwest, where prodigal internal improvement policies in the 1830s had proved disastrous, were especially emphatic in their restraint of legislative power. Their new constitutions approved in the years 1848–1851 forbade state investment in private enterprise and put strict limits on public indebtedness. They also restricted banking in various ways, such as ordering double liability for stockholders, prohibiting the suspension of specie payments, and requiring that any general banking act must be submitted to a popular REFERENDUM.

State constitutional change occurred in many ways and resulted from the work of many hands, including those of voters, convention delegates, legislators, governors, and judges. Appellate courts particularly often shaped or reshaped the fundamental law in the course of performing their routine duties, although JUDICIAL REVIEW of state legislation by state courts was a fairly rare occurrence until after the Civil War. Despite all the constitutional activity, innovation was by no means the dominant mode in the antebellum period. States borrowed much from one another, and old forms were sometimes retained well beyond the limits of their appropriateness. Vermont in 1860 still had its quaint Council of Revision, elected every seven years to examine the condition of the constitution and propose amendments. North Carolina had not yet given its governor a veto power, and in South Carolina, the legislature continued to choose the state's presidential electors. Yet the new problems of the age did encourage some experimentation. For example, certain states had begun to develop the quasi-judicial regulatory commission as an extra branch of government, and framers of the Kansas constitution in 1859 introduced the item veto, a device that most states would eventually adopt.

Although federal and state constitutional development proceeded in more or less separate grooves, the fundamental constitutional problem of the age was the relation between the nation and its constituent parts. The problem had been present and intermittently urgent since the birth of the republic, but after 1846 it became associated much more than ever before with the interrelated issues of slavery and expansion and with the dynamics of party politics.

In the federal system established by the Constitution, the national government and the state governments were each supreme within their respective spheres. This principle of DUAL FEDERALISM, even though it accorded rather well with the actual structure and distribution of governmental power in antebellum America, was by no means universally accepted as a true design of the Republic. Nationalists like Webster and Lincoln asserted the primacy of the nation, the sovereignty of its people, and the perpetuity of the Union. Sectionalists like Calhoun and Davis lodged sovereignty with the states, insisted upon strict construction of federal authority, and viewed the Union as a compact that could be abrogated. Logical consistency was not a characteristic of the intersectional debate, however. Both proslavery and antislavery forces invoked federal power and appealed to states' rights whenever either strategy suited their purposes. With regard to the recovery of fugitive slaves, for instance, Southerners demanded expansion and vigorous use of national authority, while the resistance to that authority of some northern state officials amounted to a revival of nullification. (See UNION, THEORIES OF THE.)

Most Americans agreed that slavery was a state institution, but from that premise they drew conflicting inferences. In the radical antislavery view of SALMON P. CHASE, the institution had no standing beyond the bounds of slave-state JURISDICTION, and the federal government had no constitutional power to establish it, protect it, or even acknowledge its legal existence. In short, slavery was local and freedom national. (See ABOLITIONIST CONSTITUTIONAL THEORY.) According to Calhoun, however, the federal government, as the mere agent of the states, was constitutionally obligated to give slavery as much protection as it gave any other kind of property recognized by state law. Only the sovereign power of a state could restrict or abolish the institution. In short, slavery was national and antislavery the local exception.

The practice of the United States government over the years ran closer to Calhoun's theory than to Chase's. All three branches recognized property rights in slaves and extended aid of some kind to their masters. Congress went beyond the requirements of the Constitution in making the recovery of fugitive slaves a federal business, and under congressional rule the national capital became a slave state in miniature, complete with a slave code, whipping posts, and a thriving slave trade. The image of the nation consistently presented in diplomatic relations was that of a slaveholding republic. With a persistence amounting to dedication, the Department of State sought compensation for owners of slaves escaping to foreign soil, and repeatedly it tried to secure Canadian cooperation in the return of fugitives. In the *Dred Scott* decision, Chief Justice ROGER B. TANEY laid down the one-sided rule that the federal government had no power over slavery except "the power coupled with the duty of guarding and protecting the owner in his rights."

To be sure, national authority was also used for antislavery purposes. In outlawing the foreign slave trade, Congress plainly acted within the letter and intent of the Constitution. In prohibiting slavery throughout much of the Western territory, however, the lawmakers probably drew as much sanction from the example of the NORTHWEST ORDINANCE as from the somewhat ambiguous passage in Article IV, section 3, that seemed to be relevant—namely, "The Congress shall have Power to dispose of and make all needful Rules and Regulations respecting the Territory or other Property belonging to the United States." By 1840, such prohibition had been enacted in six territorial organic acts, as well as in the Missouri Compromise. Furthermore, Chief Justice JOHN MARSHALL in AMERICAN INSURANCE COMPANY V. CANTER (1828) had given the territory clause a broad construction. In legislating for the TERRITORIES, he declared, "Congress exercises the combined powers of the general and of a State government." Since the authority of a state government to establish or abolish slavery was generally acknowledged, Marshall's words seemed to confirm Congress in possession of the same authority within the territories.

The constitutionality of legislation excluding slavery from federal territory did not become a major issue in American public life until after introduction of the WILMOT PROVISO in 1846. Although the question had arisen at times during the Missouri controversy of 1819–1820, the famous 36°30′ restriction had been approved without extensive discussion and with the support of a majority of southern congressmen. The subject had arisen again during the 1830s, but only as a secondary and academic consideration in the debate over abolitionist attacks upon slavery in the District of Columbia. As a practical matter, the Missouri Compromise had presumably disposed of the problem by reviving and extending a policy of having two different policies, one on each side of a dividing line. North of that line (first the Ohio River and then 36°30′), slavery was prohibited; south of the line, slavery was permitted if desired by the white inhabitants.

In the summer of 1846, with Texas annexed and admitted to statehood, with title to Oregon secured by treaty, and with the war against Mexico under way, the United States found itself engaged in territorial expansion on a grand scale. Texas entered the Union as a slaveholding state, and Oregon was generally understood to be free soil, but what about New Mexico and California, if they should be acquired by conquest? To many Americans, including President Polk, the obvious answer seemed to be extending the Missouri Compromise line to the Pacific Ocean. But the issue arose at a time when sectional antagonism had been inflamed by a decade of quarreling over abolitionist petitions, the GAG RULE, and the Texas question. Furthermore, whereas the 36°30′ line had meant partial abolition in a region previously open to slavery, extension of the line through New Mexico and California would have meant a partial rescinding of the abolition already achieved there by Mexican law. So David Wilmot's proposal to forbid slavery in any territory that might be acquired from Mexico won the overwhelming approval of northern congressmen when it was introduced in the House of Representatives on August 8, 1846. Southerners were even more united and emphatic in their opposition; for the Proviso would have completed the exclusion of slaveholders from all the newly acquired land in the Far West. Such injustice, they warned, could not fail to end in disunion.

The Proviso principle of "no more slave territory" quickly became the premier issue in American politics and remained so for almost fifteen years. Virtually the raison d'être of the Free Soil and Republican parties, the principle was rejected by Congress in 1850 and again in 1854, deprived of its legitimacy by the Supreme Court in 1857, and supported by less than forty percent of the electorate in the presidential contest of 1860. Yet forty percent proved sufficient to put a Republican in the White House and thereby precipitate SECESSION. During those years of intermittent sectional crisis from 1846 to 1861, the Southerners and northern conservatives who controlled government policy sought desperately and sometimes discordantly for a workable alternative to the Proviso. One thing that complicated their task was the growing tendency of all elements in the controversy to constitutionalize their arguments.

Southerners especially felt the need for constitutional sanction, partly because of their vulnerability as a minority section but also in order to offset the moral advantage of the antislavery forces. It was not enough to denounce the Proviso as unfair; they must also prove it to be unconstitutional despite the string of contrary precedents running back to the venerated Northwest Ordinance. One way of doing so was to invoke the Fifth Amendment, arguing that any congressional ban on slavery in the territories amounted to deprivation of property without DUE PROCESS OF LAW. But this argument, though used from time to time and incorporated rather vaguely in Taney's *Dred Scott* opinion, did not become a significant part of anti-Proviso strategy. For one thing, the Fifth Amendment had another cutting edge, antislavery in its effect. Free Soilers and Republicans could and did maintain that slavery was illegal in federal territory because it amounted to deprivation of *liberty* without due process of law.

More in keeping with the strict constructionism generally favored by Southerners was the principle of "nonintervention," that is, congressional nonaction with respect to slavery in the territories. Actually, nonintervention had been government policy in part of the West ever since 1790, always with the effect of establishing slavery. But in earlier years the policy had been given little theoretical underpinning. Then, after the introduction of the Wilmot Proviso, there were strenuous efforts to convert nonintervention into a constitutional imperative. The emerging argument ignored Marshall's opinion in *American Insurance Company v. Canter* and held that the territory clause of the Constitution referred only to disposal of public land. In providing government for a territory, Congress could do nothing more than what was absolutely necessary to prepare the territory for statehood. That did not include either the prohibition or the establishment of slavery. Thus nonintervention became a doctrine of federal incapacity. It left open, however, the question of what authority prevailed in the absence of congressional power. One answer, associated with Calhoun, was that property rights in slavery were silently legitimized in every territory by the direct force of the Constitution. Another answer, associated with Lewis Cass and Douglas, was that nonintervention meant leaving the question of slavery to be decided by the local territorial population. The latter theory, given the name POPULAR SOVEREIGNTY, had the advantage of seeming to be in tune with the spirit of Jacksonian democracy.

Thus, by 1848, when American acquisition of New Mexico and California was confirmed in the TREATY OF GUADALUPE HIDALGO, four distinct solutions to the problem of slavery in the territories had emerged. At one political extreme was the free soil doctrine requiring enactment of the Wilmot Proviso. At the other extreme was the Calhoun property rights doctrine legitimizing slavery in all federal territory by direct force of the Constitution. Between them were two formulas of compromise: extension of the 36°30′ line and the principle of popular sovereignty. Presumably the choice rested with Congress, but the constitutionalizing of the argument opened up another possibility—that of leaving the status of slavery in the territories to judicial determination. Legislation facilitating referral of the question to the Supreme Court was proposed in 1848 and incorporated in the historic set of compromise measures enacted two years later. The COMPROMISE OF 1850 admitted California as a free state, but for the rest of the Mexican Cession it adopted the principle of nonintervention. The effect was to reject the 36°30′ and Proviso solutions while leaving the field still open to popular sovereignty, the property rights doctrine, and judicial disposition.

Although neither of the major parties took a formal stand on the territorial question in the elections of 1848 and 1852, it was the Democrats who became closely associated with the principle of nonintervention. Cass, their presidential nominee in 1848, declared that Congress lacked the power to prohibit slavery in the territories and that the territorial inhabitants should be left free to regulate their internal concerns in their own way. This seemed to endorse popular sovereignty as the appropriate corollary to nonintervention, but for about a decade the Democratic party managed to invest both terms with enough ambiguity to accommodate both its northern and southern wings. More specifically, Southerners found that they could assimilate popular sovereignty to their own purposes by viewing it as the right of a territorial population to accept or reject slavery *at the time of admission to statehood*. That would presumably leave the Calhoun doctrine operative during the territorial period. At the same time, northern Democrats like Douglas went on believing that popular sovereignty meant the right of a territorial legislature to make all decisions regarding slavery, within the limits of the Constitution. The Whigs failed to achieve any such convenient doctrinal ambiguity, and that failure may have contributed to the disintegration of their party.

In 1854, a heavily Democratic Congress organized the territories of Kansas and Nebraska, repealing the antislavery restriction of the Missouri Compromise and substituting the principle of nonintervention. "The true intent and meaning of this act," the measure declared, "[is] not to legislate slavery into any Territory or State, nor to exclude it therefrom, but to leave the people thereof perfectly free to form and regulate their domestic institutions in their own way, subject only to the Constitution of the United States." This passage, since it could be interpreted to mean either the northern or the southern brand of popular sovereignty, preserved the ambiguity so necessary for Democratic unity. But of course the Kansas-Nebraska Act, by removing a famous barrier to slavery, provoked a storm of anger throughout the free states and set off a political revolution.

The crisis of the late 1850s was in one respect a confrontation between the emerging Republican party and the increasingly united South—that is, between the Wilmot Proviso and the principles of Calhoun. Yet it was also a struggle within the Democratic party over the meaning of nonintervention and popular sovereignty. The *Dred Scott* decision in March 1857 cleared the air and intensified the crisis. In ruling that Congress had no power to prohibit slavery in the territories, the Supreme Court officially constitutionalized the principle of nonintervention and virtually rendered illegal the main purpose of the Republican party. But Chief Justice Taney went further and disqualified the northern Democratic version of popular sovereignty. If Congress had no such power over slavery, he declared, then neither did a territorial legislature. Douglas responded with his FREEPORT DOCTRINE, insisting that a territorial government, by unfriendly legislation, could effectively exclude slavery, no matter what the Court might decide to the contrary. Southern Democrats, in turn, demanded federal protection of slavery in the territories, and on that issue the party split at its national convention in 1860.

By 1860 it had become apparent that slavery was not taking root in Kansas or in any other western territory. Yet when secession began after Lincoln's election, the efforts at reconciliation concentrated on the familiar territorial problem. The centerpiece of the abortive Crittenden compromise was an amendment reviving and extending the 36°30′ line, so recently outlawed by the Supreme Court. This continued fascination with an essentially empty issue was not so foolish as it now may seem; for the territorial question had obviously taken on enormous symbolic meaning. Because of the almost universal agreement that slavery in the states was untouchable by the federal government, the territories had come to be the limited battleground of a fierce and fundamental struggle. Thus the sectional conflict of the 1850s, whatever its origins and whatever its substance, was decisively shaped by constitutional considerations.

Bibliography

BESTOR, ARTHUR   1961   State Sovereignty and Slavery: A Reinterpretation of Proslavery Constitutional Doctrine, 1846–1860. *Illinois State Historical Society Journal* 54:117–80.

DEALEY, JAMES QUAYLE   1915   *Growth of American State Constitutions.* Boston: Ginn & Co.

FEHRENBACHER, DON E.   1978   *The Dred Scott Case: Its Significance in American Law and Politics.* New York: Oxford University Press.

PARKINSON, GEORGE PHILLIP, JR.   1972   "Antebellum State Constitution-Making: Retention, Circumvention, Revision." Ph.D. dissertation, University of Wisconsin.

POTTER, DAVID M.   1976   *The Impending Crisis, 1848–1861.* Completed and edited by Don E. Fehrenbacher. New York: Harper & Row.

WHITE, LEONARD D.   1954   *The Jacksonians: A Study in Administrative History, 1829–1861.* New York: Macmillan.

CONSTITUTIONAL HISTORY, 1861–1865

Herman Belz

If expediency and ideology ordinarily conflict with the constitutionalist desire for procedural regularity and limitations on government, in time of war they pose a fundamental challenge to CONSTITUTIONALISM and the RULE OF LAW. The first fact to be observed about the constitutional history of the Civil War, therefore, is that the federal Constitution, as in the prewar period, served as both a symbol and a source of governmental legitimacy and as a normative standard for the conduct of politics. Because the rule of the Constitution continued without interruption, it is easy to overlook the pressures that the war generated to institute a regime based exclusively on necessity and the public safety. To be sure, considerations of public safety entered into wartime constitutionalism, and there were those who believed passionately that the Union government in the years 1861 to 1865 did indeed cast aside the Constitution and resort to arbitrary rule. Yet, considered from either a comparative or a strictly American perspective, this judgment is untenable. The record abundantly demonstrates the persistence of constitutional controversy in Congress, in the executive branch, in the courts, and in the forum of public opinion—evidence that the nation's organic law was taken seriously in time of war, even if it was not applied in the same manner as in time of peace. Indeed, a constitutionalizing impulse may be said to have manifested itself in the business of warfare itself. General Order No. 100 for the government of Union armies in the field, promulgated by President ABRAHAM LINCOLN in 1863, was an attempt to limit the destructiveness of modern war that had resulted from developments in weaponry and from the emergence of other aspects of total war.

The most important constitutional question resolved by the events of the war concerned the nature of the Union. (See THEORIES OF THE UNION.) The Framers of the Constitution had created a mixed regime that in some respects resembled a confederation of autonomous states and in others a centralized unitary government. Its distinguishing feature—the chief characteristic of American FEDERALISM—was the division of SOVEREIGNTY between the federal government and the state governments. In constitutional law several decisions of the Supreme Court under Chief Justice JOHN MARSHALL had confirmed this dual-sovereignty system; yet periodically it was questioned by political groups who insisted that the Union was simply a league of sovereign states, and that the federal government possessed no sovereignty whatsoever except as the agent of the states. From 1846 to 1860 defenders of slavery asserted this state-sovereignty theory of the Union; although they never secured a congressional majority for the theory, they did force northern Democrats to adopt positions that virtually abandoned any claim to federal sovereignty in matters concerning slavery. The SECESSION policy of President JAMES BUCHANAN, which regarded secession as illegal but nonetheless tolerated the existence of the newly forming Confederate States of America, signified the constitutional and political bankruptcy of Democratic DUAL FEDERALISM and the practical repudiation of federal sovereignty.

The constitutional results of the Civil War must be measured against the effective triumph of proslavery state sovereignty which permitted the disintegration of the Union in 1860–1861. Northern victory in the war established federal sovereignty in political fact and in public policy, and by the same token repudiated the state-sovereignty theory of the Union. From the standpoint of constitutional law, this result vindicated the divided-sovereignty concept of federalism asserted in the early national period. From the standpoint of federal–state relations in the field of public policy, the war produced a significant centralizing trend, evident principally in military recruitment and organization, internal security, the regulation of personal liberty and CIVIL RIGHTS, and the determination of national economic policy.

The changes in federalism produced by the war have usually been described—sometimes in almost apocalyptic terms—as the destruction of STATES' RIGHTS and the old federal Union and their replacement by a centralized sovereign nation. In fact, however, the changes in federal–state relations that occurred between 1861 and 1865 did not seriously erode or alter the decentralized constitutional system and political culture of the United States. The centralizing of policy was based on military need rather than the appeal of a new unitary constitutional model, and it was of limited scope and duration. In no comprehensive way did the federal government become supreme over the states, nor were states' rights obliterated either in law or in policy. The theoretical structure of American federalism, as explicated by John Marshall, persisted; the actual distribution of power between the states and the federal government, the result of policy struggles on questions raised by the war, was different.

Perhaps the best way to describe the change in federalism that occurred during the Civil War is to say that after a long period of disinclination to use the constitutional powers assigned to it, the federal government began to act like an authentic sovereign state. Foremost among its achievements was the raising of armies and the providing and maintaining of a navy for the defense of the nation.

At the start of the war the decision to resist secession was made by the federal government, but the task of raising a military force fell largely upon the states. The regular United States Army, at approximately 16,000 men, was inadequate for the government's military needs, and federal authorities were as yet unprepared to call for United States volunteers. To meet the emergency it was necessary to rely on the militia, a form of military organization that, while subject to national service, was chiefly a state institution. Accordingly President Lincoln on April 15, 1861, acting under the Militia Act of 1795, issued a call to the state governors to provide 75,000 militia for three months of national service. By August 1861, in pursuance of additional presidential requests, the War Department had enrolled almost 500,000 men for three years' duty. Yet, although carried out under federal authority, the actual recruiting of troops and to a considerable extent their preparation for combat were done by the state governors, acting as a kind of war ministry for the nation.

This arrangement did not last long. Within a year declining popular enthusiasm and the utility of centralized administrative management severely impeded state recruiting efforts and led to greater federal control. Eventually national CONSCRIPTION was adopted. Congress took a half-way step toward this policy in the Militia Act of July 1862, authorizing the President, in calling the militia into national service, to make all necessary rules and regulations for doing so where state laws were defective or inadequate. Under this statute a draft was planned by the War Department, to be enforced by provost marshals nominated by state governors and appointed by the department. Political resistance in the states prevented implementation of this plan. At length, in the Enrollment Act of March 1863, Congress instituted an exclusively national system of conscription. Directed at male citizens ages twenty to forty-five and foreigners who declared their intention to become citizens, the draft law omitted all reference to the state militia. Conscription was to be enforced by federal provost marshals under a Provost Marshal General, operating under an administrative structure organized according to congressional districts. The Civil War draft, which permitted substitutes and money commutation, aroused widespread and often violent opposition and was directly responsible for inducting only six percent of the total Union military force. Nevertheless, it proved to be a decisive constitutional precedent on which the federal government relied in meeting its manpower needs in the wars of the twentieth century. (See SELECTIVE SERVICE ACTS.)

Closely related to the raising of armies was the task of maintaining internal security on the home front against the treasonable and disloyal acts of persons interfering with the war effort. In this sphere too the Union government exercised previously unused powers, asserting an unwonted sovereignty in local affairs that challenged the states' exclusive power to regulate civil and political liberty.

The law against TREASON, the elements of which had been defined in the Constitution, was the most formidable instrument for protecting national security outside the theater of war. Yet in its various manifestations—the Treason Act of 1790 requiring the death penalty and the Seditious Conspiracies Act of 1861 and the treason provisions of the CONFISCATION ACT of 1862 imposing less severe penalties—it was inapplicable in the South as long as federal courts could not operate there. It was also unsuited to the task of containing the less than treasonable activities of Confederate sympathizers and opponents of the war in the North. Loyalty oaths were a second internal security measure. The third, and by far the most important, component of Union internal security policy was military detention of persons suspected of disloyal activities, suspension of the writ of HABEAS CORPUS, and the imposition of martial law.

In April 1861 and on several occasions thereafter, President Lincoln authorized military commanders in specific areas to arrest and deny the writ of habeas corpus to persons engaging in or suspected of disloyal practices, such as interfering with troop movements or discouraging enlistments. In September 1862 the President issued a general proclamation that such persons were liable to trial by military commission or court-martial. Initially the State Department supervised civilian arrests made by secret service agents, federal marshals, and military officers. In February 1862 the War Department assumed responsibility for this practice and created a commission to examine the causes of arrests and provide for the release of persons deemed to be political prisoners. Congress further shaped internal security policy in the HABEAS CORPUS ACT of March 1863, requiring the secretaries of war and state to provide lists of prisoners to federal courts for GRAND JURY consideration. If no indictment for violation of federal law should be forthcoming, a prisoner was to be released upon taking an oath of allegiance.

The Union government arrested approximately 18,000 civilians, almost all of whom were released after brief detention for precautionary rather than punitive purposes. The policy was extremely controversial, however, for what Unionists might consider a precaution to prevent interference with the war effort could easily be regarded by others as punishment for political dissent. Evaluation of internal security policy depended upon conflicting interpretations of CIVIL LIBERTIES guarantees under the Constitution, and differing perceptions of what critics and opponents of the government were in reality doing. As with conscription, however, there was no denying that internal security measures had a significant impact on federal–state relations.

In carrying out this policy the federal government for the first time intervened significantly in local regulation of civil and political liberty. Not only did the federal government make arbitrary or irregular arrests but it also temporarily suspended the publication of many newspapers. Not surprisingly, considering the traditional exclusivity of state power over civil liberty and the partisan context in which the internal security question was debated, the states resisted this extension of federal authority. In several states persons adversely affected by internal security measures, or by enforcement of federal laws and orders concerning conscription, trade restrictions, internal revenue, or emancipation, initiated litigation charging federal officers with violations of state law, such as false arrest, unlawful seizure, kidnaping, assault, and battery. Under prewar federalism no general recourse was available to national officials involved as defendants in state litigation of this sort. Congress remedied this defect, however, in the Habeas Corpus Act of 1863.

The 1863 act provided that orders issued by the President or under his authority should be a defense in all courts against any civil or criminal prosecution for any search, seizure, arrest, or imprisonment undertaken in pursuance of such an order. The law further authorized the removal of litigation against national officers from state to federal courts, and it imposed a two-year limit on the initiation of such litigation. On only two previous occasions, in 1815 and 1833 in response to state interference with customs collection, had Congress given protection for federal officers acting under authority of a specific statute by permitting removal of litigation from state to federal courts. The Habeas Corpus Act of 1863, by contrast, protected actions taken under any federal law or EXECUTIVE ORDER. Critics argued that the law gave immunity rather than indemnity, denied citizens judicial remedies for wrongs done by the government, and usurped state power. The logic of even a circumscribed national sovereignty demanded some means of protection against state JURISDICTION, however, and during reconstruction Congress extended the removal remedy and the federal judiciary upheld its constitutionality. The wartime action marked an important extension of federal jurisdiction that made the national government, at least in time of national security crisis, more able to compete with the states in the regulation of civil liberty.

The most novel and in the long run probably the most important exercise of federal sovereignty during the Civil War led directly to the abolition of slavery and the protection of personal liberty and civil rights by the national government. No constitutional rule was more firmly established than that which prohibited federal interference with slavery in the states that recognized it. The outbreak of hostilities did not abrogate this rule, but it did create the possibility that, under the war power, the federal government might emancipate slaves for military purposes. After prohibiting slavery where it could under its peacetime constitutional authority (in the DISTRICT OF COLUMBIA and in the TERRITORIES), Congress struck at slavery in the Confederacy itself. In the Confiscation Act of 1862, it declared "forever free" slaves belonging to persons in rebellion, those who were captured, or who came within Union army lines. Executive interference with slavery went considerably farther. After trying unsuccessfully in 1862 to persuade loyal slaveholding states to accept a federally sponsored plan for gradual, compensated emancipation to be carried out by the states themselves, Lincoln undertook military emancipation. In the EMANCIPATION PROCLAMATION of January 1, 1863, he declared the freedom of all slaves in states still in rebellion and pledged executive-branch protection of freedmen's personal liberty.

Federal power over personal liberty was further made manifest in the work of local police regulation undertaken by Union armies as they advanced into southern territory. All persons in occupied areas were affected by the rule of federal military commanders, and none more so than freed or escaped slaves. From the first incursions of national force in May 1861, War and Treasury Department officials protected blacks' personal liberty, provided for their most pressing welfare needs in refugee camps, and assisted their assimilation into free society by organizing their labor on abandoned plantations and by recruiting them into the army. In March 1865 Congress placed emancipation-related federal police regulation on a more secure footing by creating the Bureau of Refugees, Freedmen, and Abandoned Lands. Authorized to control all subjects relating to refugees and freedmen for a period of one year after the end of the war, the FREEDMEN'S BUREAU throughout 1865 established courts to protect freedmen's personal liberty and civil rights, in the process superseding the states in their most traditional and jealously guarded governmental function.

Federal emancipation measures, based on the war power, did not accomplish the permanent abolition of slavery as it was recognized in state laws and constitutions. To accomplish this momentous change, and the invasion of state power that it signified, amendment of the Constitution was necessary. Accordingly, Congress in January 1865 approved for submission to the states a constitutional amendment prohibiting slavery or involuntary servitude, except as a punishment for crime, in the United States or any place subject to its jurisdiction. Section 2 of the amendment gave Congress authority to enforce the prohibition by appropriate legislation.

Controversy surrounded this terse, seemingly straightforward, yet rather delphic pronouncement, which became part of the Constitution in December 1865. Though it appeared to be a legitimate exercise of the amending power under Article V, Democrats argued that the THIRTEENTH AMENDMENT was a wrongful use of that power because it invaded state jurisdiction over local affairs, undermining the sovereign power to fix the status of all persons within a state's borders and thus destroying the unspoken premise on which the Constitution and the government had been erected in 1787. The Republican framers of the amendment for their part were uncertain about the scope and effect of the guarantee of personal liberty that they would write into the nation's organic law. At the least, the amendment prohibited chattel slavery, or property in people; many of its supporters believed it also secured the full range of civil rights appurtenant to personal liberty that distinguished a free republican society. No determination of this question was required in order to send the amendment to the states, however, and when a year later the precise scope of the guarantees provided and congressional enforcement power became issues in reconstruction, more detailed and specific measures, such as the CIVIL RIGHTS ACT OF 1866 and the FOURTEENTH AMENDMENT, were deemed necessary. Constitutionally speaking, the Thirteenth Amendment played a minor role in reconstruction.

The federal government further exercised sovereignty characteristic of a nation-state in the sphere of economic policy. This development raised few questions of contitutional propriety; the instruments for accomplishing it lay ready to hand in the ALEXANDER HAMILTON-John Marshall doctrines of BROAD CONSTRUCTION and IMPLIED POWERS. These doctrines had fallen into desuetude in the Jacksonian era, when mercantilist-minded state governments effectively determined economic policy. The exodus of Southerners from the national government in 1861 altered the political balance, however, and Republicans in control of the wartime Congress seized the opportunity to adopt centralizing economic legislation. They raised the tariff for protective purposes, authorized construction of a transcontinental railway, facilitated settlement on the public domain (HOMESTEAD ACT), provided federal aid to higher education (MORRILL ACT), established a uniform currency, asserted federal control over the nation's banking institutions, and taxed the American people in innovative ways (income tax, DIRECT TAX). These measures laid the foundation for increasing federal ECONOMIC REGULATION in the late nineteenth and early twentieth centuries. Yet they did not make the determination of economic policy an exclusively national function. In this field, as in civil rights, the federal government's acquisition of a distinct and substantial share of sovereignty diminished, but by no means obliterated, state power.

As the federal government gained power relative to the states during the war, so within the SEPARATION OF POWERS structure of the national government the executive expanded its authority relative to the other branches. Lincoln was the instrument of this constitutional change. Unlike his predecessor Buchanan, Lincoln was willing to acknowledge the necessity of an inflexible defense of the Union during the secession crisis, and after the bombardment of Fort Sumter he acted swiftly and unhesitatingly to commit the nation to arms.

To raise a fighting force Lincoln called the state militia into national service, ordered—without authority from Congress—a 40,000-man increase in the regular army and navy, requested 42,000 volunteers, and proclaimed a blockade of ports in the seceded states. He also instituted the main elements of the internal security program previously described, closed the postal service to treasonable correspondence, directed that $2,000,000 be paid out of the federal treasury, and pledged the credit of the United States for $250,000,000. Lincoln did all this without congressional authority, but not without regard for Congress. Ordering the militia into national service, he called Congress into session to meet in mid-summer. Directing the enlargement of the army and navy, he said he would submit these actions to Congress. He did so, and Congress voted approval of the President's military orders, "as if they had been done under the previous express authority and direction of the Congress." Thereafter Lincoln was ever mindful of the lawmaking branch, and in some respects deferential to it. Yet in war-related matters he continued to take unilateral actions. Thus he proclaimed martial law, suspended habeas corpus, suppressed newspaper publication, issued orders for the conduct of armies in the field, ordered slave emancipation, and directed the political reorganization of occupied southern states.

How could these extraordinary actions be rationalized under the nation's organic law? The question aroused bitter controversy at the time, giving rise to charges of dictatorship which continued to find echo in scholarly debate. No more penetrating analysis of the problem has ever been offered than that presented by Lincoln himself.

In his message to Congress of July 4, 1861, Lincoln said his actions were required by "public necessity" and "popular demand." Referring to suspension of the writ of habeas corpus, he stated that if he violated "some single law," his doing so was justified on the ground that it would save the government." . . . are all the laws, *but one,* to go unexecuted, and the government itself go to pieces, lest that one be violated?" he asked. On another occasion Lincoln posed the question whether it was possible to lose the nation and yet preserve the Constitution. "By general law life and limb must be protected," he reasoned, "yet often a limb must be amputated to save a life; but a life is never wisely given to save a limb." This appears to mean that the Constitution might be set aside, as a limb is amputated, to save the life of the nation. The inference can be drawn that emergency action, while expedient, is unconstitutional.

What is required to understand the lawfulness of the emergency measures in question, however, is not legalistic analysis of the constitutional text but rather consideration of the fundamental relationship between the nation and the Constitution. Lincoln's principal argument was that the steps taken to defend the government were constitutional because the Constitution implicitly sanctioned its own preservation. The Constitution in this view was not a mere appendage of the living nation or a derivative expression or reflection of national life, as a legal code might be considered to be. Coeval and in an ultimate political sense coterminous with it, the Constitution *was* the nation. This conception is present in Lincoln's statement of April 1864 that "measures, otherwise unconstitutional, might become lawful, by becoming indispensable to the preservation of the constitution, through the preservation of the nation." "Is there," he asked in his message of July 1861, "in all republics, this inherent and fatal weakness? Must a government, of necessity, be too *strong* for the liberties of its own people, or too *weak* to maintain its own existence?" Not that Lincoln conceded to his critics at the level of positivistic, text-based constitutional argument. Concerning habeas corpus suspension, for example, he tenaciously insisted that as the Constitution did not specify who might exercise this power, he was justified in doing so when Congress was not in session. Congress, in fact, subsequently ratified Lincoln's suspension of habeas corpus. Although his argument conformed to the requirements of American constitutional politics, his principal justification of emergency actions was that they were necessary to preserve the substance of political liberty, which was the end both of the Constitution and the Union.

It is sometimes said that Lincoln established in American public law the principle of constitutional dictatorship. Yet at no time did Lincoln exercise unlimited power. The notion of constitutional dictatorship also obscures the fact that although Lincoln applied military power on a far wider scale than previous Presidents, in doing so he merely accelerated a tendency toward expansion of the executive's defensive war-making capability. In 1827 the Supreme Court, in MARTIN V. MOTT, had upheld the President's power under the Militia Act of 1795 to call out the militia (and by extension the army and navy) in the event of actual or imminent invasion. President JAMES K. POLK had used this defensive war-making power to commit the nation to war against Mexico, and Presidents Millard Fillmore and Franklin Pierce had employed military force in circumstances that could have led to wars with foreign states. In his exercise of executive power Lincoln merely widened a trail blazed by his predecessors.

Yet in minor matters unrelated to the war, emancipation, and reconstruction, Lincoln was a passive President. Although as party leader he made effective use of his patronage powers, he did little to influence congressional legislation aside from formal suggestions in annual messages. Moreover he exercised the veto sparingly, gave broad latitude to his department heads, and made little use of the cabinet for policymaking purposes. Lincoln's respect for legislative independence complemented and encouraged another important nineteenth-century constitutional trend—the strengthening of congressional power.

To an extent that is difficult to appreciate in the late twentieth century, nineteenth-century government was preeminently legislative in nature. Lawmakers shaped public policy, resolved constitutional controversies through debate and legislation, controlled the TAXING AND SPENDING process, and exercised significant influence over administration. The years between the presidencies of THOMAS JEFFERSON and ANDREW JACKSON had been a period of legislative assertiveness, and although the struggle over slavery had brought Congress to near-paralysis, still the political foundation existed for wartime exertions of power that anticipated the era of congressional government during and after reconstruction.

Although Congress approved Lincoln's emergency measures in 1861, its action by no means signified general deference to executive power. On the contrary, reciting constitutional provisions that gave Congress power to declare war and regulate the military establishment, members made vigorous claim to exercise the WAR POWER. Accordingly, they raised men and supplies for the war, attempted through the Joint Committee on the Conduct of the War to influence military strategy, modified internal security policy, and enacted laws authorizing confiscation, emancipation, and reconstruction. The need for party unity notwithstanding, the Republican majority in Congress insisted on civilian control over the military, monitored executive department administration, and, in an unusual maneuver in December 1862, even tried to force a change in the cabinet. Tighter internal organization and operational procedures made Congress more powerful as well as more efficient during the war. The speaker of the House, for example, assumed greater control over committee memberships and the flow of legislative business; the party caucus became a more frequent determinant of legislative behavior; and standing committees and their chairmen enjoyed enhanced prestige and influence, gradually superseding select committees as the key agencies for accomplishing legislative tasks. Exercising power conferred by statute in 1857 to punish recalcitrant or uncooperative witnesses, Congress used its investigative authority to extend its governmental grasp.

In the 1930s and 1940s, Civil War historiography regarded conflict between a radical-dominated Congress and the soberly conservative Lincoln administration as the central political struggle of the war. Recent research has shown, however, that disagreement between the Democratic and Republican parties was more significant in shaping the course of political and constitutional events than was the radical versus moderate tension within the Republican party. Conflict occurred between the executive and legislative branches, as much as a result of institutional rivalry inherent in the structure of separated powers as of programmatic differences. Congressional–presidential relations were not notably more strained than they have been in other American wars. Although Lincoln demonstrated the potentially vast power inherent in the presidency, his wartime actions did not measurably extend the executive office beyond the sphere of crisis government. He evinced no tendency toward the so-called stewardship conception of the presidency advanced by THEODORE ROOSEVELT in the early twentieth century. The power of Congress waxed, its wartime achievements in policymaking and internal organization providing a solid basis for a subsequent era of congressional government.

A significant portion of American constitutional history from 1861 to 1865 occurred south of the Potomac, where were manifested many of the same problems and tendencies that appeared in the wartime experience of the United States government. The CONFEDERATE CONSTITUTION, modeled closely on that of the United States, revealed the most bitterly contested issues that had led to the war. It recognized and protected the right of slave property; proclaimed state sovereignty as the basis of the Confederacy; omitted the GENERAL WELFARE clause and the TAXING AND SPENDING POWER contained in the United States Constitution; stated that all federal power was expressly delegated; and prohibited a protective tariff and INTERNAL IMPROVEMENTS appropriations. Yet the right of secession was not recognized, evidence that the Confederacy was intended to be a permanent government.

Confederate constitutional history was marked by war-induced centralization and conflicts between federal and state authority. The Confederate government conscripted soldiers; suspended the writ of habeas corpus and declared martial law; confiscated enemy property and seized for temporary use the property of its own citizens; taxed heavily and imposed tight controls on commerce and industry; and owned and operated munitions, mining, and clothing factories. These actions and policies aroused strong opposition as expressed in the rhetoric of states' rights and through the institutions of state government. Some governors refused to place their troops under the Confederacy's authority and challenged conscription and internal security measures. Many state judges granted writs of habeas corpus that interfered with military recruitment. Lack of effective leverage over the states seriously hampered the Confederate war effort.

The most significant difference between Union and Confederate constitutionalism centered on POLITICAL PARTIES. Driven by the desire to create national unity, Southerners eschewed political party organization as unnecessary and harmful. When political differences arose, they had to find resolution in the conflict-inducing methods of the system of states' rights. In the North, by contrast, political parties continued to compete, with beneficial results. Political disagreements between the government and its Democratic critics were kept within manageable bounds by the concept of a loyal opposition, while among members of the governing party differences were directed into policy alternatives. Moreover, party organization encouraged federal–state cooperation in the implementation of controversial measures like conscription, thus helping to minimize the centrifugal effects of federal organization. Indeed, the persistence of organized party competition, even in the critical year of 1864 when military success was uncertain and the Democratic party campaigned on a platform demanding a cessation of hostilities, was perhaps the most revealing fact in Civil War constitutional history. It showed that despite important changes in federal–state relations and reliance on techniques of emergency government, the American commitment to constitutionalism was firm, even amidst events that tested it most severely.

Bibliography

BELZ, HERMAN   1978   *Emancipation and Equal Rights: Politics and Constitutionalism in the Civil War Era.* New York: Norton.

CURRY, LEONARD P.   1968   *Blueprint for Modern America: Nonmilitary Legislation of the First Civil War Congress.* Nashville, Tenn.: Vanderbilt University Press.

FEHRENBACHER, DON E.   1979   Lincoln and the Constitution. In Cullom Davis, ed., *The Public and Private Lincoln: Contemporary Perspectives.* Carbondale: University of Southern Illinois Press.

HYMAN, HAROLD M.   1973   *A More Perfect Union: The Impact of the Civil War and Reconstruction on the Constitution.* New York: Knopf.

MCKITRICK, ERIC   1967   Party Politics and the Union and Confederate War Efforts. In Walter Dean Burnham and William N. Chambers, eds., *The American Party System: Stages of Political Development.* New York: Free Press.

MCLAUGHLIN, ANDREW C.   1936   Lincoln, the Constitution, and Democracy. *International Journal of Ethics* 47:1–24.

RANDALL, JAMES G.   (1926)1951   *Constitutional Problems under Lincoln,* rev. ed. Urbana: University of Illinois Press.

WEIGLEY, RUSSELL F.   1967   *A History of the United States Army.* New York: Macmillan.

TANEY COURT

(1836–1864)

R. Kent Newmyer

The Supreme Court under Chief Justice ROGER B. TANEY (1836–1864) has not been a favorite among historians, perhaps because it defies easy generalization. There were few great constitutional moments and no dramatic lawmaking decisions comparable to those handed down by the MARSHALL COURT. The fifteen Justices who served with Taney (not counting ABRAHAM LINCOLN's Civil War appointees) varied immensely in ability—from JOSEPH STORY of Massachusetts who was the leading scholar on the bench until his death in 1845 to JOHN MCKINLEY of Alabama whose twenty-five years on the Court left barely a trace. Institutional unity and efficiency were often disrupted by abrasive personalities like HENRY BALDWIN (who became mentally unstable shortly after his appointment in 1830) and PETER V. DANIEL (whose passion for STATES' RIGHTS drove him into chronic dissent). Division was constant and bitter as the Justices disagreed openly over corporation, banking, and slavery questions—all of which tended to be seen from a sectional point of view. Fortunately for the ongoing work of the Court, most of its members shared a respect for the Constitution and had a common commitment to economic progress and property rights that cut across ideological and sectional differences. All were Democrats, too, except Story, JOHN MCLEAN, and BENJAMIN R. CURTIS. Most of the Court respected the Chief Justice—whose legal mind was of a high order—and responded well to his patient, democratic style of leadership. Still the Court under Taney did not quite cohere. There was no "leading mind," as DANIEL WEBSTER complained, and no clear-cut doctrinal unity.

Clearly the Taney Court was not the Marshall Court—but then again it was not the age of Marshall. The society that conditioned the Taney Court and defined the perimeters within which it made law was democratic in its politics, pluralistic in social composition, divided in ideology, and shaped by capitalist forces which increasingly sought freedom from traditional governmental restraints. Most threatening to judicial unity, because it was directly reflected in the opinions of the Court, was the intensification of sectional rivalry. As northern states committed themselves to commerce and manufacturing, they came to see themselves—taking their cultural cues from the abolitionists—as a section united in defense of liberty and freedom. The South found ideological conservatism an ideal umbrella for an expansive social-economic system based on cotton and organized around plantation slavery. As the sections competed for political power and control of the new West, each came to think of itself as the last best hope of mankind. And each insisted that the Constitution accommodate its policy preferences—a demand that the Supreme Court could satisfy only by compromising doctrinal purity and finally could not satisfy at all.

In short, the political and economic problems of the new age became constitutional problems just as ALEXIS DE TOCQUEVILLE had said they would. Whether the Supreme Court would be the primary agency to resolve those problems was, of course, a matter of debate. ANDREW JACKSON, armed with a mandate from the people, did not believe that the Court had a monopoly of constitutional wisdom. Newly organized POLITICAL PARTIES stood ready to dispute judicial decisions that offended their constituencies. States armed with JOHN C. CALHOUN's theory of NULLIFICATION insisted that they, not the Court, had the final word on the Constitution. Accordingly, the margin of judicial error was drastically reduced. The Court was obliged to make the Constitution of 1787 work for a new age; the high nationalism of the Marshall Court, along with its Augustan style of judging, would have to be toned down. Changes would have to come. The question—and it was as yet a new one in American constitutional law—was whether they could be made without disrupting the continuity upon which the authority of the law and the prestige of the Court rested.

The moment of testing came quickly. Facing the Court in its 1837 term were three great constitutional questions dealing with state banking, the COMMERCE CLAUSE, and corporate contracts. Each had been argued before the Marshall Court and each involved a question of FEDERALISM which pitted new historical circumstances against a precedent from the Marshall period. The Court's decisions in these cases would set the constitutional tone for the new age.

In BRISCOE V. BANK OF KENTUCKY the challenge was simple and straightforward. The issue was whether notes issued by the state-owned Commonwealth Bank were prohibited by Article I, section 10, of the Constitution, which prevented states from issuing BILLS OF CREDIT. The Marshall Court had ruled broadly against state bills of credit in CRAIG v. MISSOURI (1830), but the new Jacksonian majority ruled for the state bank. Justice McLean's opinion paid deference to legal continuity by distinguishing *Briscoe* from *Craig,* but political and economic expediency controlled the decision as Story's bitter dissent made clear. The fact was that, after the demise of the second Bank of the United States, state bank notes were the main currency of the country. To rule against the bank would put such notes in jeopardy, a risk the new Court refused to take.

Policy considerations of a states' rights nature also overwhelmed doctrinal consistency in commerce clause litigation, the Court's primary means of drawing the line between national and state power. Marshall's opinion in GIBBONS v. OGDEN (1824) had conceded vast power over INTERSTATE COMMERCE to Congress, although the Court had not gone so far as to rule that national power automatically excluded states from passing laws touching FOREIGN and INTERSTATE COMMERCE. The new age needed a flexible interpretation of the commerce clause that would please states' rights forces in both the North and the South and at the same time encourage the growth of a national market.

In MAYOR OF NEW YORK v. MILN, the second of the trio of great cases in 1837, the Court struggled toward such a reinterpretation. A New York law required masters of all vessels arriving at the port of New York to make bond that none of their passengers should become wards of the city. The practical need for such a law seemed clear enough; the question was whether it encroached unconstitutionally on federal power over interstate commerce as laid out in the *Gibbons* decision. The Chief Justice assigned the opinion to Justice SMITH THOMPSON who was prepared to justify the New York law as a police regulation and as a legitimate exercise of concurrent commerce power. His narrow definition of STATE POLICE POWER displeased some of his brethren, however, and even more so his position on CONCURRENT POWER. When he refused to compromise, the opinion was reassigned to PHILIP P. BARBOUR, who upheld the state regulation as a valid exercise of state police power. Barbour's contention that police power was "unqualified and exclusive" far exceeded anything that precedent could justify, however, as Story pointed out in his dissent. Indeed, Barbour's opinion, so far as it ruled that states could regulate interstate passengers, went beyond the position agreed upon in CONFERENCE and lacked the full concurrence of a majority.

The *Miln* case settled little except that the New York regulation was constitutional. The Court remained sharply divided over the basic questions: whether congressional power over foreign and interstate commerce was exclusive of the states or concurrent with them and, if it was concurrent, how much congressional action would be necessary to sustain national predominance. The doctrine of state police power had taken a tentative step toward maturity, but its relation to the commerce clause remained unsettled. That the states reserved some power to legislate for the health and welfare of their citizens seemed clear enough, but to establish an enclave of state power prior to, outside the scope of, and superior to powers delegated explicitly to Congress was to beg, not settle the crucial constitutional question.

The uncertainty regarding the questions generated by *Miln* contin-ued throughout the 1840s in such cases as GROVES v. SLAUGHTER (1841) where the Court refused to rule on whether the provision of the Missis-sippi Constitution of 1832 touching the interstate slave trade was a viola-tion of national commerce power. Confusion increased in the LICENSE CASES (1847) and the PASSENGER CASES (1849), which dealt with state regulation of alcohol and immigration respectively. The Justices upheld state authority in the first and denied it in the second, but in neither did they clarify the relation of state police power to federal authority over interstate commerce.

Not until COOLEY v. BOARD OF WARDENS (1852), which considered the constitutionality of a Pennsylvania law regulating pilotage in the port of Philadelphia, did the Court supply guidelines for commerce clause litigation. Congress had twice legislated on pilotage, but in neither case was there any conflict with the Pennsylvania law. The issue came, therefore, precisely and unavoidably to focus on EXCLUSIVE POWER versus concurrent power: whether the constitutional grant of commerce power to Congress automatically prohibited STATE REGULATION OF COMMERCE or whether the states could regulate commerce as long as such regulations did not actually conflict with congressional legislation.

Justice Curtis's majority opinion upheld the state law and in the process salvaged some doctrinal regularity. Starting from the undeniable premise that the commerce power granted to Congress did not expressly exclude the states from exercising authority over interstate commerce, he ruled that exclusive congressional JURISDICTION obtained only when the subject matter itself required it. The SUBJECTS OF COMMERCE, however, were vast and varied and did not require blanket exclusiveness. Some matters, he said, needed a "single uniform rule, operating equally on the commerce of the United States in every port." Some just as certainly admitted of local regulation. Power, in other words, followed function: if the subject matter required uniform regulation, the power belonged to Congress; if it did not, the states might regulate it. State police power remained to be settled, but the pressure to do so was lessened because the concurrent commerce power of the states was now clearly recognized.

SELECTIVE EXCLUSIVENESS, as the Court's approach in *Cooley* came to be called, was not a certain and final answer to the problem of allocating commerce power between the national government and the states, how-ever. The rule was clear enough but how to apply it was not, which is to say that Curtis gave no guidelines for determining which aspects of commerce required uniform regulation or which permitted diversity. What was clear was that the Court had retreated from the constitutional formalism of the Marshall period. The opinion was short, only ten pages long; it made no reference to precedent, not even *Gibbons*. The Justices now willed to do what they had previously done unwillingly: they decided cases without a definitive pronouncement of DOCTRINE. The important difference in *Cooley* was that the Court devised a rule of thumb recognizing the judicial interest-balancing that previously had been carried on covertly in the name of formal distinctions. Ordered process, not logical categories, would be the new order of the day.

The Court's flexibility also signaled a shift of power in the direction of the states. The constitutional legacy of the Marshall Court had been altered to fit Jacksonian priorities. Still, national authority had not been destroyed. The Taney Court had refused to extend the nationalist principles of McCULLOCH v. MARYLAND (1819) and *Gibbons,* to be sure, but the principles stood. The Court's new federalism did not rest on new states' rights constitutional doctrine. Neither did the new federalism threaten economic growth, as conservatives had predicted. Agrarian capitalism, for example, fared as well under the Taney Court as it had under its predecessor. The Justices did sometimes resist the most exorbitant demands of land speculators, and occasionally a dissenting Justice spoke for the little man as did Daniel in *Arguello v. United States* (1855). But the majority took their cue from FLETCHER v. PECK (1810), which is to say that plungers in the land market mostly got free rein, as for example in *Cervantes v. United States* (1854) and *Fremont v. United States* (1855). That slaveholding agrarian capitalists were to benefit from this judicial largess was clear from the decision in DRED SCOTT v. SANDFORD (1857).

The Court's promotion of commercial-industrial-corporate capitalism proved more difficult because of the sectional disagreements among the Justices. But there is no doubt that the Taney Court served as a catalyst for the release of American entrepreneurial energies. Its plan for a democratic, nonmonopolistic capitalism, Jacksonian style, was unveiled in CHARLES RIVER BRIDGE v. WARREN BRIDGE, the last of the three landmark decisions of the 1837 term. Here the question was whether the toll-free Warren Bridge, chartered and built in 1828 a few hundred feet from the Charles River Bridge, destroyed the property rights of the old bridge, in violation of its charter as protected by DARTMOUTH COLLEGE v. WOODWARD (1819). The difficulty was that the charter of 1785, although granting the Charles River Bridge the right to collect tolls, had not explicitly granted a monopoly. The fate of the old bridge depended, therefore, on the willingness of the Taney Court to extend the principle of *Dartmouth College* by implication.

Taney, who spoke for the new Jacksonian majority on the Court, refused to do so. The Chief Justice agreed that "the rights of private property are sacredly guarded," but he insisted "that the community also have rights, and that the happiness and well-being of every citizen depends on their faithful preservation." The Court should not venture into the no-man's land of inference and construction when the public interest rested in the balance, Taney argued. He cleverly supported this position by citing Marshall's opinion in PROVIDENCE BANK v. BILLINGS (1830). And the public interest, as Taney saw it, lay in extending equality of economic opportunity. "Modern science," he said with an eye on new railroad corporations, would be throttled and transportation set back to the last century if turnpike and canal companies could turn charter rights into monopoly grants.

The *Bridge* decision, like the Court's decisions in banking and commerce, revealed a distinct instrumentalist tone as well as a new tolerance for state legislative discretion. The Court also showed its preference for dynamic over static capital. Still, property rights were not generally threatened. To be sure, in WEST RIVER BRIDGE COMPANY v. DIX (1848) the Court recognized the power of state legislatures to take property for public purposes with JUST COMPENSATION, but conservatives themselves were willing to recognize that power. The Court also took a liberal view of state DEBTORS' RELIEF LEGISLATION, especially laws applying to mortgages for land, but even here the Court could claim the Marshall Court's decision in OGDEN v. SAUNDERS (1827) as its guide. There was no doubt, on the other hand, as BRONSON v. KINZIE (1843) showed, that state relief laws that impaired substantial contractual rights would not be tolerated.

Corporate property also remained secure under the *Bridge* ruling. Indeed, corporate expansion was strongly encouraged by the Taney Court despite the resistance of some of the southern agrarian Justices. After 1837 the Court consistently refused to extend charter rights by implication, but it also upheld corporate charters that explicitly granted monopoly rights even though in some cases such rights appeared hostile to community interest. Corporations also greatly profited from BANK OF AUGUSTA v. EARLE (1839), which raised the question whether corporations chartered in one state could do business in another. Taney conceded that the legislature could prohibit foreign corporations from doing business in the state and some such laws were subsequently passed. But such prohibitions, he went on to say, had to be explicit; practically speaking, this limitation assured corporations the right to operate across state lines. Hardly less important to corporate expansion was *Louisville Railroad v. Letson* (1844) which held that corporations could be considered citizens of the states in which they were chartered for purposes of DIVERSITY JURISDICTION—thus removing the increasingly unworkable fiction created in *Bank of United States v. Deveaux* (1809) and assuring corporate access to federal courts where the bias in favor of local interests would be minimized.

The Court's promotion of capitalism showed the basic continuity between the Marshall and Taney periods and the fact that antebellum law followed the contours of economic development. Acknowledgment of this continuity, however, should not obscure the real changes in constitutional federalism as the Taney Court deferred more to state power and legislative discretion. Overall the Court spoke more modestly, too, readily acknowledging former errors and generally toning down its rhetoric. In LUTHER v. BORDEN (1849), it went so far as to promise judicial self-restraint regarding POLITICAL QUESTIONS, though that promise ought not to be confused with a hard-and-fast doctrine, which it clearly was not. Although the Court avoided stridency, it did not claim less power. The constitutional nationalism which the Taney Court reduced was not the same as the judicial nationalism which it actually extended. In short, the Court did things differently, but it did not surrender its power to do them. Although the *Bridge* case conceded new power to state legislatures and promised judicial restraint, the Court still monitored the federal system in corporate contract questions. The Court's commerce clause decisions worked to make the federal system more flexible. But in every case from *Miln* through *Cooley,* the Court retained the right to judge— and often, as in *Cooley,* by vague constitutional standards. This judicial authority, moreover, was used throughout the Taney period to expand the jurisdiction of the Court, often at the expense of state judiciaries which the Court claimed to respect.

Never was federal judicial expansion more striking than in SWIFT v. TYSON (1842), a commercial law case which arose under federal diversity jurisdiction. For a unanimous Court, Story held that, in matters of general commercial law, state "laws," which section 34 of the JUDICIARY ACT OF 1789 obliged the federal courts to follow in diversity cases, did not include state court decisions. In the absence of controlling state statutes, then, federal courts were free to apply general principles of commercial law, which they proceeded to do until *Swift* was overruled in 1938. Almost as expansive was Taney's opinion in PROPELLER GENESEE CHIEF v. FITZHUGH (1851), which bluntly overturned the tidewater limitation imposed by the Marshall Court and extended the admiralty jurisdiction of the federal courts over the vast network of inland lakes and rivers.

Both these decisions were part of the Court's consistent effort to establish a system of uniform commercial principles conducive to the interstate operation of business. Both paved the way for federal judicial intrusion into state judicial authority. When state courts objected to this judicial nationalism, as the Wisconsin Supreme Court did in the slave rendition case of ABLEMAN v. BOOTH (1859), Jacksonian Roger Taney put them in their place with a ringing defense of federal judicial authority that was every bit as unyielding as was Federalist John Marshall's in COHENS v. VIRGINIA (1821). *Ableman* was an assertion of power that would have astonished conservative critics in 1837 who predicted the imminent decline and fall of the Court. Instead, by 1850 the Taney

Court was even more popular than the Marshall Court had been and the Chief Justice was praised by men of all political persuasions. All this would change when the Court confronted the issue of slavery.

Adjudicating the constitutional position of slavery fell mainly to the Taney Court; there was no escape. Slavery was the foundation of the southern economy, a source of property worth billions, a social institution that shaped the cultural values of an entire section and the politics of the whole nation. Moreover, it was an integral part of the Constitution, which the Court had to interpret. At the same time, it was, of all the issues facing the antebellum Court, least amenable to a rational legal solution—and in this respect, it foreshadowed social issues like abortion and AFFIRMATIVE ACTION which have troubled the contemporary Court. No other single factor so much accounts for the divisions on the Taney Court or its inability to clearly demarcate power in the federal system.

Given the slavery question's explosive nature, the Justices not surprisingly tried to avoid confronting it directly. Thus the obfuscation in Groves v. Slaughter (1841), where the issue was whether a provision in the Mississippi Constitution prohibiting the importation of slaves for sale after 1833 illegally encroached upon federal power over interstate commerce. The Court circumvented this issue by ruling that the state constitutional clause in question was not self-activating—a position that, while avoiding trouble for the Court, also guaranteed the collection of millions of dollars of outstanding debts owed slave traders and in effect put the judicial seal of approval on the interstate slave trade. The Court also dodged the substantive issue in STRADER v. GRAHAM (1851), which raised the question whether slaves who resided in Kentucky had become free by virtue of their temporary residence in the free state of Ohio. The Court refused jurisdiction on the ground that Kentucky law reasserted itself over the slaves on their return, so that no federal question was involved.

Where the substantive question could not be side-stepped, the Court aimed to decide cases on narrow grounds and in such a way as to please both North and South. Thus in The Amistad (1841), Justice Story ruled that Africans on their way to enslavement who escaped their Spanish captors were free by virtue of principles of international law and a close reading of the Treaty of 1794 with Spain. Extremists in neither section were pleased. Even less were they content with Story's efforts to juggle sectional differences, morality, and objective adjudication in PRIGG v. PENNSYLVANIA (1842). There the question was whether and to what extent states were allowed to pass PERSONAL LIBERTY LAWS protecting the rights of free Negroes in rendition cases. The South was pleased when Story declared the Pennsylvania liberty law of 1826 to be a violation of the constitutional and statutory obligation to return fugitive slaves. He went on to say, with his eye on northern opinion (and with doubtful support from a majority on the Court), that the power over fugitives belonged exclusively to the federal government and that states were not obliged to cooperate in their return. The decision encouraged northern states to pass personal liberty laws but also necessitated the more stringent federal fugitive slave law of 1850. Both developments fueled sectional conflict. (See FUGITIVE SLAVERY.)

The Court's strategy of avoidance aimed to keep slavery on the state level where the Constitution had put it, but the slavery question would not stay put. What brought it forth politically and legally as a national question was SLAVERY IN THE TERRITORIES, a problem which confronted the Court and the nation in *Dred Scott*. The nominal issue in that famous case was whether a Negro slave named Scott, who had resided in the free state of Illinois and the free territory of Minnesota (made free by the MISSOURI COMPROMISE of 1820) and who returned to the slave state of Missouri, could sue in the federal courts. Behind this jurisdictional issue lay the explosive political question of whether Congress could prohibit slavery in the territories, or to put it another way, whether the Constitution guaranteed it there. The future of slavery itself was on the line.

The first inclination of the Justices when they confronted the case early in 1856 was to continue the strategy of avoidance by applying *Strader v. Graham* (1851); by that precedent Scott would have become a slave on his return to Missouri with no right to sue in the federal courts. This compromise was abandoned: in part because of pressure from President JAMES BUCHANAN and Congress; in part because northern Justices McLean and Curtis planned to confront the whole issue in dissent; in part because the proslave, pro-South wing of the Court (led by Taney and Wayne) wanted to silence the abolitionists by putting the Constitution itself behind slavery in the territories; in part because the Justices pridefully believed they could put the troublesome question to rest and save the Union.

Taney's was the majority opinion so far as one could be gleaned from the cacophony of separate opinions and dissents. It was totally prosouthern and brutally racist: Scott could not sue in the federal courts because he was not a citizen of the United States. He was not a citizen because national CITIZENSHIP followed state citizenship, and in 1787 the states had looked upon blacks as racially inferior (which the states in fact did) and unqualified for citizenship (which several states did not). Scott's argument that he was free by virtue of residence in a free state was wrong, said Taney, because of *Strader* (which had been relied upon by the Supreme Court of Missouri); Scott's argument that residence in a free territory made him free carried no weight because Congress had no authority to prohibit slavery in the territories—an assertion that ignored seventy years of constitutional practice and permitted Taney to set forth the SUBSTANTIVE DUE PROCESS theory of the Fifth Amendment against the TAKING OF PROPERTY. Scott was still a slave. Congress could not prohibit slavery in the territories, because the Constitution guaranteed it there; neither, as the creatures of Congress, could territorial legislatures prohibit slavery as claimed by proponents of the doctrine of POPULAR SOVEREIGNTY. Taney's Constitution was for whites only.

Instead of saving the Union the decision brought it closer to civil war and put the Court itself in jeopardy. In effect, the decision outlawed the basic principle of the Republican party (opposition to the extension of slavery in the territories), forcing that party to denounce the Court. The Democratic party, the best hope for political compromise, was now split between a southern wing (which in 1860 chose the certainty of *Dred Scott* over the vagueness of popular sovereignty) and northern antislavery forces who, if they did not defect to the Republicans, went down to defeat with STEPHEN DOUGLAS and popular sovereignty. Sectional hatred intensified and the machinery of political compromise was seriously undercut—along with the prestige of the Court. From its peak of popularity in 1850 the Taney Court descended to an all-time low. After SECESSION it served only the section of the Union that ignored *Dred Scott* entirely, condemned the Court as a tool of southern expansionism, and looked upon the Chief Justice as an arch-traitor to liberty and national union.

Fortunately, these disabilities were not permanent. Northern hatred focused less on the Court as an institution and more on the particular decision of *Dred Scott,* which was obliterated by the THIRTEENTH and FOURTEENTH AMENDMENTS. *Dred Scott* seemed less important, too, after President Lincoln "Republicanized" the Court with new appointments (five, including a new Chief Justice who had been an abolitionist). More important, the Court brought itself into harmony with the northern war effort by doing what the Supreme Court has always done in wartime: deferring to the political branches of government and bending law to military necessity. Sometimes the Court deferred by acting (as in the PRIZE CASES of 1863 where it permitted the President to exercise WAR POWERS and still not recognize the belligerent status of the Confederacy) and sometimes it deferred by not acting (as when it refused to interfere with the broad use of martial law during the war).

The Taney Court not only survived but it also salvaged its essential powers—and with time even a grudging respect from historians. The memory of *Dred Scott* could not be totally exorcised, of course, but it diminished along with the idealism of the war years and with the recognition that the racism of the opinion was shared by a majority of white Americans. In any case, the reform accomplishments of the Taney Court helped to balance the reactionary ones. Its modest style of judging fit the new democratic age. Through its decisions ran a new appreciation of the democratic nature and reform potential of state action and a tacit recognition as well of the growing maturity of legislative government. The Court's pragmatic federalism, while it could support the evil of slavery, also embodied a tradition of cultural pluralism, local responsibility, and suspicion of power. This it did without destroying the foundations of constitutional nationalism established by the Marshall Court. Change is the essence of American experience. The Taney Court accepted this irresistible premise and accommodated the Constitution to it. The adjustment was often untidy, but the Court's preference for process over substance looked to the modern age and prefigured the main direction of American constitutional law.

Bibliography

COVER, ROBERT M.   1975   *Justice Accused: Antislavery and the Judicial Process.* New Haven: Yale University Press.

FEHRENBACHER, DON E.   1978   *The Dred Scott Case: Its Significance in American Law and Politics.* New York: Oxford University Press.

FRANKFURTER, FELIX   1937   *The Commerce Clause under Marshall, Taney and Waite.* Chapel Hill: University of North Carolina Press.

HARRIS, ROBERT J.   1957   Chief Justice Taney: Prophet of Reform and Reaction. *Vanderbilt Law Review* 10:227–257.

KUTLER, STANLEY   1971   *Privilege and Creative Destruction: The Charles River Bridge Case.* Philadelphia: J. B. Lippincott.

SWISHER, CARL B.   1974   *The Taney Period, 1836–1864.* Volume V of *The Oliver Wendell Holmes Devise History of the Supreme Court of the United States.* New York: Macmillan.

WARREN, CHARLES   1926   *The Supreme Court in United States History,* Vol. 2. New and revised ed. Boston: Little, Brown.

CONSTITUTIONAL HISTORY, 1865–1877

Michael Les Benedict

The great political and constitutional issue of the period 1865–1877 was the Reconstruction of the Union after the Civil War. Reconstruction presented several closely related issues. There were issues involving the nature of the federal system. One of these arose even before the war ended: what was the constitutional relationship to the Union of the states that had attempted to secede? Another arose after the southern states were restored to normal relations: what powers did the national government retain to protect the rights of its citizens? There was the problem of defining the constitutional status of black Americans—a problem that finally forced Americans to define American CITIZENSHIP and the rights incident to it. Also, because the President and Congress disagreed on these issues, Reconstruction brought about a crisis in legislative–executive relations that culminated in the only impeachment of an American President. Finally, the Reconstruction controversy had a powerful effect upon Americans' conception of the proper role of government, laying the groundwork for the development of laissez-faire constitutionalism.

These issues would be adjusted in the context of the established party system. During the war, the Republican party worked diligently and fairly successfully to broaden its support. Renaming their organization the Union party, Republican leaders accepted as colleagues men who had been influential Democrats until the outbreak of war. In 1864 the party nominated Tennessee's Democratic former governor and senator, ANDREW JOHNSON, to the vice-presidency. Despite this, the Union party, which would revive the name Republican after the war, was the heir to the governmental activism of the old Federalist and Whig parties. Likewise Republicans inherited nationalist theories of the federal system. (See UNION, THEORIES OF THE.) The war confirmed and extended their distrust of STATES' RIGHTS doctrines; yet many Republicans would resist going too far in the direction of "consolidation" of the Union at the expense of traditional areas of state jurisdiction. On the other hand, the majority of Democrats had remained loyal to their party and its heritage of states' rights and small government. Naturally, the Reconstruction issue, which involved both questions, found the two parties ranged against one another.

Northerners faced a paradox when they considered the status of the Confederate states at war's end. They had denied that a state could leave the Union, but few wanted the same governments that had attempted secession to return as if nothing had happened. Only so-called Peace Democrats argued that the Union should be restored through negotiations between the Confederate state governments and the national government. Somehow, Republicans and War Democrats insisted, the national government must have power to secure some changes in the South and in the federal system before final restoration. As the war progressed, and especially in 1865 and 1866, when they were forced to grapple with the problem, Republicans propounded a variety of constitutional justifications for such power. Unlike Democrats, who insisted that state government had existed before the Union and independent of it, Republicans insisted that states could exist only in the Union and by virtue of their connection with it. Thus, by trying to secede, the southern states had committed STATE SUICIDE, in the graphic language of Senator CHARLES SUMNER; or, as other Republicans put it, they had "forfeited their rights." Given this view, there were several ways to justify national power over Southerners. Many Republicans argued that if Southerners now lacked state governments, Congress must restore them under the clause of the Constitution requiring the national government to guarantee a REPUBLICAN FORM OF GOVERNMENT to each state. Moreover, in the 1849 case of LUTHER v. BORDEN the Supreme Court, citing this clause, had seemed to concede to the "political branches" of the government the power to recognize whether a state government was legitimate in case of doubt. The Court had held that the admission of state representatives to Congress was conclusive. With state governments defunct, Republicans argued, the Court's holding meant that the political branches of the national government would have final say about what government would be recognized as restored to the Union and when that recognition would take place. Implicit in this power was the authority to determine what sort of government would be acceptable.

But when some Republicans insisted that the GUARANTEE CLAUSE entitled the national government to require changes it believed necessary for states to be considered republican, most of their colleagues rebelled. Such an interpretation would give the national government power to modify "unrepublican" political and civil laws in states that had never left the Union.

Other Republicans found a safer source of power over states that had forfeited their rights: the national government had recovered control over the territory and citizens of the South through exercise of its WAR POWERS, which had overridded the peacetime provision of the Constitution that guaranteed citizens' and states' rights. The government could continue to hold Southerners in this "grasp of war" until they agreed to meet the government's conditions for the restoration of peace. On this theory, national power would be temporary, providing no precedent for intruding in states that had not been in rebellion.

Finally, other Republicans—those who wanted the most radical changes in southern society—argued that, having broken away from national authority de facto, the southern states were conquered provinces no different from any other newly acquired territory. Thus Southerners were subject to the direct control of the national government, which ought to provide ordinary territorial governments through which they could govern themselves under the revisory power of Congress. In this way the national government would retain authority to legislate directly for the South until new states were created there—establishing a public school system, for example, or confiscating the great landed estates and distributing them among the people as small farms. But this theory also seemed too radical for most Northerners, and most Republicans endorsed the more limited "grasp-of-war" doctrine.

Congress was adjourned in April and May 1865, as Lincoln was assassinated and the war ended. Lincoln's successor, the former Democrat Johnson, accepted the key elements of the WADE-DAVIS BILL developed during the war, but he followed Lincoln's policy of carrying it out under presidential authority, rather than calling Congress back into session to enact Reconstruction legislation. Johnson called for white, male voters in each southern state to elect a state constitutional convention as soon as fifty percent of them had taken a loyalty oath that would entitle them to AMNESTY. Thus blacks would have to depend on governments elected by whites for protection of life and property. The conventions were required to pronounce their states' SECESSION ordinances null and void, repudiate debts incurred by their Confederate state governments, and abolish slavery. Finally, the southern states would have to ratify the proposed THIRTEENTH AMENDMENT, which abolished slavery throughout the land. Then the conventions could organize elections to ratify the new constitutions, elect state officials, and elect congressmen. By December 1865, as Congress reconvened, this process had been completed in most of the southern states and would soon be completed in the remainder.

At first Johnson was vague about his constitutional theory of Reconstruction, but as congressional opposition developed his supporters articulated a position that left little power to Congress. Secession had merely "suspended" the operation of legal governments in the South, they insisted. As COMMANDER-IN-CHIEF of the armed forces, the President had the duty under the government's war powers to reanimate state governments. War powers were inherently presidential, Johnson insisted. He had exercised them in such a way as to preserve the traditional federal system. Congress could do no more than exercise its constitutional power to "judge of the elections, returns and qualifications of its own members" by deciding whether individual congressmen-elect were disqualified by their roles in the war; it could not deny REPRESENTATION to whole states. Gaining the support of northern Democrats for this states'-rights-oriented policy, Johnson set the stage for a bitter struggle over the relative powers of the branches of the national government.

A majority of congressmen might have acquiesced in the President's position had they been confident that loyalists would control the southern state governments or that the rights of the newly freed slaves would be respected there. However, it soon became apparent that the states were controlled by former rebels and that the rights of the freedmen would be severely circumscribed. Compounding the problem, the ex-Confederate-dominated South would increase its congressional representation now that slavery was abolished; the constitutional provision counting only three-fifths of the slave population would no longer apply. All this persuaded congressional Republicans to refuse immediate admission of southern state representatives to Congress and to seek a compromise with the President.

There were two thrusts to the congressional policy: protection of freedmen's rights and a new system of apportionment of representation in Congress. Most congressional leaders believed that the Thirteenth Amendment automatically conferred citizenship upon the freedmen when it abolished slavery. Moreover, the amendment's second section authorized Congress to pass legislation appropriate to enforce abolition. Republicans acted upon this understanding by passing a new FREEDMEN'S BUREAU bill, augmenting one passed during the war, and proposing the bill that became the CIVIL RIGHTS ACT OF 1866. The first, a temporary measure justified under the war powers, authorized an Army bureau to supervise the transition from slave to free labor, protecting the rights and interests of the freedmen in the process. The second was designed to secure permanent protection for the freedmen in their basic rights. Few Republicans thought that Americans would accept so drastic a change in the federal system as to give Congress instead of the states the job of protecting people in their ordinary rights. Therefore they adopted the idea of leaving that job to the states but requiring them to treat all groups equally. At the same time, Republicans intended to require equality only in the protection of *basic* rights of citizenship. This goal forced them to define just what those rights were. So the Civil Rights Act declared all persons born in the United States, except Indians who did not pay taxes, to be citizens of the United States; it granted all citizens, regardless of race, the same basic rights as white citizens. What were these basic rights of citizenship? "To make and enforce contracts; to sue, be parties, and give evidence; to inherit, purchase, lease, sell, hold, and convey real and personal property; and to full and equal benefit of all laws and proceedings for the security of persons and property" and to "be subject to like punishment, pains, and penalties." To secure these rights without centralizing power of ordinary legislation in Washington, the bill permitted citizens to remove legal cases from state to federal court jurisdiction in any state that did not end discrimination. (See CIVIL RIGHTS REMOVAL.) The idea was to force states to abolish RACIAL DISCRIMINATION in their own laws in order to preserve their jurisdictions. As its author explained, the act would "have no operation in any State where the laws are equal, where all persons have the same civil rights without regard to color or race."

At the same time Republicans prepared a fourteenth amendment to define citizenship and its rights; to change the way seats in Congress were apportioned, so as to reflect the number of voters rather than gross population; to disqualify leading Confederates from holding political office; and to guarantee payment of the United States debt while repudiating the Confederate debt. Congress was to have power to enforce this amendment, too, by "appropriate" legislation.

Republicans expected Johnson to endorse these measures, which after all did not attempt to replace the governments he had instituted in the South, and they expected Southerners to signify their acceptance of these "terms of peace" by ratifying the new amendment. However, Johnson insisted that the Republican program would revolutionize the federal system. He vetoed the legislation and urged Southerners to reject the proposed amendment. At the same time he attacked the Republicans bitterly. Republicans responded by passing the Civil Rights Act over Johnson's veto, enacting the new Freedman's Bureau Act, and sending the FOURTEENTH AMENDMENT to the states for RATIFICATION. To the voters, they stressed the moderation of their proposals, and Johnson's supporters were badly beaten in the congressional elections of 1866. Nonetheless, Southerners followed Johnson's advice and refused to ratify the amendment.

This refusal angered and frightened Republican congressmen. If the conflict drifted into stalemate, northern voters might tire of it and blame the Republicans for not completing restoration. Outraged at southern recalcitrance and Johnson's "betrayal," the Republicans passed new Reconstruction laws over his veto early in 1867. Designating Johnson's southern governments as temporary only, the Republicans instructed Southerners to begin the process anew. This time many leading Confederates would be disfranchised while the freedmen were permitted to vote. New state conventions would have to be elected to write new constitutions banning racial discrimination in civil and political rights. The voters would have to ratify these constitutions, and then newly elected state officials would have to ratify the Fourteenth Amendment. In 1869 the Republican Congress proposed to the states the FIFTEENTH AMEND-

MENT, banning racial discrimination in voting; southern states that had not yet finished the process of being readmitted would be required to ratify this amendment, too. In some ways the new program was a relief to Republicans. They expected that once southern blacks could vote, their state governments would have to provide them with the protection of the laws, thus rendering unnecessary the exercise of national power and preserving the old balance of the federal system.

Until the southern states complied with the new Reconstruction laws, they were to be under the control of the Army, subject to martial law and, if necessary, military courts. Southerners insisted that this whole program was unconstitutional, and they tried to persuade the Supreme Court to declare it so. In 1867 and 1868 representatives of Johnson's state governments asked the Supreme Court to enjoin Johnson and his secretary of war, respectively, from enforcing the MILITARY RECONSTRUCTION ACTS. They hoped for success, because the majority of the Justices were suspected of opposing the Republican program. In earlier cases, including EX PARTE MILLIGAN (1866), a narrow majority had held that military courts could not operate upon civilians where civil courts were functioning, and in the TEST OATH CASES the Court had ruled unconstitutional laws requiring persons to swear oaths of past loyalty in order to follow certain professions. However, even Johnson would not sustain an effort to secure Court intervention in so plainly a political issue, and the Court dismissed both suits. (See MISSISSIPPI V. JOHNSON, 1867.)

Southerners tried again in EX PARTE McCARDLE (1869), where a Southerner convicted of murder in a military court asked for a write of HABEAS CORPUS, citing the Supreme Court's Milligan decision. At least some Reconstruction laws might be jeopardized if the Court endorsed this argument, and Republicans responded by repealing the law under which McCardle had brought his suit. The Court grudgingly acquiesced in the repeal but virtually invited a new application for the writ under another law.

These developments produced ambivalent feelings about the courts among Republicans. Before the war the judiciary had tended to sustain laws protecting slavery and discrimination against black Americans. During the war Chief Justice ROGER B. TANEY had seemed to obstruct the military effort, and the Court's course since the war had hardly been reassuring. Fearing judicial interference, several leading Republicans proposed narrowing the Court's jurisdiction and requiring a two-thirds majority of Justices to rule a congressional law unconstitutional, or denying that power altogether. On the other hand, the judiciary was the only national institution besides the military capable of enforcing the new laws protecting the rights of American citizens. Not only did Congress refrain from passing the court-limitation bills but it also expanded judicial authority by making the national judiciary the forum in which citizens and even businesses were to secure justice if their rights were denied in the states. Indeed, even as Republicans worried whether the Court would impair Reconstruction, in their roles as circuit court judges the Justices were upholding the power of the national government to protect rights under the Thirteenth and Fourteenth Amendments. Altogether, the Reconstruction era witnessed a great expansion of the jurisdiction and activity of the federal courts.

While the southern attack on the Reconstruction laws failed in the Supreme Court, Johnson was able to use against the laws the fact that they employed the military in their enforcement. As COMMANDER-IN-CHIEF of the armed forces, Johnson sought to limit the authority of military commanders and to give command of occupying forces to officers sympathetic to his position. When Secretary of War EDWIN M. STANTON resisted these efforts, Johnson suspended him from office and appointed the popular General ULYSSES S. GRANT in his place. By late 1867 Johnson's obstruction was so successful that Reconstruction was grinding to a halt, with white Southerners ready to prevent ratification of their new, egalitarian constitutions.

Many Republicans denied that the President had the constitutional right to obstruct legislation in this way, and they urged the House of Representatives to impeach him. However, most Republicans were frightened of taking so radical a step, and many insisted that IMPEACHMENT lay only for indictable crimes. Despite his obstructionism, Johnson had not clearly broken any law, and they would not support impeachment until he did. Therefore in December 1867 the first impeachment resolution failed.

However, in February 1868 Johnson did finally seem to break a law. As noted, Johnson had earlier suspended Secretary of War Stanton. He had done this while the Senate was adjourned, conforming to the TENURE OF OFFICE ACT, passed in 1867, which made all removals of government officers temporary until the Senate confirmed a successor, or, in certain circumstances, voted to accept the President's reasons for removal. In Stanton's case, the Senate in 1867 refused to concur in the removal, and Stanton returned to office. Now Johnson defied the Senate and the law, ordering Stanton's permanent removal. The House impeached him immediately, and from March through May the Senate established rules of procedure, heard arguments and testimony, and deliberated.

Although many questions were raised during Johnson's trial in the Senate, the decision finally turned for most senators on whether they believed Stanton was in reality covered by the Tenure of Office Act. Despite Johnson's initial compliance with the act, his lawyers persuaded just enough Republican senators that the act did not cover Stanton, and Johnson was acquitted. But the price for acquittal was Johnson's promise to end his obstruction of the Reconstruction laws. With that interference ended, most southern states adopted new state constitutions, and in nearly all those states Republicans took control of the governments.

The new southern constitutions and Republican governments were among the most progressive in the nation. Elected mainly by black voters, southern Republican leaders thought they could secure enough white support to guarantee continued victory by using government power to promote prosperity and provide services. Thus they emulated northern Republican policies, using state taxes and credit to subsidize railroads and canals, to develop natural resources, and to control flooding along the Mississippi River. They created the first centralized state public school systems and opened state hospitals and asylums. At the same time southern Republicans were committed to improving the conditions of former slaves, both on principle and to keep the support of their largest constituency. They passed laws to provide them with the same state services that whites received, put blacks in important positions, banned discrimination in many businesses, shaped labor laws to protect workers' interests, and appointed local judges who would be sympathetic to blacks in disputes with whites.

All these activities required the states to spend and borrow far more money than they had before the war. Because it was primarily whites who owned enough property to pay taxes, the Republican policies redistributed wealth, something not acceptable to nineteenth-century Americans. Bitterly, white Southerners charged that "ignorant," "brutal" voters were being duped by venal politicians with promises of "class legislation." Southern whites denied that such governments were really democratic. Unable to defeat Republicans at the polls in most states, they turned to violence and fraud. From 1868 through 1872, midnight riders, known by such names as the Ku Klux Klan, terrorized local Republican leaders. After 1872 the violence became more organized and more closely linked to anti-Republican political organizations.

A few southern Republican governors were at first able to suppress the violence. But by 1870 they were appealing to the national government for help, thus causing serious problems for national Republican leaders. Republicans had hoped that enfranchising the freedmen would protect them without a massive expansion of national power. Moreover, everyone believed that legislation must be based on the Fourteenth and Fifteenth Amendments, ignoring the earlier view that the Thirteenth Amendment gave power to protect citizens' basic rights. But the language of the two later amendments only protected rights against STATE ACTION, and Republicans had a difficult time justifying laws protecting blacks and white Republicans from attacks by private individuals. Nonetheless, in 1871 Republicans passed such laws and also authorized President Grant to take drastic action to crush violence, including suspension of the writ of habeas corpus. They insisted that the Fourteenth Amendment required states to protect their residents; failure to do so would amount to state denial of EQUAL PROTECTION.

At first this response seemed successful, and violence abated. However, it soon flared anew. In many southern states Republicans claimed that Democratic violence and intimidation should nullify apparent Democratic majorities in elections, and they refused to count Democratic votes from areas where violence was most intense. In return Democrats organized armed militia to press their claims. In state after state Republicans had to appeal for national troops to protect them against such opponents. Where it was difficult to afford protection, the Democratic militias—often called "White Leagues"—drove Republican officials from office.

It became ever more difficult for national Republicans to respond. More and more Northerners feared that continued national intervention in the South was undermining the federal system. At the same time the Supreme Court manifested its concern to preserve a balance between state and national authority. In *Texas v. White* (1869) the Justices emphasized the importance of states in the Union, and in *Collector v. Day* (1871) they seemed to endorse the doctrine of DUAL FEDERALISM, by denying the national government's power to tax the incomes of officers of the "sovereign" states. In the SLAUGHTERHOUSE CASES (1873) the Court, in an implicitly dual federalist opinion, ruled that national and state citizenships were distinct. The Fourteenth Amendment protected only a limited number of rights inherent in national citizenship; those rights usually identified as basic remained the sole province of the states. This decision severely curtailed national power to protect black Southerners and southern Republicans from violence. In UNITED STATES V. CRUIKSHANK (1876) the Court held invalid indictments against white conspirators who had massacred blacks, in part on the grounds that the Fourteenth Amendment was aimed only at state action and could not justify prosecution of private individuals.

At the same time a growing number of Northerners were coming to share Southerners' concern about "class legislation." To these Northerners, calls for a protective tariff, for artificial inflation of the currency, for repudiation of state-guaranteed railroad bonds, for regulation of railroad rates, and for government imposition of an eight-hour work day all indicated a growing clamor for "class legislation" in the North. City political organizations, which taxed urban property holders to provide services to the less wealthy, seemed to be engaging in the same kind of "plunder" that southern whites alleged against their Republican governments. Many Northerners began to argue that the state and national constitutions required judges to overturn class legislation. They had some initial successes. The Supreme Court ruled part of the Legal Tender Act unconstitutional, only to overrule itself a year later (see LEGAL TENDER CASES, 1870), and state courts ruled that business and railroad promotion laws exceeded legislative power. However, the courts generally declined the invitation to write the doctrine of "laissez faire" into the Constitution. The majority in the *Slaughterhouse Cases* rejected the argument, and the Court sustained broad state regulatory power over businesses AFFECTED WITH A PUBLIC INTEREST—railroads, grain warehouses, and others that were left undefined. (See GRANGER CASES, 1877.)

Nonetheless, the conviction was growing that the sort of wealth-redistributing policies followed by southern Republicans was fundamentally wrong and so was fear that such ideas might spread north. More and more Northerners agreed with southern whites that southern proponents of such policies were "carpetbaggers" and "scalawags." By 1875 President Grant was refusing to help his beleaguered political allies; all but three southern states had returned to Democratic control, often through force and intimidation; and white Southerners were planning similarly violent campaigns to "redeem" the last three in 1876. Their effort to do so led to one of the greatest political and constitutional crises in American history.

In the presidential election of 1876 the violence and fraud endemic in the South threatened to engulf the nation. In the three remaining Republican states in the South—South Carolina, Louisiana, and Florida—Democrats engaged in campaigns of violence and intimidation. Republican officials threw out votes from districts they claimed Democrats had carried by force. Democrats once again charged fraud and armed to confront Republicans; southern Republicans once again appealed to the national government for protection. However, this time the outcome of the presidential election itself turned upon who had carried these three states. Without them, Democrat Samuel J. Tilden was one electoral vote short of victory. Republican RUTHERFORD B. HAYES needed the electoral votes of all three to win.

As the time drew near to count the electoral vote and declare a winner, two sets of electoral votes were sent to Congress from each of the contested states—the Republican votes certified by appropriate state agencies, and Democratic competitors. The Constitution requires electoral votes to be counted by the president of the Senate (normally the vice-president of the United States) in the presence of both houses of Congress. Republicans insisted that, absent a specific congressional resolution governing the subject, the Republican president pro tempore of the Senate would have the power to decide which set of votes were the correct ones to count (the vice-president having died in office). Controlling the Senate, Republicans prepared to block any contrary resolution that might come from the Democratic House. Democrats, on the other hand, insisted that if the two houses of Congress could not agree upon which set of votes was legitimate, neither could be counted. Then no candidate would have a majority, and according to the Constitution the House would name the winner.

With no clear precedent, and with the Supreme Court not yet accepted as the usual arbiter of such constitutional disputes, it seemed that the conflict might be resolved by force. Republican President Grant controlled the Army; if he recognized a President counted in by the Republicans, a competitor named by the House would have a hard time pressing his claim. To counter this Republican program, Democrats threatened forcible resistance.

As Americans demanded a peaceful end to the crisis, the two sides were forced to compromise. Congress passed a resolution turning all disputed electoral votes over to an Electoral Commission of ten congressmen and five Supreme Court Justices for decision. The commission decision would stand in each case unless *both* houses voted to disagree to it—an early example of a LEGISLATIVE VETO.

To the Democrats' dismay, the three Republican Supreme Court Justices joined the five Republican congressmen on the commission to decide every disputed vote in favor of the Republican candidate. In each case the majority accepted the votes certified by the agency authorized by state law. Republicans insisted the commission had no power "to go behind" these returns.

Furious, Democrats charged that this was a partisan decision. Many of them urged Democratic congressmen to prevent the completion of the count by filibustering, saying that the House could name the President if the count were not completed by the constitutional deadline of March 3. But most Democrats felt that Americans would not support such a radical course after Democrats had agreed to the compromise. To strengthen these moderates, Hayes promised not to help southern Republicans against rival claimants for state offices. As a result Hayes was declared President just within the deadline. When he honored his commitment to the Democrats, the last southern Republican governments collapsed, even though the Republicans had claimed state victories based on the same election returns that elected Hayes. (See COMPROMISE OF 1877.)

The collapse of Reconstruction was related directly to the development of constitutional commitments that would dominate the last quarter of the nineteenth century. It marked a renewal of a state-centered federalism that would characterize succeeding years. Furthermore, it was a direct result of the growing fear of "class legislation" that would lead to the acceptance of "laissez-faire constitutionalism" in the 1890s.

Bibliography

BENEDICT, MICHAEL LES   1975   *A Compromise of Principle: Congressional Republicans and Reconstruction, 1863–1869.* New York: W. W. Norton.

FAIRMAN, CHARLES   1971   *Reconstruction and Reunion, 1864–88—Part One,* Volume 6 of *The History of the Supreme Court of the United States.* New York: Macmillan.

GILLETTE, WILLIAM   1979   *Retreat from Reconstruction, 1869–1879.* Baton Rouge: Louisiana State University Press.

HYMAN, HAROLD M.   1973   *A More Perfect Union: The Impact of the Civil War and Reconstruction upon the Constitution.* New York: Knopf.

McKITRICK, ERIC L.   1960   *Andrew Johnson and Reconstruction.* Chicago: University of Chicago Press.

STAMPP, KENNETH M.   1965   *The Era of Reconstruction, 1865–1877.* New York: Knopf.

CHASE COURT
(1864–1873)

William M. Wiecek

The decade of SALMON P. CHASE's tenure as Chief Justice of the United States was one of the more turbulent in the history of the Supreme Court. Laboring under the cloud of hostility engendered by DRED SCOTT V. SANDFORD (1857), hurt by partisan attacks from without and divisions within, staggering under loads of new business, the Chase Court nevertheless managed to absorb and consolidate sweeping new jurisdictional grants to the federal courts and to render some momentous decisions.

The Chase Court displayed an unusual continuity of personnel, which was offset by political and ideological heterogeneity. Of the nine men Chase joined on his accession (the Court in 1864 was composed of ten members), seven served throughout all or nearly all his brief tenure. But this largely continuous body was divided within itself by party and ideological differences. JOHN CATRON, who died in 1865, JAMES M. WAYNE, who died in 1867, and ROBERT C. GRIER, who suffered a deterioration in his faculties that caused his brethren to force him to resign in 1870, were Democrats. NATHAN CLIFFORD, an appointee of President JAMES BUCHANAN, and STEPHEN J. FIELD were also Democrats, the latter a War Democrat. SAMUEL F. MILLER, DAVID DAVIS, and JOSEPH P. BRADLEY were Republicans. Chase himself was an ex-Democrat who had helped form the Republican party in 1854, but he drifted back to the Democratic party after the war and coveted its presidential nomination. WILLIAM STRONG, Grier's replacement, and NOAH SWAYNE were also Democrats who turned Republican before the war. Like the Chief Justice, Davis never successfully shook off political ambitions; he accepted and then rejected the Labor Reform party's nomination for the presidency in 1872. From 1870, Republicans dominated the Court, which had long been controlled by Democrats.

The work of the Supreme Court changed greatly during Chase's tenure. In 1862 and 1866, Congress realigned the federal circuits, so as to reduce the influence of the southern states, which under the Judiciary Act of 1837 had five of the nine circuits. Under the Judiciary Act of 1866, the southern circuits were reduced to two. By the same statute, Congress reduced the size of the Court from ten to seven members, mainly to enhance the efficiency of its work, not to punish the Court or deprive President ANDREW JOHNSON of appointments to it. In 1869, Congress again raised the size of the Court to nine, where it has remained ever since. More significantly, the business of the Court expanded. By 1871, the number of cases docketed had doubled in comparison to the war years. This increase resulted in some measure from an extraordinary string of statutes enacted between 1863 and 1867 expanding the JURISDICTION OF THE FEDERAL COURTS in such matters as REMOVAL OF CASES from state to federal courts, HABEAS CORPUS, claims against the United States, and BANKRUPTCY.

The Chase Court was not a mere passive, inert repository of augmented jurisdiction: it expanded its powers of JUDICIAL REVIEW to an extent unknown to earlier Courts. During Chase's brief tenure, the Court held eight federal statutes unconstitutional (as compared with only two in its entire prior history), and struck down state statutes in thirty-six cases (as compared with thirty-eight in its prior history). The attitude that produced this JUDICIAL ACTIVISM was expressed in private correspondence by Justice Davis, when he noted with satisfaction that the Court in EX PARTE MILLIGAN (1866) had not "toadied to the prevalent idea, that the legislative department of the government can override everything." This judicial activism not only presaged the Court's involvement in policy during the coming heyday of SUBSTANTIVE DUE PROCESS; it also plunged the Chase Court into some of the most hotly contested matters of its own time, especially those connected with Reconstruction. The Court also attracted the public eye because of the activities of two of its members: Chase's and Davis's availability as presidential candidates, and Chase's firm, impartial service in presiding over the United States Senate as a court of IMPEACHMENT in the trial of Andrew Johnson.

The Chase Court is memorable for its decisions in four areas: Reconstruction, federal power (in matters not directly related to Reconstruction), state regulatory and tax power, and the impact of the FOURTEENTH AMENDMENT.

Nearly all the cases in which the Supreme Court disposed of Reconstruction issues were decided during Chase's tenure. The first issue to come up was the role of military commissions. In EX PARTE VALLANDIGHAM, decided in February 1864 (ten months before Chase's nomination), the Court refused to review the proceedings of a military commission, because the commission is not a court. But that did not settle the issue of the constitutional authority of military commissions. The matter came up again, at an inopportune time, in *Ex parte Milligan,* decided in December 1866. Milligan had been arrested, tried, convicted, and sentenced to be hanged by a military commission in Indiana in 1864 for paramilitary activities on behalf of the Confederacy. The Court unanimously ruled that his conviction was illegal because Indiana was not in a theater of war, because the civil courts were functioning and competent to try

Milligan for TREASON, and because he was held in violation of the provisions of the HABEAS CORPUS ACT OF 1863. But the Court split, 5–4, over an OBITER DICTUM in Justice Davis's MAJORITY OPINION stating that the Congress could never authorize military commissions in areas outside the theater of operations where the civil courts were functioning. The Chief Justice, writing for the minority, declared that Congress did have the power to authorize commissions, based on the several WAR POWERS clauses of Article I, section 8, but that it had not done so; hence Milligan's trial was unauthorized.

Milligan created a furor in Congress and deeply implicated the Court in the politics of Reconstruction. Assuming that military commissions were essential to the conduct of Reconstruction, Democrats taunted Republicans that *Milligan* implied that they were unconstitutional, and hence that proposed Republican measures providing for military trials in the CIVIL RIGHTS ACT OF 1866 and FREEDMEN'S BUREAU Act violated the Constitution. Taken together with subsequent decisions, *Milligan* caused Republicans some anxiety. But, as Justice Davis noted in private correspondence and as Illinois Republican LYMAN TRUMBULL stated on the floor of the Senate, the decision in reality had no application to the constitutional anomaly of Reconstruction in the South.

The Court next seemed to challenge congressional Reconstruction in the TEST OATH CASES, *Ex parte Garland* and *Cummings v. Missouri*, both 1867. The court, by 5–4 decisions, voided federal and state statutes requiring a candidate for public office or one of the professions to swear that he had never participated or assisted in the rebellion. The Court's holding, that they constituted BILLS OF ATTAINDER and EX POST FACTO LAWS, seemingly threatened programs of disfranchisement and oath qualification, another part of proposed Reconstruction measures. Then, in February 1868, the Court announced that it would hear arguments in EX PARTE MCCARDLE, another challenge to military commissions. William McCardle had been convicted by a military commission for publishing inflammatory articles. A federal circuit court denied his petition for a writ of habeas corpus under the HABEAS CORPUS ACT OF 1867, a measure that had broadened the scope of the writ, and he appealed the denial to the Supreme Court. Alarmed, congressional Republicans enacted a narrowly drawn statute known as the McCardle repealer, denying the Supreme Court appellate jurisdiction in habeas petitions brought under the 1867 act. In 1869, the Court accepted the constitutionality of the repealer, because Article III, section 2, made the Court's APPELLATE JURISDICTION subject to "such Exceptions . . . as the Congress shall make." But Chief Justice Chase pointedly reminded the bar that all the rest of the Court's habeas appellate authority was left intact. This broad hint bore fruit in *Ex parte Yerger* (1869), where the Court accepted jurisdiction of a habeas appeal under the JUDICIARY ACT OF 1789. Chief Justice

Chase chastised Congress for the McCardle repealer and reaffirmed the scope of the Great Writ.

In the meantime, the Court had turned to other Reconstruction issues. As soon as Congress enacted the MILITARY RECONSTRUCTION ACTS of 1867, southern attorneys sought to enjoin federal officials, including the President and the secretary of war, from enforcing them. In MISSISSIPPI V. JOHNSON (1867), the Court unanimously rejected this petition. Chief Justice Chase drew on a distinction, originally suggested by his predecessor Chief Justice JOHN MARSHALL in MARBURY V. MADISON (1803), between ministerial and discretionary responsibilities of the President, stating that the latter were not subject to the Court's injunctive powers. In *Georgia v. Stanton* (1867), the Court similarly dismissed a petition directed at the secretary of war and General ULYSSES S. GRANT, holding that the petition presented POLITICAL QUESTIONS resolvable only by the political branches of the government. But the words of Justice Nelson's opinion seemed to suggest that if the petition had alleged a threat to private property (rather than the state's property), there might be a basis for providing relief. In May 1867, Mississippi's attorneys moved to amend their petition to specify such a threat. The Court, in a 4–4 order (Justice Grier being absent), rejected the motion. This minor, unnoticed proceeding was probably the truest index to the attitudes of individual Justices on the substantive policy questions of Reconstruction.

The Court's final involvement with Reconstruction came with TEXAS v. WHITE (1869) and *White v. Hart* (1872). In the former case, decided on the same day that the Supreme Court acknowledged the validity of the McCardle repealer, the postwar government of Texas sought to recover some bonds that the Confederate state government had sold to defray military costs. Because a state was a party, this was an action within the ORIGINAL JURISDICTION of the Supreme Court. But one of the defendants challenged the jurisdictional basis of the action, claiming that Texas was not a state in the constitutional sense at the time the action was brought (February 1867). This challenge directly raised important questions about the validity of SECESSION and Reconstruction. Chief Justice Chase, writing for the six-man majority (Grier, Swayne, Miller, dissenting) met the issue head on. He first held that secession had been a nullity. The Union was "indissoluble," "an indestructible Union, composed of indestructible States" in Chase's resonant, memorable phrasing. But, he went on, though the relations of individual Texans to the United States could not be severed, secession had deranged the status of the state within the Union. In language suggestive of the "forfeited-rights" theory of Reconstruction propounded by Ohio congressman Samuel Shellabarger which had provided a conceptual basis for Republican Reconstruction, Chase stated that the rights of the state had been "suspended" by secession and war. Congress was responsible for restoring the proper relationship, in wartime because of its authority under the military and MILITIA CLAUSES of Article I, section 8, and in peacetime under the guarantee of a REPUBLICAN FORM OF GOVERNMENT in Article IV, section 4. This was preponderantly a question to be resolved by Congress rather than the President, and hence the Lincoln and Johnson governments in power before enactment of the Military Reconstruction Acts were "provisional." Congress enjoyed wide latitude in working out details of Reconstruction policy. The sweeping language of Chase's opinion strongly implied the constitutionality of military Reconstruction. The majority opinion also offered a useful distinction between legitimate acts of the Confederate government of Texas, such as those designed to preserve the peace, and invalid ones in support of the rebellion.

In *White v. Hart* (1872) the Court reaffirmed its general position in *Texas v. White* and emphasized that the relationship of states in the union was a political question for the political branches to resolve. At the same time, the Court disposed of two lingering issues from the war in ways that reaffirmed the doctrine of *Texas v. White*. In *Virginia v. West Virginia* (1870) it accepted the creation of the daughter state, shutting its eyes to the obvious irregularities surrounding the Pierpont government's consent to the separation, and insisting that there had been a "valid agreement between the two States." And in *Miller v. United States* (1871), echoing THE PRIZE CASES (1863), a six-man majority upheld the constitutionality of the confiscation provisions of the Second Confiscation Act of 1862 on the basis of the Union's status as a belligerent.

The Chase Court decisions dealing with secession, war, and Reconstruction have stood well the test of time. *Milligan* and the *Test Oath Cases* remain valuable defenses of individual liberty against arbitrary government. The *McCardle* decision was a realistic and valid recognition of an explicit congressional power, while its sequel, *Yerger,* reaffirmed the libertarian implications of *Milligan*. The Court's position in the cases seeking to enjoin executive officials from enforcing Reconstruction was inevitable: it would have been hopeless for the Court to attempt to thwart congressional Reconstruction, or to accede to the Johnson/Democratic demand for immediate readmission of the seceded states. *Texas v. White* and *White v. Hart* drew on a sound prewar precedent, LUTHER v. BORDEN (1849), to validate actions by the dominant political branch in what was clearly a pure political question. Taken together, the Reconstruction cases evince a high order of judicial statesmanship.

The Chase Court made only tentative beginnings in issues of federal and state regulatory power, but those beginnings were significant. The first federal regulatory question to come up involved the currency. In VEAZIE BANK V. FENNO (1869) the Court sustained the constitutionality of sections of the Internal Revenue Acts of 1865 and 1866 that imposed a ten percent tax on state bank notes for the purpose of driving them out of circulation. Chase first held that the tax was not a DIRECT TAX (which would have had to be apportioned among the states) and then upheld Congress's power to issue paper money and create a uniform national currency by eliminating state paper.

The LEGAL TENDER CASES were more controversial. As secretary of the treasury, Chase had reluctantly acquiesced in the issuance of federal paper money. But when the issue came before the Court in the First Legal Tender Case (*Hepburn v. Griswold,* 1870), Chase, speaking for a 4–3 majority, held the Legal Tender Act of 1862 unconstitutional because it made greenbacks legal tender for preexisting debts. The division on the court was partisan: all the majority Justices were Democrats (Chase by this time had reverted to his Democratic antecedents), all the dissenters Republicans. Chase's reasoning was precipitate and unsatisfactory. He asserted that the act violated the OBLIGATION OF CONTRACTS, but the CONTRACT CLAUSE limited only the states. To this Chase responded that the act was contrary to the "spirit of the Constitution." He also broadly implied that the statute violated the Fifth Amendment's guarantee of DUE PROCESS.

An enlarged Court in 1871 reversed *Hepburn,* upholding the constitutionality of the 1862 statute in the Second Legal Tender Cases, with the two new appointees, Bradley and Strong, joining the three dissenters of the first case. Justice Strong for the majority averred that "every contract for the payment of money, simply, is necessarily subject to the constitutional power of the government over the currency." The Court's turnabout suggested to contemporaries that President Grant had packed the Court to obtain a reversal of the first decision. Grant was opposed to the decision, and he knew that Bradley and Strong were also opposed; but he did not secure from them any commitments on the subject, and he did not base his appointments solely on the single issue of legal tender.

Other Chase Court decisions involving federal power were not so controversial. In *United States v. Dewitt* (1870) Chase for the Court invalidated an exercise of what would come to be called the NATIONAL POLICE POWER, in this case a provision in a revenue statute prohibiting the mixing of illuminating oil with naphtha (a highly flammable mixture). Chase held that the COMMERCE CLAUSE conferred no federal power over the internal affairs of the states, and that the subject matter was remote from the topic of raising revenue. He simply assumed that there was no inherent national police power. In COLLECTOR V. DAY (1871) Justice Nelson for a divided Court held that federal revenue acts taxing income could not reach the salary of a state judge. Justice Bradley's dissent, maintaining the necessity of federal power to reach sources of income that included some functions of state government, was vindicated in GRAVES V. NEW YORK EX REL. O'KEEFE (1939), which overruled *Day.* In contrast to the foregoing cases, *The Daniel Ball* (1871) upheld the power of Congress to regulate commerce on navigable waterways, even where these were wholly intrastate.

The Chase Court decisions passing on the regulatory and taxing authority of the states caused less controversy. These cases are significant principally as evidence that the Court continued unabated its prewar responsibility of monitoring the functioning of the federal system, inhibiting incursions by the states on national authority and the national market, while at the same time preserving their scope of regulation and their sources of revenue intact. The first case of this sort, GELPCKE v. DUBUQUE (1864), involved a suit on bonds, issued by a city to encourage railroad building, which the city was trying to repudiate. The state courts had reversed their prior decisions and held that citizens could not be taxed to assist a private enterprise such as a railroad. The Supreme Court, in an opinion by Justice Swayne, reversed the result below, thus upholding the validity of the bonds. Swayne intemperately declared that "We shall never immolate truth, justice, and the law, because a state tribunal has erected the altar and decreed the sacrifice." The decision was welcomed in financial circles, particularly European ones, and presaged a Court attitude sympathetic to investors and hostile to repudiation, especially by a public agency.

The Court displayed less passion in other cases. In *Crandall v. Nevada* (1868), it struck down a state CAPITATION tax on passengers of public conveyances leaving the state as an unconstitutional interference with the right of persons to move about the country. The commerce clause aspects of the case were left to be decided later. Another case involving personal liberty, *Tarble's Case* (1872), vindicated the Court's earlier position in ABLEMAN v. BOOTH (1859) by holding that a state court in a habeas corpus proceeding could not release an individual held in federal custody (here, an allegedly deserting army volunteer).

But most cases testing the scope of state regulatory power dealt with commerce. In PAUL v. VIRGINIA (1869) the Court, through Chase, held that the negotiation of insurance contracts did not constitute commerce within the meaning of the commerce clause, and hence that a state was free to regulate the conduct of insurance companies as it pleased. This doctrine lasted until 1944. But one aspect of Justice Field's concurring opinion in *Paul* had momentous consequences. He asserted that, for purposes of the PRIVILEGES AND IMMUNITIES clause of Article IV, CORPORATIONS could not be considered "citizens," and were thus not entitled to the privileges and immunities of natural PERSONS. This caused attorneys to look to other sources, such as the due process clause (with its term "person") as a source of protection for corporations. During the same term, in WOODRUFF v. PARHAM (1868), the Chase Court upheld a municipal sales tax applied to goods brought into the state in INTERSTATE

COMMERCE even though they were still in their original package, thus limiting Marshall's ORIGINAL- PACKAGE DOCTRINE announced in BROWN v. MARYLAND (1827) to imports from other nations.

Three 1873 cases demonstrated the Court carefully adjusting the federal balance. In the State Freight Tax Case the Court struck down a state tax on freight carried out of the state. But in the *Case of the State Tax on Railway Gross Receipts* the Court upheld a state tax on a corporation's gross receipts, even when the taxpayer was a carrier and the tax fell on interstate business. And in the *Case of the State Tax on Foreign-Held Bonds* the Court struck down a tax on interest on bonds as applied to the securities of out-of-state bondholders.

The last category of major Chase Court cases dealt with the scope of the Reconstruction Amendments, and the extent to which they would alter the prewar balances of the federal system. One of Chase's circuit court decisions, *In re Turner* (1867), suggested that this potential might be broad. Chase there held a Maryland BLACK CODE's apprenticeship provision unconstitutional on the ground that it imposed a condition of involuntary servitude in violation of the THIRTEENTH AMENDMENT. This decision might have been the prelude to extensive federal involvement in matters that before the war would have been considered exclusively within the STATE POLICE POWER. But this possibility was drastically narrowed in the SLAUGHTERHOUSE CASES (1873), the last major decision of the Chase Court and one of the enduring monuments of American constitutional law. Justice Miller for the majority held that "the one pervading purpose" of the Reconstruction Amendments was the liberation of black people, not an extension of the privileges and rights of whites. Miller construed the privileges and immunities, due process, and EQUAL PROTECTION clauses of the Fourteenth Amendment in light of this assumption, holding that none of them had deranged the traditional balance of the federal system. The states still remained the source of most substantive privileges and immunities, and the states remained primarily responsible for securing them to individuals. This ruling effectively relegated the definition and protection of freedmen's rights to precisely those governments—Redeemer-dominated southern states—least likely to provide that protection. Because "we do not see in those [Reconstruction] amendments any purpose to destroy the main features of the general system," Miller rejected a substantive interpretation of the new due process clause and restricted the equal protection clause to cases of "discrimination against the negroes as a class."

The future belonged to the *Slaughterhouse* dissenters, Justices Bradley and Field. Bradley articulated the doctrine of substantive due process, arguing that the right to pursue a lawful occupation is a property right which the state may not interfere with arbitrarily or selectively. Field, in a dissent in which Chase joined (Swayne dissented in a separate opinion) relied on the privileges and immunities clause of the Fourteenth Amendment, seeing in it a guarantee of "the fundamental rights" of free men, which cannot be destroyed by state legislation. His insistence on an "equality of right, with exemption from all disparaging and partial enactments, in the lawful pursuits of life" foreshadowed the doctrine of FREEDOM OF CONTRACT.

Yet Field's and Bradley's insistence on the right to follow a chosen occupation, free of arbitrary discrimination, did not avail Myra Bradwell in her effort to secure admission to the Illinois bar (BRADWELL v. ILLINOIS, 1873). Justice Miller for the majority (Chase being the lone dissenter) refused to overturn a decision of the Illinois Supreme Court denying her admission to the bar solely on the ground of her gender. "The paramount mission and destiny of woman are to fulfill the noble and benign offices of wife and mother. This is the law of the Creator," Bradley wrote in a concurrence. "And the rules of civil society . . . cannot be based upon exceptional cases." The emergent scope of the due process, equal protection, and privileges and immunities clauses were to have a differential application as a result of the *Slaughterhouse* dissents and *Bradwell* ruling, securing the rights of corporations and men in their economic roles, while proving ineffectual to protect others from discrimination based on race and gender. (See RACIAL DISCRIMINATION; SEX EQUALITY.)

During its brief span, the Chase Court made enduring contributions to American constitutional development. It handled the unprecedented issues of Reconstruction with balance and a due recognition of the anomalous nature of issues coming before it. Yet in those decisions, Chase and his colleagues managed to preserve protection for individual rights while at the same time permitting the victorious section, majority, and party to assure a constitutional resolution of the war consonant with its military results. In non-Reconstruction cases, the Chase court continued the traditional function of the Supreme Court in monitoring and adjusting the allocation of powers between nation and states. It was more activist than its predecessors in striking down federal legislation, while it displayed the same nicely balanced concern for state regulatory power and protection of the national market that was a characteristic of the TANEY COURT.

Bibliography

FAIRMAN, CHARLES 1939 *Mr. Justice Miller and the Supreme Court, 1862–1890.* Cambridge, Mass.: Harvard University Press.
———— 1971 *Reconstruction and Reunion, 1864–88, Part One* (vol. VI of the Oliver Wendell Holmes Devise *History of the Supreme Court of the United States*). New York: Macmillan.

HYMAN, HAROLD M. and WIECEK, WILLIAM M.   1982 *Equal Justice Under Law: Constitutional Development 1835–1875.* New York: Harper & Row.

KUTLER, STANLEY I.   1968   *Judicial Power and Reconstruction Politics.* Chicago: University of Chicago Press.

SILVER, DAVID M.   1957   *Lincoln's Supreme Court.* Urbana: University of Illinois Press.

SWISHER, CARL B.   1930   *Stephen J. Field: Craftsman of the Law.* Washington, D.C.: Brookings Institution.

WARREN, CHARLES   1937   *The Supreme Court in United States History,* rev. ed. Boston: Little, Brown.

CONSTITUTIONAL HISTORY, 1877–1901

Morton Keller

American public life during the Civil War-Reconstruction years was dominated by clashes over constitutional issues of the most basic sort: race and CITIZENSHIP; FEDERALISM, STATES' RIGHTS, and the Union; the power of the President, Congress, and the courts; and the bounds of military and civil authority. This was a time when the interpretation of the Constitution held center stage in American public life. The resolution of fundamental issues was sought in Congress and the courts, in party politics and elections, ultimately through force of arms. Merely to list the milestones of the period—the great debate over SLAVERY IN THE TERRITORIES; DRED SCOTT V. SANDFORD (1857); SECESSION and CIVIL WAR; the THIRTEENTH, FOURTEENTH, and FIFTEENTH AMENDMENTS; the CIVIL RIGHTS, Reconstruction, and Enforcement Acts; and the IMPEACHMENT OF ANDREW JOHNSON—is to make the point that during the years from 1850 to 1877 the Constitution provided the context in which Americans expressed, and fought over, their most fundamental social beliefs.

How different was the period that followed! The structure of government—the relationship of the states and territories to the Union; the powers of Congress, the courts, and the President; the role of the POLITICAL PARTIES—often was a matter of political but rarely of constitutional concern. Nor were the major economic and social issues of the time confronted primarily in constitutional terms. It is revealing that no amendment to the Constitution was adopted between 1870 and 1913.

This does not mean, though, that constitutional issues had no place in American public policy between 1877 and 1900. Rather, what happened was that a sea change was taking place in American life, and the issues generated by this change took time to assume a full-fledged constitutional guise. Just as the basic constitutional issues of states' rights and slavery did not fully emerge until the 1850s, so too the constitutional issues generated by the rise of an urban-industrial society did not come into their own until after 1900, in many respects not until the 1930s.

Where should we look, in the late nineteenth century, for the seeds of the great twentieth-century effort to adapt the Constitution to the realities of an urban-industrial society? The primary structural concern

of the time was over the role of the judiciary, and here was a foreshadow-
ing of the conflict between the administrative state and the representative
state that would assume such great importance after 1900. Second, economic issues—in particular, those involving the regulation of large enterprises—were a fruitful area of contention in the late nineteenth century.
And finally, questions of citizenship and race—partly a legacy of the
Civil War-Reconstruction years but also a product of the social strains
generated by an industrializing society—continued to engage the attention of the public and of policymakers.

Frank Goodnow in his *Comparative Administrative Law* (1893) observed that while constitutional issues set the terms of debate over the
character of American government before the Civil War, administrative
issues took center stage afterward. Certainly it seemed that, as much
as anything could, the war had settled the question of the relationship
of the states to the Union. Nor did the desuetude of the post-Reconstruc-
tion Presidency, the dominance of Congress, or the still-nascent administrative state generate much in the way of constitutional debate.

Late nineteenth-century Presidents were caught up in party politics
and patronage and did relatively little to formulate and conduct public
policy. But America's evolution into a powerful industrial nation began
to leave its mark. RUTHERFORD B. HAYES and GROVER CLEVELAND used
federal troops to restore order during the railroad strikes of 1877 and
1894. The federal bureaucracy, though small, was growing; and something like a professional civil service took form, in part under the aegis
of the Civil Service Commission established by the PENDLETON ACT of
1883. Tariff and fiscal policy came to be more closely identified with
presidential leadership. But in constitutional terms the chief executive
at the end of the century was little changed from what he had been in
1877.

Congress, however, became a considerably more powerful and effective branch of government during this period. WOODROW WILSON in
1885 called "Congressional Government" the "predominant and controlling force, the centre and source of all motive and of all regulative
power." This enhanced authority came from the fact that state and
local party leaders served as senators and representatives; from congressional control over budgetary and fiscal policy; and from the increasing
regularity and stability of congressional leadership and procedure.

Perhaps the most striking change in the balance of governmental
powers during the late nineteenth century was the rise of JUDICIAL ACTIV-
ISM. The Supreme Court found only two federal laws unconstitutional
between 1790 and 1864, but it voided federal acts in seven cases between
1868 and 1877 and in eleven cases between 1878 and 1899. The Court
voided state acts in thirty-eight cases before 1865, in thirty-five cases

between 1865 and 1873, and in ninety-one cases between 1874 and 1899. A debate as old as the Constitution heated up once again in the 1890s: what were the proper limits of JUDICIAL REVIEW?

The belief was then widespread—and has been gospel since—that the late nineteenth-century courts declared open season on laws threatening corporate interests. The *American Law Review* observed in 1894 that "it has come to be the fashion . . . for courts to overturn acts of the State legislatures upon mere economical theories and upon mere casuistical grounds." Federal and state courts found in the DUE PROCESS and EQUAL PROTECTION clauses of the Fourteenth Amendment and in the doctrine of FREEDOM OF CONTRACT grounds for voiding laws that regulated working conditions or taxed CORPORATIONS. This judicial conservatism culminated in an unholy trinity of Supreme Court decisions in the mid-1890s: IN RE DEBS (1895), which sustained a federal INJUNCTION against striking railroad workers; UNITED STATES v. E. C. KNIGHT COMPANY (1895), which severely limited the scope of the SHERMAN ANTITRUST ACT; and POLLOCK v. FARMERS' LOAN AND TRUST (1895), which struck down the 1894 federal income tax law. Arnold Paul has called these decisions "related aspects of a massive judicial entry into the socioeconomic scene, . . . a conservative oriented revolution."

But the extent of the courts' antilabor and antiregulatory decision making has been exaggerated; and its purpose has been distorted. A review in 1897 of 1,639 state labor laws enacted during the previous twenty years found that 114 of them—only seven percent—were held unconstitutional. The STATE POLICE POWER to regulate working conditions was widely accepted legal doctrine: in ninety-three percent of 243 Fourteenth Amendment challenges before 1901 the Supreme Court upheld the state laws. By the late 1890s the influential New York and Massachusetts courts looked favorably on laws affecting the conditions of labor, as did the Supreme Court in HOLDEN v. HARDY (1898).

Nor did judicial policy rest only on a tender concern for the rights of property. The desire to foster a national economy was evident in many federal court decisions. And many Justices shared the widespread public sense that American society was being wrenched beyond recognition by industrialism and its consequences. Justice STEPHEN J. FIELD and jurist THOMAS M. COOLEY were as ill at ease with large corporate power as they were with legislative activism. The influential judge and treatise writer JOHN F. DILLON, who called all attempts "to pillage and destroy" private property "as baneful as they are illegal," insisted "with equal earnestness upon the proposition that such property is under many important duties toward the State and society, which the owners generally fail to appreciate."

By far the most important applications of the Constitution to issues of public policy during the late nineteenth century involved large corporate enterprise, that increasingly conspicuous and troubling presence on the American scene. Railroads led the way both in the scale of their corporate organization and in the consequent public, regulatory, and judicial response.

The roads were great beneficiaries of private and state loans before the Civil War. In the years after 1865, they received substantial federal and state land grants, and loans and subsidies from counties and townships. There were 35,000 miles of track in 1865; 93,000 in 1880. But by the mid-1870s railroads were staggering beneath the weight of their expansion. Fierce competition in the East and Midwest forced down rates and earnings. The overcapitalized lines, with high fixed costs, suffered also from the price deflation of the time. Bankruptcies and reorganizations, rate discrimination, and price-fixing pools were among the consequences. All had the effect of feeding popular anti-railroad sentiment.

That great Civil War venture in mixed enterprise, the Union Pacific Railroad, was a prolific breeder of controversy. Political and constitutional difficulties sprang up around the federal government's role in the capitalization and direction of the road. Congressmen bitterly assailed the Union Pacific's inability (or disinclination) to meet its financial obligations to the government. But not until the SINKING FUND CASES (1879) did the Supreme Court sustain the right of Congress to require this and other transcontinental lines to repay their debts. The Credit Mobilier scandal of 1872, in which stock in the construction company that built the Union Pacific was distributed to a number of influential politicians, epitomized the difficulty of fitting a semipublic enterprise into the American system of government. The Pacific Railroad Commission finally concluded: "The sovereign should not be mated with the subject."

Railroad land grants were no less a source of contention. The House unanimously resolved in 1870 that "the policy of granting subsidies in public lands to railroads and other corporations ought to be discontinued." Once again, the very principle of such aid came under attack: "These grants . . . have been made on the theory that government is an organized benevolence, and not merely a compact for the negative function of repelling a public enemy or repressing disorders."

The consequences of state and local railroad aid also were distressing, and were equally productive of doubts as to whether such aid was part of the proper role of government. The Supreme Court heard more than 350 bonding cases between 1870 and 1896. While the courts felt constrained to enforce most of those obligations, they made clear their displeasure with government subsidization. John F. Dillon condemned subsidies as "a coercive contribution in favor of private railway corporations" which violated "the general spirit of the Constitution as to the sacredness of private property." Thomas M. Cooley objected to railroad subsidies on similar grounds, arguing that "a large portion of the most urgent needs of society are relegated exclusively to the law of demand and supply." In LOAN ASSOCIATION v. TOPEKA (1875) the Supreme Court used this argument to block direct government subsidization of private enterprise.

During the years from 1880 to 1900, public, political, and (inevitably) judicial attention shifted from subsidization to regulation of the economy. The prevailing economic thought of the time, the weakness of government supervision, and the power of private interests worked against an effective system of ECONOMIC REGULATION. But inevitably the strains and conflicts attending the rise of an industrial economy produced demands on the state to intervene.

Journalist E. L. Godkin observed in 1873: "The locomotive is coming in contact with the framework of our institution. In this country of simple government, the most powerful centralizing force which civilization has yet produced must, within the next score years, assume its relation to that political machinery which is to control and regulate it." Nor surprisingly the railroads, the biggest of America's national enterprises, were the first to come under federal regulation.

During the 1870s, state railroad policy had moved from subsidy to containment. The 1870 Illinois constitution required the legislature to "pass laws establishing maximum rates of charges for the transportation of passengers and freight." That body in 1871 set maximum freight and grain elevator rates, forbade price discrimination, and created a railroad commission with supervisory and enforcement powers. Similar laws were adopted in Minnesota, Wisconsin, and Iowa. Because Grange members often were prominent advocates of rate regulation, these acts came to be known as the Granger laws.

The Supreme Court in *Munn v. Illinois* (1877), the first of the GRANGER CASES, upheld the regulatory power of the legislatures and opened up yet another path to regulation by resurrecting the old COMMON LAW doctrine that when private property was AFFECTED WITH A PUBLIC INTEREST it was subject to public accountability and control. But at the same time the Court conceded that "under some circumstances" legislation might be held to violate the Fourteenth Amendment: a portent of the conservative jurisprudence of later years.

Whatever constitutional authority might adhere to state regulation, its effectiveness was severely limited by compliant state railroad commissions, the political and legal influence of the roads, and above all the national character of the enterprise. From the mid-1880s on, federal courts increasingly struck down state railroad tax and rate laws that in their view interfered with the flow of INTERSTATE COMMERCE. The implicit policy decision was that ratemaking should be in the hands of the railroads—and be subject to the review of federal courts, not state courts and legislatures. One observer thought that "long tables of railway statistics, with the accompanying analyses, look strangely out of place in a volume of United States Reports": testimony to the fact that the courts of necessity were taking on a quasi-administrative role.

The scale and complexity of the interests affected by the railroads, the competitive problems of the lines themselves, the limited effectiveness of state regulation, and the growing intervention of the federal courts all fed a movement for national railroad regulation culminating in the INTERSTATE COMMERCE ACT of 1887. That act defined and laid down penalties for rate discrimination, and created an Interstate Commerce Commission (ICC) with the power to investigate and prosecute violators. Its primary purpose was negative: to block pooling and other cartel practices, not to secure a stable railroad rate structure. What the ICC gained thereby in constitutionality it lost in administrative effectiveness. Its early performance showed how difficult it was—given the power of private interests, popular distrust of government, and constitutional limits on the exercise of public power—to establish a bureaucratic mode of regulation. Instead, the ICC adopted what was in fact the only functioning American mode of economic supervision, that of the judiciary. Cooley, the judge and treatise writer who became the ICC's first chairman, announced: "The Commissioners realize that they are a new court, . . . and that they are to lay the foundations of a new body of American law."

During the first ten years of its existence the ICC handed down rulings on more than 800 rate controversies. But the Commission's impact was limited by the size, complexity, and competitiveness of the railroad business and by its lack of supervisory power. Demands rose in the 1890s for government ownership and operation of the lines, or at least for more rigorous supervision by a national Department of Transportation. But, as Cooley observed, these proposals were beyond the range of the late nineteenth-century American polity: "The perpetuity of free institutions in this country requires that the political machine called the United States Government be kept from being overloaded beyond its strength. The more cumbrous it is the greater is the power of intrigue and corruption under it."

The regulation of large enterprise in general posed the same problems, and produced the same response, as did that of the railroads. Mid-nineteenth-century general incorporation acts, and the competition among states to attract corporation charters, guaranteed that the terms of incorporation would remain easy, the regulation of company affairs loose and permissive. In theory the internal affairs of corporations were the business of the states; in practice, the states exercised little control.

But as in the case of the railroads, the growth of business corporations into national enterprises created a demand for federal regulation. Once again, judicial interpretation fostered the growth of a national economy.

State and federal courts strengthened the legal status of foreign (out-of-state) corporations, in effect reversing the severe constraints imposed on them by PAUL V. VIRGINIA (1869). In *Barron v. Burnside* (1887) the Supreme Court for the first time held that state regulation of foreign corporations could be of doubtful constitutionality. By the turn of the century the "liberal theory" of foreign corporations was the prevailing one.

Even more dramatic was the courts' use of the Fourteenth Amendment to protect corporate rights and privileges. During the 1870s, said Howard Jay Graham, "the rule that corporations were *not* to be regarded as constitutional 'PERSONS' theoretically was the LAW OF THE LAND." But this rule was more theory than fact, and during the late nineteenth century the judiciary explicitly brought corporations under the protection afforded to persons by the due process and equal protection clauses of the Amendment.

The rise of large enterprise in the late nineteenth century took forms that roused public concern and ultimately evoked a legislative and judicial response. The urge to override the limitations of state chartering led to the invention of the corporate trust and then the holding company. Although only about ten trusts were created during the 1880s, the word in the generic sense of a "huge, irrepressible, indeterminate" corporation came to be the object of great public concern. By 1890 several states had ANTITRUST laws, and six state supreme courts had held that trust agreements were against public policy or were illegal as monopolies or conspiracies in RESTRAINT OF TRADE. And public pressure grew for a federal antitrust law, as it had for railroad regulation.

The SHERMAN ANTITRUST ACT of 1890, passed overwhelmingly by Congress, relied on the legislature's power under the COMMERCE CLAUSE to outlaw "every contract, combination in the form of trust or otherwise, or conspiracy, in restraint of trade or commerce." The breadth of the law's formulation, and its dependence on the courts rather than on an administrative agency to define its provisions, testified to the still underdeveloped state of federal regulation. But in other ways the statute was sophisticated. By relying on the old common law concept of the illegality of conspiracies in restraint of trade, the drafters minimized the risk of having the law declared unconstitutional. And the Sherman Act was widely understood to be aimed at great combinations, not to fix an unrealistic standard of small-unit competition on the economy.

Even so, enforcement was full of difficulty. The Department of Justice in the 1890s lacked the manpower, the money, and the inclination to prosecute vigorously. The courts, too, severely limited the utility of the act. They held that a firm could come to dominate a sector of the economy without doing anything illegal, and they developed distinctions between reasonable and unreasonable restraint of trade, between legitimate business practices and "illegal commercial piracy." And in its Sugar Trust decision of 1895 (*United States v. E. C. Knight Company*) the Supreme Court dealt the law a heavy blow, holding that the Sherman Act applied only to "commerce" and not to manufacturing, and that the activities of the American Sugar Refining Company lay outside the act's coverage even though that firm controlled over ninety percent of the nation's sugar refining capacity.

The *American Law Review* called this decision "the most deplorable one that has been rendered in favor of incorporated power and greed . . . since the Dartmouth College case." In fact, the Court did take a narrow and mechanical view of interstate commerce. On that premise, its decision reflected a long-held distinction between state regulation of manufacturing and federal responsibility for interstate commerce. When private parties brought suit against trade and price cartels (particularly by those prime instances of enterprises in interstate commerce, the railroads), the Supreme Court was not reluctant to find that they violated the Sherman Act.

By the turn of the century it was apparent that the problem of corporate regulation was "rapidly assuming phases which seem beyond the scope of courts of justice." The rise of corporate capitalism, and the question of what to do about it, called as much for political-administrative will and wisdom as for legal-constitutional power and propriety.

The primary legal and, ultimately, constitutional justification for late nineteenth-century state regulation was the police power: the obligation of the states to protect the health, morals, safety, and welfare of their citizens. Many thought that the potential of that power was great indeed. The president of the American Bar Association estimated in 1897 that more than ninety percent of state legislation rested on the police power. CHRISTOPHER TIEDEMAN's *Limitations of the Police Power in the United States* (1886) was an elaborate attempt to find constitutional grounds for containing what he took to be a widely applied principle of government intervention. OLIVER WENDELL HOLMES caustically said of the police power: "We suppose the phrase was invented to cover certain acts of the legislature which are seen to be unconstitutional, but which are believed to be necessary."

The police power had its greatest appeal when public health and morals appeared to be at stake. A case in point was regulation of the liquor business. The Supreme Court upheld the right of the states to forbid the manufacture and sale of alcohol, and refused to accept the due process clause of the Fourteenth Amendment as a defense against state liquor legislation. (See INALIENABLE POLICE POWER.) Still more dramatic was judicial acceptance of extensive regulation—indeed, the near-crippling—of the oleomargarine industry. By 1886, twenty-two states either heavily taxed that product or required unattractive packaging or labeling. An 1886 federal law—"protection run mad," said an outraged critic—required that the product be called "oleo" (rather than "butterine" or other enticing names), and subjected it to a high license and manufacturing tax. The Supreme Court in *Powell v. Pennsylvania* (1888) upheld a similar Pennsylvania statute on the basis of the state's police power to protect public health.

The insufficiency of the state police power as a basis of state economic regulation became more and more apparent as the century neared its end. Corporate interests effectively espoused a laissez-faire, SUBSTANTIVE DUE PROCESS constitutionalism. More fundamentally, courts recognized the growing imbalance between state supervision and an economy that was becoming national in scope.

By 1899 the Supreme Court had held twenty-nine state laws unconstitutional because they conflicted with the commerce clause of the Constitution. In LEISY V. HARDIN (1890) the Court voided an Iowa law blocking the entry of liquor into the state, holding that the movement of an original package was protected by the national commerce power, so long as Congress had not authorized the state regulation. Responding to this invitation, Congress quickly passed the Wilson Act, which made liquor subject to state law regardless of where it was packaged. The Court validated the law on the grounds that "the common interest did not require entire freedom in the traffic in ardent spirits." But without similar congressional authorization, it continued to apply the original package doctrine against state laws restricting the entry of oleomargarine and cigarettes. And in CHAMPION V. AMES (1903) the Court upheld a statute forbidding the interstate transportation of lottery tickets, thus opening the prospect of NATIONAL POLICE POWER.

The constraints that limited the application of government authority to economic problems were at least as evident in the realm of social policy. During the period of the Civil War and Reconstruction, citizenship and race had been issues of prime importance not only in constitutional law but in politics and legislation as well. In the twentieth century these and other social concerns—education, crime, poverty, social mores, CIVIL LIBERTIES—would draw comparable attention from the public, Congress, and the courts. But such was not the case during the years between 1871 and 1900. With American society in transit from its small-unit agrarian past to its large-unit urban, industrial future, the political or constitutional standing of individual or social rights was largely ignored.

These years saw relatively little redefinition—in either constitutional law or legislative action—of the status of women, Orientals, blacks, or AMERICAN INDIANS. Legal barriers to female equality occasionally fell, but by legislation, not constitutional adjudication. Opposition to women's suffrage remained strong. Between 1870 and 1910 suffrage advocates conducted 480 campaigns in thirty-three states to get the issue on the ballot. Seventeen state REFERENDA (all but three west of the Mississippi) were held; only two were successful, in Colorado in 1893 and in Idaho in 1896.

The position of Orientals and blacks in society worsened. Organized labor agitated for the exclusion of Chinese immigrants, and anti-Chinese riots in the West testified to the intensity of public feeling. An 1882 federal law banned Chinese immigration for ten years. Supplementary acts in 1884 and 1888 tightened the exclusion law and imposed restrictions on Chinese already in the country. The Supreme Court in 1887 refused to apply the Civil Rights and Enforcement Acts of the Reconstruction period to Chinese, and in 1889 the Court upheld the restriction of Chinese immigration.

In 1892 Congress overwhelmingly renewed Chinese exclusion for another decade; it also required the registration of every resident Chinese laborer, with affidavits by one or more whites that the registrant had entered the country legally. The Supreme Court upheld this law in 1893. These policies had palpable consequences. About 100,000 lawful Chinese immigrants were in the United States in 1880; there were about 85,000 in 1900. In 1902 Chinese immigration was suspended indefinitely.

An even more pervasive white public opinion supported—or at least remained unconcerned about—discrimination against blacks. Late nineteenth-century northern courts generally upheld state laws that forbade discrimination in theaters, restaurants, and other public places, as a proper exercise of the police power. (The degree to which those laws were enforced is another matter.) But on similar grounds the courts accepted the growing number of SEGREGATION statutes. State laws separating the races in public transportation and accommodation, forbidding racial intermarriage, limiting access to the vote, and segregating schools met with no judicial obstacle.

In this sense the Supreme Court's acceptance of a Louisiana railroad segregation law in PLESSY v. FERGUSON (1896) represented the approval of an already widely established public policy, not the promulgation of new constitutional doctrine. When in 1903 the Court refused to agree that the Fifteenth Amendment might be used against Alabama officials who kept blacks from voting, Holmes suggested that relief "from a great political wrong" must come from "the legislative and political department of the government of the United States." At the same time the Court's invention of the STATE ACTION limitation on congressional power encouraged Congress to refrain from remedying private RACIAL DISCRIMINATION. (See CIVIL RIGHTS CASES, 1883.)

On the face of things, Indian public policy in the late nineteenth century had a different goal: it sought not to foster but to reduce separatism. Indian Commissioner Thomas J. Morgan declared in 1891: "The end at which we aim is that the American Indians shall become as speedily as possible Indian-Americans; that the savage shall become a citizen." But majority sentiment still regarded even nontribal Indians as inferior, and the Supreme Court went along. In *Elk v. Wilkins* (1884)—coterminous with the CIVIL RIGHTS CASES that invalidated the CIVIL RIGHTS ACT OF 1875—the Court held that Indians were not citizens within the understanding of the Fourteenth Amendment.

At the end of the century the acquisition of noncontiguous territory with substantial populations (Hawaii, the Philippines, Puerto Rico) raised old problems of statehood and citizenship in new forms. The Supreme Court in the INSULAR CASES (1901) limited the degree to which the Constitution applied to these peoples, much as the Court had been inclined to do with regard to Orientals, blacks, and Indians.

In most of the areas of social policy—education, crime, FIRST AMENDMENT freedoms—that in the twentieth century became important battlegrounds of public policy and constitutional law, there was little or no late nineteenth-century constitutional controversy. Only two such issues—prohibition and religion—raised substantial questions of constitutionality. New Hampshire Senator Henry W. Blair first proposed a national prohibition amendment to the Constitution in 1876, and a proposal to this effect was before Congress continuously until its adoption in 1918. State and local restrictions on the distribution and sale of liquor increased, and in general the courts sustained them against Fourteenth Amendment attacks, as proper applications of the police power.

The place of RELIGION IN THE PUBLIC SCHOOLS led to much political and legal conflict. State courts frequently dealt with the thorny issue of school Bible reading. Most states allowed this practice without exegesis, and the courts approved so long as attendance or participation was voluntary. The Iowa Supreme Court upheld a law that forbade the exclusion of Bible reading from the schools. But the Wisconsin court denied the constitutionality of such reading: "The connection of church and state corrupts religion, and makes the state despotic."

Protestant–Roman Catholic hostility underlay much of the conflict over school Bible reading, as it did the issue of state aid to parochial schools. Maine Republican James G. Blaine sought a constitutional amendment forbidding aid in the 1870s (see BLAINE AMENDMENT), and by 1900 twenty-three states had banned public grants to parochial schools. But the interrelationship of religion and education did not come before the Supreme Court until well into the twentieth century.

FELIX FRANKFURTER once told of a distinguished professor of property law who was called on to teach a course in constitutional law. Dutifully he did so. But he soon abandoned the effort, on the ground that the subject was "not law at all but politics." At no time in American history did this pronouncement seem more justified than in the period from 1877 to 1901. Except for the regulation of large enterprise, Americans debated the problems of a developing industrial society more in political than in constitutional terms. After 1900 the fit—or lack of fit—between those problems and the American constitutional system would be faced more directly.

Bibliography

BETH, LOREN P.   1971   *The Development of the American Constitution 1877–1917.* New York: Harper & Row.

GRAHAM, HOWARD J.   1968   *Everyman's Constitution: Historical Essays on the Four-teenth Amendment, The 'Conspiracy Theory,' and American Constitutionalism.* Chaps. 10–13. Madison, Wisc.: State Historical Society.

KELLER, MORTON   1977   *Affairs of State: Public Life in Late Nineteenth Century America.* Cambridge, Mass.: Harvard University Press.

PAUL, ARNOLD M.   1960   *Conservative Crisis and the Rule of Law.* Ithaca, N.Y.: Cornell University Press.

SKOWRONEK, STEPHEN   1982   *Building a New American State: The Expansion of National Administrative Capacities 1877–1920.* Cambridge: At the University Press.

WAITE COURT

(1874–1888)

Charles W. McCurdy

A new age of American constitutional law was at hand when MORRISON R. WAITE became CHIEF JUSTICE of the United States in 1874. Not only had the Civil War discredited many antebellum glosses on the "old" Constitution, consisting of the venerable document framed in 1787 and the twelve amendments adopted during the early republic, but it had also generated a "new" Constitution consisting of the THIRTEENTH AMENDMENT, the FOURTEENTH AMENDMENT, and the FIFTEENTH AMENDMENT. The range of choices at the Court's disposal was virtually unlimited as it reconstituted the old organic law and integrated the new. CHARLES SUMNER said it best just four years before Waite took the Court's helm. The tumultuous events of 1861–1869, he exclaimed, had transformed the Constitution into "molten wax" ready for new impression. An extraordinarily homogeneous group of men made this impression. Of the fourteen associate Justices who sat with Waite between 1874 and his death in 1888, only NATHAN CLIFFORD had been appointed by a Democrat and all but two—SAMUEL F. MILLER and JOHN MARSHALL HARLAN, both of Kentucky—had been born in the free states. All of them were Protestants. Thus the Republican party, which had subdued the South and created the "new" Constitution, had also reconstructed the federal judiciary. As the Waite Court proceeded to refashion the structure of American constitutional law, its work ineluctably reflected the values, aspirations, and fears that had animated the Republican party's northern Protestant constituency since the 1850s.

Fierce opposition to state SOVEREIGNTY concepts was a core element of Republican belief from the party's very inception. Republicans associated state sovereignty with proslavery constitutionalism in the 1850s, with SECESSION in 1861, and ultimately with the tragic war both engendered. Waite and his colleagues shared this aversion to state sovereignty dogma and repeatedly expressed it in controversies involving the IMPLIED POWERS of Congress under the "old" Constitution. In case after case the Court resisted limitations on federal power derived from state sovereignty premises and held, in effect, that Congress's authority to enact statutes deemed NECESSARY AND PROPER for the ENUMERATED POWERS had the same scope under the Constitution as it would if the states did not

162

exist. On several occasions the Court even revived the idea that Congress might exercise any power inherent in national sovereignty as long as it was not specifically prohibited by the Constitution. This doctrine, first expounded by Federalist congressmen during debate on the SEDITION ACT of 1798, had been regarded as "exploded" by most antebellum statesmen. But its revival after the Civil War did have a certain logic. If there was one impulse that every member of the Waite Court had in common, it was the urge to extirpate every corollary of "southern rights" theory from American constitutional law and to confirm the national government's authority to exercise every power necessary to maintain its existence.

The revival of the implied powers doctrine began in the often overlooked case of *Kohl v. United States* (1876). There counsel challenged Congress's authority to take private property in Cincinnati as a site for public buildings on the ground that the Constitution sanctioned federal exercise of the EMINENT DOMAIN power only in the DISTRICT OF COLUMBIA. Article I, section 8, vested Congress with authority to acquire land elsewhere "for the erection of forts . . . and other needful buildings" only "by the consent of the legislature of the State in which the same shall be." This was by no means a novel argument. JAMES MADISON and JAMES MONROE had pointed to the national government's lack of a general eminent domain power when vetoing INTERNAL IMPROVEMENT bills, and proslavery theorists had invoked the same principle as a bar to compensated emancipation and colonization schemes. In *Pollard's Lessee v. Hagan* (1845), moreover, the TANEY COURT had said that "the United States have no constitutional capacity to exercise municipal jurisdiction, sovereignty, or eminent domain within the limits of a State or elsewhere, except in the cases in which it is expressly granted." But WILLIAM STRONG, speaking for the Court in *Kohl,* refused to take this doctrine "seriously." Congress's war, commerce, and postal powers necessarily included the right to acquire property for forts, lighthouses, and the like. "If the right to acquire property for such uses be made a barren right by the unwillingness of property holders to sell, or by the action of a State prohibiting a sale to the Federal Government," Strong explained, "the constitutional grants of power may be rendered nugatory. . . . This cannot be." Congress's eminent domain power must be implied, Strong concluded, for commentators on the law of nations had always regarded it as "the offspring of political necessity, and . . . inseparable from sovereignty."

HORACE GRAY sounded the same theme in the Legal Tender Cases (*Juilliard v. Greenman,* 1884), where the Court sustained Congress's authority to emit legal tender notes even in peacetime. With only STEPHEN J. FIELD dissenting, Gray asserted that because the power to make government paper a legal tender was "one of the powers belonging to sovereignty in other civilized nations, and not expressly withheld from Congress by the Constitution," it was unquestionably "an appropriate means, conducive and plainly adapted" to the execution of Congress's power to borrow money. In Ex parte Yarbrough (1884), decided the same day, the Court spoke the language of national sovereignty in an especially significant case. At issue there was the criminal liability of a Georgia man who had savagely beaten a black voter en route to cast his ballot in a federal election. The Court unanimously sustained the petitioner's conviction under the 1870 Civil Rights Act, which made it a federal crime to "injure, oppress, threaten, or intimidate any citizen in the free exercise or enjoyment of any right or privilege secured to him by the Constitution or laws of the United States." It did so on the ground that Congress's duty "to provide in an election held under its authority, for security of life and limb to the voter" arose not from its interest in the victim's rights so much as "from the necessity of the government itself." Samuel F. Miller explained that Congress's power to regulate the time, place, and manner of holding federal elections, conferred in Article I, section 4, implied a "power to pass laws for the free, pure, and safe exercise" of the suffrage. "But it is a waste of time," he added, "to seek for specific sources to pass these laws. . . . If this government is anything more than a mere aggregation of delegated agents of other States and governments, each of which is superior to the general government, it must have the power to protect the elections on which its existence depends from violence and corruption."

The Court's decisions in *Kohl, Juilliard,* and *Yarbrough* merely jettisoned antebellum canons of strict construction. They did not impair the autonomy of state governments. The eminent domain power of the several states was not threatened by *Kohl,* the Constitution expressly prohibited the states from making anything but gold and silver a legal tender, and *Yarbrough* did not jeopardize Georgia's power to prosecute political assassins for assault or murder. Yet the Waite Court was as quick to defend exercises of Congress's powers in situations where counsel claimed that the states' autonomy was in jeopardy as in cases where their reserved powers remained unimpaired. *Ex parte Siebold* (1880) was the leading case in point. There the Court sustained a conviction for ballot stuffing under the 1871 Enforcement Act, which made it a federal crime for any state official at a congressional election to neglect duties required of him by either state or federal law. Counsel for the petitioner argued that in Prigg v. Pennsylvania (1842) and Kentucky v. Dennison (1861) the Taney Court had held that the principle of divided sovereignty precluded acts of Congress compelling the cooperation of state officials in the execution of national law. "We cannot yield to such a transcendental view of State sovereignty," Joseph Bradley proclaimed for the Court in *Siebold.* "As a general rule," he said, "it is no doubt expedient and wise that the operations of the State and National Governments should, as far as practicable, be conducted separately, in order to avoid undue jealousies and jars." But the Constitution neither mandated an immutable boundary between spheres of federal and state power nor restricted Congress's choice of means in implementing its enumerated authority to regulate federal elections.

The Court's constitutional nationalism did have limits. Like most Republicans of the age, Waite and his colleagues resisted the idea of centralization with as much ardor as the concept of state sovereignty. They regarded the national government's competence as deriving from the powers specified in the Constitution or fairly implied from it; the residual powers of government, usually called "internal police," belonged exclusively to the several states. Thus decisions like *Kohl* and *Siebold*, as Waite and his associates understood them, did not contract the ambit of state JURISDICTION. Rather the court simply refused to recognize implied limitations on the powers of Congress derived from state sovereignty premises. The *Trade-Mark Cases* (1879) underscored the Waite Court's allegiance to this view of the federal system. There a unanimous Court, speaking through Miller, held that Congress had no authority to enact a "universal system of trade-mark registration." Miller's method of analysis was more revealing than the result. His first impulse was to determine which sphere of government ordinarily had responsibility for such matters in the constitutional scheme. "As the property in trade-marks and the right to their exclusive use rest on the laws of the States, and like the great body of the rights of persons and of property, depend on them for security and protection," he explained, "the power of Congress to legislate on the subject . . . must be found in the Constitution of the United States, which is the source of all the powers the Congress can lawfully exercise." This two-tier method not only reified DUAL FEDERALISM but also put the burden of demonstrating Congress's authority to act on the government. In the *Trade-Mark Cases* it could not do so. Trade-marks lacked "the essential characteristics" of creative work in the arts and sciences, consequently the statute could not be sustained under the COPYRIGHT or PATENT powers. And the commerce power, though admittedly "broad," could not be construed as to permit federal regulation of commercial relations between persons residing in the same state.

When the Waite Court turned to cases involving the "new" Constitution, the instinct to conceptualize rights and powers in terms of dual federalism had fateful consequences. Beginning in UNITED STATES v. CRUIKSHANK (1876), the Court emasculated Congress's power "to enforce, by appropriate legislation," the rights guaranteed by the Fourteenth and Fifteenth Amendments. At issue was the validity of conspiracy convictions under the 1870 Civil Rights Act against a band of whites who had attacked a conclave of blacks in Grants Parish, Louisiana, killing from sixty to one hundred of them. The government claimed that the defendants had deprived the black citizens of their constitutional rights to hold a peaceful assembly, to bear arms, to vote, and to EQUAL PROTECTION OF THE LAWS safeguarding persons and property. The Court unanimously overturned the convictions. The CONSPIRACY law was not voided; indeed, the Court sustained a conviction under that very statute in *Yarbrough.* But Waite and his associates were determined to confine Congress's power to enact "appropriate legislation" in such a way to preserve what Miller called "the main features of the federal system." The Court had no choice in the matter, Joseph Bradley remarked on circuit in 1874, unless it was prepared "to clothe Congress with power to pass laws for the general preservation of social order in every State," or, in short, with a plenary power of "internal police."

Waite's opinion for the Court in *Cruikshank* contained two separate lines of argument. He began the first foray by pointing out that every American citizen "owes allegiance to two sovereigns, and claims protection from both." Because the two levels of government could protect the rights of citizens only "within their respective spheres," federal authorities could assert jurisdiction over perpetrators of violence only if the rights denied to victims were derived from the Constitution and laws of the United States. But in the SLAUGHTERHOUSE CASES (1873), decided ten months before Waite came to the Court, a majority of five had concluded that there were very few PRIVILEGES OR IMMUNITIES of national CITIZENSHIP and that the Fourteenth Amendment had not created any new ones. Fundamental rights of life, liberty, and property still rested upon the laws of the states, and citizens had to rely upon the states for the protection of those rights. Among the privileges of state citizenship, Waite explained in *Cruikshank,* were the rights to assemble, to bear arms, and to vote. Although guaranteed against infringement by Congress in the BILL OF RIGHTS, the rights to assemble and bear arms were not "granted by the Constitution" or "in any manner dependent upon that instrument for existence." The right to vote in state and local elections stood on the same footing because "the right to vote in the States comes from the States." The Fifteenth Amendment did give citizens a new right under the Constitution—exemption from RACIAL DISCRIMINATION when attempting to vote. Because the Grants Parish indictments did not aver that the defendants had prevented their victims "from exercising the right to vote on account of race," however, that count was as defective as the rest.

Waite's second line of argument in *Cruikshank* was designed to hold the votes of Joseph Bradley, Stephen J. Field, and NOAH SWAYNE. They had dissented in the *Slaughterhouse Cases,* claiming that the Fourteenth Amendment had been designed to reconstruct the federal system by creating a third sphere in the constitutional scheme—that of the individual whose FUNDAMENTAL RIGHTS were now protected against unequal and discriminatory state laws. Waite satisfied them by stating what came to be known as the STATE ACTION doctrine. He not only conceded that "[t]he equality of the rights of citizens is a principle of republicanism" but strongly implied that the Fourteenth Amendment had nationalized this principle under the equal protection clause, if not the privileges or immunities clause. But the amendment, he added, "does not . . . add any thing to the rights which one citizen had under the Constitution against another." The very language of the amendment's first section— "No state shall . . ."—suggested that it must be read not as a grant of power to Congress but as a limitation on the states. It followed that the exercise of fundamental rights did not come under the Constitution's protection until jeopardized by the enactment or enforcement of a state law. "This the amendment guarantees, but no more," Waite declared. "The power of the national government is limited to the enforcement of this guaranty."

The principles announced in *Cruikshank* doomed the rest of Congress's CIVIL RIGHTS program, all of which had been based on the assumption that the "new" Constitution might be employed as a sword to protect any interference with fundamental rights. A voting rights statute went down in UNITED STATES v. REESE (1876) because Congress had failed to limit federal jurisdiction over state elections to the prevention of racially motivated fraud or dereliction; the antilynching provisions of the 1871 Civil Rights Act were invalidated for want of state action in UNITED STATES v. HARRIS (1883). One latent function of *Cruikshank,* however, was to draw renewed attention to the equal protection clause as a shield for blacks and other racial minorities whose civil rights were imperiled by discriminatory state laws. Soon the docket was crowded with such cases, and the Court was compelled to wrestle with longstanding ambiguities in the Republican party's commitment to racial equality.

Republicans had always been quick to defend equal rights in the market, for it was the rights to make contracts and own property that distinguished free people from slaves. But many Republicans regarded the idea of equality before the law as wholly compatible with legalized race prejudice in the social realm. Words like "nation" and "race" were not merely descriptive terms in the nineteenth century; they were widely understood as objective manifestations of natural communities, the integrity of which government had a duty to maintain. Thus most Republicans never accepted the proposition that blacks ought to be free to marry whites and many denied the right of blacks to associate with whites even in public places. The framers of the "new" Constitution had neither abjured this qualified view of equality not incorporated it into the Fourteenth Amendment. The discretion of Waite and his colleagues was virtually unfettered. They could weave prevailing prejudices into equal protection jurisprudence or they could interpret the equality concept broadly, declare that the "new" Constitution was colorblind, and put the Court's enormous prestige squarely behind the struggle for racial justice.

Exponents of racial equality were greatly encouraged by STRAUDER v. WEST VIRGINIA (1880), the case of first impression. There a divided Court reversed the murder conviction of a black defendant who had been tried under a statute that limited jury service to "white male persons." The Fourteenth Amendment, William Strong explained for the majority, "was designed to secure the colored race the enjoyment of all the civil rights that under the law are enjoyed by white persons." This formulation was acceptable even to the two dissenters. According to Stephen J. Field and Nathan Clifford, however, jury service was not a "civil right." It was a "political right." The only rights Congress intended to protect with the Fourteenth Amendment, they contended, were those enumerated in the Civil Rights Act of 1866—to own property, to make and enforce contracts, to sue and give evidence. The equal protection clause, Field said, "secures to all persons their civil rights upon the same terms; but it leaves political rights . . . and social rights . . . as they stood previous to its adoption." But the *Strauder* majority was unimpressed by Field's version of the "original understanding" and it set a face of flint against his typology of rights. "The Fourteenth Amendment makes no attempt to enumerate the rights it designed to protect," Strong declared. "It speaks in general terms, and those are as comprehensive as possible." The very term equal protection, he added, implied "that no discrimination shall be made against [blacks] by the law because of their color."

Strauder seemed to open the door for judicial proscription of all racial classifications in state laws. John R. Tompkins, counsel for an interracial couple that had been sentenced to two years in prison for violating Alabama's antimiscegenation law, certainly read the case that way. But the idea of distinct spheres of rights—"civil" and "social" if no longer "political"—furtively reentered the Waite Court's jurisprudence in PACE v. ALABAMA (1883). Field, speaking for a unanimous Court, held that antimiscegenation laws were not barred by the Fourteenth Amendment as long as both parties received the same punishment for the crime. Equal protection mandated equal treatment, not freedom of choice; antimiscegenation laws restricted the liberty of blacks and whites alike. Underlying this disingenuous view was an unarticulated premise of enormous importance. In settings involving the exercise of "social rights" the equal protection clause did not prohibit state legislatures from enacting statutes that used race as a basis for regulating the rights of persons. The legal category "Negro" was not suspect per se. (See SUSPECT CLASSIFICATION.)

The concept of "social rights" also figured prominently in the CIVIL RIGHTS CASES (1883), decided ten months after *Pace*. There the Court struck down the CIVIL RIGHTS ACT OF 1875, which forbade the owners of theaters, inns, and public conveyances to deny any citizen "the full and equal benefit" of their facilities. Joseph Bradley, speaking for the majority, rejected the claim that the businesses covered by the act were quasi-public agencies; consequently the state action doctrine barred federal intervention under the Fourteenth Amendment. But Bradley conceded that the state action doctrine was not applicable in Thirteenth Amendment contexts. It not only "nullif[ies] all state laws which establish or uphold slavery," he said, but also "clothes Congress with power to pass all laws necessary and proper for abolishing all badges and incidents of slavery in the United States." With the exception of John Marshall Harlan, however, every member of the Waite Court equated the "badges and incidents of slavery" with the denial of "civil rights" and concluded that Congress had nearly exhausted its authority to enact appropriate legislation under the Thirteenth Amendment with the CIVIL RIGHTS ACT OF 1866. "[A]t that time," Bradley explained, "Congress did not assume, under the authority given by the Thirteenth Amendment, to adjust what may be called the social rights of man and races in the community; but only to declare and vindicate those fundamental rights which appertain to the essence of citizenship, and the enjoyment or deprivation of which constitutes the essential distinction between freedom and slavery." Bradley's opinion was circumspect in only one respect. Whether denial of equal accommodation "might be a denial of a right which, if sanctioned by the state law, would be obnoxious to the [equal protection] prohibitions of the Fourteenth Amendment," he said, "is another question." But that was true only in the most formal sense. Once the Court had identified two distinct spheres of rights under the Thirteenth Amendment, one "civil" and another "social," it was difficult to resist the impulse to link that standard with the doctrine expounded in *Pace* when deciding equal protection cases. Stephen J. Field and Horace Gray, the only members of the *Civil Rights Cases* majority still alive when PLESSY V. FERGUSON (1896) was decided, had no qualms about state laws that required SEPARATE BUT EQUAL accommodations for blacks on public conveyances. Harlan was the sole dissenter on both occasions.

Equal opportunity in the market was one civil right that every member of the Waite Court assumed was guaranteed by the equal protection clause. Thus in YICK WO V. HOPKINS (1886) the Court invalidated the racially discriminatory application of a San Francisco ordinance that required all laundries, except those specifically exempted by the board of supervisors, to be built of brick or stone with walls one foot thick and metal roofs. No existing San Francisco laundry could meet such stringent building regulations, but the ordinance had the desired effect. The authorities promptly exempted the city's white operators and denied the petitions of their 240 Chinese competitors. "[T]he conclusion cannot be resisted," STANLEY MATTHEWS asserted for a unanimous Court, "that no reason for [this discrimination] exists except hostility to the race and nationality to which the petitioners belong, and which in the eye of the law is not justified." Yet the type of right divested was at least as important in *Yick Wo* as the fact of discrimination. The Court described laws that arbitrarily impaired entrepreneurial freedom as "the essence of slavery" while laws that denied racial minorities free choice in the selection of marriage partners and theater seats were not. But that was not all. The court invoked the absence of standards for administering the laundry ordinance as an independent ground for its unconstitutionality. The boundless discretion, or, as Matthews put it, "the naked and arbitrary power" delegated to the authorities was as decisive for the Court as the fact that the ordinance had been applied with "an evil eye and an unequal hand." In the Waite Court's view, however, the same kind of concern about official discretion was neither possible nor desirable in jury-service cases. In *Strauder* Strong conceded that jury selection officials might constitutionally employ facially neutral yet impossibly vague tests of good character, sound judgment, and the like. The Court had no choice but to presume that the jury commissioners had acted properly, Harlan explained in *Bush v. Kentucky* (1883), in the absence of state laws expressly restricting participation to whites. As blacks began to disappear from jury boxes throughout the South, it became clear that although *Strauder* put jury service in the "civil rights" category, in practical application it stood on a far lower plane than the rights enumerated in the Civil Rights Act of 1866. When Booker T. Washington counseled blacks to place economic opportunities ahead of all others in 1895, he expressed priorities that the Waite Court had long since embroidered into equal protection jurisprudence.

The path of DUE PROCESS was at once more tortuous and less decisive than the development of equal protection doctrine. In *Dent v. West Virginia* (1888), decided at the close of the Waite era, the Court conceded, as it had in the beginning, that "it may be difficult, if not impossible, to give to the terms 'due process of law' a definition which will embrace every permissible exertion of power affecting private rights and exclude such as are forbidden." Yet two generalizations about the Waite Court's understanding of due process can be advanced with confidence. First, the modern distinction between PROCEDURAL and SUBSTANTIVE DUE PROCESS had no meaning for Waite and his colleagues. In their view, the Fifth and Fourteenth Amendments furnished protection for fundamental rights against arbitrary action, regardless of the legal form in which the arbitrary act had been clothed. In HURTADO V. CALIFORNIA (1884), where the majority rejected counsel's claim that the Fourteenth Amendment INCORPORATED the Bill of Rights, Stanley Matthews explained that because the due process concept embraced "broad and general maxims of liberty and justice," it "must be held to guaranty not particular forms of procedure, but the very substance of individual rights to life, liberty, and property." Even Miller, the most circumspect member of the Court, agreed in 1878 that a law declaring the property of A to be vested in B, "without more," would "deprive A of his property without due process of law." It is equally clear that the Court assumed that CORPORATIONS were PERSONS within the meaning of the Fifth and Fourteenth Amendments long before Waite acknowledged as much during oral argument in *Santa Clara County v. Southern Pacific Railroad Co.* (1886). As early as the GRANGER CASES (1877) the Court decided controversies in which railroad corporations challenged state regulation on due process grounds, and neither the defendant states nor the Justices breathed a doubt about the Court's jurisdiction. In the SINKING FUND CASES (1879), moreover, Waite stated emphatically in obiter dictum that the Fifth Amendment had always barred Congress "from depriving persons or corporations of property without due process of law."

Although every member of the Court accepted the essential premises of substantive due process, no statute was voided on due process grounds during the Waite era. Conventional assumptions about the boundary between the legislative and judicial spheres were largely responsible for the Court's reticence. In due process cases, at least, most of the period's Justices meant it when they stated, as Waite did in the *Sinking Fund Cases,* that "[e]very possible presumption is in favor of the validity of a statute, and this continues until the contrary is shown beyond a reasonable doubt." The most disarming demonstration of that Court's adherence to this principle came in *Powell v. Pennsylvania* (1888). At issue was an act that prohibited the manufacture and sale of oleomargarine. The legislature had labeled the statute as a public health measure, but it was no secret that the law really had been designed to protect the dairy industry against a new competitor. Harlan, speaking for everyone but Field, conceded that counsel for the oleomargarine manufacturer had stated "a sound principle of constitutional law" when he argued that the Fourteenth Amendment guaranteed every person's right to pursue "an ordinary calling or trade" and to acquire and possess property. Indeed, the Court had furnished protection for those very rights in *Yick Wo.* "But we cannot adjudge that the defendant's rights of liberty and property, as thus defined, have been infringed," Harlan added, "without holding that, although it may have been enacted in good faith for the objects expressed in its title . . . it has, in fact, no real or substantial relation to those objects." And this the Court was not prepared to do. Defendant's offer of proof as to the wholesomeness of his product was insufficient, for it was the legislature's duty, not the judiciary's, "to conduct investigations of facts entering into questions of public policy." Nor could the Court consider the reasonableness of the means selected by the legislature: "Whether the manufacture of oleomargarine . . . is, or may be, conducted in such a way . . . . as to baffle ordinary inspection, or whether it involves such danger to the public health as to require . . . the entire suppression of the business, rather than its regulation . . . are questions of fact and of public policy which belong to the legislative department to determine." Field, dissenting, claimed that the majority had not simply deferred to the legislature but had recognized it as "practically omnipotent."

Field overstated the predisposition of his colleagues, and he knew it. The Court seldom spoke with a luminous, confident voice in due process cases; majority opinions almost invariably revealed lingering second thoughts. Each time the Court said yes to legislatures, it reminded them that someday the Court might use the due process clause to say no. In *Powell*, for example, Harlan warned lawmakers that the Court was ready to intercede "if the state legislatures, under the pretence of guarding the public health, the public morals, or the public safety, should invade the rights of life, liberty, and property." Harlan did not explain how the Court might identify an act that had been passed "under the pretence" of exercising the police power, but he seemed to be confident that the Justices would be able to identify a tainted statute once they saw one. Waite's opinion in *Munn v. Illinois* (1877) was equally ambiguous. In one series of paragraphs he stated that the power to regulate prices was inherent in the police power; in another he suggested that price fixing was legitimate only if the regulated concern was a "business AFFECTED WITH A PUBLIC INTEREST." It followed from the latter proposition, though not from the former, that "under some circumstances" the Court might disallow regulation of prices charged by firms that were "purely and exclusively private." In *Munn* Waite was more certain about the reasonableness of rates lawfully fixed. "We know that it is a power which may be abused," he said; "but . . . [f]or protection against abuses by the legislatures the people must resort to the polls, not the courts." By 1886, however, Waite and some of his colleagues were not so sure. "[U]nder the pretense of regulating fares and freights," Waite declared in the *Railroad Commission Cases* (1886), "the State cannot require a railroad corporation to carry persons or property without reward; neither can it do that which in law amounts to a taking of private property for public use without JUST COMPENSATION, or without due process of law." This statement, like Harlan's similar remark in *Powell*, warranted many conflicting inferences. At the close of the Waite era, then, the scope of the JUDICIAL POWER under the due process clause was as unsettled as the clause's meaning.

When Waite died in 1888, a St. Louis law journal observed that he had been "modest, conscientious, careful, conservative, and safe." It was a shrewd appraisal not only of the man but of his Court's work in constitutional law. The Court's unwillingness to use judicial power as an instrument of moral leadership evoked scattered protests from racial egalitarians, who accused Waite and his colleagues of energizing bigotry, and from exponents of laissez-faire who complained that the Court had failed to curb overweening regulatory impulses in the state legislatures. But no criticism was heard from the Republican party's moderate center, where the Court had looked for bearings as it reconstructed the "old" Constitution and integrated the "new." In retrospect, it was THOMAS M. COOLEY, not Charles Sumner, who supplied the Waite Court with an agenda and suggested an appropriate style for its jurisprudence. The Republican party had resorted to "desperate remedies" and had treated the Constitution as if it were "wax" during the Civil War, he said in 1867. Now it was time for the bench and bar to ensure that postwar institutions were "not mere heaps of materials from which to build something new, but the same good old ship of state, with some progress toward justice and freedom."

Bibliography

BENEDICT, MICHAEL LES   1979   Preserving Federalism: Reconstruction and the Waite Court. *Supreme Court Review* 1978:39–79.

CORWIN, EDWARD S.   1913   *National Supremacy: Treaty Power versus State Power.* New York: Henry Holt.

——   1948   *Liberty against Government.* Baton Rouge: Louisiana State University Press.

MAGRATH, C. PETER   1963   *Morrison R. Waite: The Triumph of Character.* New York: Macmillan.

McCURDY, CHARLES W.   1975   Justice Field and the Jurisprudence of Government–Business Relations. *Journal of American History* 61:970–1005.

SCHMIDT, BENNO C.   1983   Juries, Jurisdiction, and Race Discrimination: The Lost Promise of Strauder v. West Virginia. *Texas Law Review* 61:1401–1499.

CONSTITUTIONAL HISTORY, 1901–1921

Morton Keller

American public life profoundly changed during the early twentieth century. The policy agenda during the Progressive era stands in dramatic contrast, both quantitatively and qualitatively, to its nineteenth-century predecessors. A substantial body of state and national legislation sought to subject large corporations and public utilities to far greater regulation than had been the case before. A comparable surge of enactments dealt with social issues ranging from the hours and working conditions of women and children to housing, the quality of food and drugs, the conservation of land, and the control of drinking and prostitution.

More than at any time since the Civil War and Reconstruction, Americans paid substantial attention to the structure of their government. The pace of lawmaking that dealt with politics and government quickened, stimulated by the dual motives (not always complementary) of expanding popular democracy and of bringing greater honesty and efficiency to the workings of the American state. A burst of innovation led to the creation of direct PRIMARY ELECTIONS, the INITIATIVE and REFERENDUM, and new registration and voting laws, as well as to the direct election of senators and to women's suffrage. A flood of discussion and a lesser flow of administrative, judicial, and legislative action sought to increase the effectiveness of the executive branch and the BUREAUCRACY, to improve the workings of Congress and the functioning of the courts, and to modernize the relationship between federal and state authorities and the governance of the nation's cities.

American involvement in World War I was the capstone to the Progressive era. Federal involvement in the American economy and society reached new heights; and in both technique and spirit wartime governance drew heavily on the immediate prewar experience.

THEODORE ROOSEVELT, WILLIAM HOWARD TAFT, and WOODROW WILSON were far more activist than their predecessors both in leadership styles and in domestic and foreign policy. But perhaps the most dramatic result of the quickened pace of government and the new policy agenda was the adoption between 1913 and 1920 of four constitutional amendments, providing for a federal income tax, the direct election of senators, PROHIBITION, and women's suffrage. Only at the beginning of the Republic and during the Reconstruction era had constitutional revision occurred on so large a scale.

Insofar as there was a common denominator to the public policy of the Progressive era, it lay in the belief that the time had come to deal with some of the more chaotic and unjust aspects of a mature industrial society; to bring public policy (and the nation's political and governing institutions) into closer accord with new social and economic realities. This impulse cannot be simply explained away by the once fashionable label of "reform," or the now fashionable label of "social control." A quest for social justice coexisted in complex ways with a search for order. Some Progressives wanted society (and the polity) to be more efficient: more honest and economical, less wasteful and corrupt. Others sought policies that would make society safer: more secure from the threats of big business and corrupt political machines, or from the vagaries of competition and the business cycle, or from radicals, immigrants, or blacks. Still others wanted society to be fairer: more humane and less inequitable.

This was not solely an American development. H. G. Wells observed in 1906 that "the essential question for America, as for Europe, is the rescue of her land, her public service, and the whole of her great economic process from the anarchic and irresponsible control of private owners . . . and the organization of her social life upon the broad, clear, humane conceptions of modern science."

Could it be said that a substantially changed constitutional order was one consequence of American Progressivism? Did the complex structure of ECONOMIC REGULATION embodied in the Interstate Commerce Commission, enforcement of the SHERMAN ACT, the Federal Trade Commission, railroad regulation, and a host of other economic measures fundamentally alter the relationship of the state to the economy? Did the interventionism embodied in the growing body of social legislation, accumulating restrictions on IMMIGRATION, the CIVIL LIBERTIES onslaught of the war years, and the passage of national prohibition fundamentally alter the relationship of government to American society and the individual rights of its citizens? Did the sequence of interventionist foreign policy actions, delimited at one end by the acquisition of overseas colonies after the Spanish-American War of 1898, and at the other by American intervention in World War I, fundamentally alter the place of FOREIGN AFFAIRS in the American political order?

In sum, did the early twentieth-century outburst of legislation, executive leadership, new agencies, and new government functions lead to what has been called "a qualitatively different kind of state"? Did a corporate-bureaucratic system of government supplant the nineteenth-century American "state of courts and parties"? JOHN W. BURGESS held in 1923 that the past generation had seen the transformation of American constitutional law from a stress on the protection of individual liberty to the imposition of "autocratic" governmental power over property, persons, and thought.

The distinctive American style of government that took form during the first century of the nation's history rested on the balance and SEPARATION OF POWERS among the executive, legislative, and judicial branches; on a FEDERALISM that rendered (through the POLICE POWER) to the states the things that were social; and on a conception of individual rights that, for all its abuses and distortions (the sacrifice of southern blacks to the not-so-tender mercies of southern whites; the use of the DUE PROCESS clause of the FOURTEENTH AMENDMENT to spare CORPORATIONS the indignity of state regulation and taxation), arguably gave nineteenth-century Americans more individual freedom from the interposition of the state than any other people in the world. To what degree was that constitutional order changed between 1901 and 1921?

Of course there can be no definitive answer: the glass of change inevitably will remain partially filled for some, partially empty for others. But an obscure chapter in the constitutional history of the United States may come into clearer focus if we abandon the traditional historiographical emphasis on Progressive "reform" in favor of an examination of the major instrumentalities of government: Congress, the presidency, the bureaucracy, and the mechanisms governing federal–state relations.

Congress was the branch of government that underwent the most overt and formal alteration during the early twentieth century. Two major changes, the popular election of senators through the passage of the SEVENTEENTH AMENDMENT, and the reduction of the powers of the speaker of the House of Representatives, came about in these years. These changes were products of the widespread view that Congress, like the parties, was under the control of corrupt, machine-bound politicos and sinister business interests.

Six times between 1893 and 1911 the House approved a direct election amendment. Finally, spurred by an arrangement whereby progressive Republicans agreed to drop the cause of black voting in the South in return for southern Democratic support, the Senate accepted the change. The Southerners assured that control of the time, place, and manner of holding senatorial elections would remain the province of each state.

A 1911 law sought also to assure that congressional districts would be compact, contiguous, and of roughly equal populations. But enforcement was so difficult, and the courts were so loath to intervene, that it had little effect. And although the direct election of senators gradually reversed the tendency (at least until recent times) for the Senate to become a "millionaires's club," it cannot be said that that body's role in the governmental process was substantially different in the 1920s from what it had been before 1900.

The controversy over the House speaker's authority was more intense. Joseph G. Cannon, the speaker from 1901 to 1911, appointed and was himself one of the five-member Committee on Rules, thus controlling assignments to the key committees of the House, which he populated with like-thinking conservatives. His power to expedite the work of an unwieldy legislature had been a late-nineteenth-century reform, designed to keep a boss-ridden legislature from working its will. Now it appeared to a majority of congressmen as an obstacle to the more programmatic demands of Progressive government. In 1910–1911 a coalition of Democrats and insurgent Republicans deprived Cannon of his power to serve on and appoint the Rules Committee, to choose standing committees, and to recognize members on the floor.

The seniority system came into general use as a more equitable means of choosing committee chairmen—a "reform" of the sort that Finley Peter Dunne's Mr. Dooley presumably had in mind when he commented on the Progressive predilection for structural change: "I wisht I was a German, and believed in machinery." But by the 1920s the House was as much under the control of the majority party leadership as it had ever been. During most of the decade, the Republican speaker, rules committee chairman, and floor leader ran the GOP Steering Committee and, hence, Congress. Surely Cannon would have nodded approval of floor leader John G. Tilson's estimate of his role in the 69th Congress (1929): "It will probably be said with truth that the most important work I have done during the session has been in the direction of preventing the passage of bad or unnecessary laws."

Much of the constitutional controversy of the early twentieth century focused on the character of the presidency—and of the Presidents. The Spanish-American War and the governance of territories afterward gave WILLIAM MCKINLEY's administration some of the attributes of the modern presidency, and led to concern over "The Growing Power of the President." But it was the chief executives of the Progressive years who gave a dramatically new shape to the office.

Theodore Roosevelt's executive vigor, his flamboyant efforts to turn the presidency into a "bully pulpit," his concern with issues such as the relations between capital and labor, the trusts, and conservation, and his assertiveness in foreign policy gave his presidency a cast of radicalism. Critics often spoke of him—more so than of any president since ABRAHAM LINCOLN—as having stretched the Constitution to its limits and beyond. Roosevelt himself thought that the power of the presidency enabled him "to do anything that the needs of the nation demanded. . . . Under this interpretation of executive power, I did and caused to be done many things not previously done. . . . I did not usurp power, but I did greatly broaden the use of executive power." But Roosevelt's innate conservatism, the traditionalist goals that informed most of his actions, and his political skill meant that few of his initiatives ran into constitutional difficulties. The most serious congressional objections on constitutional grounds came in the debate over the HEPBURN ACT expanding the power of the Interstate Commerce Commission (ICC); and Roosevelt adroitly compromised by leaving untouched the courts' power to review the ICC's decisions.

A contemporary said that the difference between Roosevelt and his successor, William Howard Taft, was that when a desirable course of action was proposed to Roosevelt he asked if the law forbade it; if not, then it should be done. Taft, on the other hand, tended to ask if the law allowed it; if not, then Congress must be asked. Taft brought a judicial temperament and experience (and almost no elective experience) to his office. He was thus a more self-conscious advocate of a limited presidency, and celebrator of the supremacy of law and of constitutional limitations, than any of his Republican predecessors.

Yet these views did not prevent his administration from adopting a more vigorous antitrust policy than that of Roosevelt. And Taft advocated innovations such as the establishment of a COMMERCE COURT to review ICC decisions and the institution of a federal BUDGET drawn up by the executive branch. The realities of early-twentieth-century American public life weighed more heavily than the niceties of constitutional theory.

Woodrow Wilson as a scholar of American government had long been critical of the traditional relationship between President and Congress. He often praised the British system of ministerial responsibility; his ideal President resembled the British Prime Minister. But as chief executive Wilson more closely followed Roosevelt's conception of the presidency as a bully pulpit (though perhaps with less bullying and more pulpit-pounding). And even more than Roosevelt he took the lead in formulating and seeing to the passage of legislation, a course symbolized by his breaking a tradition that dated from the time of THOMAS JEFFERSON by personally proposing legislation in a message to Congress.

The scope and coherence of Wilson's legislation was far greater than that of his predecessors. But it is worth noting that of the numerous major bills passed in his administration, including the FEDERAL RESERVE ACT, the FEDERAL TRADE COMMISSION ACT, the CLAYTON ANTITRUST ACT, the WEBB-KENYON ACT, the ESPIONAGE ACT, and the SEDITION ACT, only the KEATING-OWEN CHILD LABOR ACT was struck down by the Supreme Court.

With the entry of the United States into World War I, Wilson assumed presidential leadership of a sort that had not been seen since the time of Lincoln and the Civil War. The mobilization of American agriculture, industry, military manpower, and public opinion led to federal intervention into private activity on a massive scale. The creation of agencies such as the War Industries Board, the Food, Fuel, and Railroad Administrations, the War Finance Corporation, the National War Labor Board, and the Committee on Public Information, and statutes such as the SELECTIVE SERVICE ACT, the ESPIONAGE ACT, the Webb-Pomerene Act (which allowed exporters to organize cartels), and the Overman Act (which greatly expanded the President's power over federal bureaus and agencies) amounted to an unprecedented increase of federal power and its concentration under the President.

Did these circumstances in fact add up to a basic change in the constitutional character of the presidency? Certainly the administrations of WARREN G. HARDING and CALVIN COOLIDGE did not suggest so: they would have been comfortable with the most ardent (and least efficacious) practitioners of the limited presidency of the nineteenth century. Nor did HERBERT HOOVER, whose ambitions resembled those of his Progressive predecessors, exercise effective executive leadership on a bold new scale. And when FRANKLIN D. ROOSEVELT came into office in the trough of the Depression in 1933, he found it necessary to rest his call for a "temporary departure from [the] normal balance" of "executive and legislative authority" on the need for a "broad executive power to wage a war against the emergency as great as the power that would be given me if we were in fact invaded by a foreign foe."

For all the pressures of early-twentieth-century social, economic, and cultural change, the executive branch's constitutional position altered little if at all. After 1921, as before 1900, the powers of the presidency depended not upon alterations in Article II of the Constitution, or upon what the Supreme Court made of that article, but on the political skills of the incumbent and on the course of events: war and peace, prosperity and depression, the growth and alteration of government itself.

The argument that the character of American government underwent major change during the early twentieth century rests on the rise of an administrative state. Certainly one distinguishing characteristic of this period was the proliferation of administrative courts, boards, and commissions, with an attendant expansion of the powers, rules, and regulations of the public administration sector of the American state.

The ideal of expert administrators functioning through (or above) restraints such as party politics, federalism, or the balance of powers had a strong appeal to the Progressive generation. Abbot Lawrence Lowell warned: "If democracy is to be conducted with the efficiency needed in a complex modern society it must overcome its prejudice against permanent expert officials as undemocratic."

The courts had performed a number of essentially administrative and regulatory duties during the nineteenth century. Now, as economic and social problems became more complex and technical, so grew routinized and prescribed administrative processes, in which rule replaced discretion in public law. State laws and constitutions became ever more detailed and codelike; state regulatory agencies multiplied and gained substantially in independence. Federal laws increasingly left to administrative officers the "power to make supplementary law through rules and regulations."

The American involvement in World War I led to an exponential growth of administrative agencies and their power. The War Industries Board and its allied commissions had control over the American economy of a sort only dreamed of in Theodore Roosevelt's New Nationalism. Under the wartime ESPIONAGE ACT, the Post Office Department, the Department of Justice, and the Committee on Public Information wielded powers of suppression and persuasion over American thought and opinion that had no analogue in the nation's past.

Just where administrative law and its accompanying instrumentalities stood in the constitutional system was a matter of continuing concern. Woodrow Wilson observed in his pioneering 1887 essay "The Study of Administration" that "the field of administration is a field of business. It is removed from the hurry and strife of politics; it at most points stands apart even from the debatable ground of constitutional study." But administration was political in its relationship to law, to policy, and to interest group pressures; and it had an intimate relationship to— indeed, was very much a part of—the constitutional system of American government. In many ways the history of American public administration between 1900 and 1921 was a painful instruction in those home truths.

Administrative law of a sort had been part of the American constitutional system since the nineteenth century. Pensions, customs, internal revenue, land grants, and patents were administered by governmental agencies subject to little or no JUDICIAL REVIEW. There was continuing resistance to the idea that public administration had a distinct place in the constitutional order. Bruce Wyman, in one of the earliest systematic discussions of administrative law, set the subject in the context of Anglo-American COMMON LAW rather than constitutional law, holding that the central issue was whether public administration was subject to the same rules of law as governed the relations of citizens with one another.

Adolph Berle took another tack, arguing that administrative law was in fact the application of the will of the state by all three branches, for modern conditions made the traditional differentiation of functions impossible. Administrative law's constitutionality, he implied, rested on the proposition that all of the branches of government were essentially instruments for the expression of the popular will. Thus administrative law was "not a supplement to constitutional law. It is a redivision of the various bodies of law which previously had been grouped under the head of constitutional law."

The courts created evasive categories—"quasi-legislative," "quasi-judicial"—which enabled them to accept administrative powers without addressing the question of whether or not these threatened the separation of powers. By 1914 it appeared that "the exercise of certain discretionary power by administrative officers formally considered legislative is now held unobjectionable."

The growth of the federal bureaucracy, its increasing adherence to its own norms and standards, the fact that it was more and more under the civil service rather than political patronage—all of this has been taken to herald the arrival on the American scene of an autonomous administrative state. But the continuing subservience of government and public policy to the dictates of party politics, the competing governmental units of Congress and the courts, and underlying it all the persisting individualism, hostility to the state, and diversity of American life and thought, meant that the administrative expansion of the early twentieth century did not go on unchecked.

During the war, and immediately after, a number of intellectuals put forward schemes of postwar domestic economic and social reconstruction; they thought that the wartime infrastructure of governmental control and direction might be turned to more basic postwar problems. It soon became apparent, however, that both ideology and politics were working in another direction. Wilson himself told Congress in December 1918: "Our people . . . do not want to be coached and led. . . . [f]rom no quarter have I seen any general scheme of 'reconstruction' which . . . we could force our spirited businessmen and self conscious laborers to accept with due pliancy and obedience."

Similar forces worked to constrain the outward reach of postwar foreign policy embodied in the League of Nations. Both courts and legislatures after the mid-1920s began to turn from the radical-bashing of the Espionage Acts and the 1919–1920 Red Scare to begin the erection of the broad definition of FIRST AMENDMENT freedoms that would come to prevail in the modern American definition of civil liberties. A 1918 survey of American ADMINISTRATIVE LAW (probably by the young HAROLD LASKI, surely no enemy of the active state) warned that "with the great increase of state activity . . . there never was a time" when the value of the BILL OF RIGHTS "will have been so manifest."

As in so many other areas of American government, surface changes did not necessarily alter underlying continuities. Congressmen and party leaders may no longer have had the patronage power that once had been theirs. Yet Congress as an institution, and congressmen as party politicians, remained intensely sensitive to the political implications of administrative appointments, activities, and, perhaps most of all, budgets.

Attempts by the Presidents of the time to extend the control of the executive branch over the bureaucracy frequently ran afoul of congressional opposition. By 1921 it was an arguable point—as, indeed, it always had been—whether the bureaucracy was more subject to the direction of the President or to the will of Congress. One thing was certain: the autonomy of the bureaucracy—from Congress, from the parties, from politics—was not markedly greater than it had been a generation before.

True, administrative law as a field of theoretical concern and practical application would continue to develop. The New Deal did not spring fully armed from the brow of Franklin Roosevelt, but was built on a solid foundation of national and state precedents. From an international (and a later American) perspective, the New Deal's experiments did not seem especially bold and revolutionary. But the scale and passion of the charges of a broached constitutionalism raised by the New Deal's opponents in the 1930s suggests just how limited was the pre-1933 acceptance of an American administrative state.

One more aspect of the evolution (or non-evolution) of the American Constitution during the early twentieth century demands attention. That is the hoary principle of federalism: the distribution of functions between the state and federal governments.

In theory the Civil War and the postwar amendments had settled the nagging early-nineteenth-century question as to the degree to which the states were independent governmental entities. Relatively little attention was paid to the question of federalism during the late nineteenth century, in large part because the issues that most engaged the national government—tariff and currency policy, foreign relations, Indian affairs—were of marginal concern to the states. But as the full force of industrialism and urbanism began to change public policy in the early twentieth century, the relative roles of the federal and state governments once again became a matter of constitutional importance. The police power over health, safety, morals, and (from the late nineteenth century on) welfare, was the major legal basis for state social and economic legislation. For the most part the court accepted this; as ZECHARIAH CHAFEE, JR., observed in 1920, "The health, comfort, and general welfare of the citizens are in charge of the state governments, not of the United States."

But of the 194 Supreme Court decisions that invalidated state laws between 1899 and 1921, 102 were explained on the ground that the laws violated the distribution of powers embodied in the principle of federalism. By the 1920s and the early 1930s there was much talk of a judicial DUAL FEDERALISM that had created a "twilight zone" in which neither state nor federal power applied. And the attempt of the New

Deal to create a new level of national intervention in the realms of economic regulation and social welfare led to one of the great constitutional controversies in American history. Once again, it would appear that the policy changes of the 1900–1921 period were not accompanied by a significant alteration of the constitutional order.

Bibliography

BERLE, A. A., JR. 1916–1917   The Expansion of American Administrative Law. *Harvard Law Review* 30:430–448.

BETH, LOREN 1971 *The Development of the American Constitution 1877–1917.* New York: Harper & Row.

BLUM, JOHN M. 1954 *The Republican Roosevelt.* Cambridge, Mass.: Harvard University Press.

BURGESS, JOHN W. 1923 *Recent Changes in American Constitutional Theory.* New York: Columbia University Press.

HASBROUCH, PAUL D. 1927 *Party Government in the House of Representatives.* New York.

LOWELL, A. LAWRENCE 1913 Expert Administrators in Popular Government. *American Political Science Review* 7:45–62.

NOTE 1915 Delegation of Legislative Power to Administrative Officials. *Harvard Law Review* 28:95–97.

NOTE 1918 The Growth of Administrative Law in America. *Harvard Law Review* 31:644–646.

SKOWRONEK, STEPHEN 1982 *Building a New American State: The Expansion of National Administrative Capacities, 1877–1920.* Cambridge: At the University Press.

WYMAN, BRUCE 1903 *The Principles of Administrative Law Governing the Relations of Public Officers.* St. Paul, Minn.: Keefe-Davidson Co.

FULLER COURT

(1888–1910)

Owen M. Fiss

MELVILLE W. FULLER was Chief Justice of the United States from 1888 to 1910. Lawyers and historians know the period, and its significance for constitutional law, but do not generally identify it with Fuller's name— and for good reason. He was no leader. Fuller discharged his administrative duties effectively, and in "good humor," to borrow a phrase from OLIVER WENDELL HOLMES, one of his admirers, but he was not an important source of the ideas and vision that shaped the work of the Court.

The year of Fuller's appointment, 1888, was nonetheless an important date in the life of the Court because it marked the beginning of a period of rapid turnover. From 1888 to 1895 there were a considerable number of vacancies, and the two Presidents then in office, GROVER CLEVELAND, a Democrat, and BENJAMIN HARRISON, a Republican—whose politics were conservative and largely indistinguishable—appointed six of the Justices. One was Fuller himself. At the time of his appointment he was a respected Chicago lawyer and, perhaps more significantly, a friend of Cleveland's. The others were DAVID J. BREWER, a federal circuit judge in Kansas; HENRY BILLINGS BROWN, a federal district judge in Detroit; RUFUS PECKHAM, a judge on the New York Court of Appeals; GEORGE SHIRAS, a lawyer from Pittsburgh; and EDWARD D. WHITE, a senator from Louisiana. (LUCIUS Q. C. LAMAR and HOWELL JACKSON were also appointed during this period, but served for relatively short periods.) The intellectual leaders of this group of six were Brewer and Peckham. They appeared in their written opinions as the most powerful and most eloquent, and the Chief Justice usually turned to one or the other to write for the Court in the major cases.

In constructing their majorities, Brewer and Peckham could usually count on the support of STEPHEN J. FIELD (Brewer's uncle), who earlier had achieved his fame by protesting various forms of government regulation in the SLAUGHTERHOUSE CASES and the GRANGER CASES. In the late 1890s Field was replaced by JOSEPH MCKENNA, who was chosen by WILLIAM MCKINLEY, a President who continued in the conservative tradition of Cleveland and Harrison. Another ally of this Cleveland-Harrison group, though perhaps not so steadfast as Field or McKenna, was HORACE GRAY. Gray was appointed in 1881 by President CHESTER A. ARTHUR and served until 1902.

As a result of these appointments, the Court over which Fuller presided was perhaps one of the most homogeneous in the history of the Supreme Court. Even more striking, its composition did not significantly change for most of Fuller's tenure. Fuller died in July 1910, just months after Brewer and Peckham. It was almost as though he could not go on without them. Brown resigned in 1906 and Shiras in 1903, but their replacements—WILLIAM H. MOODY and WILLIAM R. DAY—did not radically alter the balance of power. The only important break with the past came when THEODORE ROOSEVELT appointed Oliver Wendell Holmes, Jr., to replace Gray.

At the time of his appointment, Holmes was the Chief Justice of the Supreme Judicial Court of Massachusetts and had already written a number of the classics of American jurisprudence. Brown described Holmes's appointment as a "topping off." On the Court, however, Holmes played a different role, for he had no taste for either the method of analysis or general philosophical outlook of the Cleveland-Harrison appointees. His stance was fully captured by his quip in LOCHNER V. NEW YORK (1905) that "The FOURTEENTH AMENDMENT does not enact Mr. Herbert Spencer's Social Statics." In this remark Holmes was finally vindicated in 1937 with the constitutional triumph of the New Deal, but in the early 1900s he spoke mostly for himself, at least on the bench, and had no appreciable impact on the course of decisions. No other Justice joined his *Lochner* dissent.

The other significant presence on the Court at the turn of the century was JOHN MARSHALL HARLAN. He was originally appointed by President RUTHERFORD B. HAYES in 1877 and served until 1911. He is greatly admired today for his views on the rights of the newly freed slaves and on the power of the national government. But, like Holmes, Harlan suffered the fate of a prophet: He was a loner. He had his own agenda, and though he sometimes spoke for the Cleveland-Harrison group, Harlan seemed most comfortable playing the role of "the great dissenter."

At the turn of the century, as in many other periods of our history, the Court was principally concerned with the excesses of democracy and the danger of tyranny of the majority. In one instance, the people in Chicago took to the streets and, through a mass strike, tied up the rail system of the nation and threatened the public order. President Cleveland responded by sending the army, and the judiciary helped by issuing an INJUNCTION. In IN RE DEBS (1895) Brewer, writing for a unanimous Court, upheld the contempt conviction of the leader of the union, and legitimated the use of the federal injunctive power to prevent forcible obstructions of INTERSTATE COMMERCE. For the most part, however, the people fought their battles in the legislative halls, and presented the Court with a number of statutes regulating economic relationships.

The question posed time and time again was whether these exercises of state power were consistent with the limitations the Constitution imposed upon popular majorities. Sometimes the question was answered in the affirmative, but the Court over which Fuller presided is largely remembered for its negative responses. It stands as a monument to the idea of limited government.

The most important such response consists of POLLOCK v. FARMERS' LOAN & TRUST CO. when, in the spring of 1895, the Court invalidated the first federal income tax enacted in peacetime. The statute imposed a 2 percent tax on all annual incomes above $4,000, and it was estimated that, due to the exemption, the tax actually fell on less than 2 percent of the population, the wealthy few who resided in a few northeastern states. The tax was denounced by JOSEPH CHOATE, in arguments before the Supreme Court, as an incident in the "communistic march," but the Court chose not to base its decision on a rule that would protect the wealthy few from redistribution. The Court instead largely relied upon that provision of the Constitution linking REPRESENTATION and taxation and requiring the apportionment among the states according to population of all DIRECT TAXES.

The Constitution identified a POLL TAX as an example of a direct tax. It was also assumed by all that a real estate tax would be another example of a direct tax, and the Court first decided that a tax upon the income from real estate is a direct tax. This ruling resulted in the invalidation of the statute as applied to rents (since the tax was not apportioned according to population), but on all other issues the Court was evenly divided, 4–4. The ninth justice, Howell Jackson, was sick at the time. A second argument was held and then the Court continued along the path it had started. Just as a tax on income from real property was deemed a direct tax, so was the tax on income from personal property (such as dividends). This still left unresolved the question whether a tax on wages was a direct tax, but the majority held that the portions of the statute taxing rents and dividends were not severable and that as a result the whole statute would fall. As Fuller reasoned, writing for the majority, if the provision on wages were severable, and it alone sustained, the statute would be transformed, for "what was intended as a tax on capital would remain in substance a tax on occupations and labors."

A decision of the Court invalidating the work of a coordinate branch of government is always problematic. *Pollock* seemed especially so, however, because the Court was sharply divided (5–4), and even more so because one of the Justices (whose identity is still unknown) seems to have switched sides after the reargument. The Justice who did not participate the first time (Jackson) voted to uphold the statute, yet the side he joined lost. It was no surprise, therefore, that *Pollock,* like *Debs,* became

an issue in the presidential campaign of 1896, when William Jennings
Bryan—a sponsor of the income tax in Congress—wrested control of
the Democratic Party from the traditional, conservative elements and
fused it with the emerging populist movement. Bryan lost the election,
but remained the leader of the party for the next decade or so, during
which the political elements critical of the Court grew in number and
persuasiveness. By 1913 a constitutional amendment—the first since
Reconstruction—was adopted. The SIXTEENTH AMENDMENT did not directly confront the egalitarian issue, any more than did the Court, but
simply declared that an income tax did not have to be apportioned.

The Court's first encounter with the SHERMAN ACT of 1890 was
negative and thus bore some resemblance to *Pollock.* In UNITED STATES
v. E. C. KNIGHT COMPANY, also announced in 1895, just months before
Debs and *Pollock,* the Court refused to read the Sherman Act to bar
the acquisition of a sugar refinery even though it resulted in a firm
that controlled 98 percent of the market and aptly was described (by
Harlan in dissent) as a "stupendous combination." The Court reasoned
that manufacturing was not within the reach of Congress's power over
"commerce." The difference with *Pollock,* however, lay in the fact that
this decision (written by Fuller) was in accord with long-standing interpretations of the COMMERCE CLAUSE, which equated "commerce" with the
transportation of goods and services across state lines. And this decision
was not denounced by the populists; they had no desire whatsoever to
have the federal government assume jurisdiction over productive activities such as agriculture. In any event, by the end of Fuller's Chief Justiceship, *E. C. Knight* was in effect eradicated by the Court itself. The Court
fully indicated that it was prepared to apply the act to manufacturing
enterprises, provided the challenged conduct impeded or affected the
flow of goods across state lines.

In the late 1890s, almost immediately after *E. C. Knight,* the Court,
speaking through Peckham, applied the Sherman Act to prohibit open
price-fixing arrangements by a number of railroads. There was little
issue in these cases about the reach of the commerce power, because
they involved transportation, but the Court was sharply divided over
an issue that was presented by these early antitrust cases, namely, whether
such an interference with what was then perceived as ordinary or accepted
business practices (supposedly aimed at preventing "ruinous competition") was an abridgment of FREEDOM OF CONTRACT. At first the argument
about freedom of contract was presented as a constitutional defense of
the application of the Sherman Act, wholly based on the DUE PROCESS
clause, but starting with Brewer's separate concurrence in UNITED STATES
v. NORTHERN SECURITIES COMPANY (1903) and then again in White's
opinions for a near-unanimous Court in the STANDARD OIL COMPANY
v. UNITED STATES (1911) and UNITED STATES v. AMERICAN TOBACCO

COMPANY (1911), the liberty issue dissolved into a question of statutory interpretation. The Sherman Act was read to prohibit not all but only "unreasonable" restraints of trade, and if a business practice was "unreasonable," then it was, almost by definition, the proper subject of government regulation.

In the late 1890s and early 1900s, antitrust sentiments were the principal cause of the growing Progressive movement. While populists extolled cooperative activity, progressives tried to use the legislative power to preserve the market and the liberties that it implied. They condemned activities (such as mergers or price fixing) that stemmed from the ruthless pursuit of self-interest but that, if carried to their logical extreme, would destroy the social mechanism that both legitimates and is supposed to control such self-interested activity. Progressives were also concerned, however, with stopping certain practices that did not threaten the existence of the market, but rather offended some standard of "fairness" or "decency" that had a wholly independent source. And they used the legislative power for this end.

The Justices were not unmoved by the moralistic concerns that fueled the progressives, but they were also determined—as they had been in *Pollock*—to make certain that the majorities were not using the legislative power to redistribute wealth or power in their favor. In some instances the Court allowed redistributive measures that benefited some group that was especially disadvantaged and thus could be deemed a ward of the state. On that theory, the Court, in a unanimous opinion by Brewer, upheld in MULLER V. OREGON (1908) a statute creating a sixty-hour maximum work week for women employed in factories or laundries. More generally, however, the Court voiced the same fears that had animated *Pollock* and insisted that there be a "direct" connection between the legislative rule and an acceptable (that is, nonredistributive) end such as health. The statute at issue in *Lochner v. New York,* for example, was defended on the ground that a work week for bakers in excess of sixty hours would endanger their health. Justice Peckham's opinion for the majority acknowledged that there might be some connection between a maximum work week and health, but suspected redistributive purposes and argued that if, in the case of bakers, this connection with health were deemed sufficient—that is, direct—the same could be said for virtually every occupation or profession: "No trade, no occupation, no mode of earning one's living, could escape this all-pervading power."

Just as it was fearful of state intervention to control the terms of employment, the Court was also wary of legislation regulating consumer prices—a practice initiated by the Granger movement of the 1870s but continued by the populists and progressives in the 1890s and the early 1900s. In this instance the Court feared that the customers would enrich themselves at the expense of the investors. The danger was, as Brewer formulated it, one of legalized theft. In contrast to cases like *Lochner*, however, the Court took up this issue with a viable and highly visible precedent on the books, namely, *Munn v. Illinois* (1877). Some consideration was given to OVERRULING the decision (there was no limit to the daring of some of the Justices), but the Court finally settled upon a more modest strategy—of cabining *Munn*.

For one thing, the *Munn* formula for determining which industries would be regulated—a formula that allowed the state to reach "any industry AFFECTED WITH A PUBLIC INTEREST"—was narrowed. In *Budd v. New York* (1892) the Court upheld the power of the legislature to regulate the rates of grain operators, but placed no reliance on the *Munn* public interest formula. Instead, it stressed the presence of monopoly power and the place of the grain operation in the transportation system. Second, the Court began to surround the rate-settling power with procedural guarantees. Legislatures were now delegating the power of setting prices to administrative bodies, such as railroad commissions, and the Court, in CHICAGO, MILWAUKEE & ST. PAUL RAILWAY CO. V. MINNESOTA (1890), required agencies of that type to afford investors a full, quasi-judicial hearing prior to setting rates. Finally, the Court ended the tradition of judicial deference initiated by *Munn* by authorizing judicial review of the rate actually set. The purpose was to insure against confiscation and to this end Brewer articulated in REAGAN V. FARMERS' LOAN & TRUST (1894) a right of FAIR RETURN ON FAIR VALUE. In that case the rate was set so low as to deny the investors any return at all. In the next case, SMYTH V. AMES (1898), there was some return to the investors, but the Court simply concluded that the rate was "too low."

Reagan v. Farmers' Loan & Trust and *Smyth v. Ames* were both unanimous and thrust the federal judiciary into the business of policing state rate regulations. A particularly momentous and divisive exercise of this supervisory jurisdiction occurred when a federal judge in Minnesota enjoined the attorney general of that state from enforcing a state statute that set maximum railroad rates. The attorney general disobeyed the injunction and was held in criminal contempt. Peckham wrote the opinion for the Court in EX PARTE YOUNG (1908) affirming the contempt conviction, and in doing so, constructed a theory that, notwithstanding the ELEVENTH AMENDMENT, provided access to the federal EQUITY courts to test the constitutionality of state statutes—an avenue of recourse that was to become critical for the CIVIL RIGHTS movement of the 1960s. Ironically, Harlan, who, by dissenting in the CIVIL RIGHTS CASES (1883) and in PLESSY V. FERGUSON (1896), had already earned for himself an honored place in the history of civil rights, bitterly dissented in *Ex parte Young*, because, he argued, the Court was opening the doors of federal courts to test the validity of all state statutes.

The confrontations between the Court and political branches in economic matters such as antitrust, maximum hours, and rate regulation were considerable—*Northern Securities, Lochner,* and *Ex Parte Young* were important public events of their day. Some of these decisions were denounced by political forces, particularly by the Progressive movement, which had begun to dominate national politics. Roosevelt made his disappointment with Holmes's performance in *Northern Securities* well known ("I could carve out of a banana a judge with more backbone than that"— a comment that seems only to have either amused or pleased Holmes) and finished his presidency in 1908 with a speech to Congress sharply critical of the Court. By 1912 the Supreme Court and its work were once again the subject of debate in a presidential election, as it had been in the election of 1896. It was as though the body politic was scoring the Court over which Fuller had presided for the past twenty years. Now the critical voices were more respected and covered a wider political spectrum than in 1896, but the results were mixed.

In the 1912 election the Democratic candidate, Woodrow Wilson, beat the incumbent WILLIAM HOWARD TAFT, who was generally seen as the defender, indeed the embodiment, of the judicial power. On the other hand, Wilson was less critical of the Court than Roosevelt, who ran as a Progressive. The legislation of this period also was two-sided. The CLAYTON ACT of 1914, for example, exempted labor from antitrust legislation (thus reversing the *Danbury Hatters* decision of 1908), and also imposed procedural limits on the use of the labor injunction (thus revising *Debs*), but it did not in fact have as critical an edge as the Sixteenth Amendment of 1913. The Clayton Act did not repudiate the idea of the labor injunction altogether nor did it repudiate the rule of reason in antitrust cases. Similarly, although Congress reacted in 1910 to *Ex Parte Young,* it did so only in a trivial, near-cosmetic way, by requiring three judges (as opposed to one) to issue an injunction against the enforcement of state statutes.

In attempting to construct limits on the power of the political branches, and to guard against the tyranny of the majority as it did in *Pollock, Ex Parte Young,* and *Lochner,* the Court assumed an activist posture. The Justices were prepared to use their power to frustrate what appeared popular sentiments. The activist posture was, however, mostly confined to economic reforms—redistributing income, regulating prices, controlling the terms of employment—as though the constitutional conception of liberty were structured by an overriding commitment to capitalism and the market. This characterization of their work, voiced in a critical spirit in their day and in ours, is strengthened when a view is taken of the Justices' overall receptiveness to the antitrust program of the progressives, and even more when account is taken of the pattern of decisions outside the economic domain, respecting human rights as opposed to property rights. The Justices were passive about human rights—by and large willing to let majorities have their way.

A particularly striking instance of this passivity consists of their reaction to the treatment of Chinese residents. Ever since the Civil War the Chinese were by statute denied the right to become naturalized citizens, but in the late 1880s and the early 1900s their situation worsened. The doors of the nation were closed to any further IMMIGRATION, and Congress (in the Geary Act of 1892) created an oppressive regime for those who had previously been admitted. Chinese residents were required to carry passes, and failure to have the passes subjected them to DEPORTATION proceedings that were to be conducted by commissioners (rather than judges or juries) and that put them to the task of producing "at least one credible white witness." YICK WO V. HOPKINS (1886), which invalidated, on EQUAL PROTECTION grounds, a San Francisco laundry ordinance that had disadvantaged the Chinese, was already on the books. But neither it nor the passionate dissent of Brewer ("In view of this enactment of the highest legislative body of the foremost Christian nation, may not the thoughtful Chinese disciple of Confucius fairly ask, why do they send missionaries here?") was of much avail. The Court sustained the Geary Act in *Fong Yue Ting v. United States* (1893) in virtually all its particulars.

A few years later the Court held in UNITED STATES V. WONG KIM ARK (1898) that Chinese children born here were, by virtue of the FOURTEENTH AMENDMENT, citizens of the United States. But this decision sharply divided the Court, despite the straightforward language of the amendment ("All persons born . . . in the United States and subject to the jurisdiction thereof are citizens of the United States"), and did not materially improve the quality of the process the Chinese received. There was, by virtue of *Wong Kim Ark,* a chance that a Chinese person whom the government was trying to deport was a natural born citizen, yet the Court did not even require that this claim of CITIZENSHIP be tried by a judge. Holmes wrote the opinion in these cases, *United States v. Sing Tuck* (1904) and *United States v. Ju Toy* (1905), and once again Brewer, now joined by Peckham, dissented with an intensity equal to that he had exhibited in *Fong Yue Ting.*

The same spirit of acquiescence was manifest in the cases involving the civil rights of blacks, though here it was Harlan who kept the nation's conscience. In *Plessy v. Ferguson* (1896) the Court upheld a Louisiana statute requiring racial SEGREGATION of rail cars; Harlan dissented and, borrowing a line from Plessy's lawyer, Albion Tourgee, insisted that "our Constitution is colorblind." In HODGES V. UNITED STATES (1906) the Court dismissed a federal INDICTMENT against a group of white citizens in Arkansas who forced a mill owner to discharge the blacks who had been hired. Brewer, for the majority, said that the power of the federal government under the Civil War-Reconstruction amendments (and thus under the criminal statute in question) extended only to acts by state officials. He reaffirmed the principle of the CIVIL RIGHTS CASES of 1883 by which the Court effectively ceded to the states exclusive jurisdiction to govern the treatment of one citizen by another. In *Hodges,* Harlan, the Union general from Kentucky, replayed his dissent in the *Civil Rights* cases, and denounced this principle as a fundamental distortion of the Thirteenth and Fourteenth Amendments. And in BEREA COLLEGE v. KENTUCKY (1908) the Court, over Harlan's dissent, upheld a state law that prohibited a private educational corporation from conducting its educational programs on an integrated basis.

Berea College was also written by Brewer. He was mindful of the contrast with a case such as *Lochner,* where the judicial power had been used to the utmost to protect the contractual freedom of worker and employer. Accordingly, Brewer stressed the fact that this law was applicable only to CORPORATIONS, which, to pick up a theme he had previously articulated in his concurring opinion in *Northern Securities,* were merely artificial entities created by government, not entitled to the same degree of protection as natural persons. He specifically left open the question of the validity of a similar statute if it regulated the conduct of natural persons. Harlan, in an equally equivocal dissent, said that a different result might follow if the statute regulated public rather than private education. In fact, the distorting impact of public subsidies upon the articulation of civil rights had been implicitly acknowledged some years earlier in *Cumming v. Board of Education* (1899). In that case Harlan dismissed a challenge by black parents to a decision of a local county, which ran its schools on a segregated basis, to close the only black high school and to send the black students out of the county for their education.

In the 1890s and early 1900s blacks, through one scheme or another, were disenfranchised on a grand scale. The FIFTEENTH AMENDMENT was reduced to a nullity, as Jim Crow was becoming more firmly entrenched. On several occasions, the Court was presented with challenges to these electoral practices, yet it was unable to respond with the energy that it had summoned in *Pollock* or *Lochner* or *Reagan* or, even more to the point, *Debs.* Holmes, the spokesman in these early VOTING RIGHTS cases, saw judicial relief as nothing but an "empty form": "[R]elief from a great political wrong, if done, as alleged, by the people of a State and the State itself, must be given by them or by the legislative and political department of the government of the United States." Harlan dissented, as might be expected, but so did Brewer. They realized that, because the disenfranchisement was the work of state officials, something more was at issue than the allocation of power between states and nation approved in the *Civil Rights Cases.* What was at issue, according to Brewer and Harlan, was nothing less than the integrity of the judicial power and the duty of the judiciary, to borrow a line from *Debs,* to do whatever it could to fulfill the promise of the Constitution.

The principal issue before the Court at the turn of the century was democracy and, more specifically, the determination of what limits should be placed on popular majorities. As was evident in the civil rights cases, however, the Court was also asked to allocate power between the states and the national government. The FEDERALISM issue arose in many contexts, including antitrust, labor, and rate regulation, but the one in which it proved most troublesome was PROHIBITION. By the late 1880s the prohibition movement was an active force in the states, and Fuller began his Chief Justiceship with a set of constitutional decisions that were unstable. In MUGLER V. KANSAS (1887) the Court had held that prohibition was within the STATE POLICE POWER, yet, just weeks before Chief Justice MORRISON R. WAITE's death, the Court in *Bowman v. Iowa* (1888) had also held that the states were without power to prohibit the importation of liquor from other states. The Court seemed to take away in one decision what it gave in the other. Fuller confronted this problem early on in LEISY V. HARDIN (1890), and in probably his most lasting contribution to constitutional law, fashioned an odd response. First, he announced that the commerce clause barred the states from prohibiting the sale of imported liquor (as well as its actual importation). Second, he invited Congress to intervene, and to authorize states to pass laws that would prohibit out-of-state liquor. Congress quickly responded to this invitation, and in the Wilson Act of 1890 authorized states to enact measures aimed at erecting walls to out-of-state liquor.

The state laws in question in *Leisy v. Hardin* were invalidated on the theory that they sought to regulate a matter that required nationwide uniformity. When it came to judging the congressional response, Fuller found the requisite uniformity since it was Congress that had spoken (even though it did no more than allow the states to choose) and on that theory, in *In re Rahrer* (1891), upheld the Wilson Act. In 1898, however, after some change in the composition of the Court and after the responsibility of speaking on this issue had shifted to one of the new appointees, Edward White, a sharply divided Court cut back on the Wilson Act. *Rhodes v. Iowa* (1890) held that the Wilson Act authorized a ban on sales of imported liquor within the state but not a ban on the importation itself. White insisted that any other construction would raise grave constitutional doubts as to the validity of the Wilson Act. Fuller joined White's opinion.

Over the next decade, mail order business in out-of-state liquor grew. The conflict between the Court and the prohibition movement escalated. Then in 1913 Congress, as part of the same era that saw the Sixteenth Amendment and the Clayton Act, passed the WEBB-KENYON ACT to remove any ambiguity over what it sought to accomplish in the

Wilson Act. Congress allowed states to bar both the sale and the importation of out-of-state liquor. After considerable struggle and deliberation, the Webb-Kenyon Act was upheld in an opinion by White (then Chief Justice) on the theory (if that is what it can be called) that "liquor is different." For all other goods, the common market was deemed a constitutional necessity.

The federalism issue has recurred throughout the entire history of the Supreme Court. The Court over which Fuller presided did, however, confront one issue pertaining to structure of government that was unique to the times: colonialism. The issue arose from the "splendid little war," as Secretary of State John Hay called the Spanish-American War of 1898, which left the United States with two former Spanish colonies, PUERTO RICO and the Philippines. (Much earlier the United States had purchased Alaska, and in the late 1890s it had also taken possession of Hawaii.) The assumption was that the United States would hold these territories as territories, for an indefinite period, and perhaps ultimately build a colonial empire along the European model. The question posed for the Supreme Court—not just by the litigants but by the nation at large—was whether colonialism was a constitutionally permissible strategy for the United States. Technically, the case involved a challenge to a statute imposing a tariff on goods (sugar) imported from Puerto Rico into the states. The Constitution bars Congress from imposing duties on the importation of goods from one state to another, and so the issue was whether a territory was to be treated the same as a state, or, as phrased in the language of the day, whether the Constitution followed the flag.

Three positions emerged in a series of decisions beginning in 1901 known as the INSULAR CASES. The first, most in keeping with the position of the Court in *Pollock* and the other economic cases, proclaimed the idea of limited government. The government of the United States was formed and established by the Constitution, and thus it was impossible to conceive of a separation of Constitution and government. This was the position taken by Brewer, Peckham, Fuller, and Harlan. At the opposite end of the spectrum was the so-called annexation position. It proclaimed the separation of Constitution and flag, and generally left the government unrestricted in its activities in the territories; whatever restrictions there were flowed from natural law or from a small group of provisions of the Constitution deemed essential (the tariff provision was not one). This position was most congenial to the government and yet at odds with the general jurisprudence of the Court. Only Justice Brown subscribed to it.

The remaining four Justices, in an opinion written by White, put forth what was called the incorporation theory. It tried to chart a middle course, as appeared to be White's trade. It made the Constitution fully applicable to a territory, but only after that territory was incorporated into the United States. (Prior to incorporation the government would be subject only to the restraints of natural law.) Justice White's opinion also made it clear that the decision to incorporate a territory resided in Congress. In the case before it the Court decided that the territory was not incorporated, but White also acknowledged that incorporation could be done by implication and, even more to the point, he reserved for the judiciary the power to determine whether that act of incorporation had taken place.

Ultimately incorporation was adopted as the position of the Court. But this did not occur until 1905, after an insurrection in the Philippines and other developments in the world (such as the Boer War) had made the idea of a colonial empire seem less attractive, and the danger of further imperial acquisitions seemed to have waned. In fact, incorporation became majority doctrine in *Rassmussen v. United States* (1905) in which the Court held that Alaska had been *implicitly* incorporated and that the United States was bound by the BILL OF RIGHTS in its governance of that territory. The outcome in this case affirmed the idea of limited government and JUDICIAL SUPREMACY, the hallmarks of this Court, and made it possible for Fuller, and perhaps even more significantly, for Brewer and Peckham, to abandon their absolutist position and to support the middle-of-the-road theory of White—perhaps a sign of what was to come in 1910, when Fuller died and Taft, who had once served as the commissioner in the Philippines, replaced him with White.

Bibliography

DUKER, WILLIAM   1980   Mr. Justice Rufus W. Peckham: The Police Power and the Individual in a Changing World. *Brigham Young University Law Review* 1980:47–67.
———   1980   Mr. Justice Rufus W. Peckham and the Case of *Ex Parte Young:* Lochnerizing *Munn v. Illinois. Brigham Young University Law Review* 1980:539–558.
GOODWYN, LAWRENCE   1976   *Democratic Promise: The Populist Movement in America.* New York: Oxford University Press.
KING, WILLARD   1967   *Melville Weston Fuller, Chief Justice of the United States, 1888–1910.* Chicago: University of Chicago Press.
KOLKO, GABRIEL   1963   *The Triumph of Conservatism: A Reinterpretation of American History 1900–1916.* New York: Free Press.
PAUL, ARNOLD   1960   *Conservative Crisis and the Rule of Law: Attitudes of Bar and Bench 1887–1895.* Ithaca, N.Y.: Cornell University Press.
PIERCE, CARL   1972   A Vacancy on the Supreme Court: The Politics of Judicial Appointment, 1893–1894. *Tennessee Law Review* 39:555–612.
ROCHE, JOHN   1974   *Sentenced to Life.* New York: Macmillan.

ROGAT, YOSAL   1963   The Judge as Spectator. *University of Chicago Law Review* 31:231–278.

THORELLI, HANS   1954   *The Federal Antitrust Policy: Origination of an American Tradition.* Baltimore: Johns Hopkins University Press.

TWISS, BENJAMIN   1942   *Lawyers and the Constitution: How Laissez Faire Came to the Supreme Court.* Princeton, N.J.: Princeton University Press.

WESTIN, ALAN   1953   The Supreme Court, the Populist Movement and the Campaign of 1896. *Journal of Politics* 15:3–41.

———   1958   Stephen J. Field and the Headnote to *O'Neil v. Vermont:* A Snapshot of the Fuller Court at Work. *Yale Law Journal* 67:363–383.

WOODWARD, C. VANN   1966   *The Strange Career of Jim Crow,* rev. ed. New York: Oxford University Press.

WHITE COURT
(1910–1921)

Benno C. Schmidt, Jr.

"The condition of the Supreme Court is pitiable, and yet those old fools hold on with a tenacity that is most discouraging," President WILLIAM HOWARD TAFT wrote in May 1909 to his old friend HORACE H. LURTON. Taft would have his day. One year later, Chief Justice MELVILLE W. FULLER spoke at the Court's memorial service for Justice DAVID J. BREWER: "As our brother Brewer joins the great procession, there pass before me the forms of Mathews and Miller, of Field and Bradley and Lamar and Blatchford, of Jackson and Gray and of Peckham, whose works follow them now that they rest from their labors." These were virtually Fuller's last words from the bench, for he died on Independence Day, 1910, in his native Maine. RUFUS W. PECKHAM had died less than a year earlier. WILLIAM H. MOODY, tragically and prematurely ill, would within a few months have to cut short by retirement one of the few notable short tenures on the Court. JOHN MARSHALL HARLAN had but one year left in his remarkable thirty-four-year tenure. By 1912, five new Justices had come to the Court who were not there in 1909: a new majority under a new Chief Justice.

The year 1910 was a significant divide in the history of the country as well. The population was nearly half urban, and immigration was large and growing. The country stood on the verge of enacting humane and extensive labor regulation. A year of Republican unrest in Congress and THEODORE ROOSEVELT's decisive turn to progressive agitation, 1910 was the first time in eight elections that the Democrats took control of the House. In the same year, the National Association for the Advancement of Colored People was founded. It was a year of progressive tremors that would eventually shake the Supreme Court to its foundations with the appointment of LOUIS D. BRANDEIS in 1916. But the five appointments with which President Taft rehabilitated his beloved Court between 1909 and 1912 had no such dramatic impact. There was a significant strengthening of a mild progressive tendency earlier evident within the Court, but the new appointments brought neither a hardening nor a decisive break with the DOCTRINES of laissez-faire constitutionalism and luxuriant individualism embodied in such decisions as LOCHNER v. NEW YORK (1905) and ADAIR v. UNITED STATES (1908). Taft's aim was to strengthen the Court with active men of sound, if somewhat progressive, conservative principles. Neither Taft nor the nation saw the Court, as both increasingly would a decade later, as the storm center of pressures for fundamental constitutional change.

Taft's first choice when Peckham died in 1909 was his friend Lurton, then on the Sixth Circuit, and a former member of the Tennessee Supreme Court. Lurton, a Democrat, had been a fiery secessionist in his youth, and in his short and uneventful four-year tenure he combined conservationism on economic regulation, race, and labor relations. Taft's second choice was not so modest. When Taft went to Governor CHARLES EVANS HUGHES of New York to replace Brewer, he brought to the Court for the first of his two tenures a Justice who would emerge as one of the greatest figures in the history of American law, and a principal architect of modern CIVIL LIBERTIES and CIVIL RIGHTS jurisprudence. As governor of New York, Hughes was already one of the formidable reform figures of the Progressive era, and his later career as a presidential candidate who came within a whisper of success in 1916, secretary of state during the 1920s, and Chief Justice during the tumultuous years of the New Deal, mark him as one of the most versatile and important public figures to sit on the Court since JOHN MARSHALL.

Taft's choice of the Chief Justice to fill the center seat left vacant by Fuller was something of a surprise, although reasons are obvious in retrospect. EDWARD D. WHITE was a Confederate veteran from Louisiana, who had played a central role in the Democratic reaction against Reconstruction in that state and had emerged as a Democratic senator in 1891. He had been appointed Associate Justice in 1894 by President GROVER CLEVELAND and had compiled a respectable but unobtrusive record in sixteen years in the side seat. He had dissented with able force from the self-inflicted wound of POLLOCK v. FARMERS' LOAN & TRUST CO. (1895), holding unconstitutional the federal income tax, and his antitrust dissents in TRANS-MISSOURI FREIGHT ASSOCIATION (1897) and UNITED STATES v. NORTHERN SECURITIES COMPANY (1904) embodied sound good sense. He had done "pioneer work," as Taft later called it, in ADMINISTRATIVE LAW. White had a genius for friendship and, despite a habit of constant worrying, extraordinary personal warmth. OLIVER WENDELL HOLMES summed him up in these words in 1910: "His writing leaves much to be desired, but his thinking is profound, especially in the legislative direction which we don't recognize as a judicial requirement but which is so, especially in our Court, nevertheless." White was sixty-five, a Democrat, a Confederate veteran, and a Roman Catholic, and his selection by Taft was seen as adventurous. But given Taft's desire to bind up sectional wounds, to spread his political advantage, to put someone in the center seat who might not occupy Taft's own ultimate ambition for too long, to exemplify bipartisanship in the choice of Chief

Justice, and on its own sturdy merits, the selection of White seems easy to understand.

Along with White's nomination, Taft sent to the Senate nominations of WILLIS VAN DEVANTER of Wyoming and JOSEPH R. LAMAR of Georgia. Van Devanter would sit for twenty-seven years, and would become one of the Court's most able, if increasingly conservative, legal craftsmen. Lamar would last only five years, and his death in 1915, along with Lurton's death in 1914 and Hughes's resignation to run for President, opened up the second important cycle of appointments to the White Court.

The Taft appointees joined two of the most remarkable characters ever to sit on the Supreme Court. John Marshall Harlan, then seventy-eight, had been on the Court since his appointment by President RUTHER-FORD B. HAYES in 1877. He was a Justice of passionate strength and certitude, a man who, in the fond words of Justice Brewer, "goes to bed every night with one hand on the Constitution and the other on the Bible, and so sleeps the sleep of justice and righteousness." He had issued an apocalyptic dissent in *Pollock,* the income tax case, and his dissent in PLESSY V. FERGUSON (1986), the notorious decision upholding racial SEGREGATION on railroads, was an appeal to the conscience of the Constitution without equal in our history. The other, even more awesome, giant on the Court in 1910 was Holmes, then seventy, but still not quite recognized as the jurist whom BENJAMIN N. CARDOZO would later call "probably the greatest legal intellect in the history of the English-speaking judiciary." The other two members of the Court were JOSEPH McKENNA, appointed by President WILLIAM McKINLEY in 1898, and WILLIAM R. DAY, appointed by President Theodore Roosevelt in 1903.

The Supreme Court in 1910 remained in "truly republican simplicity," as Dean Acheson would recall, in the old Senate chamber, where the Justices operated in the midst of popular government, and in the sight of visitors to the Capitol. No office space was available, and the Justices worked in their homes. Their staff allowance provided for a messenger and one clerk, and their salaries were raised in 1911 to $14,500 for the Associate Justices and $15,000 for the Chief Justice. The Court was badly overworked and the docket was falling further and further behind, not to be rescued until the JUDICIARY ACT OF 1925 gave the Court discretion to choose the cases it would review.

In the public's contemporaneous view, if not in retrospect, the most important cases before the White Court between 1910 and 1921 did not involve the Constitution at all, but rather the impact of the SHERMAN ANTITRUST ACT on the great trusts. UNITED STATES V. STANDARD OIL COMPANY (1911) and *American Tobacco Company v. United States* (1911) had been initiated by the Roosevelt administration to seek dissolution of the huge combinations, and when the cases were argued together before the Supreme Court in 1911, the *Harvard Law Review* thought public attention was concentrated on the Supreme Court "to a greater extent than ever before in its history."

The problem for the Court was to determine the meaning of restraint of trade amounting to monopoly. The answer offered by Chief Justice White for the Court was the famous RULE OF REASON, under which not all restraints of trade restrictive of competition were deemed to violate the Sherman Act, but rather only those "undue restraints" which suggested an "intent to do wrong to the general public . . . thus restraining the free flow of commerce and tending to bring about the evils, such as enhancement of riches, which were considered to be against public policy." Under this test, the Court deemed Standard Oil to have engaged in practices designed to dominate the oil industry, exclude others from trade, and create a monopoly. It was ordered to divest itself of its subsidiaries, and to make no agreements with them that would unreasonably restrain trade. The court ruled that the American Tobacco Company was also an illegal combination and forced it into dissolution.

Antitrust was perhaps the dominant political issue of the 1912 presidential campaign, and the rule of reason helped to fuel a heated political debate that produced the great CLAYTON ACT and FEDERAL TRADE COMMISSION ACT of 1914. Further great antitrust cases came to the White Court, notably *United States v. United States Steel Company*, begun in 1911, postponed during the crisis of World War I, and eventually decided in 1920. A divided Court held that United States Steel had not violated the Sherman Act, mere size alone not constituting an offense.

The tremendous public interest generated by the antitrust cases before the White Court was a sign of the temper of the political times, in which the regulation of business and labor relations was the chief focus of progressive attention. In this arena of constitutional litigation, the White Court's record was mixed, with perhaps a slight progressive tinge. On the great questions of legislative power to regulate business practices and working arrangements, the White Court maintained two parallel but opposing lines of doctrines, the one protective of laissez-faire constitutionalism and freedom from national regulation, the other receptive to the progressive reforms of the day.

In the first four years after its reconstitution by Taft, the Supreme Court handed down a number of important decisions upholding national power to regulate commerce for a variety of ends. The most expansive involved federal power to regulate railroads—and to override competing state regulation when necessary. *Atlantic Coast Line Railroad v. Riverside Mills* (1911) upheld Congress's amendment of the HEPBURN ACT imposing on the initial carrier of goods liability for any loss occasioned by a connecting carrier, notwithstanding anything to the contrary in the bill of lading. FREEDOM OF CONTRACT gave way to the needs of shippers for easy and prompt recovery. More significantly, in the second of the EMPLOYERS' LIABILITY CASES (1912), the Court upheld congressional legislation imposing liability for any injury negligently caused to any employee of a carrier engaged in INTERSTATE COMMERCE. This legislation did away with the fellow-servant rule and the defense of contributory negligence, again notwithstanding contracts to the contrary. In 1914, in the famous *Shreveport Case* (HOUSTON, EAST & WEST TEXAS RAILWAY COMPANY V. UNITED STATES) the Court upheld the power of the Interstate Commerce Commission to set the rates of railroad hauls entirely within Texas, because those rates competed against traffic between Texas and Louisiana. The Court overrode the rates set by the Texas Railroad Commission in the process. And in the most important COMMERCE CLAUSE decision of the early years of the White Court, the MINNESOTA RATE CASES (1913), the Court upheld the power of the states to regulate railroad rates for intrastate hauls, even when that regulation would force down interstate rates, so long as there had been no federal regulation of those rates. Thus, state power over rates was not invalidated because of the possibility of prospective federal regulation, and a large loophole between state and federal power was closed.

Outside the area of carrier regulation, the White Court was also friendly to national regulation by expanding the NATIONAL POLICE POWER doctrine. HIPOLITE EGG CO. V. UNITED STATES (1911) upheld the PURE FOOD AND DRUG ACT of 1906 in regulating adulterated food and drugs shipped in interstate commerce, whether or not the material had come to rest in the states. "Illicit articles" that traveled in interstate commerce were subject to federal control, the Court said, although with a doctrinal vagueness and confusion that would come back to haunt the Court in HAMMER V. DAGENHART (1918). In HOKE V. UNITED STATES (1913) the Court upheld the MANN ACT, which punished the transportation in interstate commerce of women "for the purpose of prostitution or debauchery, or for any other immoral purpose."

Taft got his opportunity for a sixth appointment—more appointments in one term than any President in our history since GEORGE WASHINGTON—when Harlan died in 1911. He filled the vacancy with MAHLON PITNEY, chancellor of New Jersey. The reasons for this appointment are obscure, but like other Taft appointments Pitney was a sound, middle-of-the-road, good lawyer with little flair or imagination. As if to prepare for the coming flap over Brandeis, the Pitney appointment ran into trouble because of the nominee's alleged antilabor positions. But Pitney prevailed, and he would serve on the Court until 1922.

If ever in the history of the Supreme Court successive appointments by one President have seemed to embrace dialectical opposites, WOODROW WILSON's appointments of JAMES C. MCREYNOLDS in 1914 and Louis D. Brandeis in 1916 are the ones. McReynolds would become an embittered and crude anti-Semite; Brandeis was the first Jew to sit on the Supreme Court. McReynolds would become the most rigid and doctrinaire apostle of laissez-faire conservatism in constitutional history, the most recalcitrant of the "Four Horsemen of Reaction" who helped to scuttle New Deal legislation in the early 1930s. Brandeis was the greatest progressive of his day, on or off the Court. McReynolds was an almost invariable foe of CIVIL LIBERTIES and CIVIL RIGHTS for black people; Brandeis was perhaps the driving force of his time for the development of civil liberties, especially freedom of expression and rights of personal privacy. What brought these opposites together in Wilson's esteem, although he came to regret the McReynolds appointment, was antitrust fervor. McReynolds's aggressive individualism and Brandeis's progressive concern for personal dignity and industrial democracy coalesced around antitrust law, and this was the litmus test of the day for Wilson. Thus, possibly the most difficult and divisive person ever to sit on the Supreme Court and possibly the most intellectually gifted and broadly influential Justice in the Court's history took their seats in spurious, rather Wilsonian, juxtaposition.

Wilson's third appointment was handed him by the resignation of his rival in the presidential election of 1916. As it became plain that Hughes was the only person who could unite the Republican party, he came under increasing pressure from Taft and others to make himself available. He did. Wilson nominated JOHN J. CLARK of Ohio to replace Hughes. One of the most pregnant speculations about the history of the Supreme Court is what might have happened had Hughes remained on the bench. He might well have become a Chief Justice in 1921 instead of Taft, and under his statesmanlike influence, the hardening of doctrine that led to the confrontation over the New Deal and the Court-packing plan might not have happened.

Although two of Wilson's three appointments were staunch progressives, the Supreme Court seemed to adopt a somewhat conservative stance as it moved toward the decade of erratic resistance to reform that would follow in the 1920s. Federal reform legislation generally continued to pass muster, but there was the staggering exception of the *Child Labor Case* in 1918. And the Court seemed to strike out at labor unions, in both constitutional and antitrust decisions.

In *Hammer v. Dagenhart* (1918) the Supreme Court stunned Congress and most of the country when it invalidated the first federal CHILD LABOR ACT. The extent of child labor in the United States during the Progressive era was an affront to humanitarian sensibilities. One child out of six between the ages of ten and fifteen was a wage earner. Prohibition and regulation of child labor became the central reform initiatives of the progressive impulse. In 1916, overcoming constitutional doubts, Wilson signed the KEATING-OWEN ACT, which forbade the shipment in interstate or foreign commerce of the products of mines where children sixteen and under had been employed, or of factories where children younger than fourteen worked, or where children fourteen to sixteen had worked more than eight hours a day, six days a week. Child labor was not directly forbidden, but was severely discouraged by closing the channels of interstate commerce.

A narrow majority of the Court, in an opinion by Justice Day, held that this law exceeded the federal commerce power. Day reasoned that the goods produced by child labor were in themselves harmless, and that the interstate transportation did not in itself accomplish any harm. This reasoning was entirely question-begging, because it was the possibility of interstate commerce that imposed a competitive disadvantage in states that outlawed child labor in comparison with less humanitarian states. Moreover, the reasoning was flatly inconsistent with the opinion in *Hipolite Egg* and *Hoke*. But the majority plainly regarded the federal child labor legislation as an invasion of the domestic preserves of the states. Holmes, joined by McKenna, Brandeis, and Clarke, issued a classic dissent.

With the preparations for an advent of American involvement in World War I, the Supreme Court recognized broad federal power to put the economy on a wartime footing. The burden of constitutional resistance to reform legislation shifted to cases involving state laws. Here the main hardening in doctrinal terms came in cases involving labor unions. Otherwise, a reasonable progressivism prevailed. Thus, in BUNTING V. OREGON (1917) the Court upheld the maximum ten-hour day for all workers in mills and factories, whether men or women. However, two minimum wage cases from Oregon were upheld only by the fortuity of an equally divided Supreme Court, Brandeis having recused himself.

The most chilling warning to progressives that laissez-faire constitutionalism was not dead came in COPPAGE V. KANSAS (1915). The issue was the power of a state to prohibit by legislation the so-called YELLOW DOG CONTRACT, under which workers had to promise their employers not to join a union. The Court in *Coppage* held such laws unconstitutional: to limit an employer's freedom to offer employment on its own terms was a violation of freedom of contract.

The Supreme Court's race relations decisions between 1910 and 1921 constitute one of the Progressive era's most notable, and in some ways surprising, constitutional developments. Each of the Civil War amendments was given unprecedented application. For the first time, in the *Grandfather Clause Cases* (1915), the Supreme Court applied the FIFTEENTH AMENDMENT and what was left of the federal civil rights statutes to strike down state laws calculated to deny blacks the right to vote. For the first time, in BAILEY V. ALABAMA (1911) and UNITED STATES V. REYNOLDS (1914), the Court used the THIRTEENTH AMENDMENT to strike down state laws that supported PEONAGE by treating breach of labor contracts as criminal fraud and by encouraging indigent defendants to avoid the chain gang by having employers pay their fines in return for commitments to involuntary servitude. For the first time, in BUCHANAN v. WARLEY (1917), it found in the FOURTEENTH AMENDMENT constitutional limits on the spread of laws requiring racial separation in residential areas of cities and towns, and also for the first time, in *McCabe v. Atchison, Topeka & Santa Fe Railway* (1914), it put some teeth in the equality side of the SEPARATE BUT EQUAL DOCTRINE by striking down an Oklahoma law that said that railroads need not provide luxury car accommodations for blacks on account of low demand.

To be sure, only with respect to peonage could the White Court be said to have dismantled the legal structure of racism in any fundamental way. After the White Court passed into history in 1921, blacks in the South remained segregated and stigmatized by Jim Crow laws, disfranchised by invidiously administered LITERACY TESTS, white PRIMARY ELECTIONS, and POLL TAXES; and victimized by a criminal process from whose juries and other positions of power they were wholly excluded. But if the White Court did not stem the newly aggressive and self-confident ideology of racism inundating America in the Progressive era, neither did it put its power and prestige behind the flood, as had the WAITE COURT and FULLER COURT that preceded it—and, at critical points, it resisted. The White Court's principled countercurrents were more symbols of hope than effective bulwarks against the racial prejudice that permeated American law. But the decisions taken together mark the first time in American history that the Supreme Court opened itself in more than a passing way to the promises of the Civil War amendments.

World War I generated the first set of cases that provoked the Supreme Court for the first time since the FIRST AMENDMENT was ratified in 1791 to consider the meaning of freedom of expression. The cases, not surprisingly, involved dissent and agitation against the war policies of the United States. The war set off a major period of political repression against critics of American policy.

In the first three cases, SCHENCK V. UNITED STATES, FROHWERK V. UNITED STATES, and IN RE DEBS (1919), following the lead of Justice Holmes, the Supreme Court looked not to the law of SEDITIOUS LIBEL for justification in punishing speech but rather to traditional principles of legal responsibility for attempted crimes. In English and American COMMON LAW, an unsuccessful attempt to commit a crime could be punished if the attempt came dangerously close to success, while preparations for crime—in themselves harmless—could not be punished. With his gift of great utterance, Holmes distilled these doctrinal nuances into the rule that expression could be punished only if it created a CLEAR

AND PRESENT DANGER of bringing about illegal action, such as draft resistance or curtailment of weapons production. Given his corrosive skepticism and his Darwinian sense of flux, the clear and present danger rule later became in Holmes's hands a fair protection for expression. But in the hands of judges and juries more passionate or anxious, measuring protection for expression by the likelihood of illegal action proved evanescent and unpredictable.

There were other problems with the clear and present danger rule. It took no account of the value of a particular expression, but considered only its tendency to cause harmful acts. Because the test was circumstantial, legislative declarations that certain types of speech were dangerous put the courts in the awkward position of having to second-guess the legislature's factual assessments of risk in order to protect the expression. This problem became clear to Holmes in ABRAMS v. UNITED STATES (1919), in which a statute punishing speech that urged curtailment of war production was used to impose draconian sanctions on a group of radical Russian immigrants who had inveighed against manufacture of war material that was to be used in Russia. In this case, Holmes and Brandeis joined in one of the greatest statements of political tolerance ever uttered.

In 1921, the year Edward Douglass White died and Taft became Chief Justice, Benjamin Cardozo delivered his immortal lectures, "The Nature of the Judicial Process." Cardozo pleaded for judges to "search for light among the social elements of every kind that are the living forces behind the facts they deal with." The judge must be "the interpreter for the community of its sense of law and order . . . and harmonize results with justice through a method of free decision." Turning to the Supreme Court, Cardozo stated: "Above all in the field of constitutional law, the method of free decision has become, I think, the dominant one today."

In this view, we can see that Cardozo was too hopeful, although his statement may have been offered more as an admonition than a description. The method of "free decision," exemplified for Cardozo by the opinions of Holmes and Brandeis, remained in doubt notwithstanding the inconsistent progressivism of the White Court, and would become increasingly embattled in the decades to come.

Bibliography

BICKEL, ALEXANDER M. and SCHMIDT, BENNO C., JR. 1984 *The Judiciary and Responsible Government 1910–1921.* Vol. IX of the Holmes Devise History of the Supreme Court. New York: Macmillan.

CARDOZO, BENJAMIN N. 1921 *The Nature of the Judicial Process.* New Haven, Conn.: Yale University Press.

CHAFEE, ZECHARIAH   1949   *Free Speech in the United States*. Cambridge, Mass.: Harvard University Press.

HIGHSAW, ROBERT B.   1981   *Edward Douglass White*. Baton Rouge: Louisiana State University Press.

SEMONCHE, JOHN E.   1978   *Charting the Future: The Supreme Court Responds to a Changing Society 1890–1920*. Westport, Conn.: Greenwood Press.

SWINDLER, WILLIAM F.   1969   *Court and Constitution in the 20th Century: The Old Legality 1889–1932*. Indianapolis: Bobbs-Merrill.

CONSTITUTIONAL HISTORY, 1921–1933

Paul L. Murphy

If reverence for the federal Constitution had diminished in the Progressive era, it was revitalized in the 1920s, as the Constitution again became a symbol of national unity and patriotism. Organizations such as the American Bar Association and the National Security League launched national campaigns of patriotism, circulating leaflets and pamphlets by the hundreds of thousands, encouraging Constitution worship, promoting an annual Constitution Day, and working for state laws to require Constitution instruction in the public schools. Forty-three states passed laws mandating the study of the the Constitution; often such laws required loyalty oaths for teachers. Such laws were intended to affirm one hundred percent Americanism from every public school instructor.

The Constitution which was so apotheosized, however, was one geared primarily to the service of property interests. This meant, on the one hand, the protection of business from government regulation and from assault by radical and liberal critics; and, on the other, active intervention of courts and the executive branch to see that constitutional ways were found to insure that the free use of one's property be protected by positive government policies, both formal and informal. Thus, while constitutional changes did occur during the decade and new emphases were developed, these modulations were contained within the dominant ideological construct of free enterprise and individual property rights— rights, it was argued, that had been secured for all time by the sacred document and its amendments.

The most influential constitutionalist of the 1920s was Chief Justice WILLIAM HOWARD TAFT. Taft set the tone for national political leadership. He was fully committed to the protection of a social order explained and justified by the tenets of JOHN LOCKE, Adam Smith, the Manchester Economists, WILLIAM BLACKSTONE, THOMAS COOLEY, and Herbert Spencer. Espousing a social ethic that stressed self-reliance, individual initiative and responsibility, and the survival of the fittest, Taft emphasized the virtually uninhibited privilege of private property and rationalized the growth of corporate collectivism in terms of individual liberty and private enterprise. For Taft it was time to move away from Progressive expansivism and restore the country to its traditional constitutional bases through a legal system that rested primarily upon judicial defense of a static Constitution and an immutable natural law.

In specific constitutional terms, these goals required restrictive, although selectively restrictive, interpretations of the federal government's taxing and commerce power; an emphasis upon the TENTH AMENDMENT as an instrument for precluding federal intrusion into the reserved powers of the states; and a limitation on the states themselves, through an interpretation of the FOURTEENTH AMENDMENT that emphasized SUBSTANTIVE DUE PROCESS and FREEDOM OF CONTRACT. These constitutional constructs would protect property against restrictive state laws but leave the states free through their police power to legislate against private activities that might threaten that property.

Operating from these assumptions, the Supreme Court majority in this period was activist in its hostility to legislative enactments that threatened or constrained the rights or privileges of the "haves" of society. Thus, between 1921 and 1933, that body ruled unconstitutional fourteen acts of Congress, 148 state laws placing governmental restraints on one or another form of business activity, and twelve city ordinances. Conversely, its majority had no trouble sustaining federal measures that aided business and sanctioning numerous state laws and city ordinances that abridged the CIVIL LIBERTIES of labor, radicals, too outspoken pacifists, and other critics of the capitalist system. In 1925, Taft took the further step of lobbying through Congress a new JUDICIARY ACT, granting the Supreme Court almost unlimited discretion to decide for itself what cases it would hear. (See CERTIORARI, WRIT OF.) Henceforth the Court could choose to take no more cases than it could handle expediently and could restrict adjudication to matters of more general interest. The result was an upgrading of the importance of the cases that the body did agree to hear and a commensurate enhancement of the Court's own prestige and power. Such a looming judicial presence dampened the enthusiasm of activist legislators, state and national, for pushing social reform legislation and made progressive members of REGULATORY COMMISSIONS cautious about exercising their frequently limited authority. Hence bodies such as the Interstate Commerce Commission and the Federal Trade Commission remained largely passive during the period, except when their business-oriented majorities sought to act solicitiously toward those being regulated.

The three presidential administrations of the period, while sharing a common constitutional philosophy, differed in concrete legislative and policy accomplishments. WARREN G. HARDING had begun his presidency with an ambitious legislative docket. His proposals included a National BUDGET AND ACCOUNTING ACT (previously vetoed by WOODROW WILSON), a new farm credit law, the creation of a system of national highways,

the enactment of a Maternity Bill, the immediate development and effective regulation of aviation and radio, the passing of an antilynching
law, and the creation of a Department of Public Welfare. A surprised
Congress was confused over priorities and wound up passing little legislation. The PACKERS AND STOCKYARDS ACT of 1921 made it unlawful for
packers to manipulate prices, create monopolies, and award favors to
any person or locality. The regulation of stockyards provided for nondis-
criminatory services, reasonable rates, open schedules, and fair charges.
The measure, which was constitutionally based on a broad interpretation
of the COMMERCE CLAUSE, gave the secretary of agriculture authority to
entertain complaints, hold hearings, and issue CEASE AND DESIST ORDERS.
The bill was a significant part of the agrarian legislation of the early
1920s, and its validation by the Supreme Court in STAFFORD v. WALLACE
(1922) provided a constitutional basis for later New Deal legislation.
The 1921 Congress also passed the FESS-KENYON ACT, appropriating
money for disabled veteran rehabilitation, and the SHEPPARD-TOWNER
MATERNITY ACT, subsidizing state infant and maternity welfare activities.
Aside from the bill setting up a Budget Bureau in the Treasury Department with a director appointed by the President, little else was forthcoming. By the end of 1921 the *New York Times* observed: "It is evident,
and it is clearly admitted in Washington, that the public is not counting
any longer upon sound and constructive legislation from Congress."
Indeed, Congress supported only occasional further legislation through
the decade. One effect of such congressional inaction, along with the
increasingly desultory Harding leadership and the even more quiescent
CALVIN COOLIDGE presidency, was to direct the attention of reformers
to the AMENDING PROCESS.

The immediate post-World War I years had seen the ratification
of the EIGHTEENTH AMENDMENT (prohibition) and the NINETEENTH
AMENDMENT (woman suffrage). In the 1920s certain fallout from both
occurred. Prohibition was unpopular from the start. In fact, noncompli-
ance became such a problem that by the late 1920s President HERBERT
HOOVER appointed a special commission, headed by former Attorney
General GEORGE WICKERSHAM to "investigate problems of the enforcement of prohibition under the 18th Amendment." As the report of
the commission stated, "the public was irritated at a constitutional 'don't'
in a matter where the people saw no moral question." More specifically,
the commission pointed to enforcement problems, emphasizing the lack
of an American tradition of concerned action between independent government instrumentalities. This, it felt, was now being painfully demonstrated by the Eighteenth Amendment's policy of state enforcement of
federal laws, with responsibility too often falling between the two stools
and enforcement occurring not at all. Not surprisingly, during the twelve
years that the Eighteenth Amendment was in force, more than 130

amendments affecting the Eighteenth in some manner were introduced. Most of these amendments provided for outright repeal; others weakened the amendment in varying degrees. When FRANKLIN D. ROOSEVELT opposed prohibition in 1932, he attracted wide support. The TWENTY-FIRST AMENDMENT repealing the Eighteenth was ratified in December 1933, although prohibition's legal residue took some years to settle. (This measure came only nine months after passage of the relatively uncontroversial TWENTIETH AMENDMENT, eliminating the "lame duck" session of Congress and changing the time for the inauguration of presidents from March to January).

The momentum that carried woman suffrage to a successful amendment continued to some degree into the early 1920s. Some feminist leaders continued to push for improved working conditions for women, for minimum wage laws, and for laws bettering the legal status of women in marriage and DIVORCE. In 1922, Congress passed the Cable Act, providing that a married woman would thereafter retain and determine her own citizenship and make her own application for naturalization after lawful admission for permanent residence, which the Act reduced to three years. Supporters of the political emancipation of women, especially the National Women's Party, got the EQUAL RIGHTS AMENDMENT (ERA) introduced in Congress in 1923 and worked for its adoption by lobbying and exerting political pressure in the early years of the decade. At that time the ERA was opposed by most of the large women's organizations, by trade unions, and by the Women's Bureau primarily because it was seen as a threat to labor-protective legislation. Opponents contended that the ERA would deprive most working women and the poor of hard-won economic gains and would mainly benefit middle and upper class women. Thus the measure floundered at the time, not to be revived until toward the end of World War II. The same period saw all native-born American Indians granted full citizenship through the Curtis Act of 1924. The measure, however, did not automatically entitle them to vote, and some states still disfranchised Indians as "persons under guardianship." In 1925 Congress passed the Federal Corrupt Practices Act, extending federal regulation of political corruption to the choice of presidential electors.

A CHILD LABOR AMENDMENT fared only slightly better. With the Supreme Court striking down federal child labor laws as unconstitutional under both the commerce and the taxing powers, advocates of children's rights turned to the amending process and Congress adopted a proposed Child Labor Amendment in June 1924. Opposed by manufacturers' associations and certain religious groups, the measure, by 1930, had secured ratification in only five states. More than three-fourths had rejected it, with the greatest hostility coming from the south and from agricultural regions, where child labor was seen as essential to family economic stability. The measure was eventually superseded by the FAIR LABOR STANDARDS ACT of 1938. By that time the evils of child exploitation were no longer felt to be beyond the constitutional reach of federal legislative power.

Other amendments were proposed: providing minimum wages for women; establishing uniform national marriage and divorce laws; giving the president an item veto in appropriation bills; abolishing congressional immunity for speeches and debates in either house; providing representation for the DISTRICT OF COLUMBIA; changing the amending process itself; providing for the election of judges; providing for the independence of the Philippine Islands; prohibiting sectarian legislation; defining the right of states to regulate employment of ALIENS; requiring teachers to take an oath of allegiance; preventing governmental competition with private enterprise; conferring upon the House of Representatives coordinate power for the ratification of treaties; limiting the wealth of individual citizens; providing for legislation by INITIATIVE; extending the civil service merit system; regulating industry; and prohibiting loans to any except allies. Varying support for all reflected, to a greater or lesser degree, public discontent with aspects of the political-constitutional system of the time. A segment of this discontent crystallized in the La Follette Progressive Party's 1924 platform, which even proposed the RECALL of judges, much to the alarm and ire of Chief Justice Taft. Such straws in the wind did not, however, portend a successful assault upon property-oriented constitutional interpretation. That assault would await the depths of the Depression.

The middle to later years of the decade saw continued congressional hostility to government interference in economic and personal activities, but no reluctance to use power when the result supported President Coolidge's aphorism that "the business of America is business." Antilynching legislation failed during the decade; northern conservatives joined white southerners in deploring it as an assault upon STATES' RIGHTS and individual freedom. In 1927, Congress enacted the McNary-Haugen Farm Bill, an elaborate measure calling for federal support for agricultural prices. The measure countered the prevailing temper of constitutional conservatism, for it extended national regulatory authority over agricultural PRODUCTION and thus not only invaded a sphere of authority traditionally reserved to the states but also interfered extensively with private property rights. President Coolidge vetoed the measure, denouncing it as "economically and constitutionally unsound." When Congress persisted, he vetoed a second McNary-Haugen Bill the following year on the same grounds.

Somewhat similar antistatist sentiments emerged when, in 1925, newly appointed Attorney General HARLAN FISKE STONE took the Bureau of Investigation out of politics and terminated its pursuit of radicals.

"There is always the possibility," Stone stated in taking the action, "that a secret police may become a menace to free government and free institutions because it carries with it the possibility of abuses of power which are not always quickly apprehended or understood. The Bureau . . . is not concerned with political or other opinions of individuals. It is concerned with their conduct, and then only with such conduct as is forbidden by the laws of the United States." Store's action was popular with all but some patriotic and right-wing groups for whom radical, or even unorthodox, ideas were a threat which the government did have a responsibility actively to check.

On the other hand, Congress met little opposition when it enacted a broad, restrictive IMMIGRATION Act in 1924 imposing stringent quotas on entry to the United States, heavily biased against southern and eastern European and Asiatic peoples. Such action was consonant with the strong tendency of the courts in the period to define the rights of aliens narrowly, with an eye to keeping such people in their proper place, particularly as easily exploitable members of the work force.

To the extent that an alternative constitutional tradition existed or was developed in the 1920s, its impact was not fully felt until Depression days. There were undertones of protest, however, coming from disparate sources. Justice LOUIS D. BRANDEIS, in his dissent in *Gilbert v. Minnesota* (1920), a decision sustaining a sedition conviction for criticism of the government's wartime policies, had stated: "I cannot believe that liberty guaranteed by the Fourteenth Amendment includes only liberty to acquire and to enjoy property." Others quickly picked up on the contradiction in this double standard, particularly when the same "liberty" was not then deemed applicable to FREEDOM OF SPEECH, FREEDOM OF THE PRESS, and FREEDOM OF ASSEMBLY. The AMERICAN CIVIL LIBERTIES UNION (ACLU), a product of the war, itself an opponent of strong government intervention in people's personal lives, worked through the decade to strengthen the power of labor and working people. The ACLU operated on the assumption that BILL OF RIGHTS freedoms flowed from economic power and that artificial impediments to the achievement of that power had to be removed. The National Association for the Advancement of Colored People was active in the decade in behalf of the constitutional rights of minorities, although its successes in producing constitutional change were decidedly limited. Similarly, organized labor saw itself as a beleaguered "minority" throughout the decade, attributing its position partly to conservation constitutionalism. Samuel Gompers stated shortly before his death: "The Courts have abolished the Constitution as far as the rights and interest of the working people are concerned."

The impact of such criticism ultimately was not so great as that from popularly elected constitutional liberals and an influential segment of the legal community. Senators William E. Borah and GEORGE NORRIS openly opposed the appointment of CHARLES EVANS HUGHES to the Chief Justiceship, arguing that there was a need for judges who would stop treating the Fourteenth Amendment only as a protection of property and recognize it as a guarantee of individual liberty. Although this opposition failed, partly because of Hughes's constitutional record and the public image of him as more progressive than reactionary, the Senate did block the subsequent nomination of John J. Parker, a prominent North Carolina Republican, to the Supreme Court in 1930; opponents particularly emphasized his racist and antilabor record. Both actions constituted unignorable Depression calls for constitutional liberalization, echoed increasingly by liberal lawyers, particularly in the law schools, many of which has been influenced by the LEGAL REALISM movement of the times. Such criticism combined with growing disillusionment with the business establishment and cynicism about a Supreme Court that could be aggressively activist in the protection of property rights and a paragon of self-restraint when it came to protecting human rights. Pressure for altered uses of government power mounted fairly early in Depression days.

Herbert Hoover was undoubtedly the most competent of the 1920s Presidents. A successful mining engineer and government bureaucrat, he had served effectively as war-time food administrator under Woodrow Wilson and as secretary of commerce in the Harding and Coolidge administrations. Hoover was eager to overhaul the executive branch of the government and reorganize it in ways that would achieve greater efficiency and greater economies in government. Saddled quickly with the worst depression in American history, Hoover was pressed to launch a large-scale national attack on the depression through federal governmental action. Such action had to fit his constitutional views, which were decidedly Taftian. For Hoover, "unless the enterprise system operated free from popular controls, constitutional freedoms would die." "Under the Constitution it was impossible to attempt the solution of certain modern social problems by legislation." "Constitutional change must be brought about only by the straightforward methods provided by the Constitution itself." Such a commitment to laissez faire economics and constitutional conservatism precluded sweeping federal actions and permitted only such remedial legislation as the AGRICULTURAL MARKETING ACT of 1929, designed to assist in the more effective marketing of agricultural commodities. Congress created the Reconstruction Finance Corporation in 1932 to rescue commercial, industrial, and financial institutions through direct government loans. Both measures so limited the scope of permissible federal activity that neither proved adequate to the challenge of providing successful depression relief.

A more specific example of Hoover's constitutionalism involved congressional enactment of the Muscle Shoals Bill of 1931. In 1918 President

Wilson had authorized, as a war-time measure, the construction of government plants at Muscle Shoals on the Tennessee River for the manufacture of nitrates and of dams to generate electric power. After the war the disposition of these plants and dams produced bitter national controversy. Conservatives insisted that they be turned over to private enterprise. Congress twice enacted measures providing for government ownership and operation for the production and distribution of power and the manufacture of fertilizers. In vetoing the second of these bills (Coolidge had vetoed the first in 1928), Hoover reiterated his belief that government ownership and operation was an approach to socialism designed to break down the initiative and enterprise of the American people. He argued that such a measure was an unconstitutional federal entrance into the field of powers reserved to the states and as such deprived the people of local communities of their liberty.

A growing number of congressmen and senators, however, were convinced that such constitutional negativism was no longer useful. In 1932, Congress passed and sent to a reluctant President the NORRIS-LaGUARDIA ACT, probably the most important measure of the period. Ever since the 1890s, labor had protested against business's turn to the courts for INJUNCTIONS to prohibit its legitimate activities. Congress's only response was a Railway Labor Act, in 1926, giving railway labor the right to bargain collectively through its own representatives. By the late 1920s, a national campaign against the labor INJUNCTION was launched with liberal congressional leaders joined by groups as disparate as the ACLU, the Federal Council of Churches, and the American Federation of Labor, all protesting the unfairness and unconstitutionality of enjoining labor's legitimate use of speech, press, and assembly. The Great Depression intensified this discontent. The Norris-LaGuardia Act made YELLOW DOG CONTRACTS unenforceable in federal courts; forbade the issuance of injunctions against a number of hitherto outlawed union practices; and guaranteed jury trials in criminal prosecutions based on violations of injunctions. The act thus removed the machinery for a variety of informal antilabor devices.

Hoover's response was to seek assurance from his attorney general, William Mitchell, that the more rigorous terms of the measure could be successfully bypassed. Having gained such assurance, he signed the bill, leaving Senator Norris to remark, bitterly, that the President dared not veto but did everything he could to weaken its effect. Yet the measure was generally popular, as was its symbolism, which presaged a more active role for the federal government in the achievement of social justice.

Such response was not lost on Franklin D. Roosevelt. During the presidential campaign of 1932, he called for a new, more liberal view of the Constitution and a BROAD CONSTRUCTION of congressional legislative power as a way of solving the nation's difficult problems. His overwhelming election victory seemed to assure that the minority liberal constitutional arguments of the 1920s would become majority ones when the New Deal program was enacted.

Bibliography

HICKS, JOHN D.   1960   *Republican Ascendancy, 1921–1933.* New York: Harper & Row.

LEUCHTENBURG, WILLIAM E.   1958   *The Perils of Prosperity, 1914–1932.* Chicago: University of Chicago Press.

MURPHY, PAUL L.   1972   *The Constitution in Crisis Times, 1918–1969.* New York: Harper & Row.

———   1972   *The Meaning of Freedom of Speech: First Amendment Freedoms from Wilson to F.D.R.* Westport, Conn.: Greenwood Press.

TAFT COURT

(1921–1930)

Robert M. Cover

WILLIAM HOWARD TAFT became Chief Justice of the United States on June 30, 1921. Never before or since has any person brought such a range of distinguished experience in public affairs and professional qualifications to the bench. Taft presided over a court that included Justices of highly varied abilities and achievements. In 1921, OLIVER WENDELL HOLMES, already a great figure of the law, had served nineteen years on the Supreme Court. He remained on the Court throughout Taft's tenure and beyond. Holmes's only equal on the Court was LOUIS D. BRANDEIS, who had been on the Court barely five years at Taft's accession. Taft, a private citizen in 1916, had vigorously opposed the appointment of Brandeis to the High Court. Although they remained ideological opponents and although some mistrust persisted on both sides, they maintained cordial relations, carrying on their opposition in a highly civil manner.

The rest of the Court that Taft inherited lacked the stature or ability of Holmes and Brandeis. Three Justices, JOHN J. CLARKE, MAHLON PITNEY, and WILLIAM R. DAY would retire within the first two years of Taft's tenure. Their retirements gave President WARREN C. HARDING a chance to reconstitute the Court. The President appointed his former Senate colleague GEORGE H. SUTHERLAND to one of the vacancies. The other two spots were filled by men strongly recommended by Taft: PIERCE BUTLER and EDWARD T. SANFORD.

The other Justices on the Court in 1921 were WILLIS VAN DEVANTER, JAMES C. McREYNOLDS, and JOSEPH McKENNA. Van Devanter had been appointed to the bench by Taft when he was President. He, like Butler and Sanford, continued to be strongly influenced by the Chief Justice. During the Taft years, he served the Chief Justice in the performance of many important institutional tasks outside the realm of decision making and opinion writing. For example, Van Devanter led the drive to revamp the JURISDICTION of the Supreme Court in the "Judges' Bill," the JUDICIARY ACT OF 1925. McReynolds, a Wilson appointee, was an iconoclastic conservative of well-defined prejudices.

Finally, Taft inherited Joseph McKenna, whose failing health impaired his judicial performance. In 1925, Taft, after consulting the other justices, urged McKenna to retire. McKenna was succeeded by HARLAN F. STONE. Though deferential to Taft at the outset, by the end of the decade Stone became increasingly identified with the dissenting positions of Holmes and Brandeis. From early 1923 through Taft's resignation only that one change took place.

Because of the substantial continuity of personnel the Taft Court can be thought of as an institution with a personality and with well-defined positions on most critical issues that came before it. Outcomes were as predictable as they ever can be, and the reasoning, persuasive or not, was consistent.

Taft was a strong Chief Justice. He lobbied powerfully for more federal judges, for a streamlined federal procedure, for reorganization of the federal judiciary, and for greater control by the Supreme Court over the cases it would decide. The most concrete of Taft's reforms was a new building for the Court itself, though the building was not completed until after his death.

A second major institutional change was completed during Taft's term. In 1925 Congress passed the "Judges' Bill." The Supreme Court's agenda is one of the most important factors in determining the evolution of constitutional law. Until 1891 that agenda had been determined largely at the initiative of litigants. In 1891 the Court received authority to review certain classes of cases by the discretionary WRIT OF CERTIORARI. However, many lower court decisions had continued to be reviewable as of right in the Supreme Court even after 1891. The 1925 act altered the balance by establishing the largely discretionary certiorari jurisdiction of the Supreme Court as it has remained for six decades. The act was one of Taft's major projects. It relieved the docket pressure occasioned by the press of obligatory jurisdiction, and placed agenda control at the very center of constitutional politics.

The successful initiatives of the Court in seizing control of its own constitutional agenda and constructing a new home should not obscure the fact that the Court's institutional position was, as always, under attack during the 1920s. A spate of what were perceived as antilabor decisions in 1921–1922 led to calls from the labor movement and congressional progressives to circumscribe the Court's powers. In the 1924 election Robert LaFollette, running as a third-party candidate on the Progressive ticket, called for a constitutional amendment to limit JUDICIAL REVIEW. Both the Republican incumbent, CALVIN COOLIDGE, and the 1924 Democratic candidate, JOHN W. DAVIS, defended the Court against LaFollette. The upshot of the unsuccessful LaFollette campaign was a heightened sensitivity to judicial review as an issue and a firm demonstration of the consensus as to its legitimacy and centrality in the American constitutional system.

Much of the labor movement had supported LaFollette's initiatives against judicial review, but labor specifically sought limitations on federal court labor INJUNCTIONS. Labor's campaign against injunctions peaked in 1927 after the Supreme Court simultaneously declined to review a series of controversial injunctions in the West Virginia coal fields and approved an injunction in BEDFORD CUT STONE COMPANY V. JOURNEYMAN STONECUTTERS, holding that a union's nationwide refusal to handle non-union stone should be enjoined as an agreement in RESTRAINT OF TRADE. Between 1928 and 1930 the shape of what was to become the NORRIS-LaGUARDIA ACT OF 1932 emerged in Congress. The impetus behind that law, the politics of it, indeed, the language and theory of the statute itself are rooted in the Taft years.

A description of the Court's institutional role must consider the relations between CONGRESS AND THE COURT in shaping constitutional law and constitutional politics. During the Taft years a dialogue between Court and Congress persisted on a variety of crucial constitutional issues. The decision of the Court striking down the first Child Labor Act in HAMMER V. DAGENHART (1918) led to congressional interest in using the taxing power to circumvent apparent limitations on the direct regulatory authority of Congress under the COMMERCE CLAUSE. The second Child Labor Act imposed an excise tax on the profits of firms employing child labor. That act was struck down as unconstitutional in 1922.

From 1922 on Congress had before it various versions of antilynching legislation—most notably the Dyer Bill, which had actually passed the House. Opponents of the antilynching legislation argued that it was an unconstitutional federal usurpation of state functions. In *Moore v. Dempsey* (1923), decided shortly after the Dyer Bill had nearly succeeded in passage, the Court held that a state criminal trial dominated by a mob constituted a denial of DUE PROCESS OF LAW, appropriately redressed in a federal HABEAS CORPUS proceeding. *Moore v. Dempsey* did not establish that an antilynching law would be constitutional. Yet a conclusion that mob domination of a criminal trial did *not* deny due process surely would have been a constitutional nail in the coffin of antilynching laws. And, prior to *Moore v. Dempsey* the relatively recent PRECEDENT of FRANK V. MANGUM (1915) had pointed toward just such a conclusion. Considerations concerning the response of Congress regularly influenced the constitutional decision making of the Taft Court. When Taft was appointed, three important labor cases were pending that had been argued but not decided by the WHITE COURT. The Court had reached an impasse. Two of the cases presented questions about the use of injunctions to restrain labor picketing. Section 20 of the Clayton Act appeared to deny the federal courts the power to issue such injunctions subject to certain exceptions, most notably the power to use the injunction to protect property from damage. *American Steel Foundries v. Tri-City Labor Council*

presented questions of construction of this section, and TRUAX V. CORRI-
GAN, involving a state law, presented a constitutional variant of the Clayton Act problem.

In *American Steel Foundries,* Taft's first significant opinion as Chief
Justice, the Court read section 20 to encompass protection of the property
interest in an ongoing business from unreasonable or intimidating picketing or from illegal BOYCOTTS or strikes. Statutory construction thus preserved the injunction as a restraint on labor.

But not all state courts saw the issue as the Taft Court did. The
Arizona Supreme Court read its statute to bar injunctions in labor disputes, at least where actual destruction of physical property was not
threatened. In *Truax v. Corrigan,* decided a week after *American Steel
Foundries,* Taft wrote for a majority of five, holding that Arizona had
unconstitutionally denied employers the injunction in labor disputes.
Truax in effect created a constitutional *right* to a labor injunction. It
did so on two grounds. First, it held that employers were denied the
EQUAL PROTECTION OF THE LAWS insofar as their particular type of property
interest was denied the same protection afforded other property interests.
Second, it held that the failure to protect the interest in the continued
operation of a business deprived the business owner of property without
due process of law. *Truax v. Corrigan* was the cornerstone of the Taft
Court edifice of industrial relations. Not only did the decision suggest
that Congress could not constitutionally prevent the federal courts from
granting labor injunctions, but it also ushered in a decade of the most
intensive use of the labor injunction the country had ever seen. A desperate battle was fought to save the unionized sector of coal from competition
from the newer, largely nonunion, southern mines. That union campaign
was broken by dozens of labor injunctions upheld by the Fourth Circuit
in a consolidated appeal. The Supreme Court's refusal to review those
decisions in 1927 attracted larger headlines than all but the most significant of Supreme Court opinions ever get. The Fourth Circuit opinion
later cost Circuit Judge John J. H. Parker a seat on the Supreme Court.
In fact, however, his conclusion was an all but inevitable consequence
of the Supreme Court's position in *Truax v. Corrigan.*

The industrial order that the Taft Court sought to protect from
labor insurgency was itself built upon uncertain constitutional foundations. The Taft Court was not committed, unambiguously, to a laissez-
faire market. The Court distinguished sharply between legislation regulating the price (wage or rent) terms of a contract and laws regulating
other terms. Thus, in the best known of its apparent inconsistencies,
the Taft Court held void a District of Columbia law prescribing a minimum wage for women, although only a year later it upheld a New
York law establishing maximum hours for women. The Court also struck

down a state statute regulating fees or commissions for employment brokers while intimating that other reasonable regulatory measures directed at employment brokerage would be upheld.

Sutherland, in his peculiar majority opinion in the minimum wage case—ADKINS v. CHILDREN'S HOSPITAL (1923)—seemed preoccupied with the redistributive aspects of the minimum wage law. There was nothing wrong with a legislative preference for a living (minimum) wage; the problem lay in imposing an obligation on the employer to pay it. One person's need, he argued, could not, in itself, justify another's obligation to satisfy it. The regulation of nonprice terms need not be redistributive in effect, for the costs of any such regulation could be recaptured by negotiated changes in price. If the Court was seeking to protect bargains against regulation with redistribution effect, then shielding price terms from governmental interference was the most visible and easily understood way to accomplish its purpose.

In general the Taft Court sought to maintain principled distinctions among three forms of economic activity. Government enterprise was subject to the usual constitutional constraints upon government. This form of economic activity was relatively unimportant in the 1920s, although in cases involving municipal utilities the Court had some opportunity to address such issues as contractual rate structure. The Court spoke more frequently to the problem of transition from private to public or from public to private enterprise. World War I had seen government control of the railroads, shipping, coal, and, to a lesser degree, labor relations generally. The Court had to develop principles of compensation to govern the takeover and return of such large-scale enterprises.

More important than the dichotomy between governmental and private economic activity was the distinction drawn between private activity AFFECTED WITH A PUBLIC INTEREST and the more general run of private economic endeavor. Upon this distinction turned the constitutionality of public regulation—including price regulation in some circumstances—of various forms of economic activity. Although the category of business affected with a public interest had been part of the Court's rhetorical stock in trade for almost half a century when Taft took his seat, it assumed particular significance through the decade beginning with a case from Kansas. In 1920, having survived the effects of a bitter coal strike, Kansas passed its Industrial Court Act, declaring all production and distribution of food, clothing, shelter, and fuel for human consumption or use to be business affected with a public interest. Public transportation and public utilities were also so labeled. The act forbade strikes, lockouts, and plant closings in all such industries except by order of the Kansas Court of Industrial Relations. Moreover, that court upon its own motion or upon the petition of virtually any person could adjudicate the fitness or adequacy of wages and prices in any such business.

The act contemplated a form of compulsory arbitration to replace labor bargaining against a background of strikes and lockouts.

In a series of unanimous opinions the Supreme Court struck down one after another of these innovative aspects of the Kansas act. Taft, in the leading opinion, WOLFF PACKING CORPORATION v. COURT OF INDUSTRIAL RELATIONS (1923) held that the state could not, by legislative fiat, declare businesses to be affected with a public interest for purposes so comprehensive as to include supervision of their wage and price structures. Taft's opinion wholly failed to state a principled distinction between those businesses traditionally subject to price regulation (such as grain elevators), on the one hand, and meat packing, on the other. In OBITER DICTUM he suggested that the competitive structure of the industry was not determinative of the legislature's power to regulate. But the opinion did acknowledge that long-established law permitted regulation of publicly conferred monopolies and of common carriers or inns even if not monopolies.

The Taft Court thus rejected a generalization, based on the war experience, that all basic economic activity could be defined as affected with a public interest. But the Court was not unmindful of the war's lessons. Unanimously it upheld the recapture provisions of the [Railroad] Transportation Act of 1920 despite the overt redistributive effect of the law. The act required the payment into a federal trust fund of half the profits earned by strong railroads, for redistribution to failing ones. The Chief Justice, at least, understood the recapture provisions as justified in part because the alternative to such a scheme might have to be nationalization. Furthermore, the Court had already gone to great lengths to uphold other, seemingly inevitable, characteristics of rate regulation in an integrated transportation system. The Interstate Commerce Commission (ICC), if it were to be effective at all, needed power to regulate joint rates over hauls using more than one line for a single journey. It was apparent that the apportionment of joint rates could be used to redistributive effect. In the *New England Divisions Case* (1923) the Court had already upheld the ICC's explicit consideration of the need to strengthen the weaker New England lines when it apportioned revenues from joint rates. It was a short step from such use of joint rates to the recapture provisions.

The Court's willingness to accept some qualifications of vested property rights in the interest of planning was not confined to such traditional areas of regulation as transportation and public utilities. The Court decided its first cases challenging general ZONING ordinances in the 1920s and, on the whole, upheld the power, though not without significant dissent and important qualifications.

Despite the Court's upholding of zoning and of regulatory initiatives such as the recapture provisions, the Taft Court has long been considered to have been ardent in imposing constitutional limits upon legislation that restricted vested property interests. That reputation is soundly based, although the extent to which the Taft Court differed from predecessor and successor Courts has been substantially exaggerated by FELIX FRANK-FURTER and his followers.

Perhaps the best known of the Taft Court pronouncements on the constitutional protection of property is Justice Holmes's opinion for the Court in *Pennsylvania Coal Company v. Mahon* (1923). Pennsylvania's Kohler Act required anthracite coal mining to be done so as to avoid subsidence of surface areas at or near buildings, streets, and other structures used by human beings. The Court held unconstitutional the application of the law to mining in an area where the mining company had conveyed surface rights, expressly reserving to itself and to its successors the subsurface mining rights.

Despite Brandeis's dissenting opinion, Holmes's opinion was moderate in tone and antithetical to the sort of dogmatics that characterized Sutherland's opinions in the wage and price regulation area. Indeed, Holmes's methodology was explicitly one that reduced the takings/regulation distinction to a matter of degree—as Holmes himself once recognized in a flippant reference to "the petty larceny of the police power." Moreover, the Court that decided *Pennsylvania Coal* decided the case of *Miller v. Schoene* (1928) five years later, upholding a Virginia law providing for the uncompensated (or less than fully compensated) destruction of cedar trees infected with cedar rust, a condition harmful only to neighboring apple trees.

The Court also had to face the implications of the constitutional protection of property in considering the methodology of public utility rate regulation. In a series of cases beginning in 1923 and proceeding throughout the Taft period, Justice Brandeis posed a major challenge to the "fair value" methodology of SMYTH V. AMES (1895). Industry during the 1920s argued that the rate base—the "property" upon which the Constitution guaranteed a reasonable rate of permissible return—should be valued according to the replacement cost of capital items—despite a general inflationary trend, accelerated by World War I. Brandeis formulated a comprehensive critique both of this particular windfall calculation and of the rule that produced it. Brandeis first reformulated the problem in a characteristically daring way. The issue was not so much a vested right to a return on capital as it was the necessity for a level of profit that could attract the new capital required for effective operation of the public utility. Brandeis lost the battle for a new approach to rate-making. Yet here, no less than in other arenas for disputes over the constitutional protection of property, doctrinal lines had been drawn that anticipated the issues of the New Deal.

Traditional, genteel conservativism is neither overtly ideological in content nor strident in manner. In most respects the Taft Court was traditionally conservative. The Court was hostile to labor and to any insurgency from the left, but the hostility usually took the form of a neutral defense of civil order. That neutrality, though it almost always worked against the left, was not explicitly one-sided and was, in fact, applied occasionally against rightist militant politics and street activity as well.

The constitutional defense of civil order entailed a strong commitment to ratify the acts of local government and of the national political branches so long as their power and authority were used to put down militant politics and especially politics of the street. Thus, the Court consistently upheld CRIMINAL SYNDICALISM LAWS, even while recognizing, in GITLOW V. NEW YORK (1925), that the FIRST AMENDMENT limited state as well as federal legislative power. Moreover, in a theoretically interesting, though practically less significant case, the Court upheld a New York law requiring the registration and disclosure of names of members of certain secret societies—a measure directed against the Ku Klux Klan. Brandeis and Holmes repeatedly dissented in the criminal syndicalism cases, sketching an alternative version of the political process far more hospitable to insurgent initiatives for change.

A second pillar of the defense of civic order was the reliance upon independent courts as guarantors of vested property rights against street politics. To this end the injunction was elevated to a constitutional pedestal. *Truax v. Corrigan,* which constitutionalized capital's right to a labor injunction, must be seen not only as a part of a larger antilabor *corpus* but also as the link between that work and the principle of civic order.

For traditional conservatives the injunction had much to commend it. It was in the hands of politically independent judges, who were less susceptible than other officials to mass pressure. It was governed—or supposed to be governed—by neutral principles rather than special interests; it permitted the adaptation of principle to local needs and adjusted the level of intervention to that necessary to shore up appropriately sound local elites. No wonder, then, that the issue of the injunction pervaded the constitutional politics of the 1920s.

If Taft was committed to the courts' playing a dominant role in labor discipline and the guarantee of civic order, he was at the same time committed to an efficient, unintimidated, and uncorrupted judiciary to do the job. In *Tumey v. Ohio* (1927) he wrote for a unanimous Court striking down as a denial of due process an Ohio scheme through which a public official judging traffic violations was paid a percentage of the fines collected. Of greater significance was MOORE V. DEMPSEY (1923), in which a divided Court upheld the power of a federal district court in federal HABEAS CORPUS proceedings to go behind the record of a state court murder conviction to determine whether the trial had been dominated by a mob.

Racist justice was a deeply rooted problem, not high on the conservative agenda for reform. Taft was, however, very concerned with the potential for corruption of the courts inherent in the great national experiment of the decade, prohibition. The Chief Justice realized that there were many opportunities for organized crime in the liquor business to buy friendly judges and other officials, especially in states where prohibition was unpopular. The Court refused to extend the protection of the DOUBLE JEOPARDY principle to cases of successive prosecutions under state and federal law for substantially the same conduct. Part of the reason for this limit upon the double jeopardy principle was the potential under any contrary rule of insulating conduct from federal prosecution by securing a state conviction and paying a small fine. The Court's interpretation of FEDERALISM to tolerate structural redundancy was thus a major prophylactic against the dangers of local corruption of courts.

Like all its predecessors, however conservative, the Taft Court paid lip service to the idea that the people are sovereign and, consequently, that popular government is a pervasive and overriding principle in constitutional interpretation. Even though dissenters within the court (Holmes and Brandeis) and critical commentators without (Frankfurter, EDWARD S. CORWIN, and THOMAS REED POWELL) claimed that the Justices ignored the presumption of constitutionality that ought to attach to the work of the popular branches, the simple fact is that no Justice denied, as an abstract principle, either the presumption of constitutionality or the deference that ought to be paid to legislative judgments. It was the application of the principle that divided the Court.

Most of the Justices were skeptical of the capacity of the masses intelligently to exercise the rights and discharge the obligations of participatory, popular government. Taft himself welcomed a leading role for elites in suppressing, or at least damping, the demands of the rabble and in representing the "better class" of citizens. But Taft's views in these matters were not very different from those of Holmes. Holmes doubted the capacity of the masses and considered a dominant role for elites in politics to be almost a natural law. Brandeis, the only real contrast, was considerably more committed to reform and to its promise. But he, in his own way, also distrusted the masses. He saw hope for change in a shift from a propertied oligarchy to a technically trained meritocracy. At the same time Brandeis understood the limits of this vision. His support of STATES' RIGHTS and localism in politics and his hostility to concentration in industry had common roots: the recognition of limits to techniques of effective organization; the affirmation of political principles limiting concentrations of power; and the affirmation of the principles of maximum participation in public affairs. Chiefly in this last respect, Brandeis stood committed to a principle that the other Justices ignored or rejected.

In what ways did the general attitudes of the Justices to popular government affect the work of the Court? Perhaps the most direct effect was visible in the great, perennial debate over the power of judicial review. The Justices appear to have been unanimous in their private opposition to schemes such as that of LaFollette to limit the power of judicial review by statute or constitutional amendment. Even Brandeis, who was personally close to LaFollette and who supported the Wisconsin senator's positions on many substantive issues, opposed initiatives to curb the Court.

In at least one important area the Taft Court initiated a significant reform in the mechanics of popular government itself. The Court struck down the first version of the Texas system of white primaries which, through official state action, denied blacks the right to vote in statewide PRIMARY ELECTIONS. NIXON V. HERNDON (1927) was the first in a line of cases that ultimately destroyed the white primary device.

The Court upheld the power of Congress to conduct LEGISLATIVE INVESTIGATIONS and to use COMPULSORY PROCESS to that end. The Court also appeared to uphold an enlarged vision of an exclusive PRESIDENTIAL POWER to remove executive officers. A special constitutional status for government of TERRITORIES was approved. Finally, the Court struggled mightily but produced no satisfactory or consistent principles in the area of STATE TAXATION OF COMMERCE and STATE REGULATION OF COMMERCE.

The 1920s saw a determined attack upon the ethnic pluralism, the cultural and ethical relativism, and the absence of traditional controls that characterized a newly emergent urban America. The prohibition movement, resurgent religious fundamentalism, virulent nativism, and racism gave rise to a reactionary program for legal reform. In the area of prohibition the Court did more than give full effect to a constitutional amendment and its implementing legislation. The Justices also decided a host of criminal procedure issues in such a way as to arm the enforcers against what was perceived as a concerted attack on law and order themselves.

But the Court was actively hostile to groups like the "new" Ku Klux Klan. It not only upheld a Klan registration statute but also, in PIERCE V. SOCIETY OF SISTERS (1925), held invalid an Oregon statute that had effectively outlawed private schools. The law was the product of a popular initiative organized and vigorously supported by the Klan as part of its nativist and anti-Catholic crusade. The decision in MEYER V. NEBRASKA (1923) striking down laws forbidding the teaching of German in the schools also reflected the Justices' unwillingness to permit nativist sentiment to cut too deeply into the social fabric.

But the Court did uphold state ALIEN land ownership laws directed principally against Asian immigrants and upheld the disgraceful national discrimination against Asian immigration in the face of constitutional attack. The Court also permitted the continuation of restrictive covenants in housing (CORRIGAN V. BUCKLEY, 1926) and segregation in public schools (GONG LUM V. RICE, 1927), though in each instance it avoided an explicit articulation of constitutional approval for these practices.

The constitutional work of the Taft Court extended over the customary broad area of national life, but it was dominated by the motif of conflict between property and labor. Civil strife, policies toward insurgency, free or regulated markets, confiscation—all were issues that arose principally from the overarching conflict. It is a measure of the Taft Court's achievement that, through Brandeis on the one hand and Taft on the other, a measure of clarity was achieved in articulating the implications of this conflict for constitutional structure and doctrine over a wide range of subjects. It was Taft's vision alone, however, that dominated the Court's action—consistently hostile to labor and its interests. The traditional conservative structure of property and order was one legacy of Taft's Court to the era of the Great Depression; Brandeis's vision— as yet wholly unrealized—was the other.

Bibliography

BERNSTEIN, IRVING   1960   *The Lean Years: A History of the American Worker, 1920– 1933*. Boston: Houghton Mifflin.

BICKEL, ALEXANDER M.   1957   *The Unpublished Opinions of Mr. Justice Brandeis: The Supreme Court at Work*. Cambridge, Mass.: Belknap Press of Harvard University Press.

DANELSKI, DAVID J.   1964   *A Supreme Court Justice Is Appointed*. New York: Random House.

FRANKFURTER, FELIX AND GREENE, NATHAN   1930   *The Labor Injunction*. New York: Macmillan.

MASON, ALPHEUS THOMAS   1946   *Brandeis: A Free Man's Life*. New York: Viking.
_____   1956   *Harlan Fiske Stone: Pillar of the Law*. New York: Viking.
_____   1964   *William Howard Taft: Chief Justice*. New York: Simon & Schuster.

MURPHY, WALTER F.   1964   *Elements of Judicial Strategy*. Chicago: University of Chicago Press.

PRINGLE, HENRY F.   1939   *The Life and Times of William Howard Taft*. New York: Farrar & Rinehart.

RABBAN, DAVID M.   1983   The Emergence of Modern First Amendment Doctrine. *University of Chicago Law Review* 50:1205–1355.

CONSTITUTIONAL HISTORY, 1933–1945

Michael E. Parrish

With the exception of the Civil War-Reconstruction era and the turbulent decade of the 1960s, no period in our history generated more profound changes in the constitutional system than the years of the Great Depression and World War II. Although the tenure of a Chief Justice of the United States often marks the boundary of a particular constitutional epoch, in this period it was a single President, FRANKLIN D. ROOSEVELT, whose personality and policies dominated the nation's political landscape, first as the leader of a domestic "war" against economic chaos, and, finally, as the architect of victory over the Axis powers. "Most of us in the Army have a hard time remembering any President but Franklin D. Roosevelt," remarked one soldier at the time of Roosevelt's death in April 1945. "He was the COMMANDER-IN-CHIEF, not only of the armed forces, but of our generation."

Roosevelt, described by Justice OLIVER WENDELL HOLMES as having a "second-rate intellect, but a first-rate temperament," was a charming, politically astute country squire from Hyde Park, New York. Crippled by polio at thirty-nine, elected President a decade later, he presided over five momentous revolutions in American life. The first, arising from his confrontation with the Supreme Court, has been aptly termed the "constitutional revolution" of 1937. The Court abandoned its long campaign, dating from the 1880s, to shape the content of the nation's economic policy by means of the judicial veto. The second revolution elevated the presidency, already revitalized by THEODORE ROOSEVELT and WOODROW WILSON in the Progressive era, to the pinnacle of leadership within the American political system. FDR did not invent the "imperial presidency," but his mastery of the radio, his legislative skills, and his twelve-year tenure went far toward institutionalizing it, despite several notable setbacks at the hands of Congress and the Court.

The third revolution, symbolized by the expansion of FEDERAL GRANT-IN-AID programs, the SOCIAL SECURITY ACT of 1935, and the efforts by the Department of Justice to protect CIVIL RIGHTS under the old Reconstruction-era statutes, significantly transformed American FEDERALISM by making the national government the chief custodian of economic security and social justice for all citizens. The fourth, marked by the revitalization of old independent REGULATORY COMMISSIONS such as the Interstate Commerce Commission, saw the final denouement of laissez-faire capitalism and the birth of state capitalism, managed by a bureaucratic elite drawn from the legal profession, the academic world, and private business. And the fifth revolution, characterized by the unionization of mass-production industries, the growing influence of urban-labor representatives in the Congress, and Roosevelt's successful effort to attract support from ethnic minorities, brought a major realignment in voting blocs and party strength that lasted three decades.

The triumph of Roosevelt and the Democratic party in the 1932 elections represented both the outcome of short-term political forces and the culmination of voting realignments that began much earlier. The inability of the HERBERT HOOVER administration to stop the slide into economic depression after the stock market crash of 1929 represented the most obvious and immediate source of Roosevelt's appeal. More significantly, his victory ended an era of Republican domination in national politics that began with WILLIAM McKINLEY in 1896, and it ushered in a Democratic reign that lasted well into the 1980s. From McKinley to Hoover, the Republicans controlled the White House, except for Wilson's two terms (1913–1921), a Democratic interlude that rested mostly upon divisions in Republican ranks.

The Republicans also controlled both houses of Congress for twenty-eight of the thirty-six years between McKinley and Franklin Roosevelt, elected a majority of the nation's governors and state legislators outside the South, and even enjoyed great popularity in big cities among trade unionists, middle class professionals, and many ethnic-religious minorities. On a platform of high tariffs, sound money, low taxes, and rising prosperity, the GOP built a formidable national coalition.

The Republican coalition developed signs of collapse during the WARREN G. HARDING–CALVIN COOLIDGE–Herbert Hoover years as economic distress increased among farmers and industrial workers despite the vaunted prosperity of the Republican New Era. In 1924, running as an independent on the Progressive party ticket, the aging Senator Robert LaFollette garnered a healthy share of votes from both urban workers and staple-crop farmers, who protested with their ballots against the economic conservatism of Coolidge and his Democratic rival, John W. Davis, a prosperous Wall Street lawyer. Hoover easily defeated New York governor Alfred E. Smith in 1928, but Smith—Irish, Roman Catholic, opposed to prohibition, and urban to the core—detached millions of ethnic, working class voters from the Republican party. Three years of economic distress which also alienated farmers, businessmen, and the once-affluent middle classes, completed the realignment process and assured Roosevelt victory in 1932.

From 1932 until his death, Roosevelt forged his own national coalition. Anchored in the lily-white South and the big cities where the Democratic party had been powerful since the days of ANDREW JACKSON and MARTIN VAN BUREN, Roosevelt welded together a collection of social, ethnic, regional, and religious minorities into a new political majority. In peace and war, the New Deal gave power, status, and recognition to those who had been outsiders in American society before the Great Depression—Irishmen, Jews, Slavs, white Southerners, and blacks.

Within this broad, diverse "Roosevelt coalition," the power and influence of organized labor and the urban wing of the Democratic party grew impressively, especially after the elections of 1934 and 1936 and the passage of the WAGNER (NATIONAL LABOR RELATIONS) ACT in 1935. Roosevelt's nomination in 1932 had been made possible by the support of key southern leaders. The success of the New Deal after 1934 and Roosevelt's electoral victories in 1940 and 1944, however, rested upon the political acumen and money provided by big labor through the political action committees of the Congress of Industrial Organizations. Roosevelt built well. His coalition ran both houses of Congress in every year but eight during the next half century. It elected HARRY S. TRUMAN in 1948, JOHN F. KENNEDY in 1960, LYNDON B. JOHNSON in 1964, and JIMMY CARTER in 1976.

Neither of the two amendments to the Constitution ratified during this period owed their inspiration directly to Roosevelt or the New Deal, although the TWENTIETH AMENDMENT, eliminating the lame-duck session of Congress, had been pushed by leading progressives for over a decade, and the TWENTY-FIRST AMENDMENT, repealing national PROHIBITION of liquor, had been endorsed by the Democratic party in its 1932 platform. Both amendments were proposed in 1932, the first time since 1789 that a single Congress had sent to the states for RATIFICATION more than one amendment. Congress also specified an unusual ratification procedure for the Twenty-First Amendment, requiring the states to convene special ratifying conventions instead of submitting the measure to their legislatures. Proponents of prohibition repeal feared that the legislatures, most of them malapportioned in favor of rural constituencies, would not be sympathetic to ratification.

Supporters of the Twentieth Amendment, led by the venerable progressive senator from Nebraska, GEORGE NORRIS, argued that the existing short session of Congress which met from December until March was a barrier to effective majoritarian democracy. By an accident of history, Congresses elected in November of even-numbered years did not meet in regular session until December of the odd-numbered year. Norris's amendment, first passed by the Senate in 1923, proposed to correct this situation by moving forward to January 3 from December the date on which sessions of Congress began and shifting back to January 3 and 20 from March 4 the date on which the terms of office began for members of Congress, and the President and Vice-President, respectively. A newly elected Congress, reflecting the fresh mandate of the people, would meet two months after an election rather than thirteen months later.

The Senate passed the Norris plan five times after 1923, but it failed to advance in the Republican-dominated House of Representatives, where the Speaker, Nicholas Longworth, opposed it. Longworth wished to keep the lame-duck session as a check upon the turbulent masses and he also objected to a provision in the Norris amendment that allowed Congress to determine the date of its own adjournment each year. Such flexibility, he believed, would only encourage more lawmaking by Congress, a prospect that he and other conservatives viewed with great distaste. The 1930 elections returned Democratic majorities to both houses of Congress, who quickly passed the Twentieth Amendment and sent it on to the states where it was ratified three years later.

American temperance organizations struggled for more than a century to achieve their goal with the adoption of the EIGHTEENTH AMENDMENT in 1919. It took the "wet" forces little more than a decade to bring the brewery, the distillery, and the saloon back to American life through ratification of the Twenty-First Amendment nine months after Roosevelt took office. Like the resurgence of the Democratic party, the repeal of national prohibition reflected a fundamental shift in political forces. The Congress that passed the Eighteenth Amendment during World War I was overwhelmingly rural, with House seats apportioned on the basis of the 1910 census, the last to record a majority for the countryside rather than the cities. The 72nd Congress, on the other hand, reflected the reapportionment of the House in 1929, where twenty-one states (mostly from the rural South and West) lost representation and eleven states (mostly in Eastern metropolitan areas) increased their share of seats.

In addition to providing urban-ethnic voters with a measure of symbolic revenge for the inconvenience of a "dry" decade, the repeal of prohibition had wide appeal in a nation reeling from economic depression and plagued by criminal violence. Sponsors argued that repeal would boost employment, raise tax revenues, and permit law enforcement personnel to concentrate upon the apprehension of major criminals such as John Dillinger. With equal vehemence, defenders of the "dry" faith claimed that repeal had been hatched by millionaires and rich corporations, eager to shift their tax burdens onto poor consumers of alcohol, and that Satan would conquer America. Thirty-six states, more concerned for the nation's fiscal problems than for the wiles of Satan, ratified the repeal amendment by December 1933.

The legislative program of the New Deal had a more direct impact upon the fate of the old CHILD LABOR AMENDMENT, which had passed

Congress in 1924 but had failed to secure ratification by three-fourths of the states. As late as 1937, only twenty-eight state legislatures had ratified the proposal which would have authorized Congress to regulate or prohibit the labor of persons under eighteen years of age. Fifteen states, mostly in the South and border regions, had rejected it; five had failed to act. The amendment became moot, however, when Congress in 1938 passed the FAIR LABOR STANDARDS ACT, which contained a similar restriction, and when the Supreme Court upheld its constitutionality in UNITED STATES v. DARBY LUMBER COMPANY (1941).

As usual, formal constitutional revision on the state level during these years was more extensive and diverse than for the federal government, although only three states (New York, Missouri, and Georgia) entirely rewrote their constitutions. At one extreme were states such as Tennessee and Illinois, where constitutional innovation remained minimal. The fundamental law of Tennessee had not been amended since 1870, while the Illinois Constitution of 1890 had been revised only twice since that date. On the other hand, voters in Louisiana were asked to adopt twenty-eight constitutional amendments in 1938, nineteen in 1940, ten in 1942, and nineteen in 1944, creating an organic law that filled nearly 300 pages with 200,000 words. California ran a distant second. By the end of World War II, its constitution of 1879 had been amended 250 times and totaled close to 50,000 words.

Unlike the United States Constitution with its broad, sweeping language, most state charters in this period included detailed declarations of public policies; the amendment process often served as a surrogate for statutory changes. In 1944, for instance, 100 proposed amendments were put before the voters in thirty different states. In California, Arizona, Oregon, and Washington the electorates defeated amendments to enact old-age pension schemes. Arkansas and Florida adopted right-to-work amendments that banned union shops, while California spurned a similar amendment. In the same year voters in other states were asked to pass upon amendments dealing with the location of airports, POLL TAXES, dog racing, and preferential civil service hiring for veterans.

Because of the era's economic crisis, which combined high unemployment, business failures, and falling tax revenues, all of the states confronted similar constitutional crises, because their organic laws usually limited state indebtedness. Escalating relief burdens placed a severe strain upon the states' fiscal resources, especially before the New Deal picked up a larger share of these costs after 1935. Legislatures and governors often found paths around these obstacles through constitutional experimentation: amendment, REFERENDUM, and judicial interpretation.

The age of Roosevelt, marked by class conflict and intense political controversy over both the economy and FOREIGN AFFAIRS, spawned many durable myths about the presidency, the growth of federal authority, and the relationship between government and the private sector. Roosevelt's critics, who hated the New Deal and distrusted his diplomacy, accused him of erecting a Presidential dictatorship. The New Deal and the mobilization of the war economy, it has been argued, also transformed the federal union as well as business–government relationships by subjecting local government and business corporations to the despotism of Washington bureaucrats. There is some truth in these generalizations but also considerable exaggeration.

Few political leaders in our history could match Roosevelt's oratorical gifts, his skill at dispensing patronage, and his deft manipulation of subordinates, the press, Congress, and opponents. But Roosevelt also experienced a number of profound setbacks between 1933 and 1939 that limited presidential power even during the unparalleled economic crisis of the Great Depression. It was World War II that shifted the balance decisively in his favor, but even during those turbulent years he usually functioned within boundaries set by Congress and public opinion.

Under the New Deal, the years of presidential preeminence in the shaping of domestic policy were remarkably fertile but brief. During the so-called Hundred Days, from Roosevelt's inauguration to early June 1933, Congress rubber-stamped dozens of White House proposals, including new banking laws, the first federal securities statute, a complete overhaul of the nation's monetary system, legislation creating the Tennessee Valley Authority, as well as laws setting up the controversial National Recovery Administration and the New Deal's basic farm program. Acting under the dubious authority of the World War I Trading with the Enemy Act, Roosevelt banned gold exports and all foreign exchange transactions until Congress approved of the administration's monetary plans that nullified gold clauses in private and public contracts and devalued the dollar by almost twenty-five percent. Equating the Depression with war, Roosevelt asked for and received from Congress the resources appropriate for a military commander battling a foreign invader.

The 1934 elections gave the President even larger majorities in Congress. This mandate encouraged a second burst of New Deal reforms in 1935. Again responding to presidential initiatives, Congress adopted a series of path-breaking laws, including the Social Security Act, the Wagner National Labor Relations Act, a $4.8 billion relief and public works measure, and a significant revision of the federal tax code that closed many loopholes and levied new surcharges on the very rich. Despite the judicial mutilation of key administration measures in 1935–1936, executive power probably stood at its peacetime zenith after Roosevelt's crushing reelection victory in 1936.

Even during these years of strong presidential leadership, Roosevelt's claims to authority did not go unchallenged. The federal courts remained a bastion of conservative Republicanism. Federal judges had issued hundreds of INJUNCTIONS against New Deal programs by early 1935, when the Supreme Court began to invalidate many of the laws of the Hundred Days, including the NATIONAL INDUSTRIAL RECOVERY ACT (NIRA) and the AGRICULTURAL ADJUSTMENT ACT. The most serious rebuff to the President came in the *Schechter* case, where the Justices invalidated the NIRA on the ground of improper DELEGATION OF POWER to the executive, and HUMPHREY'S EXECUTOR v. UNITED STATES (1935), where they curbed the President's power to remove members of independent regulatory commissions.

These judicial affronts to presidential authority became a war during FDR's second term, beginning with his ill-devised scheme to "pack" the Supreme Court with additional Justices. His proposed "Judicial Reform Act of 1937" inspired criticism both from conservatives and from many of the President's liberal friends in the Congress as well. This bitter legislative struggle divided the New Deal coalition, squandered much of the political capital that Roosevelt had accumulated during the previous four years, and gave rise to cries of "dictatorship," "tyranny," and "fascism." When the dust settled, the Court-packing plan had been defeated by Chief Justice CHARLES EVANS HUGHES and opponents in the Congress, but the Supreme Court never again seriously challenged the New Deal.

The economic recession of 1937–1938 and Roosevelt's attempt to restructure the executive branch dealt new blows to presidential leadership and prestige. Having taken credit for the economic upturn in 1935–1936, the President had to absorb the blame for the "Roosevelt recession," which had been triggered in part by his own desire to cut federal expenditures and balance the budget. Congress also scuttled his plans to reorganize the executive branch which rested upon the recommendations of a blue-ribbon committee on administrative management. The original bill called for an enlargement of the White House staff, creation of the Executive Office of the President to include the Bureau of the Budget, and a consolidation of existing bureaus, agencies, and commissions into twelve superdepartments under the President's control. The independent regulatory commissions such as the Federal Trade Commission, the Interstate Commerce Commission, and the Securities Exchange Commission would have been regrouped under the authority of these executive departments.

Congressional opponents denounced the plan as another presidential power grab. Working in tandem with rebellious bureaucrats who hoped to protect their own fiefdoms from the White House, they easily defeated the most controversial features of the plan. Roosevelt got his Bureau of the Budget and a larger staff, but little more. His political fortunes hit rock bottom in the 1938 elections, when several conservative

Democratic senators won reelection despite Roosevelt's effort to purge them during bitter primary campaigns. Confronted by an emerging conservative congressional coalition of southern Democrats and midwestern Republicans, Roosevelt had lost the initiative on domestic policy by the time German troops marched into Austria and Czechoslovakia.

The growth of presidential power, checked at the end of the 1930s, received new impetus after 1938 from the coming of World War II. Although the Supreme Court had reaffirmed in the broadest possible terms the President's constitutional authority over foreign policy in UNITED STATES v. CURTISS-WRIGHT EXPORT CORPORATION (1936), the actual limits of that authority remained to be tested. Sometimes alone and sometimes with congressional support, between 1939 and 1945 Roosevelt enlarged presidential power to an extent unknown even during World War I and the early New Deal.

Facing substantial isolationist sentiment both in Congress and among the public, Roosevelt initially attempted to counter Germany and Japan by means of EXECUTIVE AGREEMENTS and EXECUTIVE ORDERS that rested exclusively upon his claims to inherent presidential authority to conduct foreign relations and command the armed forces. He applied economic sanctions against Japan, terminating a 1911 commercial treaty, banning sales of scrap iron and steel, and freezing all Japanese financial assets in the United States. He ordered naval patrols of the western Atlantic— virtually assuring hostilities with German U-boats—and he ordered the military occupation of Iceland, with attendant naval convoys to protect ships supplying the occupation troops. In brief, Roosevelt waged an economic war in Asia and shooting war in the Atlantic without the consent of Congress.

The most extraordinary assertion of presidential power before Pearl Harbor was the destroyer-bases executive agreement in September 1940, by which Roosevelt transferred fifty over-age American destroyers to the British government in return for leases on seven naval bases in the Caribbean. This transaction, through which the President gave away a substantial portion of the United States Navy, rested upon a generous interpretation of an old nineteenth-century statute which permitted the President to dispose of worn-out ships. Most observers have believed that this action subverted the intention of Congress and violated a 1917 law specifically prohibiting the President in any foreign war "to send out of the jurisdiction of the United States any vessel built, armed, or equipped as a vessel of war." Attorney General ROBERT H. JACKSON, who advised Roosevelt on the legality of the transfer, dismissed this statute on the grounds that it applied only to ships built with the specific intention of giving them to a nation at war.

After the Japanese attack on Pearl Harbor Congress rapidly augmented presidential control over both military policy and the domestic economy. By means of the renewal of Lend-Lease, the Second WAR POWERS ACT, the EMERGENCY PRICE CONTROL ACT, the War Labor Dispute Act, and other laws, Congress gave the President the discretion, among other things, to allocate $50 billion of war supplies to America's allies, to reorganize all executive departments and agencies at will, to fix rents and prices throughout the land, and to seize industrial plants closed by strikes. In 1935, invalidating the NIRA, the Supreme Court had scolded Congress for vesting unbridled authority in the President to regulate the economy. Ten years later, as World War II drew to a close, executive discretion over the nation's economic structure far transcended that of the NIRA years.

A substantial enlargement of presidential discretion was essential for effective prosecution of World War II, but the growth of executive power carried with it threats to CIVIL LIBERTIES and unfathomable dangers to the survival of the human race. The Congress that permitted the President to restructure the executive branch also approved of the administration's plans to remove Japanese Americans from the West Coast. (See JAPANESE AMERICAN CASES.) The Congress that permitted the President to ration sugar and gasoline also gave the Commander-in-Chief a blank check for research, development, and potential use of nuclear weapons. This was truly, in Justice BENJAMIN N. CARDOZO's memorable phrase, "delegation run riot."

The expansion of federal responsibility for economic management and social services paralleled the growth of presidential power between 1933 and 1945. In a series of cases beginning with the WAGNER ACT CASES (1937) and ending with WICKARD v. FILBURN (1942), the Supreme Court laid to rest the antiquated notions of DUAL FEDERALISM, which had postulated the existence of rigid constitutional boundaries separating appropriate federal activities from those reserved exclusively to the states. In the wake of these decisions and those upholding the Social Security Act, there seemed to be no constitutional limitation upon the authority of Congress to regulate INTERSTATE COMMERCE and to tax and spend on behalf of the GENERAL WELFARE, even where these federal efforts intruded deeply into areas of social and economic life traditionally left to local government. Practice often preceded formal doctrinal legitimation. In 1934, for instance, the Bureau of Biological Survey in the Department of Commerce eradicated over seven million disease-carrying rodents in three states with a $8.7 million grant from the Civil Works Administration. Although this project produced no constitutional objection, a more sweeping federal intrusion into the domain of local health authorities is hard to imagine.

The most far-reaching instrument of expanding federal policymaking became the myriad programs of FEDERAL GRANTS-IN-AID which provided federal money for specific activities to be administered by state officials under federal guidelines. As early as 1862, the MORRILL ACT had conveyed federal lands to the states on condition that they be used for the construction and support of colleges and universities. In the Weeks Act of 1911, Congress had extended this principle to include cash grants to the states for fighting forest fires in the watersheds of navigable streams. Similar grant-in-aid programs flourished during the Wilson administration for vocational education, highways, and agricultural extension work, but budget-conscious Republican administrations had put a cap on new programs during the 1920s.

In their efforts to fight the depression, both the Hoover and Roosevelt administrations increasingly used the grant-in-aid technique. The Emergency Relief and Construction Act of 1932, approved reluctantly by Hoover, offered over $600 million in federal loans to the states for work-relief projects. The Roosevelt administration substituted grants for loans in the relief programs of the New Deal. By 1940, in addition to these vast relief activities and the continuation of old programs from the Progressive era, the New Deal had undertaken grant-in-aid programs for employment services and unemployment compensation, old age assistance, child welfare services, and maternity care. Social Security, the largest New Deal grant-in-aid program, assisted the blind, the disabled, and the unemployed through combined federal–state efforts.

The growth of federal grant-in-aid programs during the New Deal years rested upon the realization that many social and economic problems required national attention and that only the federal government commanded the fiscal resources to deal with them. Between 1932 and the end of World War II, the federal government's share of total taxes collected rose from twenty-four percent to nearly seventy-four percent. At the same time, grant-in-aid programs avoided the growth of an even larger federal bureaucracy and left many important administrative decisions in the hands of state and local officials.

In addition to grant-in-aid programs, state and local elites played a major role in the implementation of other New Deal efforts as well, a pattern of political decision making that refuted simplistic ideas about rampant centralization of power in federal bureaucrats. The heart of the New Deal's farm program, the domestic allotment system, vested important decisions in county committees composed of farmers and extension-service personnel chosen by local authorities. Under the Taylor Grazing Act, local livestock ranchers determined the extent of grazing rights on the vast public lands in the western states. And the most coercive federal program in this period, the SELECTIVE SERVICE ACT of 1940, left life-and-death decisions about the drafting of millions of American citizens in the hands of local draft boards appointed by state governors. Without the active participation of state and local officials, the wartime rationing programs for gasoline, sugar, coffee, and butter would have broken down for lack of enforcement.

When New Deal reformers ignored the interests and sensibilities of local elites, they provoked instant political protest and retaliation. Roosevelt quickly dismantled the innovative Civil Works Administration in 1934 because it drew intense criticism from governors, county supervisors, and mayors who objected to the complete nationalization of its extensive work-relief efforts. The subsequent Works Projects Administration program gave a larger share of decision making to local officials, who systematically used the machinery to punish political enemies and to discriminate against racial minorities, especially in the South. When idealistic young lawyers in the Agricultural Adjustment Administration attempted to protect sharecroppers and tenants from wholesale eviction under the farm program, they stirred up a revolt by commercial farmers, who forced their removal from the agency. Much of the opposition from southern Democrats to the New Deal after 1935 grew out of their anger at the Department of Justice for attempting to protect blacks from local violence under the old Reconstruction-era civil rights laws. The New Deal nourished a new brand of COOPERATIVE FEDERALISM in many areas of American life, but it was not a federalism without conflict and tensions, especially when national reformers challenged entrenched local customs and power relationships.

While encouraging the growth of big labor and ministering to the needs of the elderly and the poor, the New Deal also provided substantial benefits to American capitalists. Business opposition to Roosevelt was intense, but it was narrowly based in labor-intensive corporations in textiles, automobiles, and steel which had the most to lose from collective bargaining. The New Deal found many business allies among firms in the growing service industries of banking, insurance, and stock brokerage where government regulations promised to reduce cutthroat competition and to weed out marginal operators. Because of its aggressive policies to expand American exports and investment opportunities abroad, the New Deal also drew support from high-technology firms and from the large oil companies who were eager to penetrate the British monopoly in the Middle East.

Sophisticated businessmen discovered that they could live comfortably in a world of government regulation. The "socialistic" Tennessee Valley Authority lowered the profits of a few utility companies, but cheap electric power for the rural South translated into larger consumer markets for the manufacturers of generators, refrigerators, and other appliances. In addition to restoring public confidence in the stock exchanges and the securities industry, the Securities and Exchange Commission promoted self-regulation among over-the-counter dealers. Motor trucking firms received a helping hand from the Interstate Commerce Commission in reducing rate wars, and the major airlines looked to the Civil Aeronautics Board to protect them from the competitive rigors of the marketplace. When "Dr. Win-the-War" replaced "Dr. New Deal" after 1942, businessmen began to play key roles as well in the wartime agencies that regulated production, manpower, and the allocation of raw materials. The New Deal thus laid the foundations of both the welfare state and the permanent warfare state.

Bibliography

CAREY, JANE PERRY   1865   *The Rise of a New Federalism: Federal–State Cooperation in the United States.* New York: Russell & Russell.

HAWLEY, ELLIS P.   1965   *The New Deal and the Problem of Monopoly.* Princeton, N.J.: Princeton University Press.

LEUCHTENBURG, WILLIAM E.   1963   *Franklin D. Roosevelt and the New Deal.* New York: Harper & Row.

PATTERSON, JAMES T.   1969   *The New Deal and the States: Federalism in Transition.* Princeton, N.J.: Princeton University Press.

POLENBERG, RICHARD   1972   *War and Society: The United States 1941–1945.* Philadelphia: Lippincott.

SCHLESINGER, ARTHUR M., JR.   1957, 1959, 1960   *The Age of Roosevelt,* 3 vols. Boston: Houghton Mifflin.

HUGHES COURT

(1930–1941)

Archibald Cox

The years in which Chief Justice CHARLES EVANS HUGHES presided over the Supreme Court of the United States, 1930–1941, are notable for the skillful accomplishment of a revolution in CONSTITUTIONAL INTERPRE-TATION. The use of the DUE PROCESS clauses of the Fifth Amendment and FOURTEENTH AMENDMENT to protect FREEDOM OF CONTRACT and economic Darwinism against government regulation yielded to legislative supremacy and judicial self-restraint. The prevailing limits on the regulatory powers of Congress under the COMMERCE CLAUSE were swept away. The Hamiltonian view that Congress has power to spend money for any purpose associated with the general welfare was solidified by judicial approval. The Court acquiesced in the delegation of vast lawmaking power to administrative agencies. The groundwork was laid for expanding the constitutionally guaranteed FREEDOM OF SPEECH and freedom of the press.

Change was all about the Hughes Court. Of the eight Justices who flanked Hughes when he took his seat as Chief Justice, seven left the Court before he retired. The Court moved across the street from the cozy, old Senate Chamber in the Capitol to the gleaming white marble palace and ornate conference room used today. Profounder changes were occurring in the social, economic, and political conditions that give rise to constitutional litigation, that shape the briefs and arguments of counsel, and that the Court's decisions must address.

The preceding era had been marked by the rise to dominance of large-scale business and financial enterprise. Vast aggregations of men and women and material wealth were needed to develop America's resources, to harness the power unleashed by science and technology, and to capture the efficiencies of mass production for mass markets. Unlocking America's agricultural and industrial wealth made for higher standards of living and an extremely mobile society. With the gains had come corruption, hardships, injustices, and pressure for political action; but in the general prosperity of the 1920s the costs were too often ignored.

Yet the farmers were left behind and too much of the wealth was committed to speculation in corporate securities. The bursting of the latter bubble in November 1929 heralded an economic depression of unprecedented length and depth. Ninety percent of the market value of stock in industrial corporations was wiped out in three years. Twenty-five percent of the land in Mississippi was auctioned off in mortgage foreclosure sales. Factory payrolls were cut in half. One out of every four persons seeking employment was without work. The Depression destroyed people's faith in the industrial magnates and financiers, even in the ethic of individual self-reliance. The stability of American institutions seemed uncertain.

The election of FRANKLIN D. ROOSEVELT as President of the United States brought a new, more active political philosophy to government. Government, Roosevelt asserted, should seek to prevent the abuse of superior economic power, to temper the conflicts, and to work out the accommodations and adjustments that a simpler age had supposed could safely be left to individual ability and the free play of economic forces. Government should also meet the basic need for jobs and, in the case of those who could not work, for food, clothing, and shelter. For the most part these responsibilities must be met by the federal government, which alone was capable of dealing with an economy national in scope and complexity.

Roosevelt's "New Deal" not only provided money and jobs for the worst victims of the Depression; it enacted the legislation and established the government agencies upon which national economic policies would rest for at least half a century: the AGRICULTURAL ADJUSTMENT ACTS, the WAGNER NATIONAL LABOR RELATIONS ACT, the FAIR LABOR STANDARDS ACT, THE SOCIAL SECURITY ACT, and the SECURITIES AND EXCHANGE ACT.

JUDICIAL REVIEW permits those who lose battles in the executive and legislative branches to carry the war to the courts. Earlier in the century many courts, including the Supreme Court, had clung to the vision of small government, economic laissez-faire, and unbounded opportunity for self-reliant individuals. Judges had thus struck down as violations of the due process clauses of the Fifth and Fourteenth Amendments many measures now generally accepted as basic to a modern industrial and urban society: MAXIMUM HOURS AND MINIMUM WAGE LAWS, laws forbidding industrial homework, and laws protecting the organization of labor unions. The critical question for the Supreme Court in the Hughes era would be whether the Court would persevere or change the course of American constitutional law.

The response of Justices WILLIS VAN DEVANTER, JAMES C. McREY-NOLDS, GEORGE SUTHERLAND, and PIERCE BUTLER was predictable: they would vote to preserve the old regime of limited federal government and economic laissez-faire. Three Justices—LOUIS D. BRANDEIS, HARLAN F. STONE, and BENJAMIN N. CARDOZO—could be expected to eschew the use of judicial power to protect economic liberty, and might not condemn broader congressional interpretation of the commerce clause. The balance rested in the hands of Chief Justice HUGHES and Justice OWEN J. ROBERTS.

At first the Court challenged the New Deal. The National Recovery Administration sought to halt the downward spiral in wages and prices by stimulating the negotiation of industry-by-industry and market-by-market codes of "fair competition" fixing minimum prices and wages and outlawing "destructive" competitive practices. In SCHECHTER POULTRY CORPORATION V. UNITED STATES (1935) the Court held the underlying legislation unconstitutional. The major New Deal measure for dealing with the plight of the farmers was held unconstitutional in UNITED STATES V. BUTLER (1936) as "a statutory plan to regulate and control agricultural production, a matter beyond the powers delegated to the federal government." CARTER V. CARTER COAL COMPANY (1936) held that, because production was a purely local activity, Congress lacked power to legislate concerning the wages and hours of bituminous coal miners. In MOREHEAD V. NEW YORK EX REL. TIPALDO (1936) the four conservative Justices, joined by Justice Roberts, reaffirmed the 1923 decision in ADKINS V. CHILDREN'S MEMORIAL HOSPITAL invalidating a law fixing minimum wages for women. These opinions seemed to presage invalidation of such other fundamental New Deal measures as the National Labor Relations Act, a proposed federal wage and hour law, and even the Social Security Act.

President Roosevelt responded with strong criticism. The *Schechter* ruling, he said, was evidence that the Court was still living "in the horse and buggy age." On February 5, 1937, the President sent a special message to Congress urging enactment of a bill to create one new judgeship for every federal judge over the age of seventy who railed to retire. The message spoke of the heavy burden under which the courts—particularly the Supreme Court—were laboring, of the "delicate subject" of "aged or infirm judges," and of the need for "a constant infusion of new blood in the courts." No one doubted Roosevelt's true purpose. Six of the nine Supreme Court Justices were more than seventy years old. Six new Justices would ensure a majority ready to uphold the constitutionality of New Deal legislation. A month later the President addressed the nation more candidly, acknowledging that he hoped "to bring to the decision of social and economic problems younger men who have had personal experience and contact with modern facts and circumstances under which average men have to live and work."

Despite overwhelming popular support for New Deal legislation and despite the President's landslide reelection only a few months earlier, the Court-packing plan was defeated. The President's disingenuous explanation was vulnerable to factual criticism. Justice Brandeis, widely known as a progressive dissenter from his colleagues' conservative philosophy, joined Chief Justice Hughes in a letter to the Senate Judiciary Committee demonstrating that the Court was fully abreast of its docket and would be less efficient if converted into a body of fifteen Justices. Much of the political opposition came from conservative strongholds, but the current ran deeper. The American people had a well-nigh religious attachment to CONSTITUTIONALISM and the Supreme Court. They intuitively realized that packing the Court in order to reverse the course of its decisions would destroy its independence and erode the essence of constitutionalism. Yet no explanation is complete without recalling the contemporary quip: "A switch in time saves nine." The final defeat of the Court-packing plan came after a critical turning in the Court's own interpretation of constitutional limitations.

The shift first became manifest in WEST COAST HOTEL COMPANY v. PARRISH (1937), a 5–4 decision upholding the constitutionality of a state statute authorizing a board to set minimum wages for women. The Chief Justice's opinion overruled the *Adkins* case and markedly loosened the standards of SUBSTANTIVE DUE PROCESS that had previously constricted regulation of contractual relations. To the old STATE POLICE POWER doctrine confining the permissible objectives of government to health, safety, and morals, the Chief Justice added broadly the "welfare of the people" and "the interests of the community." Where the old opinions declared as an abstract truth that "The employer and the employee have equality of right and any legislation that disturbs the equality is an arbitrary interference with liberty of contract," the new majority more realistically asserted that a legislature may consider the "relatively weak bargaining power of women" and may "adopt measures to reduce the evils of the 'sweating system.'" There were also hints of greater judicial deference to legislative judgments: "regulation which is reasonable in relation to its subject and is adopted in the interests of the community is due process."

The *West Coast Hotel* case inaugurated a line of decisions sustaining every challenged economic regulation enacted by a state legislature or by the Congress. General minimum wage and maximum hour laws, price regulations, and labor relations acts—all were upheld. Even prior to Hughes's retirement, the trend was intensified by the normal replacement of all but one of the Justices who had sat with Hughes on his first day as Chief Justice. The philosophy of judicial self-restraint gradually became dominant on the Court, in the laws, and throughout the legal profession.

The troublesome problems of constitutional interpretation often call for striking a balance between the opposing ideals of democratic self-government and judicial particularization of majestic but general and undefined constitutional limitations. The philosophy of legislative supremacy and judicial self-restraint that came to dominate constitutional interpretation in the time of the Hughes Court was often asserted and widely accepted as broadly applicable to all constitutional adjudication except the enforcement of clear and specific commands. The Hughes Court thus set the stage for the central constitutional debate of the next major era in constitutional history. As claims to judicial protection of CIVIL LIBERTIES and CIVIL RIGHTS became the focus of attention, JUDICIAL ACTIVISM would be revived by substituting STRICT SCRUTINY for judicial deference in many areas of PREFERRED FREEDOMS and FUNDAMENTAL RIGHTS. Many of the new judicial activists would be liberals or progressives of the same stripe that had pressed for democratic self-government in the days when their political power confronted conservative dominance of the courts. But the opinions of the Hughes Court still mark the end of effective constitutional challenges to legislative regulation of economic activity.

The Hughes Court broke new ground in interpretation of the commerce clause only a few months after the minimum wage decision. In *National Labor Relations Board v. Jones & Laughlin Steel Corporation* (1937) the Labor Board, under authority delegated by the Wagner Act, had ordered Jones & Laughlin to reinstate four employees discharged from production and maintenance jobs in a basic steel mill because of their union activity. Both Jones & Laughlin's anti-union activities and the order for reinstatement were beyond the reach of federal power as delimited by the old line between production and interstate movement. The lower court had so decided. Led by Chief Justice Hughes, a bare majority of the Supreme Court Justices reversed that decision. Rejecting the old conceptualism that had asked whether the regulated activity had a "legal or logical connection to interstate commerce," the Court appraised the relation by "a practical judgment drawn from experience." Congress could reasonably conclude that an employer's anti-union activities and refusal to bargain collectively might result in strikes, and that a strike at a basic steel mill drawing its raw materials from, and shipping its products to, many states might in fact affect the movement of INTERSTATE COMMERCE. (See WAGNER ACT CASES.)

The *Jones & Laughlin* opinion appeared to retain some judicially enforceable constitutional check upon the congressional power under the commerce clause: "Undoubtedly the scope of this power must be considered in the light of our dual system of government and may not be extended so far as to embrace effects upon interstate commerce so indirect and remote that to embrace them, in view of our complex society, would effectually obliterate the distinction between what is national and what is local and create a completely centralized government." But the check proved illusory. The quoted admonition, while operable as a political principle guiding congressional judgment, yields no rule of law capable of judicial administration. Once the distinctions between interstate movement and production and between "direct" and "indirect" effects upon interstate commerce are rejected, the number of links in the chain of cause and effect becomes irrelevant. Federal power would reach to the local machine shop that repaired the chain saws that cut the trees that yielded the pulp wood that yielded the pulp that made the paper bought by the publisher to print the newspaper that circulated in interstate commerce. The size of the particular establishment or transaction also became irrelevant, for the cumulative effect of many small local activities might have a major impact upon interstate commerce. The new judicial deference, moreover, called for leaving such questions to Congress.

A second doctrinal development accelerated the trend. The Fair Labor Standards Act of 1938 required employers to pay workers engaged in the production of goods for shipment in interstate commerce no less than a specified minimum wage. The act also forbade shipping in interstate commerce any goods produced by workers who had not received the minimum wage. Congress claimed the power to exclude from the pipeline of interstate commerce things that would, in its judgment, do harm in the receiving state. Goods produced at substandard wages and shipped in interstate commerce might depress wages paid in the receiving states, and also in other producing states. The theory had been applied as early as 1903 to uphold a congressional law forbidding the interstate shipment of lottery tickets, but in 1918, under the doctrine barring federal regulation of production, the Court had struck down an act of Congress barring the interstate shipment of goods made with child labor. Having rejected that doctrine in the Labor Board Cases, the Hughes Court readily upheld the constitutionality of the Fair Labor Standards Act upon the theory of the lottery cases. The direct prohibition against paying less than the specified minimum wage was also upheld as a necessary and proper means of preventing goods made under substandard conditions from moving in interstate commerce and doing harm in other states. Years later similar reasoning supported broader decisions upholding the power of Congress to regulate or prohibit the local possession or use of firearms and other articles that have moved in interstate commerce.

Much more than legal logic lay behind the Hughes Court's recognition of virtually unlimited congressional power under the commerce clause. The markets of major firms had become nationwide. A complex and interconnected national economy made widely separated localities interdependent. A century earlier layoffs at the iron foundry in Saugus, Massachusetts, would have had scant visible effect in other states. During the Great Depression no one could miss the fact that layoffs at the steel mills in Pittsburgh, Pennsylvania, reduced the demand for clothing and so caused more layoffs at the textile mills in Charlotte, North Carolina, and Fall River, Massachusetts. Even as the Hughes Court deliberated the Labor Board Cases, a strike at a General Motors automobile assembly plant in Michigan was injuring automobile sales agencies in cities and towns throughout the United States.

The states were incapable of dealing with many of the evils accompanying industrialization. Many states were smaller and less powerful than the giant public utilities and industrial corporations. Massachusetts might forbid the employment of child labor, or fix a minimum wage if the due process clause permitted, but the cost of such measures was the flight of Massachusetts industries to North Carolina or South Carolina. New York might seek to ensure the welfare of its dairy farmers by setting minimum prices that handlers should pay for milk, only to watch the handlers turn to Vermont farmers who could sell at lower prices. The commerce clause barred the states from erecting protective barriers against out-of-state competition.

A shift in intellectual mode was also important. The rise of LEGAL REALISM stimulated by publication of OLIVER WENDELL HOLMES's *The Common Law* in 1881 had made it increasingly difficult for courts to find guidance in such abstractions as the equality of right between employer and employee or in such rhetorical questions as "What possible legal or logical connection is there between an employee's membership in a labor organization and the carrying on of interstate commerce?" The harsh facts of the Depression made both impossible.

The proper division of regulatory activity between the nation and the states is and may always be a much debated question of constitutional dimension. Today the question is nonetheless almost exclusively political. The Hughes Court yielded the final word to Congress.

The enormous expansion of the federal establishment that began in the 1930s and continued for half a century finds a second constitutional source in the power that Article I, Section 8, grants to Congress: "to lay and collect taxes . . . and provide for the common defense and general welfare of the United States." Here, too, the key judicial precedents of the modern era are decisions of the Hughes Court.

The scope of the TAXING AND SPENDING POWER had been disputed from the beginning. Jeffersonian localists argued that the words "general welfare" encompassed only the purposes expressly and somewhat more specifically stated later in Article I. Spending for INTERNAL IMPROVEMENTS gradually became accepted practice in the political branches, but the Supreme Court had had no occasion to adjudicate the issue of constitutional power because no litigant could show that he or she had suffered the kind of particular injury that would sustain a cause of action.

The Roosevelt administration not only spent federal funds on an unprecedented scale in order to relieve unemployment; it also broke new ground in using subsidies to shape the conduct of both state governments and private persons. The Agricultural Adjustment Act of 1933 levied a tax upon processors in order to pay subsidies to farmers who would agree to reduce the acreage sown to crops. The aim was to stabilize the prices of agricultural commodities. Linking the subsidy payments to the processing tax gave the processors STANDING to challenge the tax on the ground that the payments exceeded the limits of the federal spending power. In *United States v. Butler* (1936) the Hughes Court held the act unconstitutional because conditioning the farmer's allotments upon the reduction of his planted acreage made the whole "a statutory plan to regulate and control agricultural production, a matter beyond the power delegated to the federal government."

The decision was a prime target of President Roosevelt's criticism. It aroused fears that the Hughes Court would also invalidate the Social Security Act, a key New Deal measure establishing systems of unemployment and old age and survivors insurance. The title of the act dealing with unemployment levied a federal payroll tax upon all employers of eight or more individuals but gave a credit of up to 90 percent of the federal tax for employer contributions to a state employment fund meeting federal standards specified in the act. Very few states had previously established unemployment insurance, but the act's combination of pressure and inducement proved effective. The combination was attacked as a coercive, unconstitutional invasion of the realm reserved exclusively to the states by the TENTH AMENDMENT, which, if generalized, would enable federal authorities to induce, if not indeed compel, state enactments for any purpose within the realm of state power, and generally to control state administration of state laws. In STEWARD MACHINE COMPANY v. DAVIS (1937) the five-Justice majority answered that offering a choice or even a temptation is not coercion. Spending to relieve the needs of the army of unemployed in a nationwide depression serves the general welfare, the majority continued; the spending power knows no other limitation.

In later decades congressional spending programs would grow in size, spreading from agriculture and social insurance to such areas as housing, highway construction, education, medical care, and local LAW ENFORCEMENT. Many FEDERAL GRANTS-IN-AID to both state and private institutions are conditioned upon observance of federal standards. The balance to be struck between federal standards and state autonomy is sharply debated, but in this area, as under the commerce clause, the question is now almost exclusively left to political discretion as a result of the decisions of the Hughes Court.

Questions concerning the DELEGATION OF POWER gave rise to the fourth major area of constitutional law shaped by the Hughes Court. Congress makes the laws, it is said; the executive carries out the laws; and the judiciary interprets the laws and resolves controversies between executive and legislative officials. Never quite true, this old and simple division of functions proved largely incompatible with the new role established for federal government by the Roosevelt administration. Much law, however denominated, would have to be made by executive departments or new administrative agencies authorized by Congress, such as the Securities and Exchange Commission and the Civil Aeronautics Board. Under the traditional division the new arrangements were subject to attack as unconstitutional attempts to delegate to other agencies part of the legislative power that Congress alone can exercise.

The flow of decisions in the Hughes Court upon this question paralleled the course taken under the due process, commerce, and spending clauses. At first the majority seemed disposed to resist the new political order as in PANAMA REFINING COMPANY v. RYAN (1935) and *Schechter Poultry Corporation v. United States* (1935). Later decisions, however, reversed the initial trend. UNITED STATES v. ROCK ROYAL COOPERATIVE, INC. (1939) is illustrative. The AGRICULTURAL MARKETING AGREEMENT ACT gave the secretary of agriculture broad authority to regulate the marketing of eight agricultural commodities, including milk, with a view to reestablishing the purchasing power of farmers at the level in a base period, usually 1909–1914. In the case of milk, however, if the secretary found the prices so determined to be unreasonable, he was authorized to fix producer prices at a level that would reflect pertinent economic conditions in local milk markets, provide an adequate supply of wholesome milk, and be in the public interest. The purported standards were numerous and broad enough to impose no significant limit upon the secretary's decisions. Nevertheless, the Court upheld the delegation. It was enough that Congress had limited the secretary's power to specified commodities, had specifically contemplated price regulation, and had provided standards by which the secretary's judgment was to be guided after hearing interested parties. The decision set the pattern for all subsequent legislative draftsmen and judicial determinations.

The contributions of the Hughes Court to the law of the FIRST AMENDMENT were less definitive than in the areas of the commerce clause, economic due process, the spending power, and delegation; but they were not less important. The Hughes Court infused the First Amendment with a new and broader vitality that still drives the expansion of the constitutional protection available to both individual speakers and institutional press.

Apart from the World War I prosecution of pacifists and socialists for speeches and pamphlets alleged to interfere with the production of munitions or conscription for the armed forces, federal law posed few threats to freedom of expression. State laws were more restrictive. The illiberal decisions of the 1920s sustaining the prosecution of leftists under state CRIMINAL SYNDICALISM LAWS assumed that the First Amendment's guarantees against congressional abridgment of freedom of expression are, by virtue of the Fourteenth Amendment, equally applicable to the states. These OBITER DICTA encouraged constitutional attack upon state statutes, municipal ordinances, and judge-made doctrines restricting political and religious expression. In this area Chief Justice Hughes and Justice Roberts quickly allied themselves with the three Justices of established liberal reputation.

Two early opinions highlight the protection that the First and Fourteenth Amendments afford the press against previous restraints. NEAR v. MINNESOTA (1931) was decided upon appeal from a state court's injunction forbidding further publication of *The Saturday Press,* a weekly newspaper, upon the ground that it was "largely devoted to malicious, scandalous and defamatory articles." The newspaper had charged Minneapolis officials with serious offenses in tolerating gambling, bootlegging, and racketeering; the articles were scurrilous and anti-Semitic in tone and content. The decree was authorized by a Minnesota statute. Minnesota had experienced a rash of similar scandal sheets, some of whose publishers were believed to use their journals for blackmail. In an opinion by Chief Justice Hughes, the Supreme Court held that the injunction against publication was an infringement upon the liberty of the press guaranteed by the Fourteenth Amendment regardless of whether the charges were true or false. For any wrong the publisher had committed or might commit, public and private redress might be available; but this PRIOR RESTRAINT was inconsistent with the constitutional liberty.

The law's strong set against previous restraints was underscored a few years later by GROSJEAN v. AMERICAN PRESS COMPANY (1936), where a review of history led the Hughes Court to conclude that the First and Fourteenth Amendments bar not only censorship but also taxes that single out the press and are thus calculated to limit the circulation of information.

The chief danger to freedom or expression by the poor, the unorthodox, and the unpopular lies in state statutes and municipal ordinances that give local authorities wide discretion in preserving the peace and public order. Such laws not only invite suppression of unorthodox ideas by discriminatory enforcement but they also encourage self-censorship in hope of avoiding official interference. The Hughes Court laid the foundations for current constitutional doctrines narrowing the opportunities for abuse.

LOVELL v. CITY OF GRIFFIN (1938) introduced the doctrine that a law requiring a license for the use of the streets or parks for the distribution of leaflets, speeches, parades, or other forms of expression must, explicitly or by prior judicial interpretation, confine the licensing authority to considerations of traffic management, crowd control, or other physical inconvenience or menace to the public. From there it was only a short step to holding in CANTWELL V. CONNECTICUT (1941) that a man may not be punished for words or a street DEMONSTRATION, however offensive to the audience, under a broad, general rubric that invites reprisal for the expression of unorthodox views instead of requiring a narrow judgment concerning the risk of immediate violence. THORNHILL V. ALABAMA (1941), once important for the ruling that peaceful PICKETING in a labor dispute is a form of expression protected by the First Amendment, also introduced the then novel and still controversial doctrine that an individual convicted under a law drawn so broadly as to cover both expression subject to regulation and constitutionally protected expression may challenge the constitutionality of the statute "on its face" even though his own conduct would not be constitutionally protected against punishment under narrower legislation. (See OVERBREADTH DOCTRINE.)

Supreme Court Justices and other constitutionalists still debate the theoretical question how far the First and Fourteenth Amendments secure individuals a right to some PUBLIC FORUM for the purposes of expression. The Hughes Court's decision in HAGUE V. CONGRESS OF INDUSTRIAL ORGANIZATIONS (1939) recognized such a right to the use of streets, parks, and like public places traditionally open for purposes of assembly, communication, and discussion of public questions: "Such use of the streets and public places has, from ancient times, been a part of the privileges, immunities, rights and liberties of citizens. The privilege . . . to use the streets and parks for communication of views on national questions may be regulated in the interest of all; . . . but must not in the guise of regulation be abridged or denied." On this ground *Schneider v. State* (1939) invalidated four city ordinances banning the use of the streets to hand out leaflets. Against this background later Justices would wrestle with the constitutional problems raised by restrictions upon house-to-house canvassing and the use of other government properties for the purpose of expression.

The Hughes Court presided over a revolution in constitutional interpretation. Many conservatives were convinced that in joining the liberal Justices, the Chief Justice and Justice Roberts unconscionably distorted the law to suit the winds of politics. Yet while the revolution is plain, the ground-breaking decisions did appreciably less violence than some reforming decisions of the later WARREN COURT and BURGER COURT to the ideal of a coherent, growing, yet continuing body of law binding the judges as well as the litigants. Doubtless the presence of two competing lines of authority in the Court's earlier decisions often made it easier for the Hughes Court to perform this part of the judicial function. Liberty of contract had never been absolute. The Court had previously sustained, in special contexts, the power of Congress to regulate local activities affecting interstate commerce. Acceptance of the Hughes

Court's changes was also the easier because the Hughes Court was diminishing judicial interference with legislative innovations whereas the Warren and Burger Courts pressed far-reaching reforms without legislative support and sometimes against the will expressed by the people's elected representatives. That the old structure and powers of government should be shaped to industrialization, urbanization, and a national economy seemed more inevitable than that public schools should be integrated by busing, that prayer and Bible-reading should be banned from the public schools, or that abortion should be made a matter of personal choice. Yet even when the differences are acknowledged, much of the success of the Hughes Court in managing its revolution in constitutional interpretation seems attributable to the Chief Justice's belief in the value of a coherent, though changing, body of law, to his character, and to his talents combining the perception and sagacity drawn from an earlier, active political life with his extraordinary legal craftsmanship, earlier fine-honed as an Associate Justice.

Bibliography

ALSOP, JOSEPH and CATLEDGE, TURNER   1938   *The 168 Days*. Garden City, N.Y.: Doubleday.

JACKSON, ROBERT H.   1941   *The Struggle for Judicial Supremacy*. New York: Knopf.

MURPHY, PAUL   1972   *The Constitution in Crisis Times 1918–1969* New York: Harper & Row.

PUSEY, MERLO J.   1951   *Charles Evans Hughes*. New York: Macmillan.

STERN, ROBERT L.   1946   The Commerce Clause and the National Economy, 1933–1946. *Harvard Law Review* 59:645–693.

SWINDLER, WILLIAM F.   1970   *Court and Constitution in the Twentieth Century*, Part I. Indianapolis: Bobbs-Merrill.

STONE COURT

(1941–1946)

Archibald Cox

When Associate Justice HARLAN FISKE STONE moved over to the central seat of the Chief Justice in October 1941, he presided over a bench seven of whose nine members had been appointed to the Court by President FRANKLIN D. ROOSEVELT. All seven, who were sympathetic to the mass of new regulatory laws and welfare measures sponsored by the President, could be expected to develop approvingly the constitutional revolution of 1937. Surely they would sustain vast congressional expansion of federal power under the COMMERCE CLAUSE and drastically curtail the scope of JUDICIAL REVIEW. Stone himself had been appointed Associate Justice by President CALVIN COOLIDGE, but he had long advocated newly dominant constitutional principles in dissenting opinions. OWEN J. ROBERTS, now the senior Associate Justice, was a Republican appointed by President HERBERT C. HOOVER, but it was the shift of his vote, along with Chief Justice CHARLES EVANS HUGHES's, that had tipped the scales for change. Outside observers expected "a new unity in Supreme Court DOCTRINE, based upon a clearer philosophy of government than has yet been expressed in the swift succession of decisions rendered by a Court standing in the shadow of political changes."

But there was no unity. The new Chief Justice soon came to view his brethren as "a team of wild horses." DISSENTING OPINIONS and CONCURRING OPINIONS proliferated in numbers previously inconceivable. The controversies ranged from major jurisprudential differences to unworthy personal squabbles over such matters as the phrasing of the Court's letter to Justice Roberts upon his retirement.

The sources of disunity were both philosophical and temperamental. All but one or two of the Justices were highly individualistic, each was accustomed to speak his mind. All, with the possible exception of Justice Roberts, accepted the new regulatory and welfare state; but there were sharp differences over the proper pace and extent of change. The Chief Justice and Justices Roberts, STANLEY F. REED, JAMES F. BYRNES, and to a lesser degree Justices FELIX FRANKFURTER and ROBERT H. JACKSON, were more conservative in disposition than Justices HUGO L. BLACK, WILLIAM O. DOUGLAS, FRANK MURPHY, and Justice Byrnes's successor, WILEY B. RUTLEDGE. The temperamental differences were sometimes matched by differences in legal philosophy. The Chief Justice, Justice Frankfurter, and to a lesser degree Justice Jackson, were craftsmen of the law deeply influenced by a strong sense of the importance of the judge's loyalty to a growing, changing, but still coherent set of legal principles. For them, such institutional concerns were often more important than immediate, practical consequences. Justices Black, Douglas, and Murphy gave far more emphasis to the redistribution of social and economic power and to progressive reform. In conflicts between the individual and his government outside the economic area, the conservatives' instinct for order would often clash with the progressive liberals' enthusiasm for CIVIL LIBERTIES and CIVIL RIGHTS. The marked dissension indicates the difficulty any President of the United States faces in stamping one pattern upon the work of the Court.

Viewed in the sweep of constitutional history, the Stone years, 1941–1946, were the first part of a period of transition also encompassing the VINSON COURT, 1946–1953. By 1940 the main lines of CONSTITUTIONAL INTERPRETATION under the commerce clause and GENERAL WELFARE CLAUSE had been adapted to centralized ECONOMIC REGULATION and the welfare state. After 1953, when EARL WARREN became Chief Justice of the United States, the driving force would be a new spirit of libertarianism, egalitarianism, and emancipation. It remained for the Stone Court to complete the reinterpretation of the commerce clause and to pursue the philosophy of judicial deference to legislative determinations, whether state or federal. But harbingers of the new age of reform by constitutional adjudication also began to appear. The first explicit challenges to an across-the-board philosophy of judicial self-restraint were raised in the Stone Court. From the seeds thus scattered would grow the doctrinal principles supporting the subsequent vast expansion of constitutionally protected civil liberties and civil rights.

In interpreting the commerce clause, the Stone Court, whenever faced with a clear assertion of congressional intent to exercise such wide authority, did not shrink from pressing to its logical extreme the doctrine that Congress may regulate any local activities that in fact affect INTERSTATE COMMERCE. For example, in WICKARD V. FILBURN (1942) the Court sustained the imposition of a federal penalty upon the owner of a small family farm for sowing 11.9 acres of wheat in excess of his 11.1 acre federal allotment, upon the ground that Congress could rationally conclude that small individual additions to the total supply, even for home consumption, would cumulatively affect the price of wheat in interstate markets. The reluctance of the more conservative Justices to sanction unlimited expansion of federal regulation into once local affairs took hold when federal legislation was couched in terms sufficiently ambiguous to permit limitation. Decisions putting marginal limits upon the coverage of the federal wage and hour law are the best examples. Only a bare majority of four of the seven Justices participating could be mustered in UNITED STATES v. SOUTHEASTERN UNDERWRITERS ASSOCIATION (1944) for holding the insurance industry subject to the SHERMAN ANTITRUST ACT. In PAUL v. VIRGINIA (1879) the Court had first ruled that writing an insurance policy on property in another state was not interstate commerce. Later decisions and an elaborate structure of regulation in every state were built upon that precedent. Congress had essayed no regulation of insurance. The executive branch had not previously sought to apply the Sherman Act. Justices Black, Douglas, Murphy, and Rutledge seemed not to hesitate in sustaining the Department of Justice's novel assertion of federal power, a position supportable by the literal words of the statute and the logic of the expansive view of the commerce power. Respect for precedent and a strong sense of the importance of institutional continuity led the Chief Justice and Justices Frankfurter and Jackson to protest so sharp a departure from the status quo in the absence of a specific congressional directive: "it is the part of wisdom and self-restraint and good government to leave the initiative to Congress. . . . To force the hand of Congress is no more the proper function of the judiciary than to tie the hands of Congress." Congress responded to the majority by limiting the application of the Sherman Act to the insurance business, and by confirming the states' powers of regulation and taxation.

New constitutional issues that would lead to the next major phase in the history of constitutional adjudication began to emerge as wartime restrictions and the multiplication of government activities stirred fears for personal liberties. The war against Nazi Germany reinvigorated ideals of human dignity, equality, and democracy. As more civil liberties and civil rights litigation came upon the docket, a number of Justices began to have second thoughts about the philosophy of judicial deference to legislative determinations. That philosophy had well fitted the prevailing desire for progressive social and economic reform so long as the states and the executive and legislative branches of the federal government were engaged in the redistribution of power and the protection of the disadvantaged and distressed. The recollection of past judicial mistakes and the need for consistency of institutional theory cautioned against activist judicial ventures even in so deserving an area as civil liberty. On the other hand, continued self-restraint would leave much civil liberty at the mercy of executive or legislative oppression. The libertarian judicial activist could achieve a measure of logical consistency by elevating civil liberties to a PREFERRED POSITION justifying stricter standards of judicial review than those used in judging economic measures. The older dissenting opinions by Justices OLIVER WENDELL HOLMES and LOUIS D. BRANDEIS pleading for greater constitutional protection for FREEDOM OF SPEECH pointed the way even though they had failed to rationalize a double standard.

Stone himself, as an Associate Justice, had suggested one rationale in a now famous footnote in UNITED STATES v. CAROLENE PRODUCTS Co. (1938). Holding that the Court should indulge a strong presumption of constitutionality whenever the political processes of representative government were open, he nonetheless suggested that stricter judicial review might be appropriate when the challenge was to a statute that interfered with the political process—for example, a law restricting freedom of speech—or that was a result of prejudice against a DISCRETE AND INSULAR MINORITY—for example, a law discriminating against black people.

The issue was first drawn sharply under the FIRST and FOURTEENTH AMENDMENTS in the FLAG SALUTE CASES (1940, 1943). The substantive question was whether the constitutional guarantees of the freedom of speech and free exercise of religion permitted a state to expel from school and treat as truants the children of Jehovah's Witnesses, who refused to salute the United States flag. In the first case, the expulsions were sustained. Speaking for the Court, Justice Frankfurter invoked the then conventional rationale of judicial self-restraint. National unity and respect for national tradition, he reasoned, were permissible legislative goals. The compulsory flag salute could not be said to be an irrational means of seeking to secure those goals, even though the Court might be convinced that deeper patriotism would be engendered by refraining from coercing a symbolic gesture. To reject the legislative conclusion "would amount to no less than the pronouncement of pedagogical and psychological dogma in a field where courts possess no marked and certainly no controlling competence." The lone dissent came from Stone, who was still an Associate Justice.

Three years later the Court reversed itself. Justice Jackson, for the Court, summarized the core philosophy of the First Amendment: "If there is any fixed star in our constitutional constellation, it is that no official, high or petty, can prescribe what shall be orthodox in politics, nationalism, religion, or other matters of opinion or force citizens to confess by word or act their faith therein." First Amendment freedoms, the Court reasoned, rejecting Justice Frankfurter's plea for consistent application of the principle of judicial self-restraint, might not be curtailed for "such slender reasons" as would constitutionally justify restrictions upon economic liberty. Freedom of speech, of assembly, and of religion were susceptible of restriction "only to prevent grave and immediate danger to interests that the State may lawfully protect. We cannot because of modest estimates of our competence in such specialities as public education, withhold the judgment that history authenticates as the function of this Court when liberty is infringed."

Even in the 1980s, the deep and pervasive cleavage between the advocates of judicial self-restraint and the proponents of active judicial review in some categories of cases still divides both the Justices and constitutional scholars. It is now pretty clear, however, that judicial review will be stricter and there will be little deference to legislative judgments when restrictions upon freedom of expression, religion, or political association are at stake. (See JUDICIAL ACTIVISM AND RESTRAINT.)

In later years the Court would come also to scrutinize strictly, without deference to the political process, not only some laws challenged as denials of the EQUAL PROTECTION OF THE LAWS guaranteed by the Fourteenth Amendment but even statutes claimed to infringe FUNDAMENTAL RIGHTS in violation of the DUE PROCESS clauses of the Fifth and Fourteenth Amendments. The Stone Court broke the ground for STRICT SCRUTINY of statutory classifications prejudicing an "insular minority" in a opinion in one of the JAPANESE AMERICAN CASES declaring that "all legal restrictions which curtail the civil rights of a single racial group are immediately suspect . . . the courts must subject them to the most rigid scrutiny." In later years the constitutional standard thus declared became the basis for many decisions invalidating hostile RACIAL DISCRIMINATION at the hands of government, segregation laws, and other "invidious" statutory classifications.

Earlier the Stone Court opened the door to strict review in a second and still highly controversial class of cases under the equal protection clause. An Oklahoma statute mandated the STERILIZATION of persons thrice convicted of specified crimes, including grand larceny, but not of persons convicted of other crimes of much the same order and magnitude, such as embezzlement. The somewhat obscure opinion by Justice Douglas in SKINNER v. OKLAHOMA (1942), holding the differential treatment to violate the equal protection clause, emphasized the need for "strict scrutiny" of classifications made in a sterilization law, and referred to procreation as "a basic liberty." Later reforms by constitutional adjudication in the area of VOTING RIGHTS and legislative REPRESENTATION would be based upon the proposition that a legislative classification is subject to strict scrutiny not only when it is invidious but also when it differentiates among individuals in their access to a basic liberty. The precedent would also be invoked to support still later controversial decisions upholding claims of individual liberty in matters of sexual activity, childbirth, and abortion.

The Stone Court also sharpened the weapons for challenging crucial discrimination in the processes of representative government. In most of the states of the Old South, nomination as the candidate of the Democratic party still assured election to office. A political party was regarded as a private organization not subject to the equal protection clause of the Fourteenth Amendment or to the FIFTEENTH AMENDMENT's prohibition against denial or abridgment of VOTING RIGHTS by reason of race or color. Even after PRIMARY ELECTIONS regulated by state law became the standard method for nominating party candidates, "white primaries" remained an accepted method of excluding black citizens from participation in self- government.

The first step in upsetting this neat device was taken in an opinion by Justice Stone just before he became Chief Justice. Interference with the right to cast an effective ballot in a primary held to nominate a party's candidate for election as senator or representative was held in UNITED STATES v. CLASSIC (1938) to interfere with the election itself and thus to be punishable under legislation enacted by Congress pursuant to its power to regulate the time, place, and manner of holding elections under Article I, section 4. Next, in SMITH v. ALLWRIGHT (1944) the Stone Court ruled that if black citizens are excluded because of race or color from a party primary prescribed and extensively regulated by state law, their "right . . . to vote" has been denied or abridged by the state in violation of the Fifteenth Amendment. Opening the polls to effective participation by racial minorities throughout the South, in accordance with the promise of the Fifteenth Amendment, would have to await the civil rights revolution and the enactment of the VOTING RIGHTS ACT OF 1965, but these decisions eliminating "white primaries" were the first major steps in that direction.

While marking its contributions to the mainstream of constitutional history, one should not forget that the Stone Court was a wartime court subject to wartime pressures as it faced dramatic cases posing the underlying and unanswerable question, "How much liberty and judicial protection for liberty may be sacrificed to ensure survival of the Nation?" Economic measures were uniformly upheld, even a scheme for concentrating the review of the legality of administrative price regulations in a special EMERGENCY COURT OF APPEALS, thus denying a defendant charged in an ordinary court with a criminal violation the right to assert the illegality of the regulation as a defense. Extraordinary deference to military commanders under wartime pressures alone can account for the Court's shameful decision sustaining the constitutionality of a military order excluding every person of Japanese descent, even American-born United States citizens, from most of the area along the Pacific Coast.

More often, the majority resisted the pressures when individual liberty was at stake. In DUNCAN v. KAHANAMOKU (1946), an opinion with constitutional overtones, the substitution of military tribunals for civilian courts in Hawaii was held beyond the statutory authority of Army commanders. Prosecution of a naturalized citizen of German descent who had befriended a German saboteur landed by German submarine and who took his funds for safekeeping was held in CRAMER v. UNITED STATES (1945) not to satisfy the constitutional definition of TREASON because the only overt acts proved by the testimony of two witnesses—meetings with the enemy saboteur in public places—were not shown to give aid and comfort to the enemy. In *Schneiderman v. United States* (1943) the Court held that proof that a naturalized citizen was an avowed Marxist and long-time active member, organizer, and officer of the Communist Party of the United States, both before and after his NATURALIZATION, was insufficient to warrant stripping him of CITIZENSHIP on the ground that, when naturalized, he had not been "attached to the principles of the Constitution . . . and well disposed to the good order and happiness of the United States."

The delicate balance that the Stone Court maintained between the effective prosecution of the war and the constitutional safeguards of liberty is perhaps best illustrated by the dramatic proceedings in EX PARTE QUIRIN (1942). In June 1942 eight trained Nazi saboteurs were put ashore in the United States by submarine, four on Long Island and four in Florida. They were quickly apprehended. President Roosevelt immediately appointed a military commission to try the saboteurs. The President was determined upon swift military justice. The proclamation declared the courts of the United States closed to subjects of any nation at war with the United States who might enter the United States and be charged with sabotage or attempt to commit sabotage. The trial was prosecuted with extraordinary speed and secrecy. Before the trial was complete, counsel for the saboteurs sought relief by petition for HABEAS CORPUS. By extraordinary procedure the case was rushed before the Supreme Court. The Justices broke their summer recess to hear oral argument. An order was promptly entered denying the petitions and promising a subsequent opinion. Within a few days the military tribunal passed sentence and six of the saboteurs were executed.

In the post-execution opinion the Court explained that the offense was triable by military commission; that the military commission was lawfully constituted; and that the proceedings were conducted without violation of any applicable provision of the Articles of War. The Justices were greatly troubled upon the last question. Some realized that in truth the swift and secret procedure ordained by the President left them with little ability to give meaningful protection to the saboteurs' legal rights in the military proceedings. Yet, even while recognizing that wartime pressures bent traditional legal safeguards in this as in other instances before the Stone Court, one should not conclude "inter arma silent leges." The hard core of the Court's decision was that judicial review of the saboteurs' constitutional contentions could not be barred even by the President as COMMANDER-IN-CHIEF. One may therefore hope that, if similar circumstances again arise, the Stone Court's basic defense of CONSTITUTIONALISM in time of war will prove more significant than its occasional yielding to the pressures of emergency.

Bibliography

MASON, ALPHEUS   1956   *Harlan Fiske Stone, Pillar of the Laws.* Chaps. 34–42. New York: Viking Press.

ROSTOW, EUGENE   1945   The Japanese American Cases: A Disaster. *Yale Law Journal* 54:489–533.

SWINDLER, WILLIAM F.   1970   *Court and Constitution in the Twentieth Century,* Vol. 2, chaps. 6–10. Indianapolis: Bobbs-Merrill.

WOODWARD, J.   1968   *Mr. Justice Murphy.* Chaps. 11–13. Princeton, N.J.: Princeton University Press.

CONSTITUTIONAL HISTORY, 1945–1961

Paul L. Murphy

Reconversion to a peacetime society required reestablishing balance among the branches of the government and a careful reassessment of the role of each. The same process occasioned a reexamination of the relations between government and private power. These immediate problems of reconstruction were joined by the emergence of a "cold war" with the Communist bloc of nations. Americans defined that struggle as one against totalitarian rule—the antithesis of constitutional democracy.

The wartime period had seen massive government regulation of the economy and the personal lives of citizens. Congress had authorized governmental reorganization in 1941, reenacting a World War I measure giving the President almost unlimited power to reorganize federal agencies directing the nation's resources in wartime. (See WAR POWERS ACT.) At the end of World War II, Congress created a bipartisan Commission on Organization of the Executive Branch of the government headed by ex-President HERBERT HOOVER. It recommended reforms designed to reduce administrative disorder and bureaucracy. Congress in 1947 proposed the TWENTY-SECOND AMENDMENT (ratified in 1951) limiting presidential service to two terms.

Although many congressional conservatives hoped to roll back various New Deal programs, few were prepared to return the nation's economy to the unregulated control of private business leaders. Depression lessons had been painful. The FULL EMPLOYMENT ACT of 1946 declared that it was the government's task to take all steps necessary to maximize employment, production, and purchasing power. And while certain conservative congressmen were disturbed by the economic management this measure obviously necessitated, few opposed its goal of securing national economic stability. The Housing and Rent Act of 1947, continuing the wartime Price Control Act, raised an important question: does the WAR POWER continue after the shooting has ceased? The Supreme Court, in WOODS v. MILLER (1948), answered affirmatively as to legislation responding to wartime dislocations.

The issue of restraints on organized labor dissolved presidential–congressional harmony. President HARRY S. TRUMAN in 1946 vetoed the TAFT-HARTLEY ACT, an amendment to the 1935 WAGNER ACT, the nation's principal labor law. Taft-Hartley sought to eliminate an alleged prolabor bias by arming management with new rights and imposing limitations on long-established trade union practices. Truman called the act "completely contrary to the national policy of economic freedom," and "a threat to the successful working of our democratic society." But Congress passed it over his veto, and thirty states also enacted antilabor statutes, including RIGHT-TO-WORK LAWS and antipicketing measures. The LANDRUM-GRIFFIN ACT of 1959 sought to combat growing charges of union scandal, extortion, and deprivation of members' rights by imposing more direct federal authority over internal union procedures.

Executive-legislative cooperation resulted in passage of the Cellar-Kefauver Act of 1950, authorizing more rigid enforcement of the antitrust laws against corporate mergers. Two years later, following a Supreme Court ruling striking at "fair trade" laws, Congress passed the McGuire Act exempting state-approved fair trading from the federal antitrust laws. Seen as a consumer protection law, the measure was politically acceptable at the time.

In the FOREIGN AFFAIRS area, Congress and the President clashed. Truman had inherited a presidency whose prerogatives in foreign policy had been greatly expanded. Committed to the realization of Roosevelt's postwar programs, Truman backed American participation in the new United Nations. Such action entailed expanding presidential prerogatives at the expense of congressional power. American participation meant applying military sanctions against an aggressor state at the discretion of the United States delegate to the Security Council, who was under the control of the President. By the United Nations Participation Act of 1945 Congress recognized that the President could not commit the United States to participation in United Nations military sanctions without congressional consent, but it acknowledged implicitly that Congress's warmaking power was conditioned by the necessity of international security action. Similarly, when the United States joined the NORTH ATLANTIC TREATY Organization in 1950, it pledged automatic intervention if any member suffered armed attack. The question was raised whether such a commitment upset the traditional balance between the executive and legislative branches in questions of war and peace.

With the invasion of South Korea by Communist forces, presidential discretion rather than congressional action provided a dramatic answer. Truman, on June 25, 1950, without asking for a formal DECLARATION OF WAR or consulting Congress, ordered United States POLICE ACTION in the area. This order brought charges from Senator ROBERT A. TAFT that Truman had "usurped power and violated the Constitution and the laws of the United States." In the "great debate" that followed, Truman's actions and presidential war power generally were condoned, but not without a strong attempt, led by Senator John Bricker, to curb the treaty-making power of the President by constitutional amendment. One form of the unsuccessful BRICKER AMENDMENT would have declared: "A provision of a treaty or other international agreement which conflicts with this Constitution shall not be of any force or effect."

The Supreme Court ultimately eased the minds of Bricker's supporters. The circumstances were constitutionally significant. As new treaties of alliance grew in the late 1940s and early 1950s, American military and civilian personnel spanned the globe. Questions grew regarding the legal status of American citizens living abroad. Did the Constitution follow the flag? In REID v. COVERT (1957) the Court held that an EXECUTIVE AGREEMENT was subject to the limits of the Constitution, and thus could not confer on Congress power to authorize trial by COURT-MARTIAL of a civilian dependent of a serviceman stationed overseas. "We must not," wrote Justice HUGO L. BLACK, "break faith with this nation's tradition of keeping military power subservient to civilian authority."

Earlier, Congress had enacted a NATIONAL SECURITY ACT, creating the National Security Council and reorganizing the means by which war powers were exercised. The measure constricted the President's foreign policy prerogatives by requiring him to consult Congress before taking certain actions. In practice, however, it did not constrain willful Presidents. The ATOMIC ENERGY ACT of 1946 sought to insure civilian control over atomic energy production and precluded dissemination of technical information to other nations. By the 1950s, however, President Eisenhower sought and obtained an amendment, as the basis for an international cooperation program, to develop peaceful applications of nuclear energy. Nuclear power was apparently to become an important bargaining chip in the international arena.

One incident growing out of the KOREAN WAR revealed public feelings regarding the swelling authority of the executive and the proper nature of constitutional government. During the war, the President felt that constitutional history was on his side, given earlier validated presidential interventions in national emergency crises. He authorized his secretary of commerce to seize and operate struck steel mills, thereby insuring production of vital defense materials. His executive order was not based on statutory authority, but only on the ground that a threatened strike of the nation's steelworkers created a national emergency. When the steel companies sought an INJUNCTION against the government, federal spokesmen argued that the seizure was based upon Article II of the Constitution, and "whatever inherent, implied, or residual powers may flow therefrom." The President's actions drew sharp criticism, especially his refusal to use the Taft-Hartley Act provisions hated by his labor constituency. Before the Supreme Court, government counsel stressed expanded presidential prerogative during national emergencies, but the Supreme Court drew a line between public regulation and governmental operation of private business. In one of its most celebrated postwar constitutional decisions, the Court, speaking through Justice Black, rejected claims for presidential EMERGENCY POWERS and INHERENT POWERS in domestic affairs. Truman promptly announced compliance with the ruling, and the public reacted favorably to JUDICIAL ACTIVISM in curtailing excessive federal power. (See STEEL SEIZURE CONTROVERSY; YOUNGSTOWN SHEET & TUBE V. SAWYER.)

Constitutional development in the Truman years had been heavily influenced by considerations of national security at home and abroad, some serious, some specious, and all heavily political. Republican and conservative southern Democratic opponents of the New Deal had begun in 1938 to "red-bait" the Roosevelt administration by associating its personnel with un-Americanism or by representing the government's extension of powers as socialistic or communistic. Wartime investigations of federal employees and postwar revelations of inadequate security procedures intensified conservative demands for a housecleaning of the executive branch. Capitalizing on this issue during the 1946 congressional elections, the Republicans secured control of both houses of Congress, insuring that the subsequent Congress would investigate the loyalty of federal employees. During this period, the HOUSE COMMITTEE ON UN-AMERICAN ACTIVITIES (HCUA) was given permanent committee status, and between 1947 and 1948 Congress instituted thirty-five committee investigations of federal personnel and policies.

Lacking Roosevelt's political capital, and alarmed by leaks of classified information, Truman moved quickly to take control of the loyalty issue. In November 1946 he appointed a special presidential commission to investigate the problem, and in 1947 he formally instituted, by EXECUTIVE ORDER 9835, a permanent federal employee LOYALTY-SECURITY PROGRAM. To disarm congressional opposition further, Truman appointed conservatives to the loyalty program's major administrative positions. Under this program, negative information from any source was the potential basis for a security dismissal or the denial of government service. An ATTORNEY GENERAL'S LIST of subversive organizations was drawn up, with membership a basis for dismissal. The only guideline the order provided was that a designated organization must be "totalitarian, Fascist, Communist, or subversive," or one adopting a policy "approving the commission of acts of force or violence to deny to others their constitutional rights."

Civil libertarians attacked the program on constitutional grounds, charging that it presumed employees to be subversive and subject to dismissal unless they could prove themselves innocent. Critics of the program also charged that it lacked procedural protections, a charge raised chronically against HCUA. However, the administration moved with regard for justice and fair play during its loyalty probes, and by early 1951 the Civil Service Commission had cleared more than three million federal employees; the Federal Bureau of Investigation had made 14,000 investigations of doubtful cases; over 2,000 employees had resigned, although in very few cases because of the investigation; and 212 persons had been dismissed because of reasonable doubts of their loyalty. In 1948 the executive branch also sought to demonstrate concern for national security by obtaining indictments of the eleven national leaders of the Communist party under the Smith Act. A long and bombastic trial followed, ending in convictions for conspiracy to advocate overthrow of the government by force and violence. (See Dennis v. United States.)

Conservative critics claimed that the Truman administration's loyalty efforts were window dressing to divert attention from more serious problems. The sensational Alger Hiss-Whittaker Chambers hearings and the resultant conviction of Hiss, a former New Deal official, for perjury in connection with disclosures of secret security information, catalyzed Congress into launching its own loyalty program. The Mundt-Nixon Bill, seeking to force communists out into the open by requiring them to register with the Justice Department, was caught in 1948 election year politics and failed passage; but by 1950, following the reelection of Truman, the Internal Security Act, a similar measure, was passed resoundingly over the President's veto. The act went beyond the Truman loyalty program for government employees. It attempted to extend loyalty probes into nongovernmental areas of American life and generally assumed a need to shift the authority for security matters to congressional leadership. Civil libertarians challenged the measure as violative particularly of First Amendment guarantees. But in the Korean War period, with burgeoning security apprehensions fed aggressively by Senator Joseph R. McCarthy of Wisconsin, the possibility of launching a successful test case of even the act's most extreme provisions promised little success. Instead, Senator Patrick A. McCarran of Nevada, one of the measure's principal champions, persuaded Congress in 1952 to pass, over another Truman veto, a revised immigration law. The act contained provisions to prevent the admission of possible subversives, and it authorized Deportation of immigrants with communist affiliations even after they had become citizens.

The expanded activities of congressional committees in Legislative Investigations of loyalty and security raised important constitutional questions about committee prerogatives and behavior. While practice varied, some of the more flamboyant committees, such as HCUA, Senator McCarthy's Committee on Governmental Operations, or McCarran's Senate Internal Security Committee with large, aggressive, and ruthless staffs, pried into federal activities and even investigated subversion in the movie and entertainment industries, various private organizations, the academic community, and the churches. Committee actions alarmed civil libertarians, because of growing disregard for the type of procedural guarantees and safeguards of individual liberty normally afforded any citizen in a court of law. The committees browbeat witnesses, denied a RIGHT TO COUNSEL, and afforded no opportunity to examine charges, which were often irresponsible and from dubious sources. Opportunity to cross-examine witnesses was denied. Individuals' past affiliations and activities were used as evidence of guilt, and they were expected to prove themselves innocent to an obviously biased congressional "jury." As a result many witnesses invoked the Fifth Amendment, refusing to testify on the grounds that any statement made might tend to incriminate them. This led to charges that such citizens were "Fifth Amendment Communists." Congress in 1954 passed a FEDERAL IMMUNITY ACT to force testimony in return for promises of immunity from prosecution. (See IMMUNITY GRANT.) Generally the courts, including the Supreme Court, were cautious about thwarting government measures, deciding cases on the narrowest of grounds and proscribing only the most overt abuses.

Postwar demands for greater constitutional protections for minorities within American society expanded CIVIL RIGHTS. Many Americans believed that the United States should extend first class CITIZENSHIP to all. The struggle with the Communist world for the minds of Third World people added urgency. Early in 1946, President Truman established a Committee on Civil Rights affirming that "the preservation of civil rights, guaranteed by the Constitution, is essential to domestic tranquillity, national security, the general welfare, and the continued existence of our free institutions." In 1947 the committee proposed extension of an approach initiated by Attorney General FRANK MURPHY in the late 1930s, stressing that the federal government should be a shield in protecting citizens against those who would endanger their rights, and a sword to cut away state laws violating those rights. The report called for strengthening the CIVIL RIGHTS DIVISION of the Justice Department, using the Federal Bureau of Investigation in cases involving violations of civil rights, enacting antilynching and anti-POLL TAX laws, and establishing a permanent Fair Employment Practices Commission. However, with Southerners dominating many key congressional committees, prospects were dim for any program extending full civil rights to black Americans.

Truman determined to make the effort. In early 1948 he sent Congress a message calling for prompt implementation of the commission's report. A southern revolt in the Congress culminated in the secession of members from the Democratic Party. These "Dixiecrats" ran their own presidential candidate, J. Strom Thurmond, on a STATES' RIGHTS platform calling for "segregation of the races" and denouncing national action in behalf of civil rights as a "totalitarian concept, which threatens the integrity of the states and the basic rights of their citizens." Although Truman won the election, in the civil rights area he had available only executive remedies. These he utilized, strengthening the Civil Rights Division and encouraging the Justice Department to assist private parties in civil rights cases. He also ordered that segregation be ended in federal employment and that the armed services be fully integrated. (See EXECU-TIVE ORDERS 9980 AND 9981.) These developments encouraged civil rights activists to look to the courts for constitutional action in behalf of minority rights. Truman's Supreme Court appointees, however, were consistently conservative and espoused a narrow view of the judicial power. Only a few cautious rulings proscribed some forms of RACIAL DISCRIMINATION. (See SHELLEY V. KRAEMER, 1948; SWEATT V. PAINTER, 1950.)

Although DWIGHT D. EISENHOWER shared many of Truman's views regarding the President's vital and dominant leadership role in foreign policy, he conceived the domestic presidency in a different light. No social crusader, Eisenhower also had no desire to undo major programs of the New and Fair Deals. Rather he saw the presidency as a mediating agency, harmonizing the functioning of the team, and ratifying decisions and policies carefully prepared by responsible subordinates or by congressional leadership. Thus during Eisenhower's eight years in office Congress reasserted considerable domestic initiative, and when the President acted he usually complemented congressional desires.

During the 1952 campaign, Republicans made much of the "Communists in government" issue. Eisenhower realized that loyalty-security actions had to be taken to satisfy a nervous public. In 1953, he established a new executive loyalty program that expanded the criteria of the earlier Truman program. Discharge from federal service was now based on a simple finding that the individual's employment "may not be clearly consistent with the interests of national security." Several thousand "security risks" were dismissed. HCUA, cheering from the sidelines, then attempted to subpoena former President Truman to explain his security inadequacies. Truman responded with a polite letter giving the committee a lecture on SEPARATION OF POWERS and the independence of the executive.

Critics of the program focused on the absence of PROCEDURAL DUE PROCESS, the prevalence of GUILT BY ASSOCIATION, and the use of "faceless informers" as sources of damaging accusations. As long as Senator McCarthy was riding high such allegations remained just that. Tired of being smeared as "soft on Communists," frustrated liberal Democrats pushed through Congress a COMMUNIST CONTROL ACT in 1954, outlawing the party and initially seeking to make party membership a crime. The act proved virtually unenforceable. With the Senate censure and eventual demise of Senator McCarthy and the growing lack of enthusiasm of the Eisenhower administration for fueling the loyalty hysteria, security issues drifted into the background. By the late 1950s respectable bodies such as the New York City Bar Association and the League of Women Voters called for more precise standards for the federal government's loyalty-security program. With the Supreme Court also questioning aspects of that program's constitutional insensitivity, the President in early 1960 established a new industrial security program with vastly improved procedural safeguards. It included FAIR HEARINGS, the right of CONFRONTATION, and the right to examine all charges under ordinary circumstances. The same spirit came to prevail in the operation of other security programs.

The Eisenhower administration showed concern for state prerogatives and the need for balancing them against the rights of the individual. The federal government's growth in size and power since the late 1930s had been paralleled in state governments. During this period the states collected more money, spent more, employed more people, and engaged in more activities than ever before. When the expenditure and employment were assisted by FEDERAL GRANTS-IN-AID, lack of state compliance with federal standards meant potential loss of federal revenues. But states acted enthusiastically on their own in areas ranging from education and social services to a struggle with the federal government over control of natural resources. In 1947 the Supreme Court ruled that the United States had dominion over the soil under the marginal sea adjoining California. That state had maintained it was entitled, by virtue of the "equal footing" clause in the act admitting it to the Union, to the rights enjoyed by the original states and that those states owned such offshore areas. The Court concluded that such ownership had not been established at the time of the Constitution, and the interests of SOVEREIGNTY favored national dominion. But following the victorious Eisenhower campaign of 1952, in which the Republicans had courted the West and the South with promises of offshore riches, Congress passed the Submerged Lands Act of 1953, vesting in the states the ownership of lands beneath the marginal sea adjacent to the respective states. The Supreme Court subsequently denied leave to file complaints challenging the statute's constitutionality.

At another level, states and municipalities became so concerned in the 1950s with employees' loyalty that they enacted restrictive security measures. These included prohibiting the employment of Communist party members, LOYALTY OATHS as a condition of employment for teachers, service personnel, and candidates for public office, and measures authorizing state prosecution for SEDITION against the United States. State bar associations in turn moved to exclude from admission candidates who were allegedly former Communist party members or who refused to answer questions regarding former suspect affiliations. When the

Supreme Court struck at such state sedition laws (PENNSYLVANIA V. NELSON, 1956) and bar restraints (SCHWARE V. NEW MEXICO BOARD OF BAR EXAMINERS, 1958; KONIGSBERG V. CALIFORNIA STATE BAR, 1957) its actions were denounced by the Conference of Chief Justices of the States as "the high-water mark . . . in denying to a state the power to keep order in its own house." Bills were introduced in Congress to deny the Court APPELLATE JURISDICTION in cases of this kind.

In this atmosphere, national leaders were hesitant to push for early implementation of the Supreme Court's DESEGREGATION mandate, and preferred to interpret the command "with ALL DELIBERATE SPEED" by emphasizing deliberation. A pattern of "massive resistance" emerged in the southern states, constituting a crazy quilt of INTERPOSITION proclamations, pupil-assignment or placement laws, freedom-of-choice laws, TUITION GRANT plans, and state statutes prescribing discipline of teachers for violation of state policies on the school segregation question. Meanwhile, federal authorities sat on their hands until after the 1956 election. Then they took cautious steps to bring the federal government more directly into the civil rights area. Eisenhower's attorney general proposed a federal statute to authorize an investigation of rights violations, particularly VOTING RIGHTS. The CIVIL RIGHT ACT OF 1957 passed after Southerners had so amended it as to make it virtually toothless. When Eisenhower signed the act into law early in September, he could have used a much stronger bill. One week earlier Governor Orville Faubus of Arkansas, an acknowledged segregationist, had ordered state troops into Little Rock to prevent implementation of a federal court order approving the admission of a handful of black students into that city's Central High School. Confronted with military defiance of federal authority, Eisenhower had no choice but to respond. He reluctantly dispatched several companies of the United States Army to Little Rock, under a provision of the United States Code, which authorized the suppression of insurrection and unlawful combinations that hindered the execution of either state or federal law. (See POSSE COMITATUS ACT.) He also nationalized and thus neutralized the Arkansas National Guard. Black children attended school for a year under military protection and Arkansas's massive resistance was held at bay by bayonets.

After the Little Rock case was decided by the Supreme Court in COOPER V. AARON (1958), which sustained the school desegregation order, Congress also acted. The CIVIL RIGHTS ACT OF 1960 made it a federal crime for a person to obstruct or interfere with a federal court order, or to attempt to do so by threats of force. Other provisions expanded federal remedies for enforcing voting rights. The measure, for which the Republicans claimed credit in their 1960 platform, put Congress and the executive branch on record as committed to push ahead with rights enforcement.

For minority groups without the political constituency of blacks, little positive action was forthcoming. Women's rights in this period was a subliminal theme at best. Women's work in World War II had gone a long way toward shattering the stereotype of the helpless, weaker sex in need of protective legislation. Some leaders in Congress moved toward proposal of the EQUAL RIGHTS AMENDMENT as a vote of thanks to women for their magnificent wartime performance. Both parties endorsed the measure at war's end, and Harry Truman spoke publicly in its support. But Eleanor Roosevelt, with the support of organized labor, insisted that protective legislation was more valuable for working women than the establishment of an abstract principle of legal rights. Despite two attempts in the Senate to pass a bill proposing the amendment in the late 1940s, and a third in 1953 with a rider specifying that no protective legislation was to be affected, the measure was not seriously revived in this period.

The rights of American Indians suffered even more. In 1953, the Eisenhower administration set out on a policy of "termination," supporting a program designed to reduce the federal government's involvement in Indian affairs and to "free" Indians from federal supervision. Specifically, termination sought to end the existing supportive federal–tribal relationship and transfer almost all responsibilities and powers from the federal government to the states. The effects on "terminated" tribes was disastrous; many tribal members were soon on public assistance rolls. Indians detested the law embodying this policy, seeing it as an instrument for tribal extinction. They expended their energies to defeat it, and finally achieved victory in 1968. The Indian Civil Rights Act of that year encouraged Indian self-determination with continuing government assistance and services.

The judicial branch in the period from 1945 to 1961 changed from a cautious and accommodating agency, under Chief Justice FRED M. VINSON, to an active, aggressive, and controversial storm-center under Chief Justice EARL WARREN. Just as WILLIAM HOWARD TAFT had made the Supreme Court the principal instrument for the determination of constitutionality in the 1920s, Earl Warren, who assumed the chief justiceship 1953, came to play a similar role in the late 1950s. Often backlash resulted, but in Warren's case, from conservatives and not liberals. Statistically, the WARREN COURT's record was not so activist as that of the 1920s. Four acts of Congress, eighty-five state acts, and sixteen ordinances were ruled unconstitutional from 1945 through 1960, with the Justices overruling twenty-two prior decisions. But the activist image was strong because the Court entered explosive areas of sensitive public policy.

The Court's unanimous decision in BROWN V. BOARD OF EDUCATION (1954) had shocked southern states-righters into defensive and retaliatory actions. The Court's consistent pushing ahead in the civil rights area sustained and intensified this antipathy. But Warren, supported by a liberal majority, was not prepared to stop. In the loyalty-security area, the Court limited the more sweeping provisions of the Smith Act, the Internal Security Act of 1950, and state loyalty measures. The rights of individuals and their protection from the abuses of government seemed to come first to the Justices' minds. The Court struck at departures from fair procedure by congressional committees. In *Jencks v. United States* (1957) it ruled that a defendant in a criminal case should have access to prior recorded statements of witnesses against him. Congress promptly sought to limit that ruling by the passage of the JENCKS ACT. By the late 1950s, the Justices began the process of critically examining state anti-OBSCENITY and censorship laws. In Congress there was talk of the need to curtail the Court's authority through legislation limiting its appellate jurisdiction. National action by right-wing groups quickly emerged to bolster such a movement, contributing to a broad public dialogue on the Court's proper function.

Defenders and critics of the Warren Court's liberal activism debated the proper role of the Constitution in the American polity. Champions of liberal judicial activism defended the legitimacy of judicial activity to shape constitutional law in accordance with democratic values. Supporters of judicial restraint advocated deference to popularly elected legislatures with courts confined to a narrowly circumscribed role. To conservative constitutionalists, the rule of law meant more than the imposition by a liberal Court of its own ethical imperatives, with little concern for orthodox doctrinal consistency.

There were no winners in this debate. But it proved apropos to the developments of the 1950s and to the institutional interrelationships of those years.

Bibliography

MURPHY, PAUL L.   1969   *The Constitution in Crisis Times, 1918–1969*. New York: Harper & Row.

MURPHY, WALTER F.   1962   *Congress and the Court*. Chicago: University of Chicago Press.

PRITCHETT, C. HERMAN   1954   *Civil Liberties and the Vinson Court*. Chicago: University of Chicago Press.

VINSON COURT

(1946–1953)

C. Herman Pritchett

FRED M. VINSON was Chief Justice of the United States from June 24, 1946, until his death on September 8, 1953. During his seven-year period of service the Supreme Court was considerably less interesting, colorful, or originative of significant constitutional DOCTRINE than its predecessor, the STONE COURT, or its successor, the WARREN COURT. However, the Vinson Court did deal with serious and important issues, particularly Cold War challenges to CIVIL LIBERTIES and awakening concerns about RACIAL DISCRIMINATION.

Vinson was a close friend of President HARRY S. TRUMAN and an active Democrat who had had the unique experience of serving in all three branches of the federal government. Immediately preceding his appointment to the Court he had been secretary of the treasury. President Truman had made one previous appointment, naming HAROLD BURTON, a Republican and former Senate colleague of Truman, to replace OWEN ROBERTS in 1945. The other seven justices were of course all holdovers from the Stone Court, which guaranteed a continuation of the judicial dialogue that had pitted the liberal activism of HUGO L. BLACK, WILLIAM O. DOUGLAS, FRANK MURPHY, and WILEY B. RUTLEDGE against the brilliant critiques of FELIX FRANKFURTER and ROBERT H. JACKSON, with the moderate STANLEY F. REED somewhere in the center.

The four-judge liberal bloc had within itself the votes required to grant CERTIORARI petitions, which ensured that civil liberties issues would continue to appear on the Court's agenda. When the liberals agreed, they needed only one additional vote to constitute a majority. But in the summer of 1949 Justices Murphy and Rutledge died, cutting the liberal bloc in half. President Truman filled these two vacancies by the appointment of TOM C. CLARK, his attorney general, and SHERMAN MINTON, who had been a New Deal senator from Indiana. The two new justices joined with Vinson, Reed, and Burton in a moderately conservative bloc which dominated the remaining four terms of the Vinson Court. An indication of the balance of power on the Court is provided by the number of dissents registered by each of the Justices during this four-year period: Clark 15, Vinson 40, Burton 44, Minton 47, Reed 59, Jackson 80, Frankfurter 101, Douglas 130, Black 148.

The most famous decision of the Vinson Court in terms of public reaction, and probably the most noteworthy as a contribution to constitutional theory, was YOUNGSTOWN SHEET & TUBE CO. v. SAWYER (1952), generally known as the Steel Seizure Case. Here the Court by a vote of 6–3 held unconstitutional President Truman's seizure of the nation's steel mills in 1952, an action he justified as necessary to avert a nationwide strike that might have affected the flow of munitions to American troops in Korea. The President had no statutory authority for the seizure, which consequently had to be justified on a theory of inherent presidential power to meet emergencies.

Justice Black, supported by Douglas, flatly denied the existence of any inherent presidential powers. Justices Jackson and Frankfurter were less dogmatic, and the doctrine of the case is generally drawn from their opinions. As they saw it, the controlling factor was that Congress had considered granting the President seizure power to deal with nationwide strikes when adopting the TAFT-HARTLEY ACT in 1947 but had decided against it. In addition, Jackson contributed a situational scale for ruling on claims of executive emergency power. Vinson, in his most famous dissent, upheld the President as having moved in an emergency to maintain the status quo until Congress could act, and he rejected the majority's "messenger boy" concept of the presidential office.

The fact that the Court could have avoided the constitutional issue in the Steel Seizure Case by various alternatives suggested that most of the justices believed it important to announce a check on presidential power. The decision was enormously popular with the press and public and has subsequently been accepted as an authoritative statement on the SEPARATION OF POWERS, establishing that actions of the president are subject to JUDICIAL REVIEW. There had been some doubt on this point since the failure of the post-Civil War suit against the president in MISSISSIPPI v. JOHNSON (1867). It established also that executive claims of power for which statutory authority is lacking, and which must consequently rely on the President's general Article II authority, are subject to strict judicial scrutiny.

Less significant in its doctrine than the Steel Seizure Case but almost as controversial was the Court's contempt ruling against John L. Lewis, leader of the coal miners, in 1947 (UNITED STATES v. UNITED MINE WORKERS). The government had seized the nation's bituminous coal mines in 1946 to end a crippling strike and had entered into a contract with Lewis on wages and working conditions. When Lewis subsequently terminated the contract unilaterally and resumed the strike, the government secured a contempt JUDGMENT and heavy fine against Lewis and the union. In his first major opinion Vinson upheld the conviction for contempt, ruling that the NORRIS-LAGUARDIA ACT limiting the issuance of labor INJUNCTIONS was not binding on the government as an employer.

A significant difference between the Stone and Vinson Courts was that World War II had ended and the Cold War against communism had begun. The hunt for subversives in which the nation was caught up soon after the shooting war was over tainted the entire period of the Vinson Court and created difficult civil liberties issues. The government's principal weapon against suspected subversion was the Smith Act of 1940, which made it unlawful to teach and advocate the overthrow of the United States government by force and violence, or to organize a group for such a purpose.

Convictions of eleven leaders of the American Communist party under the Smith Act were upheld by the Supreme Court in DENNIS V. UNITED STATES (1951). In the most memorable event of his judicial career, Chief Justice Vinson wrote the Court's majority opinion defending the Smith Act against contentions that it violated the FIRST AMENDMENT. The defendants admittedly had taken no action with the immediate intention of initiating a revolution. But Vinson held that the CLEAR AND PRESENT DANGER TEST, developed by Justice OLIVER WENDELL HOLMES and LOUIS D. BRANDEIS, did not require the government to wait until a "putsch" was about to be executed before acting against a conspiracy. Vinson accepted the reformulation of the test developed by Judge LEARNED HAND: "Whether the gravity of the 'evil,' discounted by its improbability, justifies such invasion of free speech as is necessary to avoid the danger." He considered the communist "evil" to be that grave. Justices Black and Douglas dissented; Douglas pointed out that the prosecution had introduced no evidence of Communist party action aimed at overthrow of the government.

Vinson also wrote the Court's opinion in AMERICAN COMMUNICATIONS ASSOCIATION V. DOUDS (1950), upholding the Taft-Hartley Act noncommunist oath. This statute denied the protections and services of the WAGNER (NATIONAL LABOR RELATIONS) ACT to any labor organization whose officers failed to file affidavits that they were not members of the Communist party. The Chief Justice held that Congress in adopting this statute was acting to prevent the obstruction of commerce by "political strikes." The law was not aimed at speech but rather at harmful conduct carried on by persons who could be identified by their political affiliations and beliefs.

The Vinson Court was caught up in the final moments of the Cold War's most spectacular event, the execution of Julius and Ethel Rosenberg, who were charged with passing atomic "secrets" to the Russians. Review of the lower court conviction and subsequent APPEALS was routinely denied by the Supreme Court in 1952 and early 1953, as were also the initial petitions for STAY OF EXECUTION. But Justice Douglas thought that one final petition filed the day before execution was scheduled raised a new legal issue deserving consideration. He consequently granted a stay which the full Court set aside the next day, and the executions were then carried out. Douglas's action caused a brief furor and a congressman demanded his IMPEACHMENT. In the last opinion before his death Vinson defended Douglas's action as a proper response to protect the Court's JURISDICTION over the case pending a consideration of the legal issue raised. Black and Frankfurter joined Douglas in asserting that the stay should have been granted.

During the era of the Vinson Court, congressional committee investigations of communism developed into major political and media events. Senator Joseph McCarthy's pursuit of "Fifth Amendment Communists" got under way in 1950, too late to create issues for the Vinson Court. But the HOUSE COMMITTEE ON UN-AMERICAN ACTIVITIES had begun operations in 1938, and by 1947 petitions for review of contempt citations against witnesses who had refused to reply to committee interrogation began to reach the Supreme Court. However, it declined review of all the cases that would have required a ruling on the constitutionality of the use of investigatory power, and it dealt only with certain less controversial issues of committee procedure and use of the Fifth Amendment privilege by witnesses.

A prominent feature of the Cold War period was concern about the loyalty of government employees. A LOYALTY OATH fad developed in nearly every state, which the Vinson Court legitimated in GERENDE v. BOARD OF SUPERVISORS OF ELECTIONS (1951) by upholding a Maryland law that required candidates for public office to file affidavits that they were not "subversive persons."

A loyalty program covering federal employees was set up by President Truman in 1947 and was continued by President DWIGHT D. EISENHOWER. It required checking the loyalty of all incumbent employees and all applicants for federal employment. A complex administrative organization of loyalty review boards was created, and to assist the boards the attorney general issued a list of organizations he found to be "totalitarian, fascist, communist, or subversive." Consideration of the constitutionality of this program split the Court 4–4 in *Bailey v. Richardson* (1951). But in JOINT ANTI-FASCIST REFUGEE COMMITTEE V. MCGRATH (1951), decided the same day, the Court by a vote of 5–3 challenged the attorney general's list as having been drawn up without appropriate investigation or DUE PROCESS. The dissenters were Reed, Vinson, and Minton. In spite of this opinion the list continued to be used for a number of years in government hiring and investigation.

At the state level a New York law providing for the removal of public school teachers on grounds of membership in listed subversive organizations was upheld in ADLER V. BOARD OF EDUCATION OF CITY OF NEW YORK (1952), Justice Minton reasoning that the purpose was constitutional and that procedural protections provided by the statute were adequate. Justices Black and Douglas dissented, and Frankfurter would have denied the appeal on technical grounds of STANDING and RIPENESS.

Apart from Cold War cases, FREEDOM OF SPEECH and FREEDOM OF THE PRESS did not suffer seriously at the hands of the Vinson Court. BURSTYN V. WILSON (1952) was in fact an advance in its holding that a motion picture could not be censored on the ground that it was "sacrilegious." A law censoring magazines featuring bloodshed and lust was struck down in *Winters v. New York* (1948) as void for vagueness. *Poulos v. New Hampshire* (1953) upheld licensing of meetings in public parks and streets, but only if the licenses were granted without discrimination, and the use of licensing ordinances to prevent unpopular religious groups or preachers from holding meetings in public parks was rebuffed in NIEMOTKO V. MARYLAND (1951) and KUNZ V. NEW YORK (1951).

In TERMINIELLO V. CHICAGO (1949) a divided Court reversed on rather technical grounds the conviction of a rabble-rouser for BREACH OF THE PEACE resulting from an incendiary speech. But FEINER V. NEW YORK (1951) upheld the conviction of a soap-box orator even though the situation was much less inflammatory than in *Terminiello*. Moreover, BEAUHARNAIS V. ILLINOIS (1952) approved a state law treating critical comments about racial groups as criminal and subjecting their authors to prosecution for GROUP LIBEL.

The Vinson Court dealt with a number of conflicts between freedom of expression and privacy but without producing any theories justifying or limiting privacy claims such as those subsequently developed in GRISWOLD V. CONNECTICUT (1965) by the Warren Court. Use of sound trucks in streets and parks was initially upheld in *Saia v. New York* (1948) against contentions of infringement on privacy, but in the following year the Court conceded that "loud and raucous" sound trucks could be forbidden (KOVACS V. COOPER). Radio broadcasts including commercial messages in DISTRICT OF COLUMBIA streetcars were permitted to continue by *Public Utilities Commission v. Pollak* (1952), even though CAPTIVE AUDIENCES might suffer, but *Breard v. City of Alexandria* (1951) protected householders by approving an ordinance forbidding door-to-door selling of magazine subscriptions. Justice Black charged that the latter decision violated the "preferred position" for First Amendment freedoms originated by the Roosevelt Court. The severest blow to that philosophy was *United Public Workers v. Mitchell* (1947) which upheld by a vote of 4–3 the HATCH ACT limits on political activity by public employees.

In a 1940 case, THORNHILL V. ALABAMA, the Court had strongly asserted that PICKETING in labor disputes was protected by the First Amendment. Almost immediately, however, the Court found it necessary to announce limits on this holding, a process the Vinson Court continued. The most significant case was GIBONEY V. EMPIRE STORAGE & ICE CO.

(1949), where the Court ruled unanimously against a union that was picketing to force an employer to enter into an illegal restrictive contract.

The issue of public financial aid to religious schools required the Vinson Court to make the first significant effort to interpret and apply the First Amendment ban on ESTABLISHMENT OF RELIGION. EVERSON V. BOARD OF EDUCATION (1947) involved a state arrangement under which parents could be reimbursed from public moneys for their children's bus fare to parochial schools. An unusual five-judge majority composed of three liberals (Black, Douglas, and Murphy) and two conservatives (Vinson and Reed) held that the subsidy was simply a social welfare measure and that the First Amendment did not require exclusion of persons of any faith from the benefits of "public welfare legislation." Rutledge's vigorous dissent regarded payment for transportation to church schools as a direct aid to religious education and so unconstitutional.

The following year McCOLLUM V. BOARD OF EDUCATION presented another church–state issue. The case involved a RELEASED TIME program of religious education under which public school children attended classes in Protestant, Roman Catholic, or Jewish religious instruction during school hours and in the school building. The Court's almost unanimous verdict of UNCONSTITUTIONALITY aroused a storm of criticism in church circles, and within four years the Court substantially reversed this ruling, upholding a New York City released time program that differed from McCollum only in that the classes were held off the school grounds (ZORACH V. CLAUSEN, 1952.) A similar reluctance to disturb the religious community was seen as the Court avoided on technical grounds of standing a ruling on the constitutionality of Bible-reading in the public schools (DOREMUS V. BOARD OF EDUCATION).

The Vinson Court's civil liberties record was distinctly better than that of its predecessors in one area, protection of minorities from discrimination. The prevailing constitutional rule was that established by PLESSY V. FERGUSON in 1896—that SEGREGATION of the races was constitutional provided treatment or facilities were equal. In practice, they were never equal, but over the years the Court had consistently avoided the difficult task of enforcing the Plessy rule. In the field of education, none of the few efforts to challenge unequal facilities had been successful. But in 1938 the HUGHES COURT made a small beginning, ruling in MISSOURI EX REL. GAINES V. CANADA that Missouri, which denied blacks admission to state law schools, must do so or set up a separate law school for blacks. MORGAN V. VIRGINIA (1946) invalidated a state Jim Crow law requiring racial segregation of passengers on public motor carriers, but the constitutional ground given was burden on INTERSTATE COMMERCE rather than denial of EQUAL PROTECTION.

The Vinson Court undertook cautiously to build on these beginnings.

The COMMERCE CLAUSE justification used in the Virginia bus case was likewise employed in BOB-LO EXCURSION CO. v. MICHIGAN (1948). But the Vinson Court's boldest action against segregation came shortly thereafter in SHELLEY v. KRAEMER (1948). With Vinson writing the opinion, the Court declared that RESTRICTIVE COVENANTS binding property owners not to sell to minorities, although within the legal rights of property owners, were unenforceable. For a court to give effect to such a discriminatory contract, Vinson held, would amount to STATE ACTION in violation of the FOURTEENTH AMENDMENT.

The separate law school for blacks that Texas had established was declared unequal in SWEATT v. PAINTER (1950). The University of Oklahoma, forced to admit a black graduate student, required him to sit in a separate row in class, at a separate desk in the library, and at a separate table in the cafeteria. McLAURIN v. OKLAHOMA STATE REGENTS (1950), with Vinson again writing the opinion, held these practices to be an unconstitutional impairment of the student's ability to learn his profession.

Vinson's opinion, however, rejected the opportunity to consider the broader issue of the *Plessy* SEPARATE BUT EQUAL rule. So attacks on the segregation principle continued, and the TEST CASES moved from the universities and graduate schools to the primary and secondary schools. In December 1952 BROWN v. BOARD OF EDUCATION OF TOPEKA and four other school segregation cases were argued for three days before the Court. But instead of a decision in June, the Court set the cases for reargument in October. The Chief Justice died in September, and so the Vinson Court's most momentous issue was passed on to the Warren Court.

Although the Stone Court had broken some new ground in CRIMINAL PROCEDURE, its record was mixed, particularly in guaranteeing the RIGHT TO COUNSEL and protection against UNREASONABLE SEARCHES and seizures. This latter issue surfaced in the Vinson Court's first term. One of the oldest problems in American constitutional law is whether the due process clause of the Fourteenth Amendment "incorporated" and made effective in state criminal proceedings the protections of the Fourth through the Eighth Amendments. As recently as 1937 in PALKO v. CONNECTICUT the Court had reiterated the principle that all state procedures consistent with ORDERED LIBERTY are acceptable.

In ADAMSON v. CALIFORNIA (1947) the *Palko* doctrine survived on the Vinson Court, but by only a 5–4 vote. Justice Black led the minority. He relied on legislative history to establish his version of the intention of the framers of the Fourteenth Amendment and attacked the ORDERED LIBERTY test as substituting natural law and the notions of individual Justices for the precise and protective language of the BILL OF RIGHTS.

Although Black lost in *Adamson,* "ordered liberty" was a standard powerful enough to bring state criminal processes within the ambit of the FOURTH AMENDMENT in WOLF V. COLORADO (1949). However, Justice Frankfurter for the six-judge majority held only that SEARCHES AND SEIZURES by state law officers are bound by the standard of reasonableness; he declined to go further and impose on state prosecutions the EXCLUSIONARY RULE which prevents EVIDENCE secured by unconstitutional means from being offered in federal prosecutions. Justices Murphy, Douglas, and Rutledge, dissenting, contended that the exclusionary rule provided the only effective protection against police violation of the Fourth Amendment, and their view was finally adopted on the Warren Court in MAPP V. OHIO (1961).

With respect to right to counsel, the Vinson Court accepted the rule announced by the Stone Court in BETTS V. BRADY (1942) that the necessity for counsel depended upon the circumstances, such as the seriousness of the crime, the age and mental capacity of the defendant, and the ability of the judge. Applying the "special circumstances" rule in twelve cases, the Vinson Court concluded that in six the absence of counsel had resulted in denial of a FAIR TRIAL. In only one of the twelve was the Court unanimous. This experience was a factor in the Warren Court's decision in GIDEON V. WAINWRIGHT (1963) to abolish the confusing special circumstances rule and make counsel mandatory in all state felony prosecutions.

What was potentially one of the Vinson Court's most significant decisions for the federal system was nullified by Congress. In 1947 the Court ruled that subsurface land and mineral rights in California's three-mile coastal area belonged to the federal government (*United States v. California*), and in 1950 the Court applied the same rule to Texas. Congress retaliated in 1953 by ceding to the states ownership of land and resources under adjoining seas up to a distance of three miles from shore or to the states' historic boundaries.

In summary, the tendency of the Vinson Court was to follow a policy of judicial restraint, rejecting innovation or activism. The number of cases decided by full opinion fell below one hundred during three of the last four years, far less than the number typically decided by earlier Courts. The five justices who dominated the Court in its latter period were capable but lacking in style or originality. The four Justices of intellectual distinction—Black, Douglas, Frankfurter, and Jackson—generally paired off and pulled in opposite directions.

The pall of the Cold War hung over the Court. Confronted with the scandal of McCarthyism, it was quiescent. Facing Smith Act prosecutions, the loyalty inquisition of federal employees, lists of subversive organizations, scrutiny of school teachers' associates, loyalty oaths, and deportation of ex-communists, the Court's response was usually to legitimate the government's action.

But in one field, significantly, there was a different kind of response. The Vinson Court did not evade the issue of racial discrimination. Although moving cautiously, as was appropriate considering the enormity of the problem, the Court nevertheless proceeded to bring denial of equal protection out of the limbo of neglect and unconcern into the focus of national consciousness and thereby prepared the way for its successor's historic decision on May 17, 1954.

Bibliography

FRANK, JOHN P. 1954 Fred Vinson and the Chief Justiceship. *University of Chicago Law Review* 21:212–246.

MURPHY, PAUL L. 1972 *The Constitution in Crisis Times, 1919–1969.* New York: Harper & Row.

PRITCHETT, C. HERMAN (1954)1966 *Civil Liberties and the Vinson Court.* Chicago: University of Chicago Press.

SWINDLER, WILLIAM F. 1970 *Court and Constitution in the Twentieth Century: The New Legality, 1932–1968.* Indianapolis: Bobbs-Merrill.

WARREN COURT

(1953–1969)

G. Edward White

It was surely the best known Supreme Court in history, and probably the most controversial. Its grand themes—racial equality, REAPPORTION-MENT, the separation of religion and education, DUE PROCESS—became matters of public consciousness. Its leading judges—HUGO L. BLACK, WILLIAM O. DOUGLAS, FELIX FRANKFURTER, JOHN MARSHALL HARLAN, and EARL WARREN—became personages in whom the general public took an interest. When the Warren Court came into being in October 1953, the Supreme Court was the least known and least active of the major branches of government; by the retirement of Chief Justice Warren in June 1969, nearly everyone in American life had been affected by a Warren Court decision, and a great many Americans had firm opinions about the Supreme Court. When Warren was appointed Chief Justice, few commentators took note of the fact that he had had no previous judicial experience and had spent the last twelve years as a state politician. By the time WARREN E. BURGER succeeded Warren as Chief Justice the process of nominating a Justice to the Supreme Court had become an elaborate search for the "experienced," uncontroversial, and predictable nominee, and the Court was to lower its profile again.

The Warren Court years, then, were years in which the Supreme Court of the United States made itself a vital force in American culture. A striking pattern of interchange between the Court and the general public emerged in these years. As public issues, such as CIVIL RIGHTS or legislative malapportionment surfaced, these issues became translated into constitutional law cases. The Court, expanding the conventional ambit of its JURISDICTION, reached out to decide those cases, thereby making an authoritative contribution to the public debate. As the Court continued to reach out, the public came to rely on its presence, and the American JUDICIAL SYSTEM came to be perceived as a forum for the resolution of contemporary social problems. The use of the Supreme Court as an institution for redressing grievances ignored by Congress or state legislatures became common with the Warren Court.

The origins of the Warren Court can officially be traced to September 8, 1953, when Chief Justice FRED M. VINSON died of a heart attack. By September 30, President DWIGHT D. EISENHOWER had named Warren, the governor of California who had been a rival candidate for the Republican presidential nomination in 1952, as Vinson's successor. This nominal creation of the Warren Court did not, however, hint at its character. Indeed that character was not immediately apparent. Even the Court's first momentous decision, BROWN v. BOARD OF EDUCATION (1954), announced in May of its first term, was in some respects a holdover from the VINSON COURT. *Brown* had been argued before the Vinson Court, was based in part on Vinson Court precedents chipping away at RACIAL DISCRIMINATION in education, and was decided by a Court whose only new member was its Chief Justice. It was a cautious decision, apparently assuming that DESEGREGATION would be a long and slow process.

But *Brown* was also the Warren Court's baptism of fire. All the elements that were to mark subsequent major Warren Court decisions were present in *Brown*. *Brown* involved a major social problem, racial discrimination, translated into a legal question, the constitutionality of SEPARATE BUT EQUAL public schools. It posed an issue that no other branch of government was anxious to address. It raised questions that had distinctively moral implications: in invalidating racial SEGREGATION the Court was condemning the idea of racial supremacy. And it affected the lives of ordinary citizens, not merely in the South, not merely in public education, for the Court's series of PER CURIAM decisions after *Brown* revealed that it did not consider racial segregation any more valid in other public facilities than it had in schools. The Warren Court had significantly altered race relations in America.

The context of the Warren Court's first momentous decision was decisive in shaping the Court's character as a branch of government that was not disinclined to resolve difficult social issues, not hesitant to foster social change, not reluctant to involve itself in controversy. By contrast, the legislative and executive branches appeared as equivocators and fainthearts. The Warren Court was deluged with criticism for its decision in *Brown,* both from persons who resisted having to change habits of prejudice and from scholars who faulted the reasoning of the Court's opinion. This response only seemed to make the Court more resolute.

The deliberations of *Brown* also served to identify some of the Justices whose presence was to help shape the character of the Warren Court. Earl Warren transformed a closely divided Court, which had postponed a decision on *Brown* because it was uncertain and fragmented on the case's resolution, into a unanimous voice. That transformation was a testament to Warren's remarkable ability to relate to other people and to convince them of the rightness of his views. In *Brown* he had argued that those who would support the separate but equal doctrine should recognize that it was based on claims of racial superiority. That argument struck home to at least two Justices, TOM C. CLARK and STANLEY F. REED, who had grown up in the South. When Warren had finished his round of office visits and discussions, he had secured nine votes for his majority opinion and had suppressed the writing of separate concurrences. ROBERT H. JACKSON, a long holdout in *Brown* who was dubious about the possibility of finding a doctrinal rationale to invalidate the separate but equal principle, joined Warren's opinion and left a hospital bed to appear in court the day the decision was announced.

A silent partner in the *Brown* decision had been Felix Frankfurter. By the late 1950s Frankfurter's jurisprudence, which stressed a limited role for judges in reviewing the constitutionality of legislative decisions, had rigidified, isolating Frankfurter from many other justices and identifying him as one of the guardians of a theory of judicial self-restraint. Judicial self-restraint in *Brown* would have supported the separate but equal doctrine, since that doctrine itself signified a judicial reluctance to disturb legislative enactments forcibly separating persons on the basis of race. Frankfurter, however, could not abide the consequences of continued deference to the separate but equal doctrine, but he did not want to expose the lack of "restraint" that his position assumed. He accordingly confided his views on *Brown* only to Warren and worked toward fashioning a decree—containing the controversial phrase ALL DELIBERATE SPEED as a guideline for implementing desegregation—that would temper the shock of the *Brown* mandate. At the appropriate moment he joined Warren's opinion.

The partnership of Warren and Frankfurter in the segregation cases contrasted with the usual posture of both Justices on the Warren Court. Warren's approach to judging, with its relative indifference to doctrinal reasoning and to institutional considerations, its emphasis on the morally or ethically appropriate result, and its expansive interpretation of the Court's review powers, was the antithesis of Frankfurter's. For the most part the two men sharply disagreed over the results or the reasoning of major Warren Court decisions, with Frankfurter enlisting a stable of academic supporters in his behalf and Warren seeking to bypass doctrinal or institutional objections to make broad ethical appeals to the public at large.

The presence of two other significant Warren Court Justices, Hugo Black and William O. Douglas, was also felt in *Brown*. Black, a native of Clay County, Alabama, and fleetingly a member of the Ku Klux Klan, had been an opponent of racial discrimination since being elected to the Senate in 1926. He had supported the Vinson Court precedents crippling "separate but equal," for which he had received outspoken criticism in his home state. His position in *Brown* was well known early on: an uncompromising opposition to discriminatory practices. Such positions were characteristic of Black on the Warren Court. He staked out positions decisively, held them with tenacity, and constantly sought to convert others to his views. His theory of constitutional adjudication, which placed great emphasis on a "literal" but "liberal" construction of

BILL OF RIGHTS protections, was a major contribution to Warren Court jurisprudence.

Equally outspoken and tenacious, and even more activist than Black, was William O. Douglas, whose academic experience, which paralleled Frankfurter's, had generated a strikingly different conception of judicial behavior. Douglas did not agonize over issues of institutional deference and doctrinal principle; he took his power to make law as a given and sought to use it to promote values in which he believed. The values were principally those associated with twentieth-century libertarianism and egalitarianism. Douglas spoke out for small business, organized labor, disadvantaged minorities, consumers, the poor, dissidents, and those who valued their privacy and their freedom from governmental restraint. Douglas's role on the Warren Court was that of an ideologue, anxious to secure results and confident that he could find doctrinal justifications. Together, Black and Douglas prodded the Court to vindicate even the most unpopular forms of free expression and minority rights.

While the Warren Court was generally regarded as an activist Court and a liberal Court, it was not exclusively so, and not all its members could be characterized as either activists or liberals. Until his retirement in 1962, at the midway point of Warren's tenure, Frankfurter had vociferously protested against an excessively broad interpretation of the Court's review powers, a position that resulted in his supporting the constitutionality of a number of "conservative" legislative policies. Other Justices on the Warren Court were either disinclined to exercise sweeping review powers or less enthusiastic than Warren, Black, or Douglas about the policies of twentieth-century liberalism. Most influential among those Justices was John Harlan, an Eisenhower appointee who joined the Court in 1955 and remained until 1971.

Harlan frequently and adroitly rejected the assumptions of Warren Court majorities that "every major social ill in this country can find its cure in some constitutional 'principle'" and that the Court could be "a general haven for reform movements." Moreover, in a group of Justices who were often impatient to reach results and not inclined to linger over the niceties of doctrinal analysis, Harlan distinguished himself by producing painstakingly crafted opinions. Often Harlan's quarrels with a majority would be over the method by which results were reached; his concurrences and dissents regularly demonstrated the complexities of constitutional adjudication.

The Warren Court will be best known for its identification with three themes: egalitarianism, liberalism, and activism. From *Brown* through POWELL v. McCORMACK (1969), Earl Warren's last major opinion, the Court demonstrated a dedication to the principle of equality, a principle that, in Archibald Cox's felicitous phrase, "once loosed . . . is not easily cabined." Race relations were the initial context in which the Court attempted to refine the meaning of equal justice in America. Once the ordeal of *Brown* was concluded, that meaning seemed comparatively straightforward. In a series of *per curiam* opinions, the Court extended *Brown* to public beaches, parks, recreational facilities, housing developments, public buildings, eating facilities, and hospitals. The conception of equality embodied by these decisions was that of equality of opportunity: blacks could not be denied the opportunity of access to public places.

Brown had been rationalized by the Court on similar grounds: the gravamen of the injustice in a segregated school system was a denial of equal educational opportunities to blacks. But equality of opportunity became difficult to distinguish, in the race cases, from the conception of equality of condition. The Court presumed that classifications based on race were constitutionally suspect and seemed to suggest that equal justice in the race relations area required something like color-blindness. Classifications based on race or skin color not only denied black Americans equal opportunities, they also were not based on any rational judgment, since the human condition transcended superficial differences of race. After the *per curiams,* the massive resistance to *Brown,* and the civil rights movement of the 1960s, the Court gradually perceived that equality in race relations necessitated the eradication of stigmas based on skin color. This momentum of egalitarianism culminated in *Loving v. Virginia* (1967), in which the Court invalidated state prohibitions of miscegenous marriages, thereby affirming the absence of fundamental differences between blacks and whites.

Between the *per curiams* and *Loving* had come skirmishes between the Court and groups resisting its mandates for change in race relations. COOPER V. AARON (1963) involved a challenge by the governor of Arkansas to compulsory integration in the Little Rock school system. The Court, in an unprecedented opinion signed individually by all nine Justices, reaffirmed the obligations of Southern schools to integrate. *Goss v. Board of Education* (1963) invalidated minority-to-majority transfer plans whose purpose was to allow students to attend schools outside their districts in which their race was in the majority. HEART OF ATLANTA MOTEL V. UNITED STATES (1964) and *Katzenbach v. McClung* (1964) used the Constitution's COMMERCE CLAUSE and the CIVIL RIGHTS ACT OF 1964 to prevent hotels and restaurants from refusing service to blacks. BURTON V. WILMINGTON PARKING AUTHORITY (1961) and *Evans v. Newton* (1966) showed the Court's willingness to use the DOCTRINE of "STATE ACTION" to compel ostensibly private establishments (restaurants and parks) to admit blacks.

After *Loving* the Court grew impatient with resistance to the implementation of its decrees in *Brown.* In GREEN V. NEW KENT COUNTY SCHOOL BOARD (1968) the Court scrutinized the actual effect of "freedom of choice" plans, where students attended schools of their own choice.

The Court found that the system perpetuated segregation when eighty-five percent of the black children in a school district had remained in a previously all-black school and no white child had chosen to attend that school, and advised that "delays are no longer tolerable." Finally, in ALEXANDER V. HOLMES COUNTY BOARD OF EDUCATION (1969) the Court declared that the time for racial integration of previously segregated school systems was "at once." *Green* and *Alexander* compelled integration of schools and other public facilities. Equality of condition had become the dominant means to achieve the goal of equality.

One can see a similar trend in the area of reapportionment. For the first half of the twentieth century, including the early years of the Warren Court, state legislatures were not apportioned solely on the basis of population. Upper houses of legislatures had a variety of means for electing their members, some deliberately unresponsive to demographic concerns, and few states apportioned legislative seats on the basis of ONE PERSON, ONE VOTE. In *Baker v. Carr* (1962), however, the Court announced that it would scrutinize Tennessee's system of electing state legislators to see if it conformed to the population of districts in the state. Justice WILLIAM J. BRENNAN, a former student of Frankfurter's, rejected the POLITICAL QUESTION doctrine Frankfurter had consistently imposed as a barrier to Court determination of reapportionment cases. Frankfurter wrote an impassioned dissent in *Baker,* but the way was clear for constitutional challenges to malapportioned legislatures. By 1964 suits challenging legislative apportionment schemes had been filed in more than thirty states.

Chief Justice Warren's opinion for the Court in REYNOLDS V. SIMS (1964), a case testing Alabama's reapportionment system, demonstrated how the idea of equality had infused the reapportionment cases. "We are cautioned," he wrote, "about the dangers of entering into political thickets and mathematical quagmires. Our answer to this: a denial of constitutionally protected rights demands judicial protection; our oath and our office require no less of us. . . . To the extent that a citizen's right to vote is debased, he is that much less a citizen." Equality did not mean merely an equal opportunity to have representatives from one's district in a state legislature, but that all votes of all citizens were to be treated equally: voting, like race relations, was to be an area in which equality of condition was to prevail.

The Court provided for such equality even where the state's citizens had indicated a preference for another scheme. In LUCAS V. FORTY-FOURTH GENERAL ASSEMBLY (1964), the Court invalidated Colorado's districting plan apportioning only one house of the legislature on a population basis. This plan had been adopted after a statewide referendum in which a majority rejected population-based apportionment for both houses. Warren found that the scheme did not satisfy the equal protection clause because it was not harmonious with the principle of one person, one vote. Voting was a condition of CITIZENSHIP, not just an opportunity to participate in government.

In free speech cases, the Warren Court struggled to move beyond a "marketplace" approach, in which majorities could perhaps suppress speech with distasteful content, to an approach where all speakers were presumed to have an equal right to express their thoughts. The approach was first developed in "communist sympathizer" cases, where a minority of the Court objected to laws making it a crime to be a member of the Communist party or to advocate Communist party doctrine. Eventually, in BRANDENBURG V. OHIO (1969), a unanimous Court distinguished between "mere advocacy" of views and "incitement to imminent lawless action." That case involved statements made by a member of the Ku Klux Klan at a rally that were derogatory of blacks and Jews. The fact that the speaker was known to belong to an organization historically linked to racism and violence was not enough to hinder expression of his views.

Brandenburg united, without entirely clarifying, a number of strands of Warren Court FIRST AMENDMENT doctrine. In the OVERBREADTH cases, such as *NAACP v. Alabama ex rel. Flowers* (1964), APTHEKER V. SECRETARY OF STATE (1964), KEYISHIAN V. BOARD OF REGENTS (1967), and UNITED STATES V. ROBEL (1967), the Court found that legitimate governmental prohibitions on speech that employed "means which sweep unnecessarily broadly" violated the First Amendment, because they might deter the behavior of others who could not legitimately be prohibited from speaking. In the SYMBOLIC SPEECH cases, the Court considered the permissibility of wearing black arm bands (TINKER V. DES MOINES COMMUNITY SCHOOL DISTRICT, 1969) or burning draft cards (UNITED STATES V. O'BRIEN, 1968) or mutilating flags (STREET V. NEW YORK, 1969) as a means of protesting the Vietnam War. Finally, in the "sit-in" and "picketing" cases, such as COX V. LOUISIANA (1964), BROWN V. LOUISIANA (1966), and ADDERLEY V. FLORIDA (1966), the Court sought to distinguish protected "expression" from unprotected but related "conduct." In none of these areas was the Court's doctrinal position clear—draft card burners and picketers were denied constitutional protection, although flag mutilators and "sit-in" demonstrators were granted it—but the decisions revealed the Warren Court's interest in carving out an area of First Amendment protection that was not dependent on public support for the speaker or his actions.

The Warren Court also attempted to extend the First Amendment's reach into other doctrinal areas, notably defamation and OBSCENITY. In NEW YORK TIMES V. SULLIVAN (1964) the Court concluded that common law libel actions could raise First Amendment issues. The Court's opinion, which found that the First Amendment gave rise to a constitutional privilege to make false and defamatory statements about public officials if the statements were not made with recklessness or malice, expressed concern that libel law could be used as a means of punishing "unpopular" speech. Justice Brennan's majority opinion referred to "a profound national commitment to the principle that debate on public issues should be uninhibited, robust, and wide-open," and spoke of the "inhibiting" effects of civil damages on "those who would give voice to public criticism."

Once the First Amendment was seen as relevant to defamation cases, the future of common law principles in the area of libel and slander seemed precarious. *New York Times v. Sullivan* had established a constitutional privilege to publish information about "public officials." *Rosenblatt v. Baer* (1966) widened the meaning of "public official" to include a supervisor of a county-owned ski resort; *Curtis Publishing Co. v. Butts* (1967) and *Associated Press v. Walker* (1967) included "public figures" as well as public officials in the category of those in whose affairs the general public had a special interest; *Time, Inc. v. Hill* (1967) found a privilege to disclose "private" but newsworthy information.

The defamation cases showed the tendency of the equality principle to expand once set in motion: it seemed hard to distinguish different rules for public officials, public figures, and matters of public interest. Such was also true in the area of obscenity. Once the Court recognized, as it did in ROTH V. UNITED STATES (1957), that First Amendment concerns were relevant in obscenity cases, and yet a core of unprotected expression remained, it was forced to define obscenity. Thirteen obscenity cases between 1957 and 1968 produced fifty-five separate opinions from the Justices, but the meaning of "obscene" for constitutional purposes was not made much clearer. Some Justices, such as Black and Douglas, decided that obscene speech was entitled to as much constitutional protection as any other speech, but a shifting majority of the Court continued to deny protection for expressions that, by one standard or another, could be deemed "obscene." Among the criteria announced by Court majorities for labeling a work "obscene" was that it appeal to a "prurient interest," and that it be "patently offensive" and "utterly without redeeming social value." Justice Stewart, in JACOBELLIS V. OHIO (1964), announced a different criterion: "I know [obscenity] when I see it." Eventually, after *Redrup v. New York* (1967), the Court began to reverse summarily all obscenity convictions whenever five Justices, for whatever reason, adjudged a work not to be obscene.

A final area of unprotected expression involved the FIGHTING WORDS doctrine of CHAPLINSKY V. NEW HAMPSHIRE (1942). A series of Warren Court cases, including *Edwards v. South Carolina* (1963), *Gregory v. Chicago* (1969) and even *New York Times v. Sullivan*, with its language about "vehement, caustic, and sometimes unpleasantly sharp attacks on government and public officials," may have reduced *Chaplinsky* to insignificance.

The pattern of First Amendment decisions, taken with its opinions on race relations and reapportionment, not only demonstrated the Warren Court's shifting conceptions of equality but stamped it in the popular mind as a "liberal" Court. Liberalism has been identified, in the years after World War II, with support for affirmative government and protection of civil rights; the Warren Court was notable for its efforts to insure that interventionist government and civil libertarianism could coexist. But in so doing the Warren Court redefined the locus of interventionist government in America. *Brown v. Board of Education* was a classic example. Congress and the state legislatures were not taking sufficient action to preserve the rights of blacks, so the Court intervened to scrutinize their conduct and, where necessary, to compel them to act. This role for the Court was a major change from that performed by its predecessors. "Liberal" judging in the early twentieth century, according to such defenders of interventionist government as Felix Frankfurter and Louis D. Brandeis, meant judicial self-restraint: the Supreme Court was to *avoid* scrutiny of state and federal legislation whose purpose was to aid disadvantaged persons. The Warren Court eschewed that role to become the principal interventionist branch of government in the 1950s and 1960s.

In addition to its decisions in race relations and reapportionment, two other areas of Warren Court activity helped augment its public reputation as a "liberal" Court. The first area was CRIMINAL PROCEDURE: here the Court virtually rewrote the laws of the states to conform them to its understanding of the Constitution's requirements. The most important series of its criminal procedure decisions, from a doctrinal perspective, were the INCORPORATION DOCTRINE cases, where the Court struggled with the question of whether, and to what extent, the due process clause of the FOURTEENTH AMENDMENT incorporates procedural protections in the Bill of Rights, making those protections applicable against the states. The Warren Court began a process of "selective incorporation" of Bill of Rights safeguards, applying particular protections in given cases but refusing to endorse the incorporation doctrine in its entirety. This process produced some landmark decisions, notably MAPP v. OHIO (1961), which applied FOURTH AMENDMENT protections against illegal SEARCHES AND SEIZURES to state trials, and BENTON v. MARYLAND (1969), which held that the Fifth Amendment's DOUBLE JEOPARDY guarantee applied to the states. Other important "incorporation" cases were GRIFFIN v. CALIFORNIA (1965), maintaining a RIGHT AGAINST SELF-INCRIMINATION; MALLOY v. HOGAN (1964), applying the Fifth Amendment's self-incrimination privilege to state proceedings; and DUNCAN v. LOUISIANA (1968), incorporating the Sixth Amendment's right to TRIAL BY JURY in criminal cases.

A major consequence of selective incorporation was that fewer criminal convictions were obtained in state trials. Particularly damaging to state prosecutors were the decisions in *Mapp* and *Mallory*, which eliminated from state court trials illegally secured evidence and coerced statements of incrimination. The Court also tightened the requirements for police conduct during the incarceration of criminal suspects. *Malloy v. United States* (1957) insisted that criminal defendants be brought before a magistrate prior to being interrogated. MIRANDA V. ARIZONA (1966) announced a series of constitutional "warnings" that the police were required to give persons whom they had taken into custody. *Miranda* had been preceded by another significant case, ESCOBEDO V. ILLINOIS (1964), which had required that a lawyer be present during police investigations if a suspect requested one. Further, the landmark case of GIDEON V. WAINWRIGHT (1963) had insured that all persons suspected of crimes could secure the services of a lawyer if they desired such, whether they could afford them or not.

The result of this activity by the Warren Court in the area of criminal procedure was that nearly every stage of a POLICE INTERROGATION was fraught with constitutional complexities. The decisions, taken as a whole, seemed to be an effort to buttress the position of persons suspected of crimes by checking the power of the police: some opinions, such as *Miranda,* were explicit in stating that goal. By intervening in law enforcement proceedings to protect the rights of allegedly disadvantaged persons—a high percentage of criminals in the 1960s were poor and black— the Warren Court Justices were acting as liberal policymakers.

Church and state cases were another area in which the Court demonstrated its liberal sensibility, to the concern of many observers. Affirmative state action to promote religious values in the public schools—heretofore an aspect of America's educational heritage—was likely to be struck down as a violation of the establishment clause. In ENGEL V. VITALE (1962) the Court struck down nondenominational prayer readings in New York public schools. A year after *Engel* the Court also invalidated a Pennsylvania law that required reading from the Bible in ABINGTON TOWNSHIP SCHOOL DISTRICT V. SCHEMPP (1963) and a Maryland law that required recitation of the Lord's Prayer in *Murray v. Curlett* (1963). (See RELIGION IN PUBLIC SCHOOLS.) In *McGowan v. Maryland* (1961), however, the Court permitted the state to impose SUNDAY CLOSING LAWS. Chief Justice Warren, for the Court, distinguished between laws with a religious purpose and laws "whose present purpose and effect" was secular, even though they were originally "motivated by religious forces." The Court invoked *McGowan* in a subsequent case, BOARD OF EDUCATION V. ALLEN (1968), which sustained a New York law providing for the loaning of textbooks from public to parochial schools.

Liberalism, as practiced by the Warren Court, produced a different institutional posture from earlier "reformist" judicial perspectives. As noted, liberalism required that the Court be both an activist governmental institution and a defender of minority rights. This meant that unlike previously "activist" Courts, such as the Courts of the late nineteenth and early twentieth century, its beneficiaries would be nonelites, and unlike previously "reformist" Courts, such as the Court of the late 1930s and 1940s, it would assume a scrutinizing rather than a passive stance toward the actions of other branches of government. Had the Warren Court retained either of these former roles, *Brown, Baker v. Carr,* and *Miranda* would likely not have been decided as they were. These decisions all offended entrenched elites and required modifications of existing governmental practices. In so deciding these cases the Warren Court was assuming that activism by the judiciary was required in order to produce liberal results. With this assumption came a mid-twentieth-century fusion of affirmative governmental action and protection for CIVIL LIBERTIES.

Maintaining a commitment to liberal theory while at the same time modifying its precepts required some analytical refinements in order to reconcile the protection of civil liberties with claims based on affirmative governmental action. In *Brown* the desires of some whites and some blacks to have a racially integrated educational experience conflicted with the desires of some whites and some blacks to limit their educational experiences to persons of their own race. The Court chose to prefer the former desire, basing its judgment on a theory of the educational process that minimized the relevance of race. That theory then became a guiding assumption for the Court's subsequent decisions in the race relations area.

Similar sets of intermediate distinctions between goals of liberal theory were made in other major cases. In the REAPPORTIONMENT cases the distinction was between REPRESENTATION based on population, a claim put forth by a disadvantaged minority, and other forms of proportional representation that had been endorsed by legislative majorities. The Court decided to prefer the former claim as more democratic and then made the one-person, one-vote principle the basis of its subsequent decisions. In the school prayer cases the distinction was between the choice of a majority to ritualize the recognition of a public deity in the public school and the choice of a minority to deny that recognition as out of place. The Court decided to prefer the latter choice as more libertarian. In the criminal procedure cases the distinction was between a majoritarian decision to protect the public against crime by advantaging law enforcement personnel in their encounters with persons suspected of committing crimes, and the claims of such persons that they were being unfairly disadvantaged. The Court chose to prefer the latter claims as being more consistent with principles of equal justice.

When the Warren Court reached the end of its tenure, liberalism clearly did not merely mean deference toward the decisions of democratic and representative bodies of government. It meant deference toward these decisions only if they promoted the goals of liberal policy: equality, fairness, protection of civil rights, support for disadvantaged persons. Under this model of liberal policymaking, the Supreme Court was more concerned with achieving enlightened results than it was with the constitutional process by which these results were reached. Liberalism and judicial activism went hand in hand.

As it became clear that the Court's activism was designed to promote a modified version of liberalism, the Court became vulnerable to public dissatisfaction with liberal policies. Such dissatisfaction emerged in the 1970s. The internal contradictions of liberalism became exposed in such areas as AFFIRMATIVE ACTION in higher education and forced busing in primary education, and the saving distinctions made by the Court in earlier cases appeared as naked policy choices whose legitimacy was debatable. If affirmative preference, based on race, for one class of applicants to an institution of higher learning results in disadvantage to other classes, equality of condition has not been achieved and equality of educational opportunity has been undermined. If some families are compelled to send their children to schools where they are racial minorities in order to achieve "racial balance" throughout the school system, the resulting "balance" may well disadvantage more people than it advantages. Equality and social justice have turned out to be more complicated concepts than mid-twentieth-century liberalism assumed.

The egalitarianism and the liberalism of the Warren Court paled in significance when compared to its activism. If contemporary America has become a "litigious society," as it is commonly portrayed, the Warren Court helped set in motion such trends. Social issues have habitually been transformed into legal questions in America, but the Warren Court seemed to welcome such a transformation, finding constitutional issues raised in contexts as diverse as reapportionment and prayers in the public schools. As the Court created new sources of constitutional protection, numerous persons sought to make themselves the beneficiaries. Sometimes the Court went out of its way to help the organizations litigating a case, as in the civil rights area. The result was that the lower courts and the Supreme Court became "activist" institutions—repositories of grievances, scrutinizers of the conduct of other branches of government, havens for the disadvantaged.

In the academic community, Warren Court activism was from the first regarded as more controversial than Warren Court egalitarianism. The reason was the prominence in academic circles of a two-pronged theory of JUDICIAL REVIEW, one prong of which stressed the necessity of grounding judicial decisions, in the area of constitutional law, in textually supportable principles of general applicability, and the other prong of which resurrected Frankfurter's conception of a limited, deferential role for the Court as a lawmaking institution. The Warren Court, according to academic critics, repeatedly violated the theory's dual standards. Decisions like *Brown v. Board, Baker v. Carr,* GRISWOLD V. CONNECTICUT (1965), a case discovering a RIGHT OF PRIVACY in the Constitution that was violated by statutes forbidding the use of BIRTH CONTROL pills, and HARPER V. VIRGINIA BOARD OF ELECTIONS (1966), a case invalidating POLL TAX requirements on voting as violating the EQUAL PROTECTION clause because such requirements conditioned VOTING RIGHTS on wealth, had not been sufficiently grounded in constitutional doctrine. There was no evidence that the Fourteenth Amendment was intended to reach segregated schools and there were no judicial decisions supporting that position. The Constitution did not single out for protection a right to vote, let alone a right to have one's vote weighed equally with the votes of others. "Privacy" was nowhere mentioned in the constitutional text. The framers of the Constitution had assumed a variety of suffrage restrictions, including ones based on wealth. In short, leading Warren Court decisions were not based on "neutral principles" of constitutional law.

Nor had the Court been mindful, critics felt, of its proper lawmaking posture in a democratic society where it was a conspicuously nondemocratic institution. In *Brown* it had ostensibly substituted its wisdom for that of Congress and several Southern states. In *Baker* it had forced legislatures to reapportion themselves even when a majority of a state's voters had signified their intention to staff one house of the legislature on grounds other than one person, one vote. In *Engel v. Vitale* it had told the public schools that they could not have government-formulated compulsory prayers, even though the vast majority of school officials and parents desired them. It had fashioned codes of criminal procedure for the police, ignoring Congress's abortive efforts in that direction. It had decided, after more than 200 years of defamation law, that the entire area needed to be reconsidered in light of the First Amendment.

A role for the Court as a deferential, principled decision maker was, however, not sacrosanct. Few Supreme Courts had assumed such a role in the past. All of the "great cases" in American constitutional history could be said to have produced activist decisions: MARBURY V. MADISON (1803), establishing the power of judicial review; McCULLOCH V. MARYLAND (1819) and GIBBONS V. OGDEN (1824), delineating the scope of the federal commerce power; DRED SCOTT V. SANDFORD (1857), legitimizing SLAVERY IN THE TERRITORIES; the LEGAL TENDER CASES, deciding the constitutionality of legal tender notes; POLLOCK V. FARMERS LOAN AND TRUST (1895), declaring an income tax unconstitutional; LOCHNER V. NEW YORK (1905), scuttling state hours and wages legislation; UNITED STATES V. BUTLER (1936), invalidating a major portion of the New Deal's administrative structure. Activism was an ancient judicial art.

The Warren Court's activism differed from other Courts' versions principally not because its reasoning was more specious or its grasp of power more presumptuous but because its beneficiaries were different. Previous activist decisions had largely benefited entrenched elites, whether slaveowners, entrepreneurs, "combinations of capital," or businesses that sought to avoid government regulation. The activist decisions of the Warren Court benefited blacks, disadvantaged suburban voters, atheists, criminals, pornographers, and the poor. The Warren Court's activism facilitated social change rather than preserving the status quo. The critics of the Court had forgotten that the role they espoused for the judiciary had been created in order to facilitate change and promote the interests of the disadvantaged. In the 1950s and 1960s the "democratic" institutions charged with that responsibility had become unresponsive, so the Warren Court had acted in their stead. It was ironic that the same critics who were shocked at the Court of the 1930s' resistance to the New Deal should protest against a Court that was reaching the results they had then sought.

Activism was the principal basis of the Court's controversiality; egalitarianism its dominant instinctual reaction; liberalism its guiding political philosophy. The combination of these ingredients, plus the presence of some judicial giants, gave the Warren Court a prominence and a visibility that are not likely to be surpassed for some time. But even though countless persons in the American legal profession today were shaped by Warren Court decisions, one can see the Warren Court receding into history. That Court seemed to have been led, in the final analysis, by a conception of American life that appeared vindicated by the first fifty years of twentieth-century experience. That conception held that American society was continually progressing toward a nobler and brighter and more enlightened future. As Earl Warren wrote in a passage that appears on his tombstone:

> Where there is injustice, we should correct it;
> where there is poverty, we should eliminate it;
> where there is corruption, we should stamp it out;
> where there is violence, we should punish it;
> where there is neglect, we should provide care;
> where there is war, we should restore peace;
> and wherever corrections are achieved we should add them
> permanently to our storehouse of treasures.

In that passage appears the Warren Court sensibility: a sensibility dedicated to the active pursuit of ideals that have seemed less tangible and achievable with the years.

Bibliography

BICKEL, ALEXANDER 1970 *The Supreme Court and the Idea of Progress.* New York: Harper & Row.

BLACK, CHARLES 1970 The Unfinished Business of the Warren Court. *University of Washington Law Review* 46:3–45.

COX, ARCHIBALD 1968 *The Warren Court.* Cambridge, Mass.: Harvard University Press.

KURLAND, PHILIP 1970 *Politics, the Constitution, and the Warren Court.* Chicago: University of Chicago Press.

LEVY, LEONARD W., ed. 1972 *The Supreme Court under Earl Warren.* New York: Quadrangle Books.

MCCLOSKEY, ROBERT 1960 *The American Supreme Court.* Chicago: University of Chicago Press.

WECHSLER, HERBERT 1959 Toward Neutral Principles of Constitutional Law. *Harvard Law Review* 73:1–23.

WHITE, G. EDWARD 1976 *The American Judicial Tradition.* New York: Oxford University Press.

——— 1982 *Earl Warren: A Public Life.* New York: Oxford University Press.

CONSTITUTIONAL HISTORY, 1961–1977

Richard C. Cortner

An examination of nonjudicial constitutional development from the administration of President JOHN F. KENNEDY to that of President GERALD R. FORD reveals at the outset an unusual amount of constitutional change through the process of constitutional amendment. Indeed, counting the adoption of the BILL OF RIGHTS in 1791 as only one episode of constitutional change via the AMENDMENT PROCESS, the period from 1961 to 1977 was characterized by an exceptionally high level of constitutional amending activity, with four amendments adopted during the period. In contrast, again counting the adoption of the Bill of Rights as one amendment episode, there were thirteen constitutional amendments adopted between 1789 and 1961.

Three of the constitutional amendments adopted during the 1961–1977 period were clear reflections of the expansion of egalitarianism that found expression in other fields in the policies of DESEGREGATION, REAPPORTIONMENT, and the enlargement of the protection of CIVIL RIGHTS. The TWENTY-THIRD AMENDMENT, adopted on March 19, 1961, extended the right to vote in presidential elections to the residents of the DISTRICT OF COLUMBIA although restricting the District to the number of electoral votes allotted to the least populous state. The TWENTY-FOURTH AMENDMENT, ratified on January 23, 1964, outlawed the imposition of POLL TAXES in presidential and congressional elections and therefore removed a form of WEALTH DISCRIMINATION in federal elections. The addition of this amendment to the Constitution was subsequently rendered superfluous by the Supreme Court's holding in HARPER V. VIRGINIA BOARD OF ELECTIONS (1966) that poll taxes were a form of INVIDIOUS DISCRIMINATION prohibited by the Constitution. Further extension of VOTING RIGHTS occurred with the adoption of the TWENTY-SIXTH AMENDMENT on June 30, 1971, which extended the right to vote in both federal and state elections to eighteen-year-old citizens. The Twenty-Sixth Amendment was necessitated by the Supreme Court's holding in OREGON V. MITCHELL (1974) that Congress lacked the constitutional power to legislate the eighteen-year-old vote in state and local elections.

In contrast with the Twenty-Third, Twenty-Fourth, and Twenty-Sixth Amendments, the Twenty-Fifth Amendment, relating to PRESIDEN-

TIAL SUCCESSION and disability and adopted in 1967, was the result of years of debate with regard to the problems that might arise if an incumbent president were temporarily or permanently disabled. Serious consideration of such an amendment to the Constitution was prompted by the illnesses afflicting President DWIGHT D. EISENHOWER during his term of office, and additional impetus for constitutional change in this area was created by the assassination of President Kennedy in 1963.

Under the provisions of the Twenty-Fifth Amendment, the President may declare his own disability to perform the duties of the office by informing the president pro tempore of the Senate and the speaker of the House of Representatives in writing of his own disability. Alternatively, the President's disability may be declared in writing to the same congressional officers by the vice-president and a majority of the Cabinet. In either instance, the vice-president assumes the duties of the presidency as acting President. A period of presidential disability may be ended either by the President's informing the congressional officers in writing of the termination of his disability, or if there is disagreement between the President and the vice-president and a majority of the Cabinet on the issue of the President's disability, the Congress may resolve the dispute. A two-thirds majority of both houses of Congress, however, is required to declare the President disabled; otherwise, the President resumes the duties of his office.

Although the disability provisions of the Twenty-Fifth Amendment have not been applied, Section 2 of the amendment had an important impact on the succession to the presidency during the administration of President RICHARD M. NIXON. Section 2 provides that whenever a vacancy in the office of vice-president occurs, the President shall appoint a new vice-president with the approval of a majority of both houses of Congress. These provisions of the Twenty-Fifth Amendment came into play when Vice-President Spiro T. Agnew resigned his office in 1973 under the threat of prosecution for income tax evasion. Pursuant to Section 2, President Nixon appointed Congressman Gerald R. Ford of Michigan as Agnew's successor, and the Congress confirmed Ford as vice-president. Subsequently, President Nixon resigned his office on August 9, 1974, when his IMPEACHMENT for his involvement in the WATERGATE affair and other abuses of office seemed imminent, and Vice-President Ford succeeded Nixon in the office of President. Under the provisions of the Twenty-Fifth Amendment, Ford thus became the first appointed vice-president as well as the first unelected vice-president to assume the office of the presidency.

The Watergate affair that led to President Nixon's resignation involved not only charges of bugging the Democratic National Committee headquarters, and the obstruction by the executive of the subsequent investigation of that incident, but also more generalized abuses of power by the executive. In addition to the issue of the scope of EXECUTIVE PRIVILEGE, which was ultimately resolved by the Supreme Court adversely to the President's claims in UNITED STATES v. NIXON (1974), the Watergate affair raised major constitutional issues concerning the nature of the impeachment process, as the impeachment of a President was seriously considered by the Congress for the first time since the impeachment of President ANDREW JOHNSON in 1868. Because the Constitution provides that governmental officers including the President may be removed from office on impeachment for TREASON, bribery, or other high crimes and MISDEMEANORS, the consideration of the impeachment of President Nixon by the Congress involved the determination of what constituted an impeachable offense, an issue that had also been at the heart of the debate over the Johnson impeachment.

In the deliberations of the Judiciary Committee of the House of Representatives regarding ARTICLES OF IMPEACHMENT against President Nixon, the President's supporters argued that the President could be impeached only within the meaning of the Constitution for an indictable criminal offense. The President's opponents, on the other hand, contended that articles of impeachment could embrace political offenses, such as the abuse of power by the President, which were not indictable under the criminal law. The latter position ultimately prevailed among a majority of the Judiciary Committee when the committee adopted three articles of impeachment against President Nixon that contained charges that were essentially political, abuse of power offenses which were not indictable.

Article one of the articles of impeachment charged the President with obstruction of justice and with violating his oath of office requiring him to see to it that the laws were faithfully executed, but the second and third articles charged him with violating the constitutional rights of citizens, impairing the administration of justice, misusing executive agencies, and ignoring the SUBPOENAS of the Judiciary Committee through which it had sought EVIDENCE related to its impeachment inquiry. Although these charges included some indictable offenses, in adopting the articles the majority of the committee obviously construed the words "high crimes and misdemeanors" to include offenses that did not involve indictable crimes. In reaching this conclusion, the committee majority took a position that conformed with the view of the nature of the impeachment process that the House of Representatives had adopted in the Johnson impeachment proceedings in 1868.

Whether this broad view of the nature of impeachable offenses would have been sustained by a majority of the House of Representatives or the required two-thirds majority in the Senate remained an unanswered question because of President Nixon's resignation in August 1974. The Supreme Court rejected the President's claim of executive privilege and ordered the disclosure of the White House tape recordings relevant to the trial of those indicted in the Watergate affair. On the tapes thus released there appeared conversations clearly indicating President Nixon's participation in a conspiracy to obstruct justice, an indictable offense. In light of almost certain impeachment by the House of Representatives and likely conviction in the Senate, President Nixon resigned. With the impeachment process thus aborted, the answer to what properly could be considered an impeachable offense was left unresolved, as it had been in the proceedings against President Johnson over a hundred years earlier.

The Watergate affair and the abuses of presidential power associated with it, along with the involvement of the United States in the Vietnam War, had a profound impact upon the principal nonjudicial constitutional issue during the 1961–1977 period—the issue of the proper relation between the powers of the executive branch of the government and the powers of the Congress. Beginning at least as early as the administrations of FRANKLIN D. ROOSEVELT in the 1930s and 1940s, the presidency had increasingly become the dominant political institution at the national level, and Roosevelt's successors refined and added to the assertions of PRESIDENTIAL POWER that had characterized his administrations. By the late 1960s and early 1970s, therefore, the "Imperial Presidency" had become the focus of considerable attention and constitutional controversy, and a reassertion of congressional power against the aggrandizement of presidential power had clearly begun.

This reassertion of congressional power was to a great extent a reaction to the expansion of the powers of the presidency to new extremes during the administration of President Nixon. Although previous presidents had asserted the power to impound and to refuse to expend funds appropriated by Congress in limited areas, President Nixon asserted a much broadened IMPOUNDMENT power as a presidential prerogative. Instead of the relatively isolated instances of presidential refusals to spend congressionally appropriated monies that had occurred previously, during the 1970s the Nixon administration impounded billions of dollars in congressional appropriations and effectively asserted a presidential power to enforce only those congressionally authorized programs that received the president's approval.

The involvement of the United States in the war in Vietnam and Southeast Asia contributed to further controversy regarding the scope of presidential power to commit the armed forces to foreign military conflicts in the absence of a DECLARATION OF WAR by the Congress. The involvement of the United States in Vietnam had begun under President Kennedy with the dispatch of military advisers to the South Vietnamese armed forces, but under Presidents LYNDON B. JOHNSON and Nixon the American military presence in Southeast Asia grew to hundreds of thousands of troops. The failure of the American military efforts in Southeast Asia and the high cost of those efforts in lives and resources bolstered the arguments of critics that the power of the President to commit the United States to foreign military conflicts must be reined in.

Because of the impoundment policy of the Nixon administration and the presidential war in Southeast Asia, a reassertion of congressional power occurred in the field of domestic as well as FOREIGN AFFAIRS. The congressional response to the impoundment controversy was the enactment of the CONGRESSIONAL BUDGET AND IMPOUNDMENT CONTROL ACT OF 1974. This legislation provided that if the President resolved to eliminate the expenditure of funds appropriated by Congress, he was required to inform both houses of Congress of: the amounts involved; the agencies and programs affected; and the fiscal, budgetary, and economic effects of, and the reasons for, the proposed impoundment of funds. Both houses of Congress, the act provided, must approve the impoundment within forty-five days. If the President proposed instead to defer the spending of congressionally authorized appropriations, the act provided that he must similarly inform Congress of his intention to defer expenditures, and within forty-five days either house of Congress could require the expenditure of the funds by passing a resolution disapproving the President's proposed action. If the President refused to abide by congressional disapproval of impoundments, the act further authorized the Comptroller General to initiate legal action in the federal courts to force compliance with the will of the Congress.

In addition to addressing the problem of presidential impoundments, the Congressional Budget and Impoundment Control Act was directed at strengthening the powers of Congress over the budgetary process. To replace the practice of enacting appropriations without regard to the total amount that should be appropriated in a given fiscal year, the act provided that the Congress should agree upon a BUDGET resolution at the outset of the appropriations process, setting the total amount of money to be appropriated during the fiscal year. The amount so specified would then govern the actions of Congress in considering individual appropriations bills.

Finally, the act created a new agency, the Congressional Budget Office, and authorized that agency to advise Congress regarding revenue estimates, the likely amount of deficits or revenue surpluses and other economic data important to the budgetary process. Congress thus created a congressional agency, beyond the control of the executive, which would be an independent source of economic and budgetary information in competition with the executive branch's Treasury Department and Office of Management and Budget.

This reassertion of congressional power over domestic policy was matched in the field of foreign policy by the WAR POWERS RESOLUTION of November 7, 1973, passed over the veto of President Nixon. In the War Powers Resolution, Congress sought to deal with the problem of presidential wars such as the military involvement of the United States in Southeast Asia. Congress therefore not only imposed restrictions upon the power of the President to commit the country's armed forces in foreign conflicts but also sought to define the war-making powers of both the President and the Congress.

With regard to the war-making power of the President, the War Powers Resolution declared that the President could introduce United States armed forces into hostilities, or into a situation in which imminent involvement in hostilities was clearly indicated by the circumstances, only pursuant to a declaration of war, or under specific statutory authorization, or in response to a national emergency created by an attack upon the United States, its territories or possessions, or its armed forces. The language of the resolution thus clearly repudiated the argument, frequently asserted in the past, that the President was constitutionally authorized to take whatever action deemed necessary to protect the national interest. The impact of the resolution as an authoritative congressional interpretation of the President's constitutional war-making power was diluted, however, by the decision of Congress to include the interpretation of the President's war-making power in the "Purpose and Policy" section of the act, with the result that it did not purport to have legally binding effect.

The parts of the War Powers Resolution that did purport to be legally binding required the President to consult with Congress in every possible instance before committing the armed forces in hostilities or hostile situations. If the armed forces are introduced by the President into hostilities or hostile situations in the absence of a declared war, the resolution provided, the President must report the situation in writing to the presiding officers of the Congress within forty-eight hours and continue to report every six months thereafter. The resolution further required that in the absence of a declared war, the introduction of the armed forces must be terminated within sixty days, or ninety days if the military situation makes their safe withdrawal impossible within sixty days. Finally, in the absence of a declared war or congressional authorization, the President must withdraw the armed forces from hostilities occurring outside the territory of the United States if Congress directs him to do so by CONCURRENT RESOLUTION, which is not subject to the President's veto power.

Although the War Powers Resolution was plainly an attempt by Congress to reassert its authority over presidential war-making and over the conduct of foreign affairs generally, its impact upon presidential power did not appear to have been so great as its supporters hoped or it critics feared at the time of its passage. During the administration of President Ford, American armed forces were introduced into hostile situations during the evacuation of Vietnam as well as during the recapture of the American merchantman *Mayaguez* and its crew from Cambodia. President Ford nevertheless did not feel bound in these actions by the terms of the War Powers Resolution but rather made plain his conviction that he was acting under his constitutional powers as COMMANDER-IN-CHIEF and as chief executive. The War Powers Resolution was thus subjected to early challenge as an authoritative construction of the President's war-making power. Given the ability of Presidents to marshal public support for their actions in foreign affairs, particularly in times of crisis, it was clear that the act could not be considered the last word regarding the relative power of Congress and the President in the field of foreign policy and war-making.

Just as the War Powers Resolution and the Congressional Budget and Impoundment Control Act symbolized the reassertion of congressional power in relation to the executive, both also embodied the device which Congress increasingly used in reasserting power over executive policymaking—the LEGISLATIVE VETO. The legislative veto first emerged as a congressional device for controlling the executive during the 1930s when Congress reserved the right to veto presidential proposals to reorganize the executive branch, but by the 1970s the legislative veto in various forms had proliferated and had been embodied in almost two hundred statutes enacted by Congress. The increased use of the legislative veto reflected Congress's dissatisfaction with its relationship with the executive and a desire to reassert policymaking power that had been eroded during the previous decades of heightened executive power.

Congress employed the legislative veto to disapprove proposed presidential actions, to disapprove rules and regulations proposed by the executive branch or administrative agencies, and to order the termination of presidential actions. The device took several forms, with some statutes requiring a resolution of approval or disapproval by only one house of Congress, others requiring both houses to act through a concurrent resolution, and still others conferring upon congressional committees the power to exercise the legislative veto.

Despite its increased use by Congress, the legislative veto was frequently opposed by the executive branch since its introduction in the 1930s on the grounds that the practice violates the Constitution. The executive and other critics of the legislative veto argued that the practice violated the principle of SEPARATION OF POWERS, ignored the principle of bicameralism in the exercise of legislative power, and allowed Congress to avoid the President's veto power which is normally applicable to legislation passed by Congress.

The constitutional principle of separation of powers, critics of the legislative veto noted, permits Congress to shape national policy by passing statutes, but, properly construed, does not permit Congress to interfere in the enforcement or administration of policy—a power properly belonging to the executive branch. The legislative veto, it was argued, thus violated a fundamental constitutional principle, especially insofar as it was used to allow Congress to veto rules and regulations proposed by executive or administrative agencies under DELEGATIONS OF POWER from the Congress.

Opponents also argued that the Constitution contemplates that Congress's policy-making role ordinarily requires the passage of statutes by both houses of Congress with the presentation of the statutes to the President for his approval or disapproval. By allowing the approval or disapproval of national policy through single house resolutions, JOINT RESOLUTIONS, or decisions of congressional committees, it was argued, the legislative veto ignored the bicameral legislative process contemplated by the Constitution and in addition permitted congressional policymaking through mechanisms not subject to the President's veto power, as the Constitution also contemplated.

Congress, on the other hand, clearly viewed the legislative veto as a useful weapon in exercising oversight over the executive and the bureaucracy, both of which were recipients of massive delegations of legislative power since the 1930s. Striking at another source of the imperial presidency, Congress thus embodied the legislative veto in the National Emergencies Act of 1976, which terminated national emergencies declared by the President in 1933, 1950, 1970, and 1971, and required the President to inform the Congress of the existence of national emergencies and the powers the executive intends to use in managing the emergency. Such emergencies, the act provided, could be terminated at any time by Congress via a concurrent resolution. (See EMERGENCY POWERS.)

Despite the long-standing controversy regarding the constitutional legitimacy of the legislative veto, the Supreme Court did not pass upon the validity of the device until 1983. In IMMIGRATION AND NATURALIZATION SERVICE v. CHADHA (1983), however, the Court declared the legislative veto invalid on the ground that it violated the constitutional principles requiring legislative enactments to be passed by both houses of Congress and to be subject to the veto powers of the President.

Just as the period from the administration of President Kennedy to that of President Ford witnessed significant readjustments of presidential–congressional relations, dramatic changes also occurred during the period in the nature of the political party system and the electoral process. Perhaps the most significant development was the decline in the power and influence of the major political parties. The decline in the percentage of the public who identified with the Republican and Democratic parties that began in the 1950s continued during the 1960s and 1970s. In 1952 twenty-two percent of the voters indicated a strong identification with the Democratic party, while thirteen percent indicated such an identification with the Republican party. By 1976, these percentages had declined to fifteen and nine percent, respectively, while the number of voters identifying themselves as independents had risen significantly.

This decline in voter identification with the two major political parties was accompanied by a decline in the importance of the national conventions of the two parties in the selection of presidential candidates. In 1960, only sixteen states selected their delegations to the national party conventions through presidential primaries, but by 1976 thirty states used the primary system for the selection of national party convention delegates, with the result that almost three-quarters of the Democratic national convention delegates and well over sixty percent of the Republican delegates were selected through the presidential primary process. Nominations of presidential candidates were consequently no longer the products of negotiations among party leaders at the national conventions; rather the national conventions merely ratified the selection of a presidential candidate as determined in the presidential primaries. And this decline in the significance of the national conventions was furthered, in the Democratic party, by the adoption of rules during the 1970s diminishing the power of party leaders and requiring proportional representation of women, minority groups, and other constituent groups within the party.

The decline of power of the political parties was furthered by the adoption of federal CAMPAIGN FINANCING laws in 1971, 1974, and 1976 which limited the amounts that could be contributed to election campaigns by individuals and groups and provided for federal financing of presidential elections. The result was a further diminution of the importance of traditional party organizations to presidential candidates, who increasingly relied upon personal campaign organizations both to win nomination and to conduct their national election campaigns. In a governmental system based upon the separation of powers, the decline of the party system, which traditionally had served to bridge the gap between the executive and legislative branches, could only have profound effects upon the capacity of Presidents to lead as well as upon the formation of national policy.

The period between 1961 and 1977 witnessed an acceleration of a long-term trend toward the centralization of power in the national government, although by the end of the period a significant reaction to this trend had become apparent. Two primary factors contributed to this centralizing trend: increased subsidization by the national government of programs at the state and local levels, and the assumption of responsibility by the national government over vast areas that had traditionally been left to state and local governments.

When John F. Kennedy was elected in 1960, for example, FEDERAL GRANTS-IN-AID to state and local governments stood at just over seven billion dollars and accounted for approximately fifteen percent of the total expenditures of state and local governments. By 1976, these federal grants-in-aid had mushroomed to almost sixty billion dollars and constituted almost twenty-five percent of total state and local expenditures.

Not only did state and local governments become increasingly dependent financially upon federal largess during this period but the character of federal grant-in-aid programs was also significantly altered. Before the 1960s, federal aid was primarily directed at subsidizing programs identified by state and local governments, but during the 1960s the identification of program needs increasingly shifted to the national government, with federal funds allocated according to national priorities. In addition, many federal grants, especially during President Johnson's War on Poverty program, were distributed at the local community level, by-passing state governors and officials who had traditionally had a voice in the administration of federal grants. As a result of the ensuing outcry from state and local officials, during the late 1960s and 1970s the federal government resorted to the device of block grants to state and local governments, grants involving fewer nationally imposed restrictions on their use and thus allowing the exercise of greater discretionary power by state and local officials. In 1972, Congress also adopted the State and Local Fiscal Assistance Act, which embraced the principle of federal revenue sharing with state and local governments. Despite the greater flexibility allowed state and local decision makers under REVENUE SHARING and block grants, the financial dependence of state and local governments on the national government in 1976 was eight times what it had been in 1960.

During the same period, the federal government's power was significantly expanded through congressional passage of a host of new statutes that expanded the regulatory role of the federal government in numerous new fields. Civil rights, the environment, occupational safety, consumer protection, and many other fields for the first time were subjected to extensive federal regulation. Since almost all of the new regulatory statutes involved extensive delegation of legislative power by Congress to the bureaucracy, the new expansion of federal regulatory authority involved a massive increase in administrative rules and regulations, as the bureaucracy exercised the legislative powers that had been delegated to it.

This increased intrusion of the federal government into the lives and affairs of the public ultimately produced a backlash of hostility toward the federal bureaucracy. John F. Kennedy had campaigned for the presidency in 1960 with the promise to get the country moving again, a promise suggesting an activist role for the national government. Because of the backlash against the expansion of the regulatory role of the federal government, however, presidential candidates in 1976 found that attacks on the federal bureaucracy and the national government as a whole hit a responsive chord with the public and proved to be popular campaign rhetoric.

This unpopularity of the bureaucracy, however, was only one symptom of the American public's shaken confidence in its major political institutions that had become manifest by the mid-1970s. Between 1961 and 1976, one President had been assassinated, one had resigned in disgrace, the long and costly war in Vietnam had concluded in disaster, and the Watergate affair had revealed the betrayal of the public trust at the highest levels of the government as well as abuses of power with sinister implications for the liberties of the American people. Such traumatic events not only undermined public confidence in political institutions but also profoundly affected the course of constitutional development. The office of the presidency, which since the 1930s had evolved into the dominant political institution at the national level, was consequently diminished considerably by 1976 in both power and prestige. Although a resurgence of congressional power had occurred in the 1970s, there was little evidence that Congress was institutionally capable of assuming the role of national leadership previously performed by the presidency, and effective national leadership had been made even more difficult by the decline of the political party system.

The most basic problem confronting the American polity by 1976 was nevertheless the problem of the loss of public confidence in governmental institutions. And the restoration of that confidence was the most profoundly difficult and fundamentally important task American public leadership faced as this period of constitutional development came to a close.

Bibliography

ALEXANDER, HERBERT   1976   *Financing Politics: Money, Elections and Political Reform.* Washington, D.C.: Congressional Quarterly.

DRY, MURRAY   1981   The Congressional Veto and the Constitutional Separation of Powers. In Bessette, Joseph M. and Tulis, Jeffry, *The Presidency in the Constitutional Order.* Baton Rouge: Louisiana State University Press.

JACOB, HERBERT AND VINES, KENNETH N., eds. 1976   *Politics in the American States: A Comparative Analysis,* 3rd ed. Boston: Little, Brown.

KEECH, WILLIAM R. AND MATTHEWS, DONALD R. 1977   *The Party's Choice.* Washington, D.C.: Brookings Institution.

KURLAND, PHILIP B.   1977   *Watergate and the Constitution.* Chicago: University of Chicago Press.

SCHLESINGER, ARTHUR M., JR.   1973   *The Imperial Presidency*. Boston: Houghton Mifflin.

SCIGLIANO, ROBERT   1981   The War Powers Resolution and the War Powers. In Bessette, Joseph M. and Tulis, Jeffry, *The Presidency in the Constitutional Order*. Baton Rouge: Louisiana State University Press.

SUNDQUIST, LEONARD D.   1981   *The Decline and Resurgence of Congress*. Washington, D.C.: Brookings Institution.

CONSTITUTIONAL HISTORY, 1977–1985

Dennis J. Mahoney

As America moved from commemorating the bicentennial of the DECLA-RATION OF INDEPENDENCE to commemorating the bicentennial of the Constitution, the political order was in apparent disarray. Constitutional history is, primarily, an account of changes in the distribution of power and authority within a regime. At least since 1933, political power in the American regime had shifted toward the federal government, and, within the federal government, toward the executive branch. Commentators referred to an "imperial presidency"; and yet no one since DWIGHT D. EISENHOWER had held the presidential office for two full terms. JOHN F. KENNEDY had been assassinated; LYNDON B. JOHNSON had abandoned the quest for reelection; RICHARD M. NIXON had been forced to resign; GERALD R. FORD, the appointed vice-president who succeeded Nixon, lost his bid for election in his own right. JIMMY CARTER, who defeated Ford, was to prove unable to carry the burden of the presidency, and so to be crushed in his bid for reelection by the landslide that elected RONALD REAGAN.

The national consensus about what the government should be and should do, at bottom a consensus about the meaning of the Constitution, was breaking down. No longer did national majorities automatically form behind the notions of positive government, of redistribution of wealth and incomes, or of solving anything identified as a "national problem" by creating a new administrative agency within the federal BUREAUCRACY. There were indications that a new consensus was forming, but it was not yet fully formed. Less clearly than in the past—say, in 1800, 1832, 1860, or 1932—was the new consensus readily identified with the program of a particular POLITICAL PARTY, although the revitalization of the Republican party gave it the better claim to such identification.

Constitutional history can be understood either broadly or narrowly. In the broad sense, the constitution is the arrangement of offices and the distribution of powers in a country, it is how the country governs itself. In a narrow sense, the Constitution is a document in which the framework for self-government is spelled out. The process of constitutional change in the United States most often involves redistribution of power without constitutional amendment.

306

Formal amendment of the Constitution is a rare event. Only thirty-two amendments have ever been proposed by Congress, and two of those were pending as 1977 began; by 1985 both had died for want of RATIFICATION. The EQUAL RIGHTS AMENDMENT (ERA), ostensibly a guarantee that women and men would be treated equally under the law, but potentially a blank check for expansion of federal and judicial power, had been proposed in 1972. The DISTRICT OF COLUMBIA REPRESENTATION AMENDMENT, which would have made the national capital the equivalent of a STATE for most purposes, had been proposed in 1978. Even as those proposals failed to obtain the necessary votes in state legislatures, there was popular demand for more amendments: to mandate a balanced federal BUDGET; to proscribe SCHOOL BUSING as a remedy for de facto school segregation; to permit prayer in public schools; and to overturn the Supreme Court's proclamation of a constitutional right to abortion.

Amendments to accomplish each of these objectives were introduced in Congress, and the ERA was reintroduced, but none was proposed to the states. Indeed, only one amendment received a two-thirds vote in either house of Congress: the balanced budget amendment passed the Senate, but died when the House of Representatives failed to act on it. In the case of the balanced budget amendment, there were petitions from thirty-three states (one less than constitutionally required) calling for a convention to frame the proposal. Although there was much speculation among politicians, academicians, and pundits about how such a convention might work and whether it could be restricted in its scope, the failure of a thirty-fourth state to act made the speculation at least temporarily moot.

For three decades, constitutional innovation had been centered on the judicial branch. Between 1977 and 1985, however, constitutional development centered on the contest between Congress and the executive branch for predominance. The most important constitutional decision of the Supreme Court during the period, IMMIGRATION AND NATURALIZATION SERVICE v. CHADHA (1983), passed on a phase of that contest.

The only uniquely American constitutional doctrine is that of the SEPARATION OF POWERS attended by CHECKS AND BALANCES. The embodiment of that doctrine in the Constitution set up a constant rivalry for preeminence between the political branches and an intense jealousy of powers and prerogatives. Beginning in the FRANKLIN D. ROOSEVELT era, the President—or the institutionalized presidency—seemed to acquire ever more power within the political system, and appeared to have acquired a permanent position of dominance. But the VIETNAM WAR and the WATERGATE crisis led to a resurgence of Congress, represented especially in the War Powers Resolution of 1973 and the CONGRESSIONAL BUDGET AND IMPOUNDMENT CONTROL ACT of 1974.

The seizure of the American embassy in Iran by Islamic revolutionary guards in 1979 set the stage for reassessment of the constitutional status of the WAR POWERS. President Carter in April 1980 ordered the armed forces to attempt a rescue of the American citizens held hostage in Tehran. The secrecy necessarily surrounding such an attempt precluded the "consultations" mandated by the War Powers Resolution. When, through the coincidence of bad planning and bad weather, the operation proved a costly failure, congressional critics were quick to denounce Carter for his defiance of the law—some going so far as to call for his IMPEACHMENT. The hostages subsequently were released as the result of an EXECUTIVE AGREEMENT by which Carter canceled the claims of some Americans against the revolutionary government of Iran and caused other claims to be submitted to an international tribunal rather than to American courts. This settlement of the hostage crisis appeared to some observers to exceed the scope of presidential power, but it was upheld by the Supreme Court in DAMES & MOORE v. REGAN (1981).

The War Powers Resolution continued to bedevil presidential conduct of FOREIGN AFFAIRS during the Reagan administration; but the real character of that controversial resolution was revealed by the contrast between two incidents involving American military forces. In 1981 President Reagan, at the request of all of the governments of the region, and in conjunction with two foreign allies, detailed a battalion of marines to Beirut, Lebanon, as part of an international peacekeeping force. The operation was not of the sort explicitly covered by the War Powers Resolution, and Reagan, although he communicated with members of Congress, did not take steps to comply with the consultation or reporting requirements of the resolution. Congress, however, unilaterally acted to approve the President's course of action rather than precipitate a confrontation over either the applicability of the resolution or its constitutionality. Several months after a suicide bomber killed more than 200 marines, the President withdrew the rest of the marines from Lebanon, conceding a major foreign policy failure; but Congress, because it had acted affirmatively to approve the operation, was in no position to condemn the President for that failure.

Subsequently, in 1984, the President authorized a military operation to rescue American citizens trapped in the small Carribean nation of Grenada and to liberate that country from a Cuban-sponsored communist dictatorship. Such an operation was precisely within the terms of the War Powers Resolution, but it was planned and executed in secrecy and, again, the President complied with neither the consultation nor the reporting requirements of the resolution. However, because the operation was perceived as a success, most members of Congress refrained from complaining about the breach of the War Powers Resolution.

As the War Powers Resolution represented the resurgence of Congress in the foreign policy arena, the Congressional Budget Act was designed to reassert congressional control over government spending priorities. The federal budgetary process had been introduced in the 1920s to replace the chaotic amalgam of uncoordinated appropriations by which Congress had theretofore allocated federal revenues. But the executive budget, while coordinating expenditures and subjecting them to a common annual plan, remained detached from the appropriations process; hence disputes arose between the branches, especially when the aggregate of appropriations exceeded the executive's estimate of revenues. The deferral and cancellation of appropriated expenditures—called IMPOUNDMENT—became especially controversial when President Nixon was accused of using them for political, rather than economic, reasons.

The 1974 act purported to solve the problem by making budget planning a congressional function and by linking budgeting and appropriations in a single process. But, because the internal structure of Congress is not conducive to unified decision making and because the executive branch has not conceded that the detailed planning of expenditures is properly a legislative activity, the revised budget process has not been successful. The national government commonly operates for most of the year on the basis of resolutions authorizing continued spending at some percentage increase over the previous year's spending plus numerous special appropriations.

Between 1977 and 1985, as, to a lesser degree, between World War II and 1977, one of the great tests of constitutional government in America was the fiscal crisis resulting from persistent excesses of governmental expenditures over governmental revenues. Under constant political pressure to maintain or increase expenditure levels, but facing the unpopularity of increases in taxation (combined with the economic difficulty that increased tax rates may, by diminishing the tax base, actually result in lower revenues), Congress has resorted to borrowing to finance chronic deficits. At the end of 1985, Congress enacted, and President Reagan signed, a law providing for automatic reductions of appropriations when projected deficits reached specified levels. However, the ink was hardly dry before that measure (the GRAMM-RUDMAN-HOLLINGS ACT) was challenged as unconstitutional, even by some members of Congress and some representatives of the administration.

State legislatures, commonly required by their state constitutions to balance their own annual budgets, have petitioned Congress for a convention to propose a balanced budget amendment to the federal constitution. How even a constitutional mandate could be enforced to make Congress do what it seems unable to do, that is, to make difficult choices about public affairs, remains unclear. Meanwhile, the Congressional Budget Act exists to frustrate any attempt of the executive branch to supply the decision making.

Yet another device by which Congress attempted to reassert itself in the contest for dominance under a constitution that separates powers was the LEGISLATIVE VETO. Long before 1977, the DELEGATION OF POWER to the executive branch and to various INDEPENDENT REGULATORY AGENCIES was so great that the published volumes of federal regulations exceeded in number by many times the volumes of federal statutes. In statutes delegating legislative power to administrative bodies, Congress began to include provisions allowing Congress, or one house of Congress, to deprive agency actions of effect by simple resolution. In June 1983 the Supreme Court, in IMMIGRATION AND NATURALIZATION SERVICE V. CHADHA, held that the legislative veto, in some or all of its forms, was unconstitutional. The effect of the *Chadha* decision on legislative veto provisions that differed significantly from that in the Immigration and Nationality Act remained unclear for some time after the decision, and Congress continued to enact new legislative veto provisions after the decision. The real winner in that struggle for power, however, was not the President, but the bureaucracy.

Congress also asserted itself in more traditional ways, especially by exploiting the constitutional requirement that certain presidential actions have the Senate's ADVICE AND CONSENT. One category of such action is treaty making. President Carter suffered embarrassment over the PANAMA CANAL TREATIES and defeat on the second Strategic Arms Limitation Treaty. The Panama Canal debate was the first extended debate on a major treaty since that on the Treaty of Versailles in 1919. The treaty was signed in September 1977 but the Senate did not consent to its ratification until the spring of 1978. The vote was 68–32 (only one affirmative vote more than required) and the Senate attached a "reservation" to the treaty, asserting that the United States could intervene militarily if the canal should ever be closed; the reservation nearly caused Panama to rescind its ratification of the treaty. President Carter signed the strategic arms treaty in July 1979 at a summit meeting with President Leonid Brezhnev of the Soviet Union. Although trumpeted as a major foreign policy achievement, the treaty was delayed in Senate hearings and finally shelved in 1980 after the Soviet Union invaded Afghanistan.

President Carter vigorously asserted the presidential treaty power when, after recognizing the People's Republic of China in Beijing as the lawful government of all of China he unilaterally abrogated the long-standing mutual defense treaty between the United States and the Republic of China on Taiwan. An affronted Congress immediately provided for a United States Institute to represent American interests in the Republic of China while delaying for over a year Carter's request that trade preferences be granted to the mainland regime. Congress was unable to salvage the mutual defense treaty, however; and the Supreme Court held in GOLDWATER V. CARTER (1979) that members of Congress lacked STANDING to challenge the President's action in court.

The other category of action requiring Senate approval is appointments. The Senate, although nominally controlled by the President's own party, frequently used confirmation hearings and votes to express disapproval of certain Reagan administration policies, especially the administration's reluctance to impose and enforce AFFIRMATIVE ACTION requirements. The Senate delayed for over a year appointment of Edwin Meese to be ATTORNEY GENERAL, and rejected outright the promotion of William Bradford Reynolds to be associate attorney general. Although Reagan's nomination of SANDRA DAY O'CONNOR to the Supreme Court (the only nomination to the Court between 1977 and 1985) was approved rapidly and without serious controversy, several other judicial appointments were delayed or rejected.

Another signal characteristic of American constitutionalism is FEDERALISM. From the mid-1930s on, the balance of power between the national government and the states has been shifting steadily in favor of the national government. President Reagan came to office pledging a reversal of that trend. However, his proposal for a "new federalism," in which governmental functions assumed by the national government would be relinquished to the states, was coolly received not only by Congress but also by state politicians, who feared that their responsibilities would increase even as their revenues continued to decrease. Somewhat more successful was Reagan's proposal to replace the myriad of categorical FEDERAL GRANTS-IN-AID, by which the national government partially funded certain mandated programs and set the standards by which the programs were to be run, with block grants.

Congress, however, has increasingly imposed conditions and restrictions on the use of block grant funds; so even the limited victory may prove hollow. Although conservatives like President Reagan frequently express a principled aversion to the use of conditional grants of money as a means to coerce the states into acceding to federal goals and programs, they have not been so averse in practice. Examples of new uses of the TAXING AND SPENDING POWER to accomplish legislative goals not strictly within Congress's ENUMERATED POWERS include: a requirement that hospitals receiving federal funds perform certain lifesaving measures on behalf of handicapped newborn children; a requirement that states, as a condition of receiving highway building funds, enact certain provisions to counter drunken driving; and a requirement that schools, as a condition of receiving federal aid, permit religious groups to meet in their facilities on the same basis as do other extracurricular organizations.

Whether the election of 1980 wrought an enduring change in the constitution of American government remains an open question. Al-

though President Reagan decisively defeated former Vice-President Walter F. Mondale in 1984, the House of Representatives remained under
the control of Carter's and Mondale's party. And the Senate, even with
a Republican majority, did not prove to be so committed as the President
to reduction of the role of the federal government in American society.
Nevertheless, Reagan had considerable success in achieving the deregula-
tion of some kinds of businesses and in returning to private enterprise
some activities that had come under the ownership and management
of the federal government. On the other hand, the heralded "new federalism" did not cause a resurgence in the relative importance of the state
governments, and federal control continued to be maintained through
the use of conditions attached to grants-in-aid. At the bicentennial of
the Constitution, it is still too early to say whether Reagan effected, as
he said he would, "another American revolution."

Bibliography

CARTER, JIMMY 1984 *Keeping the Faith.* New York: Bantam.
FISHER, LOUIS 1984 *Congressional Conflicts between Congress and the President.*
    Princeton, N.J.: Princeton University Press.
GINSBERG, BENJAMIN 1987 *Reconstituting American Politics: Cleavages and Coali-
    tions in the Age of Ronald Reagan.* New York: Oxford University Press.
HOWITT, ARNOLD M. 1984 *Managing Federalism: Studies in Intergovernmental
    Relations.* Washington: Congressional Quarterly.
SCHRAMM, PETER W. and MAHONEY, DENNIS J., EDS. 1986 *The 1984 Election
    and the Future of American Politics.* Durham, N.C.: Carolina Academic Press.

BURGER COURT

(1969–1986)

A. E. Dick Howard

The roots of the Burger Court lie in the JUDICIAL ACTIVISM of the WARREN COURT. The social vision of the Supreme Court under EARL WARREN was manifested on many fronts—dismantling racial barriers, requiring that legislative apportionment be based upon population, and vastly expanding the range of rights for criminal defendants, among others. At the height of its activity, during the 1960s, the Warren Court became a forum to which many of the great social issues of the time were taken.

Such activism provoked sharp attacks on the Court. Some of the criticism came from the ranks of the academy, other complaints from political quarters. In the 1968 presidential campaign, RICHARD M. NIXON objected in particular to the Court's CRIMINAL PROCEDURE decisions—rulings which, he said, favored the country's "criminal forces" against its "peace forces."

During his first term as President, Nixon put four Justices on the Supreme Court—WARREN E. BURGER, HARRY A. BLACKMUN, LEWIS F. POWELL, JR., and WILLIAM H. REHNQUIST. Rarely has a President been given the opportunity to fill so many vacancies on the Court in so short a time. Moreover, Nixon was explicit about the ideological basis for his appointments; he saw himself as redeeming his campaign pledge "to nominate to the Supreme Court individuals who share my judicial philosophy, which is basically a conservative philosophy."

Thus was born the Burger Court. For a time, pundits, at least those of liberal persuasion, took to calling it "the Nixon Court." Reviewing the 1971 TERM, *The New Republic* lamented that the "single-mindedness of the Nixon team threatens the image of the Court as an independent institution."

Inevitably, the work of the Burger Court was compared with that of its predecessor, the Warren Court. During the early Burger years, there was evidence that, with Nixon's four appointees on the bench, a new, and more conservative, majority was indeed in the making on the Court.

By the summer of 1976, a conservative Burger Court seemed to have come of age. For example, near the end of the 1975 term the Court closed the doors of federal courts to large numbers of state prisoners by holding that a prisoner who has had a full and fair opportunity to raise a FOURTH AMENDMENT question in the state courts cannot relitigate that question in a federal HABEAS CORPUS proceeding. In other criminal justice decisions, the Court whittled away at the rights of defendants, showing particular disfavor for claims seeking to curb police practices.

Decisions in areas other than criminal justice likewise showed a conservative flavor. For example, in the same term the Court used the TENTH AMENDMENT to place limits on Congress's commerce power, rejected the argument that claims of AGE DISCRIMINATION ought to trigger the higher level of JUDICIAL REVIEW associated with SUSPECT CLASSIFICATIONS (such as race), and refused to hold that CAPITAL PUNISHMENT is inherently unconstitutional.

By the mid-1970s, a student of the Court might have summarized the Burger Court, in contrast with the Warren Court, as being less egalitarian, more sensitive to FEDERALISM, more skeptical about the competence of judges to solve society's problems, more inclined to trust the governmental system, and, in general, more inclined to defer to legislative and political processes. By the end of the 1970s, however, such generalizations might have been thought premature—or, at least, have to be tempered. As the years passed, it became increasingly more difficult to draw clean distinctions between the years of Earl Warren and those of Warren Burger.

Cases involving claims of SEX DISCRIMINATION furnish an example. In 1973 four Justices (WILLIAM J. BRENNAN, WILLIAM O. DOUGLAS, BYRON R. WHITE, and THURGOOD MARSHALL) who had been on the Court in the Warren era sought to have the Court rule that classifications based on sex, like those based on race, should be viewed as "inherently suspect" and hence subject to STRICT SCRUTINY. The four Nixon appointees (together with Justice POTTER STEWART) joined in resisting such a standard. Yet, overall, the Burger Court's record in sex discrimination cases proved to be one of relative activism, even though the Court applied an intermediate STANDARD OF REVIEW in those cases, rather than one of strict scrutiny. In the 1978 term, for example, there were eight cases that in one way or another involved claims of sex discrimination; in six of the eight cases the Justices voted favorably to the claim, either on the merits or on procedural grounds.

In the early 1980s, with the Burger Court in its second decade, there was evidence that a working majority, conservative in bent, was taking hold. Two more Justices from the Warren era (William O. Douglas and Potter Stewart) had retired. Taking their place were appointees of Republican presidents—JOHN PAUL STEVENS (appointed by President GERALD R. FORD) and SANDRA DAY O'CONNOR (named by President RONALD REAGAN). While Stevens tended to vote with the more liberal Justices,

O'Connor appeared to provide a dependable vote for the more conservative bloc on the Court.

In the 1983 term the conservatives appeared to have firm control. The Court recognized a "public safety" exception to the MIRANDA RULES and a "good faith" exception to the EXCLUSIONARY RULE in Fourth Amendment cases. The Justices upheld a New York law providing for the PREVENTIVE DETENTION of juveniles and sustained the Reagan administration's curb on travel to Cuba. As one commentator put it, "Whenever the rights of the individual confronted the authority of government this term, government nearly always won." The AMERICAN CIVIL LIBERTIES UNION's legal director called it "a genuinely appalling term," one in which the Court behaved as a "cheerleader for the government."

No sooner had such dire conclusions been drawn than the Burger Court once again confounded the Court-watchers. The very next term saw the Court return to the mainstream of its jurisprudence of the 1970s. The Court's religion cases are an example. Between 1980 and 1984 the Court appeared to be moving in the direction of allowing government to "accommodate" religion, thus relaxing the barriers the FIRST AMENDMENT erects between church and state. The Court rebuffed challenges to Nebraska's paying a legislative chaplain and Pawtucket, Rhode Island's displaying a Christmas crèche. Yet in the 1984 term the Court resumed a separationist stance, invalidating major programs (both federal and state) found to channel public aid to church schools, invalidating an Alabama statute providing for a "moment of silence or prayer" in public schools, and striking down a Connecticut law making it illegal for an employer to require an employee to work on the employee's chosen Sabbath. The Reagan administration had filed briefs in support of the challenged laws in all four cases, and in each of the four cases a majority of the Justices ruled against the program.

Even so brief a sketch of the Burger Court's evolution conveys something of the dialectical nature of those years on the Court. In reading Burger Court opinions, one is sometimes struck by their conservative thrust, sometimes by a liberal result. Here the Burger Court is activist, there it defers to other branches or bodies. There is continuity with the Warren years, but discontinuity as well. One is struck, above all, by the way in which the Court in the Burger era has become a battleground on which fundamental jurisprudential issues are fought out.

No simple portrait of the Burger Court is possible. Some measure of the Burger years may be had, however, by touching upon certain themes that characterize the Burger Court—the questions which observers of the Court have tended to ask and the issues around which decision making on the Court has tended to revolve.

At the outset of the Burger era, many observers thought that a more conservative tribunal would undo much of the work of the Warren

Court. This prophecy has been unfulfilled. The landmarks of the Warren Court remain essentially intact. Among those landmarks are BROWN V. BOARD OF EDUCATION (1954) (school desegregation), REYNOLDS V. SIMS (1964) (legislative REAPPORTIONMENT), and the decisions applying nearly all of the procedural protection of the BILL OF RIGHTS in criminal trials to the states.

In all of these areas, there have been, to be sure, important adjustments to Warren Court doctrine. Sometimes, a majority of the Burger Court's Justices have shown a marked distaste for the ethos underlying those precedents. Thus, while leaving such precedents as MIRANDA V. ARIZONA (1956) and MAPP V. OHIO (1961) standing, the Burger Court has frequently confined those precedents or carved out exceptions. Yet, despite criticisms, on and off the bench, of the INCORPORATION DOCTRINE, there has been no wholesale attempt to turn the clock back to the pre-Warren era.

In school cases, while the Burger Court has rebuffed efforts to provide remedies for de facto SEGREGATION, where de jure segregation is proved the Court has been generous in permitting federal judges to fashion effective remedies (it was an opinion of Chief Justice Burger, in SWANN V. CHARLOTTE-MECKLENBURG BOARD OF EDUCATION (1971) that first explicitly upheld lower courts' use of busing as a remedy in school cases). In legislative apportionment cases, the Burger Court has permitted some deviation from strict conformity to a population basis in drawing state and local government legislative districts, but the essential requirement remains that REPRESENTATION must be based on population.

A common complaint against the Warren Court was that it was too "activist"—that it was too quick to substitute its judgment for decisions of legislative bodies or other elected officials. In opinions written during the Burger years, it is common to find the rhetoric of judicial restraint, of calls for deference to policy judgments of legislatures and the political process generally.

Some Burger Court decisions reflect a stated preference for leaving difficult social issues to other forums than the courts. In rejecting an attack of Texas's system of financing public schools through heavy reliance on local property taxes, Justice Powell argued against judges' being too ready to interfere with "informed judgments made at the state and local levels."

Overall, however, the record of the Burger Court is one of activism. One of the hallmarks of activism is the enunciation by the Court of new rights. By that standard, no judicial decision could be more activist than the Burger Court's decision in ROE V. WADE (1973). There Justice Blackmun drew upon the vague contours of the FOURTEENTH AMEND- MENT'S DUE PROCESS clause to decide that the RIGHT TO PRIVACY (itself a right not spelled out in the Constitution) implies a woman's right to have an ABORTION.

In the modern Supreme Court, the Fourteenth Amendment's due process and EQUAL PROTECTION clauses have been the most conspicuous vehicles for judicial activism. The Warren Court's favorite was the equal protection clause—the so-called new equal protection which, through strict scrutiny and other such tests, produced such decisions as *Reynolds v. Sims*. With the advent of the Burger Court came the renaissance of SUBSTANTIVE DUE PROCESS.

An example of the Burger Court's use of substantive due process is Justice Powell's plurality opinion in MOORE V. EAST CLEVELAND (1977). There the Court effectively extended strict scrutiny to a local ordinance impinging on the "extended family." Powell sought to confine the ambit of substantive due process by offering the "teachings of history" and the "basic values that underlie our society" as guides for judging. It is interesting to recall that, only a few years before *Roe* and *Moore*, even as activist a Justice as Douglas had been uncomfortable with using substantive due process (hence his peculiar "emanations from a penumbra" opinion in GRISWOLD V. CONNECTICUT, 1965). The Burger Court, in opinions such as *Roe* and *Moore*, openly reestablished substantive due process as a means to limit governmental power.

Another index of judicial activism in the Supreme Court is the Court's willingness to declare an act of Congress unconstitutional. Striking down a state or local action in order to enforce the Constitution or federal law is common, but invalidation of congressional actions is rarer. The Warren Court struck down, on average, barely over one federal statute per term; the Burger Court has invalidated provisions of federal law at about twice that rate. More revealing is the significance of the congressional policies overturned in Burger Court decisions. Among them have been CAMPAIGN FINANCE (BUCKLEY V. VALEO, 1976), the eighteen-year-old vote in state elections (OREGON V. MITCHELL, 1970), special bankruptcy courts (NORTHERN PIPELINE CONSTRUCTION CO. V. MARATHON PIPE LINE CO., 1982), and the LEGISLATIVE VETO (IMMIGRATION AND NATURALIZATION SERVICE V. CHADHA, 1983).

Yet another measure of judicial activism is the Court's oversight of the behavior of coordinate branches of the federal government, apart from the substantive results of legislative or executive actions. The Burger Court thrust itself directly into the WATERGATE crisis, during Nixon's presidency. Even as the IMPEACHMENT process was underway in Congress, the Supreme Court, bypassing the Court of Appeals, expedited its hearing of the question whether Nixon must turn over the Watergate tapes. Denying Nixon's claim of EXECUTIVE PRIVILEGE, the Court set in motion the dénouement of the crisis, resulting in Nixon's resignation. The Burger

Court has similarly been willing to pass on the ambit of Congress's proper sphere of conduct. For example, the Court's narrow view of what activity is protected by the Constitution's SPEECH OR DEBATE CLAUSE would have surprised WOODROW WILSON, who placed great emphasis on Congress's role in informing the nation.

Closely related to the question of judicial activism is the breadth and scope of the Court's business—the range of issues which the Court chooses to address. Justice FELIX FRANKFURTER used to warn against the Court's plunging into "political thickets" and was distressed when the Warren Court chose to treat legislative apportionment as appropriate for judicial resolution.

Reviewing the record of the Burger Court, one is struck by the new ground it has plowed. Areas that were rarely entered or went untouched altogether in the Warren years have since 1969 become a staple of the Court's docket. In the 1960s Justice ARTHUR J. GOLDBERG sought in vain to have the Justices debate the merits of capital punishment, but the Court would not even grant CERTIORARI. By contrast, not only did the Burger Court, in *Furman v. Georgia* (1972), rule that capital statutes as then administered were unconstitutional, but also death cases have appeared on the Court's calendar with regularity. (See CAPITAL PUNISHMENT CASES, 1972, 1976.)

Sex discrimination is another area that, because of Burger Court decisions, has become a staple on the Justices' table. In *Hoyt v. Florida* (1961) the Warren Court took a quite relaxed view of claims of sex discrimination in a decision upholding a Florida law making jury service for women, but not for men, completely voluntary. By the time Warren Burger became Chief Justice, in 1969, the women's movement had become a visible aspect of the American scene, and since that time the Burger Court has fashioned a considerable body of law on women's rights.

The Burger Court has carried forward—or has been carried along with—the "judicialization" or "constitutionalization" of American life. The victories won by blacks in court in the heyday of the CIVIL RIGHTS movement have inspired others to emulate their example. Prisoners, voters victimized by malapportionment, women, juveniles, inmates of mental institutions—virtually any group or individual failing to get results from the legislative or political process or from government bureaucracies has turned to the courts for relief. And federal judges have woven remedies for a variety of ills.

The Burger Court might have been expected to resist the process of constitutionalization. On some fronts, the Justices have slowed the process. SAN ANTONIO INDEPENDENT SCHOOL DISTRICT V. RODRIGUEZ (1973) represents a victory for a hands-off approach to SCHOOL FINANCE (although it is undercut somewhat by the Court's subsequent decision in *Plyler v. Doe,* 1982). But such decisions seem to be only pauses in the expansion of areas in which the judiciary is willing to inquire.

The Burger Court may sometimes reach a "liberal" result, sometimes a "conservative" one. In some cases the Justices may lay a restraining hand on the EQUITY powers of federal judges, and in some they may be more permissive. All the while, however, the scope of the Supreme Court's docket expands to include wider terrain. In constitutional litigation, there seems to be a kind of ratchet effect: once judges enter an area, they rarely depart. This pattern characterizes the Burger era as much as it does that of Warren.

Even in areas that seemed well developed in the Warren Court, the Burger Court has added new glosses. It was long thought that COMMERCIAL SPEECH fell outside the protection of the First Amendment; the Burger Court brought it inside. It was Burger Court opinions that enlarged press rights under the First Amendment to include, at least in some circumstances, a right of access to criminal trials. The jurisprudence by which government aid to sectarian schools is tested is almost entirely of Burger Court making. Most of the case law sketching out the contours of personal autonomy in such areas as abortion, BIRTH CONTROL, and other intimate sexual and family relations dates from the Burger era. If idle hands are the devil's workshop, the Burger Court is a temple of virtue.

The contour of rights consists not only of substantive doctrine; it also includes jurisdiction and procedure. Who shall have access to the federal forum, when, and for the resolution of what rights—these have been battlegrounds in the Burger Court. If a case may be made that the Burger Court has achieved a retrenchment in rights, it may be that the case is the strongest as regards the Court's shaping of procedural devices.

Warren Court decisions reflected a mistrust in state courts as forums for the vindication of federal rights. Burger Court decisions, by contrast, are more likely to speak of the COMITY owed to state courts. Thus, in a line of decisions beginning with YOUNGER V. HARRIS (1971), the Burger Court has put significant limitations on the power of federal judges to interfere with proceedings (especially criminal) in state courts. The Court also has sharply curtailed the opportunity for state prisoners to seek federal habeas corpus review of state court decisions.

Technical barriers such as STANDING have been used in a number of cases to prevent plaintiffs' access to federal courts. For example, in *Warth v. Selden* (1976) black residents of Rochester were denied standing to challenge exclusionary ZONING in the city's suburbs. Similarly, in SIMON V. EASTERN KENTUCKY WELFARE RIGHTS ORGANIZATION (1976) poor residents of Appalachia were held not to have standing to challenge federal tax advantages granted to private hospitals that refused to serve the INDIGENT.

By no means, however, are Burger Court decisions invariable in restricting access to federal courts or in limiting remedies for the violation of federal law. Some of the Court's interpretations of SECTION 1983, OF TITLE 42, UNITED STATES CODE (a civil rights statute dating back to 1871) have made that statute a veritable font of litigation. The Warren Court had ruled, in 1961, that Congress, in enacting section 1983, had not intended that municipalities be among the "persons" subject to suit under the statute; in 1978, the Burger Court undertook a "fresh analysis" of the statute and concluded that municipalities are subject to suit thereunder.

Going further, the Court ruled, in 1980, that municipalities sued under section 1983 may not plead as a defense that the governmental official who was involved in the alleged wrong had acted in "good faith"; the majority disregarded the four dissenters' complaint that "ruinous judgments under the statute could imperil local governments." And in another 1980 decision the Court held that plaintiffs could use section 1983 to redress claims based on federal law generally, thus overturning a long-standing assumption that section 1983's reference to federal "laws" was to equal rights legislation. The Burger Court's section 1983 rulings have been a major factor in the "litigation explosion" which in recent years has been the subject of so much legal and popular commentary.

The reach of federal courts' equity powers has been another hotly debated issue in the Burger Court. CLASS ACTIONS seeking to reform practices in schools, prisons, jails, and other public institutions have made INSTITUTIONAL LITIGATION a commonplace. Such suits go far beyond the judge's declaring that a right has been violated; they draw the judge into ongoing supervision of state or local institutions (recalling the quip that in the 1960s federal district judge Frank Johnson was the real governor of Alabama). Institutional litigation in federal courts raises serious questions about federalism and often blurs the line between adjudication, legislation, and administration.

Some Burger Court decisions have attempted to curb federal judges' equity power in institutional cases. For example, in RIZZO V. GOODE (1976) Justice Rehnquist, for the majority, reversed a lower court's order to the Philadelphia police department to institute reforms responding to allegations of police brutality; Rehnquist admonished the judge to refrain from interfering in the affairs of local government. Similarly, in prison cases, the Burger Court has emphasized the importance of federal judges' deference to state prison officials' judgment about questions of prison security and administration.

In important respects, however, the Burger Court has done little to place notable limits on federal courts' equity powers. Especially is this true in school DESEGREGATION cases. A wide range of remedies has been approved, including busing, redrawing of attendance zones, and other devices. Although the Court has maintained the distinction between DE FACTO AND DE JURE segregation (thus requiring evidence of purposeful segregation as part of a plaintiff's prima facie case), decisions such as those from Columbus and Dayton (both in 1979) show great deference to findings of lower courts used to support remedial orders against local school districts.

Painting a coherent portrait of the Burger Court is no easy task. An effort to describe the Court in terms of general themes, such as the Justices' attitude to judicial activism, founders on conflicting remarks in the Court's opinions. Likewise, an attempt to generalize about the Burger Court's behavior in any given area encounters difficulties.

Consider, for example, the expectation—understandable in light of President Nixon's explicit concern about the Warren Court's rulings in criminal justice cases—that the Burger Court would be a "law and order" tribunal. In the early years of the Burger Court (until about 1976), the Court, especially in its rulings on police practices, seemed bent on undermining the protections accorded in decisions of the Warren years. The majority showed their attitude to the exclusionary rule by referring to it as a "judicially created remedy," one whose benefits were to be balanced against its costs (such as to the functioning of a GRAND JURY). In the late 1970s, the Court seemed more sympathetic to *Miranda* and to other devices meant to limit police practices. But in the early 1980s, especially in SEARCH AND SEIZURE cases, the Court seemed once again markedly sympathetic to law enforcement.

Or consider the Court's attitudes to federalism. In some decisions, the Burger Court has seemed sympathetic to the interests of states and localities. In limiting state prisoners' access to federal writs of habeas corpus, the Court shows respect for state courts. In rebuffing attacks on inequalities in the financing of a state's public schools, the Court gives breathing room to local judgments about running those schools. In limiting federal court intervention in prison affairs, the Court gives scope for state judgments about how to run a prison.

Yet many Burger Court decisions are decidedly adverse to state and local governments' interests. The Court's section 1983 rulings have exposed municipalities to expensive damage awards. The Burger Court has been more active than the Warren Court in using the dormant COMMERCE CLAUSE to restrict state laws and regulations found to impinge upon national interests. And in the highly controversial decision of GARCIA V. SAN ANTONIO METROPOLITAN TRANSIT AUTHORITY (1985) the Court said that, if the states have Tenth Amendment concerns about acts of Congress, they should seek relief from Congress, not from the courts (in so ruling, the Court in *Garcia* overturned National League of Cities v. Usery, 1976, itself a Burger Court decision).

How does one account for such a mixed record, replete with conflicting signals about basic jurisprudential values? The temperament and habits of the Justices of the Burger Court play a part. Pundits often imagine the Justices coming to the Court's conference table with "shopping lists," looking for cases on which to hang doctrinal innovations. For most (although not necessarily all) of the Justices, this picture is not accurate. By and large, the Justices tend to take the cases as they come. This tendency is reinforced by the Court's workload pressures. Far more cases come to the Burger Court than came to the Warren Court. Complaints by the Chief Justice about the burden thus placed on the Court are frequent, and in 1975 it was reported that at least five Justices had gone on record as favoring the concept of a National Court of Appeals to ease the Supreme Court's workload.

The Burger years on the Court have lacked the larger-than-life figures of the Warren era, Justices like Hugo L. Black and Felix Frankfurter, around whom issues tended to polarize. Those were judges who framed grand designs, a jurisprudence of judging. Through their fully evolved doctrines, and their arm-twisting, they put pressure on their colleagues to think about cases in doctrinal terms. Since the departure of the great ideologues, the Justices have been under less pressure to fit individual cases into doctrinal tableaux. Ad hoc results become the order of the day.

The Burger Court has been a somewhat less ideological bench than was the Warren Court. Many of the Court's most important decisions have turned upon the vote of the centrists on the bench. It is not unusual to find, especially in 5–4 decisions, that Justice Powell has cast the deciding vote. Powell came to the bench inclined to think in the pragmatic way of the practicing lawyer; as a Justice he soon came to be identified with "balancing" competing interests to arrive at a decision. The Burger Court's pragmatism, its tendency to gravitate to the center, blurs ideological lines and makes its jurisprudence often seem to lack any unifying theme or principle.

A Burger Court decision—more often, a line of decisions—often has something for everyone. In *Roe v. Wade* the Court upheld the right of a woman to make and effectuate a decision to have an abortion. Yet, while invalidating state laws found to burden the abortion decision directly, the Court has permitted state and federal governments to deny funding for even therapeutic abortions while funding other medical procedures. In Regents of the University of California v. Bakke (1978) a majority of the Justices ruled against racial quotas in a state university's admissions process, but a university, consistent with *Bakke*, may use race as a factor among other factors in the admissions process.

Burger Court decisions show a distaste for categorical values. The Warren Court's fondness for prophylactic rules, such as *Miranda* or the Fourth Amendment exclusionary rule, is not echoed in the Burger Court. The Burger bench may not have jettisoned those rules outright, but most Justices of this era show a preference for fact-oriented adjudication rather than for sweeping formulae.

Burger Court opinions are less likely than those of the Warren Court to ring with moral imperatives. Even when resolving so fundamental a controversy as that over abortion, a Burger Court opinion is apt to resemble a legislative committee report more nearly than a tract in political theory. A comparison of such Warren Court opinions as *Brown v. Board of Education* and *Reynolds v. Sims* and a Burger Court opinion such as *Roe v. Wade* is instructive. Warren Court opinions often read as if their authors intended them to have tutorial value (Justice Goldberg once called the Supreme Court "the nation's schoolmaster"); Burger Court opinions are more likely to read like an exercise in problem solving.

For most of its existence, the Burger Court has been characterized by a lack of cohesive voting blocs. For much of its history, the Burger years have seen a 2–5–2 voting pattern—Burger and Rehnquist in one wing, Brennan and Marshall in the other wing, the remaining five Justices tending to take more central ground. Justice Stewart's replacement by Justice O'Connor (a more conservative Justice) tended to reinforce the Burger-Rehnquist wing, while Justice Stevens gravitated more and more to the Brennan-Marshall camp. Even so, the Burger Court was a long way from the sharp ideological alignments of the Warren years.

The Court's personalities and dynamics aside, the nature of the issues coming before the Burger Court help account for the mixed character of the Court's record. The Warren Court is well remembered for decisions laying down broad principles; *Brown, Mapp, Miranda,* and *Reynolds* are examples. The task of implementing much of what the Warren Court began fell to the Burger Court. Implementation, by its nature, draws courts into closer judgment calls. It is one thing to lay down the principle that public schools should not be segregated by race, but quite another to pick one's way through the thicket of de facto-de jure distinctions, interdistrict remedies, and shifting demographics. Had the Warren Court survived into the 1970s, it might have found implementation as difficult and splintering as has the Burger Court.

If the Warren Court embodied the heritage of progressivism and the optimistic expectations of post-World War II America, the Burger years parallel a period of doubt and uncertainty about solutions to social problems in the years after the Great Society, the VIETNAM WAR, and Watergate. In a time when the American people might have less confidence in government's capacity in other spheres, the Supreme Court might well intuitively be less bold in imposing its own solutions. At the same time, there appeared, in the Burger years, to be no turning back the clock on the expectations of lawyers and laity alike as to the place of an activist judiciary in public life. Debate over the proper role of the judiciary in a democracy is not insulated from debate over the role of government generally in a society aspiring to ORDERED LIBERTY. Judgments about the record of the Burger Court, therefore, tend to mirror contemporary American ideals and values.

Bibliography

BLASI, VINCENT, ED.   1983   *The Burger Court: The Counter-Revolution That Wasn't.* New Haven, Conn.: Yale University Press.

FUNSTON, RICHARD Y.   1977   *Constitutional Counterrevolution?: The Warren Court and the Burger Court: Judicial Policy Making in Modern America.* Cambridge, Mass.: Schenkman.

LEVY, LEONARD W.   1974.   *Against the Law: The Nixon Court and Criminal Justice.* New York: Harper & Row.

MASON, ALPHEUS T.   1979   *The Supreme Court from Taft to Burger,* 3rd ed. Baton Rouge: Louisiana State University Press.

WOODWARD, BOB and ARMSTRONG, SCOTT   1979   *The Brethren: Inside the Supreme Court.* New York: Simon & Schuster.

EMERSON, THOMAS I.   1980   First Amendment Doctrine and the Burger Court. *California Law Review* 68:422–481.

HOWARD, A. E. DICK   1972   Mr. Justice Powell and the Emerging Nixon Majority. *Michigan Law Review* 70:445–468.

REHNQUIST, WILLIAM H.   1980   The Notion of a Living Constitution. *Texas Law Review* 54:693–706.

SALTZBERG, STEPHEN A.   1980   Foreword: The Flow and Ebb of Constitutional Criminal Procedure in the Warren and Burger Courts. *Georgetown Law Journal* 69:151–209.